Road to Wapatomica

A modern search for the Old Northwest

ROAD TO WAPATOMICA

A MODERN SEARCH FOR THE OLD NORTHWEST

BY BOB HUNTER

CULLODEN BOOKS

Columbus

Published by Culloden Books in the United States of America.

ISBN: 978-1-7366917-2-4 (hardcover)
ISBN: 978-1-7366917-0-0 (softcover).
ISBN: 978-1-7366917-1-7 (electronic).

On the cover – Landscape with Covered Wagon, painting by
Asher Brown Durand in 1847. Collection of the Indianapolis
Museum of Art.

TABLE OF CONTENTS

III.   SOLDIERS AND SETTLERS

IV.   CONTESTED GROUND

V.   LAKES AND STRAITS

VI.   FRENCH INDIANA-ILLINOIS

VII.   FURS AND PORTAGES

ACKNOWLEDGMENTS

The success of this book depended, at least in part, on the willingness of strangers to help a writer on a search that may not have made much sense to them. That so many proved so helpful is a testament to the accommodating nature of most Americans, even times of domestic strife, economic hardship and political division.

The best example of this occurred in the tiny Ohio River community of Hanging Rock, Ohio, where I stopped a guy mowing his lawn to ask directions to a rock ledge that was barely visible through the trees at the top of a nearby hill. The grass cutter – Mike Chatfield -- offered to give me a ride up to the house of the man who owned the property. When we got there, Chatfield introduced me to the owner – Chris Hopper – who said that the terrain was too rough for me to walk the rest of the way, and offered to take me up there in his UTV. From there, he also took me to another site he thought I should see. Over the course of an hour, two guys who had never seen me before interrupted their days and went out of their way to help.

The list of people who have aided this search in ways both big and small is immense. From library workers who fielded phone queries from me and sought out others when they couldn't find the answer to historians and archaeologists who were never too busy to give me as much time I needed to understand the nature of a site, historical event or fiction masquerading as fact.

It would be difficult to name every librarian who helped, but I want to offer special thanks to Gayle Martinson and Lisa R. Marine (Wisconsin Historical Society), Marta Ramey, (Briggs library in Ironton, Ohio), Gary Meek (Piqua Public Library), Valerie Elliott and Kaitlynn Carroll (Smith Library of Regional History in Oxford, Ohio), Renee Hopper (Defiance Public Library) and Stephen Headley (Cincinnati Public Library).

I also want to thank Bill Pickard, Erin Bartlett and Bill Eichenberger of the Ohio History Connection, J. Colby Bartlett of the Ouiatenon Preserve, Catherine Wilson of the Greene County Historical Society, Tilda Philpot of the Shelby County Historical Society, Mary Elise Antoine of the Prairie du Chien Historical Society, Susan G. Little and Marjorie A. Smith of the Daughters of the American Revolution, Jim Walker of the *Ironton Tribune*, Defiance city historian Randy Buchman, Fred K, Snyder of the Ohio Sea Grant Extension, Rich Halquist of The History Center in Fort Wayne, Indiana, Denise Simms Sunderland of the Pickaway County Historical Society and Dr. Clay Johnson, Brenda Arnett and Nancy Stump of the Garst Museum

Special thanks are also offered to Michael Nassaney, Katina Elwood, Ed Rambacher and Judith Vierling Close.

Finally, I want to give special thanks to my son, Rob, who helped create several maps that are found in these pages. He saw me working on one of these early in the process and knowing of my embarrassing lack of artistic skills, offered his assistance.

"I've got it, Dad," he said. "This will give you a chance to get a little payback for all of those art classes that you paid for me when I was a kid."

INTRODUCTION

When I set out to find the Old Northwest in today's Midwest much of it was hiding in plain sight. This seemed odd only until I realized how few people were looking for it.

What does the Old Northwest mean to you? Probably not much. You may recognize it as another name for the old Northwest Territory, officially created by the Northwest Ordinance in 1787 and intact only until Ohio began preparing for its admission to the union as a state in 1803. But the region between the Ohio and Mississippi rivers near the Great Lakes was sometimes referred to as the "Northwest" even before it received its formal title as the "Territory Northwest of the River Ohio" by the Second Continental Congress in the days immediately following the American Revolution.

For my purposes, the geographic boundaries of this book will adhere relatively closely to those political borders – the modern states of Ohio, Michigan, Indiana, Illinois, Wisconsin, and northeast Minnesota. The Old Northwest's life span is being defined much more broadly however, beginning with the initial interactions of European explorers, missionaries and traders with Native Americans.

It's obvious that most places in the mostly forested land mass of the Old Northwest bore little resemblance, in both appearance and value, to these spots today. Rivers, lakes and mountains defined the geography of that world. The three portages that each earned a visit and a chapter in this book because of their supreme importance in those distant days are fortunate if we have even a vague awareness of them now. Most residents of Portage, Wisconsin, probably know that the Fox-Wisconsin river portage that gave the city its name served an important connector in the fur trade, but most people outside of Wisconsin are probably unconsciously ignorant of it. Portage locations don't get much love from modern travelers. The average twenty-first century man or woman doesn't spend much time lugging canoes from one stream or lake to the next. Hence, they see little practical value in portages' existence.

Rivers and lakes that are now primarily used for recreational purposes functioned as the primary highways of Native Americans, explorers and settlers, offering a means of traveling great distances much faster than they could on old Indian and buffalo trails. Mountains were impediments to travel or places of spiritual significance. Now they're National Parks, ski resorts and good cover photos for Facebook.

Many villages and towns settled early and hugely important back in the day – Kaskaskia, Illinois, and Prairie du Chien, Wisconsin, for example -- survive as relatively small, out of the way places that many of us know little about. Many villages and towns that pioneers thought would someday become major cities aren't much larger now than when they were settled.

Some significant sites have seemingly vanished altogether. Farm fields cover some of the most important places, including Pickawillany, Loramie's trading post and Fort Ouiatenon. The site of Fort Junandat, a French fort/trading post on the south shore of Sandusky Bay, is a victim of shoreline erosion and higher water levels and has been reclaimed by the bay. A few miles west of Springfield, Ohio, a motorist on Interstate 70 between Columbus and Dayton drives directly through the site of one of the major Shawnee villages and doesn't have a clue.

My mission of discovery occurred on many different levels. It didn't take long to realize that important Native Americans and their historic sites aren't remembered in the same way as those of the white settlers and their heroes, if they are remembered at all. This is an extension of a sad story that most of us know.

For much of the first two centuries of our nation's existence, history treated Native Americans as conquered foes who stood in the way of our manifest destiny. It praised courageous missionaries who introduced civilization and Christianity to pagan tribes, esteemed the frontier spirit that fueled the pioneers' relentless push westward and celebrated the feats of heroic soldiers who made the land safe for settlers.

As I made my rounds, it became clear that the widespread lack of attention to Native American history had affected even my own perception of places and events. The last addition to the book, a chapter on the Shawnee village of Wapatomica, had been briefly considered and rejected earlier because I had been unaware of its importance. The site has a marker erected by the Eastern Shawnee tribe of Oklahoma in recent years and a crumbling one erected long ago and is located in an isolated forest choked with weeds and brush surrounded by private property. It was one of the last visits I made and the last chapter I wrote (even though it doesn't appear last in the book). It represented an awakening of sorts for me and hence is the basis for the title, *Road to Wapatomica.*

The stories told by many historical markers and plaques, particularly those erected or dedicated decades ago, are written from the perspective of European explorers and white soldiers and settlers. The little historical information offered from the Indian side is often incomplete and inaccurate.

But then historical markers from important non-Indian events are often misplaced and/or wrong. A poor history-minded soul who ponders a tablet explaining that the history he is seeking happened here, might find it disconcerting to learn that the marker was placed in 1902 when historians thought it happened here and have since been proven wrong. There might be another stone bearing a plaque or a bronze plate on a building somewhere else that corrects the earlier gaffe, but he has no way of knowing it.

While writing this book, I watched a historical series on The History Channel that made William Henry Harrison the hero of the Battle of Fallen Timbers and didn't even mention the general who led the American forces, Anthony Wayne. The show apparently needed to segue to the next scene, one involving Harrison, so it re-wrote history and made Wayne's aide-de-camp – Harrison – the hero.

If you can't believe a historical marker or the History Channel, it should be clear that understanding the history of the people, places and things that came before us isn't always easy.

A twenty-first century world that offers an attractive array of electronic detours doesn't help much. Even many who love history have difficulty putting down their smart phones long enough to spend much time thinking about Native Americans whose footsteps we trace when we walk our dogs and run our lawn mowers. And while genealogy websites such as Ancestry and MyHeritage are wildly popular, I wonder how many users look beneath their family trees and actually consider the perils and risks faced by the poor, inconvenienced souls who slogged through the thick woods of the Old Northwest to both clear the land and make it safe enough for us to grow corn, play youth soccer or work in an insurance office.

The effort is worth it, though. A search for the past can unlock the imagination. The modern soul who can look at the parking lot of a popular bar-restaurant in Sandusky, Ohio, and somehow see the mayhem a tribe of angry Native Americans wreaked on the soldiers of an ancient British fort will enjoy a deeper, more personal experience beyond any that can be witnessed on Netflix or HBO. If the surroundings have changed, the space is the same. For those who have never taken that kind of mental journey, the sudden realization that incredible, memorable events happened in places where we work, eat, play and sleep can feel like an epiphany.

History has always been more than the succession of names and dates many of us learned in school. You can Google the biography of an eighteenth-century Indian chief, soldier or pioneer and discover a half-dozen fun facts about them in less time than it takes to peel an orange. But if this were your life, would a half-dozen fun facts be enough to describe the real life you have lived?

My quest to find the Old Northwest in the modern Midwest was an enlightening experience, one I hope the reader enjoys even half as much as I did. Read the stories, scout the routes and hit the road yourself, as soon as the pandemic eases enough to permit safe travel. It is definitely a trip worth taking.

1 INDIAN TRAILS

Any modern search for the Old Northwest probably begins on an old Indian trail. That isn't as crazy as it seems. We spend much of our time tracing these ancient footpaths in our daily lives, even if we are unaware of it.

Mackinac Trail was the first Indian path I ever met. The part of it I knew as a small boy had another name, U.S. Route 2, and it ran from St. Ignace to Sault Ste. Marie in Michigan's Upper Peninsula. Interstate 75 replaced the eastern leg of U.S. 2, but the two-lane paved road still covers the trail as H-63 and much of it is still bordered by thick woods of white birch and pine.

When I was in my 20s, we used to stay at a campground located on Mackinac Trail, not far from a natural limestone formation called Castle Rock that had reputedly been an Ojibwa lookout. Knowing that Native American hunters, fur traders and French missionaries had come by this way gave a little more meaning to those nights by the campfire, although those early travelers probably would have found our use of the fire to roast sticky white cubes we called marshmallows more than a little curious.

Without the name, we might never have made the connection between a paved, two-lane road and the "trail" that preceded. It made it obvious that the trail had once been just that, a path made by moccasins through a dense forest.

I loved the idea that progress hadn't stolen its name over the centuries. What I didn't know is that others called it the Sault and Green Bay Trail, because it turned west (with modern U.S. 2) at St. Ignace and connected those two important fur trade centers (via modern Michigan Route 33 and U.S. 41). I also didn't know that the Mackinac Trail continued south on the other side of the straits to modern Saginaw, or that there are still places in the lower peninsula where the name has survived the creativity of modern real estate developers. It's Mackinaw Street in Saginaw and Mackinaw Road west of Bay City, but you get the idea. It's still better than Sunny Day Drive.

A mission of discovery of Old Northwest sites takes a modern time traveler over dozens of old Native American trails that haven't existed as such for centuries. The street names make the history connection easy in only a small number of cases. Those who know about the other trails have made a conscious effort to find them and you could easily hold a convention of those folks inside your neighborhood Pizza Hut. Most of us won't pore over old maps and books to make the association between Indian trails and the modern roads that trace them. Without a sign, there's no reason to know that a section of I-94 was once a foot path known as the St. Joseph Trail, especially from a seat in a car going 70 miles per hour.

Many of the early trails have been obscured by freeways, state and national highways, railroads and canals. Some took routes that weren't preferred by the later settlers and are lost in woods or fields that have been churned up by farmers for centuries. But many are beneath our wheels and feet.

If you know the history, there are times when it's not hard to guess where Native American trails once lay. Long, diagonal roads that cut across the neat paths of townships created by the surveyor's compass, roads which connect modern towns built on sites of Indian villages, generally follow the routes of old Indian trails.

But others were followed by Native Americans. The Indians trusted the instincts of wild animals to lead them to the easiest grades, springs and salt licks. Tribal settlements often sprung up where the trail passed over a riffle of a river or creek where crossing was easy.

The Indians who originally traversed these routes didn't set out to blaze modern highways. If a huge tree fell in the path of the trail, they would find their way around it and might create a new route for the path in the process. Because of that, trails may take routes that seem incomprehensible to us today. The Indian may have avoided a marsh that no longer exists and is now crossed by a modern highway. He may have taken a higher route in order to have a better view and avoid an ambush by his enemies. Property lines didn't exist, so there were no arbitrary barriers to the Indians' travels. The Indian didn't bother to improve a pathway by clearing dead timber or fallen rocks. Having a straight trail through the forest was unimportant to him; straight roads are usually the work of highway planners who "improved" the Indians' work much later. Even if the Indian preferred the shortest route, a longer but easier route may have been more practical.

The canoe served as the Indians' primary means of travel. Many creeks and rivers that are unnavigable today served as conduits of travel in those early days. Trails offered another means of communication and interaction among the tribes and were utilized as war paths to help thwart the increasing encroachment of white settlers.

When we are cruising along a highway between open farm fields at speeds that would have been incomprehensible to those early Native Americans, it's obvious that there is a tremendous difference between the trackless wilderness of the Indian and most of our modern terrain. Even in forested areas of harsh terrain where hiking can be a challenge, the modern experience is radically different from that of our ancestors. We know the rustle of leaves we hear or the movement we catch in the dark shadows of today's forest were probably created by a squirrel or rabbit and aren't those of a vengeful warrior ready to split our skulls with a tomahawk.

The first pioneers to utilize the Ohio River as a route to discovery and settlement faced a forbidding wall of trees and vegetation and unwelcome terrain on the early part of the route. A dense forest served as the shoreline north and west of the Ohio and most of the streams that offered routes into the interior of Indian country were relatively narrow and confined to small spaces. In many cases, they were overhung with trees and vines that created a dangerous tunnel of hiding places for unfriendly locals. A slow journey on a stream choked with driftwood must have seemed daunting to even the most courageous traveler. Foolhardy folks who entered were susceptible to ambush, and the price of admission might be capture or the loss of life.

The mouth of the Muskingum River offered the first wide entrance to the Ohio country and a more welcome invitation to the interior, and the Scioto and the Miami rivers had even wider bottom lands and offered more hospitable routes north. Favorable geography is only half of the equation, however. The Scioto and Miami rivers were guarded by Shawnee and Miami tribes mostly hostile to settlers.

Although trails crisscrossed the Old Northwest, some were more important than others and some are still easy to follow today.

The Scioto Trail is one of the best examples of both. It ran from the Ohio River at modern Portsmouth, Ohio, to Lake Erie at the site of the Indian village of Dunqueindundeh and the French post of Junandat. It lay on the second bottom of the broad flats of the Scioto River, and is unusual in that modern U.S. 23 covers most of it for 155 miles from Portsmouth to Upper Sandusky. The route is now mostly a four-lane highway that bypasses some of the towns that the trail (and old U.S. 23) passed through such as Waverly, Chillicothe and Circleville. But most of the highway still covers the trail, sometimes referred to as the Great Highway of the Shawnee.

This was probably the most heavily used trail in the Ohio country, used by Indians to get to the neutral hunting grounds of Kentucky and to the fertile fishing grounds of Sandusky Bay.

From Upper Sandusky, the trail continued north on current Ohio Route 53 until it reached Sandusky Bay at Dunqueindundeh, where it met the Lake Trail (Ohio 163) to Detroit.

The trail ran near many important Indian villages and is steeped in history. Christopher Gist is believed to be the first white man to use the trail in 1750 when he descended it after starting from the headwaters of the Licking River near modern Lancaster, Ohio, following a trip through Muskingum River country. The famous Logan Elm, under which Mingo Chief Logan made his eloquent address in 1774, lay one mile east of the trail, just south of modern Circleville. Cornstalk's Town, home of the famous Shawnee chief, was located not far from there, a mile east of the trail. Battle Island, site of Colonel William Crawford's defeat to a combined force of British rangers and Indians in 1782, was located on the trail three miles north of Upper Sandusky. He was eventually captured and burned at the stake three miles from it. The trail served as an important artery for the Shawnee (in the south), Mingo (central, in and near Columbus) and Wyandot (north).

The Great Trail is harder to follow, in part because of the hilly terrain and deep woods of eastern Ohio, but there is no denying its importance. It led from Logstown, an important Indian trading post at the mouth of the Beaver River across the Ohio River from today's Aliquippa, Pennsylvania, approximately 20 miles northwest of Fort Pitt, to Fort Detroit.

Following it today would be a test for Rand McNally: It led due west over the ridges, jogged north on Ohio 164 to Dungannon, then turned west across the hills to modern Hanoverton, where the trail turned west on what is now U.S. 30. It went south at modern Malvern on Ohio 43 and eventually crossed the Tuscarawas a quarter of a mile north of Fort Laurens. U.S. 250 traces most of its route to modern Wooster where U.S. 30 again has taken its path.

This is a good place to take a breather and remind ourselves that the Indian didn't have to make any of these turns. It was one trail, not pieces of a half-dozen routes with so many numbers that our GPS might have to ask for directions.

OK, to continue. . . south of Ashland the trail turned north and joins what is today's Ohio 96 near Olivesburg, and at Plymouth it headed north on what is now Ohio 61. At Monroeville, the trail headed west on what is now U.S. 20. It may have joined the Lake Trail near the Blue Hole at Castalia, although it is also possible that it took a more southerly route to the mouth of the Maumee, where Peter Navarre's trading post stood on the east side of the mouth of the Maumee River near Ironville. The combined trails crossed the river here and followed the defunct U.S. 25 (now mostly I-75) to Detroit.

The Wabash Trail was the route used by Arthur St. Clair and Anthony Wayne in their respective 1791 and 1794 campaigns against the Indians. It led from the Ohio River opposite the Licking River (Cincinnati) up the Mill Creek Valley to the Cincinnati neighborhood of Northside, where it follows Spring Grove Avenue and Vine Street to Ohio 4 to the modern city of Hamilton. St. Clair built Fort Hamilton there.

The trail crossed the Great Miami River here, crossed Four Mile Creek and then joined U.S. 127 in New Miami. (Wayne elected to stay on the east side of the river to that point.) It tracks on 127 through Eaton to a point about seven miles south of Greenville, where it bent westward, near Fort St.

Clair (built by Wayne) before heading to Greenville. From Greenville, the trail heads northwest on Ohio 49 to Fort Recovery, where St. Clair's army was crushed by the Indians under Little Turtle.

If you know the story of that massacre, it is difficult to drive the final part of this peaceful route (Ohio 49) without thinking of the frantic survivors, some of whom ran much of the 52 miles back to the safety of Fort St. Clair in a desperate attempt to stay alive. These panic-stricken souls weren't runners who had spent months training to run a marathon, but terrified folks running for their lives.

The Lake Trail served as a war trail for the Iroquois on their raids against Erie tribes. It ran from Buffalo to Detroit on a bench of an earlier Lake Erie and mimics U.S. 20. Euclid Avenue covers this trail through most of Cuyahoga County to Cleveland's Public Square. It followed Superior Avenue from there across the Cuyahoga River to Detroit Avenue, which takes the trail to Rocky River. Here, there path splits in two, one following the modern route of U.S. 20 and other following U.S. 6, close to the lake.

In 1764, British Colonel John Bradstreet and an expedition of 1,500 men was returning from Fort Detroit to Fort Niagara and he found the safe harbor of Rocky River too treacherous for his 46-foot bateaux. He had his fleet of 60 boats row 1.7 miles west -- an inexplicable move that would have been analyzed for weeks by retired generals and good-looking news anchors on cable news networks today -- where an expected swell swamped his boats, incapacitating 25 and severely damaging may others. The spot where this occurred is just north of U.S. 6 at a park now called Bradstreet's Landing. (A touch of irony there?) The trail continues to a spot four miles southeast of the Blue Hole at Castalia, where the Lake Trail meets the Great Trail. The combined trail goes to Junandat and then on to Fort Detroit.

In the lower peninsula of Michigan several trails survive as modern highways. The Grand River Trail is marked by Grand River Avenue, old U.S.16, from downtown Detroit though modern Grand Rapids to Lake Michigan at the mouth of the Grand River, the site of modern Grand Haven.

The Saginaw Trail, from Toledo through Saginaw and Midland and connecting to the Mackinac Trail, forms what in some places (between Saginaw, Flint and Pontiac, for example) is called Dixie Highway. In many locations, it used what is now U.S. Route 23 and old U.S. Route 10.

The Great Sauk Trail ran from Detroit to the Mississippi River at modern Rock Island, Illinois. In Michigan, modern U.S. 12 closely follows or covers the trail until it reaches what is now northern Indiana, where it takes a route that is now U.S. 30 near Michigan City to Valparaiso.

Noted explorer and ethnologist Henry Schoolcraft, writing from Michigan City in 1820, described the trail, as a "plain horse path, which is considerably traveled by traders, hunters, and others..." He also wrote that a stranger could not follow it without the services of a guide because of the numerous side trails.

U.S. 30 swings west past Merrillville, Indiana, where a Great Sauk Trail marker is in the median on Van Buren Street, about 400 feet south of Homer Iddings Elementary School. It continued on to Joliet, Illinois, where it crossed the Illinois River and follows the route on the north side of the river that is now taken by U.S. 6. This route takes it directly past the "Grand Village of the Illinois," a village that once housed as many as 6,000 people, and sat across the river from Starved Rock, a site steeped in history. The trail continues on U.S. 6 to the Mississippi River.

The St. Joseph Trail was an ancient Indian footpath that ran from the mouth of the St. Joseph River on Lake Michigan (St. Joseph, Michigan), to a spot a few miles east of Ann Arbor. It roughly paralleled the Great Sauk Trail, which lay to the south. When Michigan became a state, the trail became a roadway and was designated as Territorial Road, and it still exists with that name in some places. Most of the route is covered today by U.S. 12, I-94 and Michigan Avenue.

René-Robert Cavelier, Sieur de La Salle reputedly used this route to travel to Detroit in 1680 on a return trip that began on the ill-fated Griffon, which he separated from on an off-shore island near the mouth of Green Bay. (The Griffon is believed to have been the largest sailing vessel on the Great Lakes up to that time.) La Salle had decided to stay behind with four canoes to explore the head of Lake Michigan. La Salle eventually made it back to Fort Frontenac. The wreck of the Griffon has never been found.

Not all of the Native American routes area are as easily followed today. The Buffalo Trace, also called the Vincennes Trace, ran between Louisville, Kentucky, and Vincennes, Indiana. It started as a natural migration route for millions of American bison or buffalo from the grasslands and salt licks of Kentucky to the prairies of Illinois and became a Native American trail. Today it is part of the Historic Pathways National Scenic Byway.

No one is sure of the trail's exact route at the time of the first historical mentions of it. It is known to have gone through present-day New Albany, Indiana, and headed west through Harrison and Floyd counties to the Little Blue River in Crawford County. From there it tracked northwest and ran just north of today's Valeene. The Trace's main line subsequently split into numerous smaller trails that converged near several large ponds or mud holes north of Jasper where buffalo would wallow. Due to the large number of buffalos that used it, the well-worn path measured 12 to 20 feet wide in some places.

The French are believed to be the earliest white men to use this overland route during the time of the founding of Vincennes in 1731. But the trace didn't become a major thoroughfare until after George Rogers Clark's expedition to Vincennes in 1779. Surveyor and explorer John Filson made two waterway trips from Louisville to Vincennes in 1785 and 1786 and returned by two separate overland routes. Filson's first trip to Vincennes took 18 days and he wrote that the French, using the overland route or "the Trace," covered the same distance in half that time. Clark used the Buffalo Trace again in 1786 when he and 1,000 men marched from Louisville to the forts at Vincennes for the Battle of Vincennes. General Josiah Harmar and his army traveled over the trace in 1788, covering the 130 miles in six days.

You'd think a trail created by millions of bison, taken up by the Indians and used by thousands of soldiers would have been difficult to lose, but that's what happened. Parts of the trace have been uncovered in southern Indiana and there is a hiking trail in the Hoosier National Forests Spring Valley Recreation Area south of French Lick that follows a portion of the trace. There is also small tract within Buffalo Trace Park, a preserve maintained by Harrison County. Modern U.S. 150, created in 1820 as an improved stagecoach line that Indiana Territory governor William Henry Harrison had proposed in 1805, lies north of the old path and serves as the Louisville-Vincennes route today. Its construction helped give the old route back to nature.

Another route created by wild animals, the Old Jambeau Trail or Green Bay Road, has been treated much better by history than its abandoned cousin in southern Indiana. When deer, elk and possibly bison traveled north in their search of new grazing lands in Wisconsin in prehistoric times they inadvertently created a path that would someday become as a well-used trail between modern Chicago and Green Bay, Wisconsin.

Not sure how the animals got there but the Indian trail begins at the north end of Chicago's Michigan Boulevard bridge. (Conspiracy theorists can insert their tales of flying saucer-toting deer, buffalo and elk here.) It ran north along the height of land between the Lake Michigan shore and the North Branch of the Chicago River, then went north on Rush Street as far as Chicago Avenue. It assumed a northwest course for a mile (a diagonal that has long since disappeared) to the intersection of Clark Street and North Avenue. Clark Street (which becomes Chicago Street) merges with Green Bay Road in Evanston.

It picked up the name Jambeau in Racine County, Wisconsin, from an American Fur Company trader named Jacques Vieau Sr., who established a trading post at a Potawatomi village at Skunk Grove (now Franksville, about a mile east of I-94) in 1792. Indians supposedly had difficulty pronouncing his name and called him Jean Beau, which for some reason became Jambeau.

The U.S. Army surveyed for a trail to connect Fort Dearborn in Chicago and Fort Howard in Green Bay in 1832 and incorporated some of the Old Jambeau Trail in it. That route, called the Green Bay Trail, is now a much straighter State Route 31 in the southern part of it, which shouldn't be surprising. In the early days of the nineteenth century, white settlers annually worked to straighten the zig-zagging trail each winter using sleds to offer a new, easier routes for travelers in the spring.

A 27-acre woods in Pleasant Prairie, Wisconsin, named for the Momper family which owned a farm there for generations, has a preserved a 400-foot section of the trail and a plaque-bearing boulder. It has been closed to the public while local officials debate how to use it.

From Milwaukee to Green Bay, this route ran in a direct line (as Green Bay Avenue or Green Bay Road) to Saukville on Milwaukee River. From here it followed the general course of the Lake Michigan shore (State routes 32. 42 and I-43) to Manitowoc Rapids and Green Bay. Sauk Trail Road near Sheboygan may have been part of this.

An alternative route ran northwest from Milwaukee, through Menominee Falls, Rubicon Post Office and Fond du Lac. It followed the eastern edge of Lake Winnebago and reached the Fox River at Wrightstown, and followed the southern bank (Wisconsin 22) through De Pere to Green Bay.

The area that became metropolitan Chicago had more than a dozen Native American trails. The Vincennes Trail (or Vincennes Trace), also called the Hubbard Trail after prominent area fur trader Gurdon S. Hubbard, was one of the most important ones. Indians doubtless created this route because it lay on a ridge that ran from south to west from what is now the center of Chicago; the area we know as the Loop was all marsh. The Illinois, Fox and Potawatomi tribes are thought to have used the trail primarily as a route to and from Wisconsin to southern Indiana and Illinois.

State Street was the northern tip of the route. From there it ran to Vincennes Avenue to Winchester Avenue to Western Avenue, which turns into Dixie Highway and Illinois Route 1. It goes through modern Hoopeston and Danville, and the trail veers off the state route at Lawrenceville and goes five miles east and crosses the Wabash River to Vincennes, Indiana.

In Chicago, the trail originally ran about a mile west of the current Vincennes Avenue. As the city drained the marshy land, the street was moved several blocks to the east in 1854 and then moved east again in the early twentieth century to make for a shorter, more direct route. That explains a small stone and plaque erected by the Daughters of the American Revolution in 1928 that honors the Vincennes Trail at the southeastern tip of the Dan Ryan Woods Forest Preserve at 91st Street and Pleasant Avenue. The trail served as an important stagecoach route and a small inn called the Rexford House stood there.

Army Trail Road in Chicago's western suburbs covers an Indian trail that started west of Chicago and ended at a Winnebago village in modern Beloit, Wisconsin. It got its name because U.S. Army troops used this route in 1832 during the Black Hawk War. The tracks left by heavy army wagons formed a road for early settlers.

It didn't cost the taxpayers anything.

I.

ACROSS THE OHIO

2 MARIETTA

When you think of all of the calamities that might have befallen a wooden house in more than 330 years, its survival into the twenty-first century seems almost a miracle. Then when you hear the story of the Rufus Putnam house and see where it is – on its original foundation inside the Campus Martius Museum in Marietta, Ohio – its remarkable life span begins to sharpen into focus.

This probably isn't the first place to build a museum over a historic house, although it is the only one I have ever seen. If that hadn't happened, we might be listening to a sad lament that sounds vaguely similar to those of a thousand other long-departed frontier houses, or even buying what some modern snake oil salesman says are surviving pieces of the historic structure on eBay:

"Wanna buy a door knob that was once part of a house owned by Revolutionary War officer Rufus Putnam? He probably had his hand on it hundreds of times. But you don't have to take our word for it. We have this, uh, certificate of authenticity."

Thankfully, we don't need a salesman to tell us that Putnam's house is the real deal. Once a part of an outside wall of the Campus Martius fortification that Ohio Company settlers built for safety from hostile Indian tribes in 1788, it is a survivor of everything that time, Mother Nature, men and boys could throw at it.

In fact, an elderly docent who conducts tours of the structure told a story showing that boys may have been the biggest threat of all.

"Around the turn of the twentieth century the house was in bad shape and it was a real eyesore in the neighborhood," he said. "There were those who wanted to see the house torn down, and some of the neighborhood boys decided to take matters into their own hands. They started firing flaming arrows at the house from a porch across the street, thinking that when it burned down, everyone would find the arrows and think that the Indians had done it."

He let that thought sink in for a moment.

"Of course, by that point, there weren't any Indians. . ."

The guide snickered at his joke, which seemed lost on a troupe of touring fourth graders who probably weren't listening anyway. But the incident may have helped spur local citizens into doing something to save the building, which still stands (inside the museum) near the corner of Washington and Second streets, a modern block and a half from the Muskingum River. The local chapter of the Daughters of the American Revolution began leasing the structure in 1905. They cleaned it up and operated it until 1917, when the state bought it and placed it under the control of the Ohio Historical Society. The OHS started building a museum around it in 1929, enabling it to stay exactly where it was.

The civilian fortification it was part of measured 180 by 180 feet, with a 140 by 140-foot courtyard in the middle. A blockhouse stood on each corner of the structure and houses between the blockhouses formed the outside walls. The houses were made of sawed timbers, not logs, and were typical of the New England construction methods of the time. The workers used standardized sizes of lumber, which sped up construction; Putnam believed this important because he didn't think local Indian tribes would stay friendly long.

A model of Campus Martius (the name is from the Latin for Field of Mars, the military camp of ancient Rome) sits inside the four-room shell of a 1795 addition to the rear of the house that was constructed from the adjoining blockhouse; the Treaty of Greenville that year ended the Indian threat in the region and the dismantling of the fort began.

The docent pointed to a little two-story building on that model to show where former Revolutionary War General Rufus Putnam lived, but it took a little prodding to get the man to show where the blockhouse that stood next to the house would be today. That helps a modern visitor visualize this as more than an old house, but also as a part of the fortification erected here to protect nervous settlers from hostile Indians.

Simply as a surviving house from that distant time, the place is amazing, a window into that distant frontier period. The guide explains that these structures were designed to hold at least eight persons to a room – there are two rooms upstairs and two downstairs in the original house -- and as many of 20 during dangerous times. So settlers who were looking for wide open spaces in the West were probably best served by staying outside. It's not difficult to imagine a large family or families gathered around the open-hearth fireplace during cold winter months. Fact is, the rooms were small enough that those cozy "gatherings" in the first-floor kitchen/dining room/living room could be probably considered part of the routine, 365 days a year.

RUFUS PUTNAM HOUSE AS IT APPEARED IN 1895

But that's getting ahead of the story, which goes right to the beginnings to the Northwest Territory. Even before 48 former Revolutionary War soldiers came from Ipswich, Massachusetts, to what became Marietta, Ohio, in April, 1788, with their shares of an Ohio Company grant of 1,500,000 acres in hand, the army had erected a fortification on the west shore of the Muskingum where it enters the Ohio River in 1785 to protect the rights of – you may not believe this -- Native Americans.

The treaties the Indian tribes had signed gave the white intruders the right to settle on lands south of the Ohio River in modern-day Kentucky, but not north of it in lands that became Ohio, Indiana and Illinois. So Major John Doughty and a detachment of troops built Fort Harmar, named for Doughty's commanding officer, General Joshua Harmar, at the mouth of the Muskingum beginning in the fall of 1785 to help keep the settlers on the south side of the river and keep the peace.

This is a textbook example of wishful thinking. From June to December, 1787, the soldiers greeted 146 down bound boats, with 3,196 people, 1,381 horses, 165 wagons, 171 cattle, 245 sheep and 24 hogs. Most of those early pioneers did settle on lands that became Kentucky, but some of them eyed the fertile lands on the Ohio side of the river and squatted on what was supposed to be Indian land in violation of those treaties. Rather than discouraging squatters, Fort Harmar's presence may have even encouraged some of them, giving them reason to hope that the American soldiers were there for their protection. Congress' passage of the Ordinance of 1785, which authorized the surveying of a strip of easternmost Ohio called the Seven Ranges for revenue-raising land sales, didn't help much either. It told would-be squatters that settling the rest of the region would only be a matter of time.

Fort Harmar had five sides 125 feet in length with a bastion of some type on each corner. Its hewed log walls stood 12 feet high. It stood on the second bank of the river on a site occupied today by Harmar Elementary School, an odd synergy that somehow invites the visitor to merge ancient images with current views. Like the fort, the school faces the water; a row of parking spaces in front occupies space once populated by horses and soldiers.

The riverside drive that the school faces is called Fort Street. The intersecting street on the north side of the school is Fort Square. A rectangular, gray, granite marker in the weeds near the downslope of the riverbank announces this as the site of Fort Harmar, which would be a disappointing memorial if the fort hadn't been honored with a street and a square. Harmar's name is also attached to the entire neighborhood and the hill behind it.

While this spot didn't have much time in the spotlight, it was a busy place for a while. Putnam and his 48 would-be settlers landed here in two broad flatboats and three long canoes on the misty morning of April 7, 1788. They intended to land on the opposite side of the Muskingum but missed the shore in the thick weather. A party of about 70 Delaware men, women and children under a principal chief named Captain Pipe were encamped near the mouth of the river at the time, having come here a few days before to trade with the soldiers at the fort, and they greeted the newcomers with smiles and handshakes. Later that day, the soldiers towed the travelers across the river and some of the curious Delawares watched them unload. After they finished, the men began hacking away at massive, old growth trees that created the thick forest. They cleared land for their new settlement as quickly as they could, while their hungry horses grazed in a pasture of pea vines and buffalo clover nearly knee high. That night the lonely soldiers at Fort Harmar must have been heartened to see campfires across the water, flickering in the dark.

Former Revolutionary War General Arthur St. Clair, the first governor of the Northwest Territory, landed here in July in a twelve-oared barge and he made his office in one of the blockhouses at Fort Harmar. A few days later, he crossed the Muskingum to the uncompleted Campus Martius for the first time, escorted by the territory's secretary, Winthrop Sargent, and the officers from Fort Harmar. General Putnam led the delegation that welcomed them.

St. Clair set up the government of the new territory as his first order of business. His second was to secure peace with the Indians. The two sides agreed to hold a council sixty miles up the Muskingum where Taylorsville, Ohio, now stands the following June. When complications cancelled it, St. Clair changed course and insisted that peace negotiations be held at Fort Harmar. That finally happened on January 9, 1789, when the governor completed two treaties. The first came with twenty-four chiefs and warriors of the Six Nations; it reaffirmed the terms of the 1784 treaty at Fort Stanwix whereby the Iroquois relinquished all claims to land in the western territory. The second, a new one with chiefs from the Wyandot, Delaware, Chippewa, Pottawatomie and Sac nations, didn't accomplish much.

The Indians could see white settlers encroaching on their land and saw no need to make any new concessions or even abide by the old treaty's terms. St. Clair demanded that the chiefs agree to the reservation boundary established in the Treaty of Fort McIntosh in 1785. The Indians refused. An irritated St. Clair threatened them with attack and bribed them with three thousand dollars in presents, which got their signatures on a treaty they didn't plan to follow. The absence of representatives from the Shawnee and Miami tribes meant more than the presence of the others. The land St. Clair thought he was buying would have to be won on the battlefield.

To a large extent, those negotiations marked the end of Fort Harmar's significance. St. Clair's sons and daughters moved to Marietta during the fall of 1790 (his wife remained at his estate in Pennsylvania) and St. Clair moved them into the southwest blockhouse at Campus Martius. In December, St. Clair and the troops stationed at Fort Harmar moved to Fort Washington where the fledgling community of Cincinnati was sprouting, marking the end of Fort Harmar's importance as a military post. While Indians remained a threat in the Ohio Company tract, the real war for the settlement of the Ohio Valley had moved farther west.

After the Indian wars ended, the fort was eventually abandoned and torn down. It received equally rude treatment from the nearby rivers, which chomped away at some of the ground where the historic structure stood. In an 1848 book, Samuel P. Hildreth wrote about how much the fort site had changed in just a little over sixty years:

"Between the fort and the bank of the river there was sufficient space to muster a battalion of men. A part of the ground was occupied by three stout log buildings, for the use of the artificers attached to the garrison. The rivers have made sad inroads on the site of the old fort. At this day, not only the whole space between it and the river is washed away, but more than half of the ground occupied by the walls; so that the stone wall of the well, which was near the center, is now tumbling down the bank of the river. This continual wasting of the banks had widened the mouth of the Muskingum so much that during the summer months a sand bar or island occupies the spot that used to afford 10 or 12 feet of water. Before any clearings were made, the huge sycamore trees, as they inclined over the water on the opposite shores, narrowed the mouth of the river so much that a person passing hastily by in the middle of the Ohio, would hardly notice its outlet, so darkly was it shadowed by these giants of the forest."

Campus Martius' presence on the east side of the Muskingum partially explains why Fort Harmar's usefulness waned. While it stood a half-mile up river, new settlers cleared the land near the point opposite Fort Harmar and by the outbreak of war in 1791, 20 houses had already sprouted there. While the houses were mostly made of round logs and didn't have the finished appearance of those at Campus Martius, they had started to multiply. No blockhouses of any kind had been built there, so the Ohio Company hired Colonel William Stacey to build palisades around this area to keep the families safe.

A few houses remained outside the pickets, but four acres were enclosed, four blockhouses were built and sentries were posted every night. The Lafayette Hotel, a Marietta landmark at 101 South Front Street since 1917, would lie on the eastern boundary of this area, with the Muskingum River on the west. It stretched north of the Ohio only a couple of blocks, so it's apparent what a small area those crude early buildings covered.

Unfortunately, all of those structures were gone before anyone had a chance to build a museum over them. Only one pre-1800 structure in Marietta besides Putnam's house has survived and it even predates it: the Ohio Company land office.

Putnam built the simple one-story log structure with a gabled roof and one window and a door in front, near the Muskingum River west of the Campus Martius site in 1788, shortly after the settlers landed. Because it was completed before Putnam's house, it is regarded as the oldest building in the state of Ohio.

Inside this little office, early maps of the Northwest Territory were made, surveys were platted and the sale and allocation of land was carried out. It was moved up Washington Street between Front and Second streets in 1791, almost opposite the Putnam house, so the guns of Campus Martius could protect it. As the superintendent of the Ohio Company, Putnam used it as his business office; from 1796 to 1803 he also served as the first surveyor-general of the United States. The building has since been moved again to become part of the Campus Martius Museum complex.

Putnam lived in his house on the opposite side of the street from the old land office until he died at the age of 87 in 1824. He was the last surviving American-born officer of the American Revolution. When he went to his grave in Mound Cemetery, six blocks southeast on Fifth Street, he took his place next to his wife. Persis, and among many of his soldier friends. The old graveyard is said to be the final resting place of more Revolutionary War officers than any cemetery in the nation.

Thirty-seven Revolutionary War veterans, including Putnam, Commodore Abraham Whipple, General Benjamin Tupper and his son Major Anselm Tupper (who was 11 when he signed up to fight the British) are buried here. But an ancient 30-foot high mound built by the Adena Culture between 800 B.C. and 100 A.D. that sits in the center of the cemetery is the real star.

Numerous mounds dotted the landscape here when the Ohio Company settlers landed, and unlike those in most of Ohio's larger cities, many of these have survived. Captain Jonathan Hart, the commander of Fort Harmar, first investigated the site in 1786 and he drew a plan of the site that appeared in the May 1787 issue of Columbian Magazine. Between 1788 and 1796 members of the Ohio Company made provisions for the mounds to be surveyed and protected, gave them their Latin names, and placed the mounds under the domain of the future mayor of Marietta. This kept the mounds relatively secure for almost a century before the residents of Marietta began dismantling them for various construction projects.

In 1789, Reverend Manasseh Cutler had several trees growing out of the earthworks chopped down so he could count the growth rings; he determined that the trees had begun to grow 441 years earlier in approximately 1347. He determined that the trees had been preceded by another round of growth of at least equal age, pushing the date for the construction of the earthworks back to least 1000 years before the 1780s.

Sacra Via Park, located at a landing site on the Muskingum, was once the site of a ceremonial walled path that led from the river to the various mounds. One of these that stands three blocks to the northeast, the Quadranaou platform mound, has been preserved as Quadranaou Park. The Capitolium, a truncated pyramidal mound with three ramps leading to its summit, was mostly preserved because the Washington County Library was erected on its summit in 1916.

The Great Mound, or Conus, in the cemetery is the most visible reminder what the Ohio Company settlers found here and a good place for reflection. Forty-six steps take visitors to the top, where benches invite the curious to survey the landscape and realize that this place was settled by another people hundreds of years before the Indian tribes that Harmar, St. Clair and eventually Anthony Wayne confronted.

The Revolutionary War veterans who lie in Mound Cemetery are late comers, another reminder of why Marietta is such a special place.

3 BIG BOTTOM

On the beautiful spring day that I visited the site of Big Bottom Massacre, I didn't see another person. My solemn stroll around the three acres of riverfront property that make up Big Bottom Memorial Park consumed more than an hour. I read the base of a 12-foot marble obelisk inscribed with the names of the 12 men and women killed in a surprise attack by a passing band of Indian warriors. I eyed the massive sycamores and silver maples and wondered if any had been a witness to the attack. During the visit, I didn't notice one car or truck pass on Ohio Route 266, the tortuous road which brought me here. Even with my total lack of expertise in such matters, it struck me that there were probably safer places to build a settlement among hostile Indians.

The village of Stockport, a mile up river, had 503 residents in the 2010 census, but it was founded in 1843. That was a year after Samuel and William Beswick constructed the first of several mills there (the Stockport Mill Inn occupies the last one) and more than 50 years after a dozen would-be settlers died a mile down river.

A visitor to the park is struck with how isolated it seems, even today. For that reason, it may be as good a place as any to understand the differences between the hardy, independent souls who came to the Ohio frontier in the eighteenth century and the rest of us. The nagging thought of any modern visitor: A party of 36 would-be settlers risked their lives and some even died for this?

The back story behind the Big Bottom Massacre, which occurred on that small, isolated strip of parkland on the east side of the Muskingum River, on January 2, 1791, brings those differences out in sharp relief.

Former Revolutionary War general Rufus Putnam had led 48 Ohio Company settlers in the founding of Marietta near the mouth of the

Muskingum only 22 months before. They built a walled fortification with four blockhouses called Campus Martius to discourage Indian attacks, and were just a short distance up river from Fort Harmar, which had been perched on the opposite side of the Muskingum at its entrance into the Ohio to discourage squatters from trying to settle north of the Ohio since 1785.

Putnam and his group arrived in April, 1788. That little settlement, one of only four on the Ohio between Pittsburgh and modern-day Louisville, immediately attracted many of those who couldn't resist the magnetic draw of the Ohio country. There were 137 "arrivals" that first year, 153 in 1789 and 203 in 1790, figures that must have made Marietta seem like a metropolis to the land-hungry settlers who came out here.

Most of those early pioneers were farmers who knew good land when they saw it, which is why they selected wide river bottoms for their farms and villages. In making early land assignments, section lines of the original survey were often ignored and the land was laid out in long strips, giving settlers frontage on the rivers, which then served as the only highways.

Presumably by late 1790, most of the river frontage near Marietta had already been claimed. Probably for that reason, the Ohio Company sponsored small settlements nearby that wouldn't alarm the local Indians – Belpre, Waterford and Wolf Creek are examples of these – and offered each settler 100 acres of land as long as they improved the property within a few years.

This may have motivated the party of 36 men who left Marietta and headed up the Muskingum River into the heart of Indian country in the fall of 1790, although Putnam reportedly counseled against it. But the 36 pioneers were apparently determined to settle on the chunk of flat, rich riverside ground that they found 40 miles north at Big Bottom. It is worth nothing that the land there wasn't part of the million and a half acres that the Ohio Company had secured for Revolutionary War veterans, not that that probably would have mattered much to local tribes. Although 1785 and 1786 treaties at Fort McIntosh and Fort Finney had opened up land north of the Ohio River to the intruders, most of the tribes still didn't recognize the white man's right to settle on any of it.

Even today, an unfortified camp at Big Bottom seems like an easy target for Indian tribes. The group started the construction of a blockhouse of large beech logs when it arrived and apparently started looking after their own interests before they completed it. They took no other precautions. They didn't construct palisades around the blockhouse, even though an Indian path on the other side of the river ran from Sandusky to the mouth of the Muskingum. They didn't post sentries or even leave their dogs outside to alert them when intruders were lurking. For some reason, they apparently didn't see the need for such precautions.

BIG BOTTOM PARK

Isaac and Francis Choate built a cabin a short distance from the blockhouse and began clearing their lots. James Patten, another member of the company, and hired laborer Thomas Shaw lived with them. Asa and Eleazar Bullard took a small cabin that had been erected in a clearing a few years before and finished it. The others obviously had similar plans, but within a few weeks of their arrival, the weather turned bitterly cold. The river froze over a few days before Christmas. Clay also froze under those conditions, so the frigid settlers didn't chink between the logs.

Forty miles from the comparative safety of Campus Martius and Fort Harmar and hundreds of miles from any comparable military installation, the Big Bottom settlers might be considered fearless, reckless, stupid or all of the above. But again, they saw the world through a much different lens than those trying to understand them from a neatly-manicured lawn in the twenty-first century. Even seeing the smoke from a distant cabin seemed like an encroachment on the liberty to some of these early settlers.

For those with that perspective, Marietta could never be more than a jumping off point. The Big Bottom group wanted to claim their own piece of prime property and build their own settlement, even if it meant putting their lives in imminent danger. And in this case, that is exactly what they did.

On the evening of January 2, the settlers were eating dinner when a party of about 25 Delaware and Wyandot warriors passed on that trail on the opposite side of the river, possibly with the intent to attack a small settlement at Waterford 12 miles downriver. The sight of the little settlement of Big Bottom surprised the Indians, who quickly discerned its vulnerabilities. They separated into two parties and quietly stole across the frozen river and attacked.

The smaller group of Indians entered the Choate cabin as if they were dinner guests, greeted the settlers with a smile and sat down for a repast. With the men's guard lowered, the Indians seized them and used some leather thongs they found in the corner of the room to restrain them. Maybe because the Choates didn't resist, they were the lucky ones.

The other group approached the blockhouse undetected. A "large, resolute Indian" smashed the door open and held it while his comrades rushed through and began shooting the surprised settlers. Some of the Indians slipped their guns between the un-chinked logs and shot a few men by the fire. Isaac Meeks' wife grabbed an axe and plunged it into the shoulder of one of the attackers. It proved to be her dying act; some of her companions were dead before they had a chance to resist. In another example of their reckless disregard for their own safety, all of their guns stood against the wall in the corner of the room.

A young man named John Stacy escaped through a window and climbed onto the roof in search of an escape. He was shot and killed there while he pleaded for his life. The Bullards exited their cabin when they heard the shots. They heard the man's desperate pleas, retrieved their guns and disappeared into the woods, seconds before they heard the doors to their own cabin burst open. Their relay of the news at Samuel Mitchell's hunting camp four miles downriver sent Mitchell and Captain Joseph Rogers, a former Revolutionary War officer, on a mission to inform those at Wolf Creek and Waterford of the disturbing news and to alert them to the possibility of additional attacks.

Sixteen-year-old Philip Stacy, John's younger brother, had somehow hidden himself under some bedding in the corner of the blockhouse. The Indians found him and planned to kill him as well, but his pleas for mercy at the feet of one of the lead warriors saved his life. For the time being, he became a prisoner and not a corpse.

The marker at the base of the white obelisk erected in 1905 reports that nine men (John Stacy, Zebulon Throop, Ezra Putnam, John Camp, Jonathan Farewell, James Couch, William James, Joseph Clark and Isaac Meeks), one woman (Meeks' wife) and two Meeks children were killed in the attack, and that Asa Bullard, Eleazer Bullard and Philip Stacy escaped.

Five men were also reportedly taken captive by the Indians – James Patten, Thomas Shaw, brothers Francis and Isaac Choate Jr., and Philip Stacy. Stacy's inclusion in both groups is curious. He died of sickness when his captors reached the British post at the rapids of the Maumee River, so maybe someone saw this as a form of escape.

Those killed in the attack share a common grave. After removing everything of value, the Indians tore up the floor of the blockhouse, piled the wood on top of the settlers' dead bodies and set the pile on fire, intending for the bonfire to consume both the blockhouse and the bodies of their enemies. But because the green beach logs of the blockhouse's exterior didn't burn well, the fire destroyed only the floor and roof and left the walls mostly standing. Searchers found that macabre scene with the charred, unrecognizable bodies of the settlers when they arrived the next day. The obelisk sits on that site today.

After the warriors burned the cabins and the blockhouse, the deserted village remained that way. No attempt was made to resettle the ground.

The other captives fared better. Francis Choate's release was secured by "Colonel (Alexander) McKee, the Indian agent," at the Maumee rapids; he was sent to Detroit and eventually made his way home to Massachusetts. His brother Isaac remained captive until he reached Detroit, where he secured his release by promising to work at his trade as a coppersmith, until he repaid his debt. After a few months, he also made his way back East.

The Indians kept Thomas Shaw at the Maumee rapids for a few months until his release was secured by "the noted Colonel (Joseph) Brant." He worked for a French farmer near Detroit until Brant discovered that he was an expert axe-man and he persuaded him to work for his brother-in-law a few miles from Fort Niagara.

James Patten remained a captive until the Indians released him as a result of a prisoner exchange at Fort Defiance in 1795. Richard Walker researched Patten for the Belpre Historical Society and he came across some letters where the former captive spoke of the attack.

"There's not a large volume of materials, but there are some letters," Walker told the *Parkersburg News and Sentinel* in 2015. "He mentions at the time of the attack he was in a cabin while the others were eating supper. They were taken captive before the others were attacked. They were taken across the Muskingum River and held while the warriors came back and attacked the block house where the rest of the settlers were – so they were really out of harm's way at the time of the attack."

Patten was 37 years old at the time of the attack and he was the only survivor who returned to the Belpre\Marietta area. He had fought in the Revolutionary War and in March, 1797, the Ohio Company granted him 100 acres of land near Belpre, where he farmed the rest of his life.

As such, he may have fared better than some of his captors. After a steady buildup of frustration over random Indian attacks in the years immediately prior to it, the Big Bottom Massacre marked the outbreak of four years of frontier warfare in the Ohio country.

The fighting ended only when General Anthony Wayne defeated the Indians at Fallen Timbers and the defeated tribes signed the Treaty of Greenville.

4 GALLIPOLIS

Most modern visitors to Gallipolis arrive by car on Ohio Route 7, part of what those creative folks at the Federal Highway Administration call the Ohio River Scenic Byway. I arrived from the north, after exiting from U.S. 5 onto Ohio 7 near the Silver Memorial Bridge to West Virginia. The passing scenery on the riverside route into town reminded me of time spent counting the rings from the outside in on the stump of an ancient oak tree.

There's a Super 8 motel, a Buffalo Wild Wings and a Subway; a Wal-Mart, a Chevrolet dealership and a McDonald's; then a glass service, a church, and a couple of local pizza parlors. As we move closer to the center of the tree, Gallipolis' businesses and houses start to show their age. There's a paint store, a second-hand furniture store and a coin laundry; a library, two more churches and some well-kept houses that would have long since retired if they were human, and finally a crowded collection of old commercial buildings that existed long before McDonald's was a gleam in the McDonald brothers' eyes.

At its center, Gallipolis is, to use a little modern slang, older than dirt. It is a charming town, which is what you would expect from one settled by more than 500 mostly well-to-do French citizens (some indentured servants infiltrated the group) fleeing from horrors of the French Revolution. But in fact, the nobles, merchants and craftsmen who left on seven boats from Le Havre de Grace, France, in February, 1790, had relatively little to do with the development of the town of just over 3,000 that we know today.

The French 500, as those founding settlers are called, came here as the victims of a swindle, buying unseen land in an Ohio paradise from the Scioto Company of investors who never paid Congress for its grant. In fact, because of survey errors the property sold to them in France actually belonged to the Ohio Company. The French settlers knew something was wrong when they arrived in Alexandria, Virginia, and no one showed up to greet them and transport them to the finished town as they had been promised. It got worse when they discovered that the deeds they carried were worthless.

As weeks of uncertainly passed, some of the immigrants began to run out of money and their plight became public knowledge, the Ohio Company agreed to locate the French colony on its land – while maintaining title to it, of course. It had founded the settlement of Marietta upriver two years before, so General Rufus Putnam, acting as an agent for the trustees of Scioto Company, hired John Burnham of Essex, Massachusetts, to enlist a company of fifty young men who were expert woodmen. He assigned them to clear a wooded, tangled site on the Ohio shore near Chickamauga Creek, two miles from the mouth of the Kanawha River, for the new city. (The settlement was actually supposed to be opposite the mouth of the Kanawha, but Burnham and the wood cutters found the low-lying bottom land too susceptible to floods.) The Scioto Company employed them for six months at 26 cents a day to build 80 log huts and four blockhouses for protection for 500 settlers and to assist in clearing the lands adjacent to the settlement. They also hunted game to provide food for the travelers and even helped protect them from assault from Indian tribes.

Burnham and 36 woodmen from Massachusetts reported to Putnam in Wellsburg, Virginia, (now West Virginia) on May 29, 1790 – four ax men had already deserted and ten had yet to join the group – and then continued on down river to begin work. Meanwhile, the first group of French immigrants started westward from Alexandria on June 29 under the direction of two experienced woodsmen, Major Isaac Guion and James Backus, with no idea what an arduous journey lay ahead.

The glowing prospectus that described the property admitted that they would have to travel to their new city after landing in America, but the author was either a blatant liar or woefully ignorant of geography:

"The land transit is about thirty miles, but will probably be diminished in a little while, by means of a plan which is actually in contemplation for opening a communication between the Potomac and Ohio rivers."

The distance to their new home was, in fact, about 400 miles, much of it over narrow, rough roads over mountains and some through thickets and wet mud. As for the plan to connect the Potomac and the Ohio, well, we're still waiting. The last part of the journey came on flatboats, down the Monongahela and then the Ohio, and the first boats finally swung ashore on a wet, gray October 19.

The paradise they had been promised was anything but. They faced a high, steep bank which fronted a square of cleared land with 80 dark, one-room cabins in four rows framed by a thick forest, hardly a Garden of Eden worthy of a 4,000-mile journey. A blockhouse stood on each of four corners and a log stockade enclosed company stores and some larger log houses that had been built for the party's wealthier members. That speck in the Ohio woods those hearty Massachusetts men cleared is City Park today.

When you see the park and merge that vision with drawn images of 80 cabins crammed into it surrounded by a thick, forbidding, primeval forest, it isn't difficult to see why many of those original settlers didn't stay, or for that matter, why some even died in the harsh conditions.

John Heckewelder paused in Gallipolis for a day on June 27, 1792, on his way down the Ohio, and he estimated that the town had about 150 dwellings and between 300 and 400 residents at that point, less than two years after landing. But he was fascinated by the workmen he found there and offered a favorable impression of the place that wasn't shared by most who stopped there in succeeding years:

"The most interesting shops . . . were those of goldsmiths and watchmakers. They showed us work on watches, compasses and sun-dials finer than any I had ever beheld. Next in interest was the sculptor and stonecutter. The latter had two finished mantels, most artistically carved. General Putnam at once purchased one of them for twelve guineas, the other was intended for a Dutch gentleman who had built a two-story house here, fifty feet long . . . .. The worker in glass seemed to be a born artist. He made us a thermometer, a barometer, a glass tobacco pipe, a small bottle (which could contain about a thimble full), and a most diminutive stopper. As we were on a journey, and were in daily need of light, he presented us with a glass full of dry stuff, which burns as soon as a match is applied. The stuff, he told us, was manufactured from bones."

Heckewelder may have let his astonishment at finding skilled artisans in a remote wilderness outpost blind him to the exodus that was taking place from there. Haberdasher Antoine Laforge arrived with those early settlers and became justice of the peace before he eventually removed to New Madrid, in Spanish Louisiana. He was still living in Gallipolis in August, 1792, when he wrote: "Of the 500 who came here in the beginning, we are now not more than 200; because some had not sufficient patience while others were driven far away by fear. And as to those who remain, more than half are arranging to move away at the earliest opportunity."

For people used to the comforts of French civilization, conditions were harsh. The bitter winters, shortage of food, recurrent sickness, danger of Indian attacks and fear of dispossession of their property – the Ohio Company still held title to it – tested the courage and endurance of those early settlers.

At the onset of spring, many residents cane down with racking fevers that persisted for a long time, and most of the victims suspected that the marshes just beyond the town caused these outbreaks. The lack of food doubtless also made the locals susceptible to all manner of illnesses than they would have been otherwise.

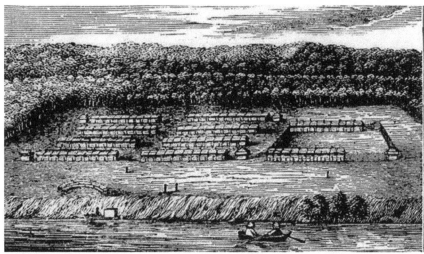

GALLIPOLIS IN 1790

A traveler named Thomas Chapman visited the town for a few hours on November 10, 1795, and described a place (poor spelling and all) that didn't seem long for this world:

". . . came to at Gallipolis, a Small miserable looking village of upwards of 100 little wretched Log Cabins, all Occupied by poor starved sickly-looking Frenchmen . . . The whole of the Inhabitants of this Town, the Governor not excepted, have Starvation and Sickness strongly pictured in their faces . . . We left this wretched place at 2 P. M."

Despite the conditions, some of the French gamely held on and continued to hope that the property they had paid for while in France would eventually be theirs. In March, 1795, Congress finally tried to rectify the wrongs. The French settlers still living in Gallipolis were each offered 217.4 acres of free land in the so-called French Grant, 40 miles west of town on the Ohio River in today's Scioto County. Few apparently wished to move there and instead made pleas to Ohio Company officials in Marietta in December for an outright gift of their home sites. The company rejected this request and instead offered to sell them their lots for $1.25 an acre. Some of them gave in, repurchasing 912 acres for $1,140.

None of these developments encouraged the French to stay in the area, but some did and there is physical evidence of their presence over two centuries later. The riverside houses on the streets that border the park on the east (State Street) and west (Court Street) were both constructed in 1811 by Frenchmen who stayed here. Pete LeClercq arrived with the French 500 at the age of 17 and built the two-story brick house at 1 Court Street; he became one of the little town's leading citizens, serving as clerk of courts and postmaster for 25 years. Across the park at the corner of First Avenue and State Street, J.P.R. Bureau built his two-story brick house in the same year. Bureau, another of the original settlers, ran a general store on the river side of his house that given its location must have been popular.

But it's clear that there weren't many Frenchmen like LeClercq and Bureau. The 1806 tax list for Gallia County shows only 16 French among its 145 surnames. Of the 367 persons on the tax list in 1810, there are 25 French surnames that match those of settlers prior to 1795.

A visitor can find lots of business names which refer to the city's distant past – Frenchtown Apartments, French City Chiropractic, French Town Veterinary Clinic, etc. – but little in the way of French surnames.

Suffice it to say that when I crossed City Park and entered the office of the Gallia County Historical Society on Second Street in search of answers, I didn't see any posters announcing the French 500's annual cookout and family reunion. Cheryl Enyart described herself as the unpaid facilities coordinator/director of the society, and she shook her head when I asked her how many direct descendants of the French 500 are still in Gallipolis.

"Every so often, one will walk through that door, but they're not from here," she said. "Well, Paul Eich would have a straight line, I think. His ancestor would be Robert Safford, who married Catherine Cameron, and he's the only one I know of living here in town. Denee Pellegrini was one – she was a Duteil – but she died."

Just for the record, Colonel Safford was here before the French 500 – as one of the ax men. But he wasn't French and neither was his wife, who was born in Canada. And so it goes.

"I think Ruth Haft was working on something for somebody who was a Chevalier," Enyart continued. "There were Chevaliers here, but whether they were connected to those on those boats is another thing. You have to dig. But as far as somebody walking around, Paul is the only one that comes to mind."

Disappointing as that might be for a modern time traveler hoping to find a small version of the New Orleans' famous French Quarter perched on the banks of the Ohio, it actually makes sense. The small settlement of Gallipolis grew into the place it is today when the Welsh and Germans migrated here later.

"The Welsh came and stayed," Enyart said. "The Germans came and stayed. The French were pantywaists. They said 'I will not do this.' They were the upper crust. Some of the men had smoother hands and complexion than the women did. They were fleeing for their necks. They were fleeing France to get away from the guillotine and anything else that might happen to them."

Still, it's the French who gave the city its name and much of its rich history. A block and a half east of the park at 432 First Avenue is a two-story, brick building constructed in 1819 as Our House Tavern. In May, 1825, the

Marquis de Lafayette visited there on his tour of America and apparently exchanged greetings with some Gallipolis citizens whom he had known back in France during the days of the American Revolution. The building is a museum today, and stands across the street from another ancient tavern, the Eagle, which was built in 1809. The white frame building backs up to the Ohio River, as many on First Avenue do. Another one that does, the so-called Berthelot House, lies two blocks to the east. Its 1802 birth makes it the oldest frame dwelling in town.

So if this isn't New Orleans, it is has enough history, ancient houses and southern Ohio scenery to make it interesting even before a visitor inquiries about the burials of those early French settlers. Those who fell sick and died before the thick forest surrounding the original settlement was cleared doubtless ended up in the woods somewhere and could be sleeping in someone's backyard. But a handful of those who stuck around and lived into the nineteenth century were buried in Pine Street Cemetery, seven or eight blocks northeast of City Park.

It looks like just another old cemetery in another small town, at least until it springs what is almost certainly Gallipolis' biggest surprise. Marie Bobin Menager, one of the bit players in the French settlement here, lies under a deteriorating tombstone that has had a bronze plaque affixed to it so we don't forget who is buried there.

Marie (or Mary) was born in France in 1772. She came to America as one of the French 500, and her marriage to Claudius Roman Menager in 1790 has been called the first to take place in the village. Before she died in 1857, she was one of the last survivors of the original settlers.

OK, that's all interesting enough until we get to this: Before she came here, she had been the sweetheart of a young French lieutenant named Napoleon Bonaparte, who would become the French emperor fourteen years later. Supposedly Bonaparte fell hard for the beautiful Bobin and he considered following her to America and marrying her.

Could Gallipolis have become the capital of Napoleon's empire? Might he have become Anthony Wayne's aide de camp instead of William Henry Harrison and become a hero at Fallen Timbers, or a southern Ohio farmer. The thought boggles the mind. He obviously changed his mind and decided to remain in France, and at some point he supposedly sent guards to America hoping to bring her back to France. But by that time, she had become romantically interested in someone she met on the boat to America, the young Frenchman who became her husband.

Napoleon didn't marry for the first time himself until 1796 – make of that what you will – but years later, he supposedly sent a medallion with his image on it to show Marie that he had not forgotten one of his first loves. That medallion is on display in the Our House Museum, a gift of Ruth Hamilton, a Menager descendant who lived in Columbus.

Is the medallion real? No clue.

But if Menager was indeed Napoleon's sweetheart, and it's difficult to imagine a story that incredible being totally made up, then little Gallipolis has a tale that may actually be more amazing than the story of Gallipolis itself.

While standing on Menager's grave, it occurred to me that this is as close as I would ever be to anyone who has been this close to Napoleon. You can't get much more French than that.

5 POINT PLEASANT

When a friend asked why I went to Point Pleasant, West Virginia, when I was writing a book about the Old Northwest, I offered all of the practical reasons first.

It is two miles and two bridges from Gallipolis, Ohio, or about five minutes by car. The Battle of Point Pleasant occurred there in 1774 because Shawnee chief Cornstalk and about one thousand warriors from his tribe's villages in the Pickaway Plains (Ohio) near the Scioto River attacked about an equal number of Virginian troops that were camped there. While the Americans suffered more casualties, the Indians' retreat (back to Ohio country) ended Lord Dunmore's War with a treaty signed at Camp Charlotte (Ohio).

It is also the site of a four-ton stone obelisk bearing the name "Cornstalk," which holds the remains of the famous Shawnee war chief. But Cornstalk wasn't killed in battle. Three years later, he came to the fort that had been constructed on the site of the battle under the white flag of truce and was taken prisoner. While he was being held, he was murdered by some vengeful soldiers and frontiersmen and buried there.

Tu-Endie-Wei State Park, a pretty, four-acre patch of green space at the confluence of the Ohio and the Great Kanawha rivers and only a few blocks from the center of town, is the site of both the fort and part of the battle; the ebbs and flows of the battle also occurred in what is now the central business district, which stretches for six blocks up Main Street from the park.

For anyone in search of frontier history, that is more than enough reason to visit here. But many of today's visitors come for paranormal reasons that some have tenuously linked to a so-called curse placed on the area by Cornstalk. A 2002 movie called *The Mothman Prophecies* links reported appearances of a red-eyed, seven-foot tall, moth-like creature for a year before the tragic Silver Bridge collapse in 1967. The Mothman supposedly wasn't seen again after 46 died in the tragedy.

Today, there is a Mothman statue on Fourth Street that is taller than Cornstalk's stone obelisk and a Mothman Museum nearby on Main Street. In a frequently repeated version of the story, Cornstalk sent the Mothman to terrorize the town's citizens before exacting his vengeance with a bridge collapse that engineers mistakenly think occurred because of structural problems.

In case you're wondering, Cornstalk also gets the blame for a laundry list of tragedies that have befallen the region over the years; I found one writer on the web who listed the 1930 Ohio Penitentiary fire that killed 322 inmates in Columbus – 110 miles away – as part of the "region's" many tragedies. There is even the text of a speech Cornstalk was supposed to have made before he died in a hail of bullets where he put his curse on the area. Some historians have traced the origin of this to a local play that may have created the curse for dramatic effect in 1921.

Neither the battle nor the murder needs embellishment. Some historians (and even more West Virginia tourism types) cite the conflict as the battle of the first of the American Revolution. That seems a stretch second only to the centuries-old death of an Indian chief being somehow linked to a moth-like creature and a bridge collapse.

The battle's roots can be traced to 1768, when the Iroquois gave up all of their lands east and south of the Ohio River to the British in the Treaty of Fort Stanwix. There was one problem with this: The Iroquois didn't occupy any of this land; the Shawnee, Delaware and the Seneca-Cayuga (Wyandot) did.

So when white settlers began streaming into the region, the Indians from those tribes reacted by attacking the settlers, and by the spring of 1774, the conflicts had become a serious problem. In May when family members of peace-loving Chief Logan were murdered at Yellow Creek, many Wyandots and Shawnees demanded retribution. Although Cornstalk urged conciliation and promised to protect innocent British fur traders in the Ohio Country from retaliatory attacks, most Shawnees wanted war and he reluctantly agreed to abide by their wishes. In the meantime. Logan and his followers were conducting raids and killing settlers.

This prompted Lord Dunmore, the royal governor of Virginia, to offer his assistance, in part because he wanted to place Virginia militiamen in these regions and open them to white settlement. Dunmore devised a plan where his army of approximately 1,200 troops would advance from Fort Pitt down the Ohio and Colonel Andrew Lewis would lead a force of 1,000 Colonial militia through the rugged terrain from the southeast. Eventually the troops would converge and attack the Shawnee villages in the Pickaway Plains.

Some historians think Dunmore wanted to make Lewis look bad and sow seeds of discord among his troops with the difficult march, but it didn't happen. When it became clear that Lewis would arrive first, Dunmore sent word for Lewis to immediately cross the Ohio and engage the enemy with the troops he had, rather than wait for Dunmore to arrive. Dunmore said his troops would go up the Hocking River and join Lewis' force in a pincher action against the Indians.

Lewis knew Dunmore's force would arrive too late to be of any assistance, so when his troops reached the Ohio he had his men camp on the triangle of land where the Kanawha empties into the Ohio in order to recuperate from the difficult march. When Cornstalk's scouts discovered them there, the Shawnee chief led his Indian force in a quiet crossing of the Ohio in the dead of night and launched a surprise attack of the Virginia troops from the rear.

Lewis scouts alerted him to the Indians presence, so he marched his troops into the woods to confront them; they were a half-mile from the point and the sun was just peeking through the treetops on October 10, 1774, when the gunfire broke out. This would put the beginnings of the battle somewhere in the vicinity of the Mason County Courthouse on Sixth Street, the street which would later connect with the Silver Bridge. (Believers of the curse gasp here.)

MONUMENT HOLDS CORNSTALK'S REMAINS.

Within the first fifteen minutes of fighting, a line of militia had formed, giving the Virginians the third side of a triangle that was also sided by the two rivers. An intense battle marked by vicious bursts of hand-to-hand combat raged in those woods for over five hours with Lewis aided by company commanders James Fleming and Charles Lewis (his brother) and Cornstalk supported by Blue Jacket and Pucksinwah, father of Tecumseh. Each side gained and gave ground at various points in furious fighting in an area less than 200 yards deep.

Fighting finally began to taper off at noon. Although shots were fired for the rest of the afternoon, there was no more hand-to-hand fighting. Around five o'clock, Cornstalk received word from his scouts that another detachment of Lewis' army would be joining the Colonial force from the south in about three hours. As darkness descended, the Indian troops disappeared into the woods and were eventually seen crossing the Ohio, giving the white militia the victory, albeit a debatable one. Seventy-five Virginians had been killed, including Charles Lewis and half (23) of their non-commissioned officers. One hundred forty men had also been wounded, 88 of whom could no longer fight during this campaign. The "losing" Indians had 22 killed, including Pucksinwah, and 18 wounded.

When Cornstalk and his warriors reached the Pickaway Plains and reported what had happened, he discovered that his Shawnee brothers now had lost their taste for battle and wanted peace. Cornstalk and Lord Dunmore gave it to them a few weeks later at Camp Charlotte, a few miles up Scippo Creek from Cornstalk's town. In the terms of the agreement, the Shawnees ceded all claims to land south and east of the Ohio (today's West Virginia and Kentucky), and they also agreed to return all white captives and stop attacking barges of immigrants traveling on the Ohio River.

Peace didn't last, which is how Cornstalk ended up back in today's Point Pleasant three years later. The treaty negotiated at Camp Charlotte was supposed to have been signed by all of the parties at Fort Pitt later, but never was. And because hostility had picked up on both sides, Cornstalk decided to go under a flag of truce to Fort Randolph (the fort had been built at the forks of the Ohio and Kanawha) to explain to that camp commander that the Indians could no longer abide by the agreement. It was October 10, 1777 – three years to the day after the battle – that Cornstalk returned with his son, Elinipsico, and sub chief Red Hawk to explain the Shawnees' position.

"The grievances are too great to be borne," Cornstalk said. "I can no longer restrain my young men from joining the raiding parties encouraged by our friends, the British. I no longer wish to restrain them. We have suffered much at the hands of the Shemanese who have repeatedly broken the treaty. Now there is a treaty no longer. It is a matter of honor that we have come here to tell you of this."

Honor apparently meant little to Captain Matthew Arbuckle, who promptly had the trio taken prisoner and led to a small room with only three small slits for a window. The news of Cornstalk's capture spread like a wildfire in the garrison, and it wasn't long before the door flew open and a large group of soldiers and frontiersman with rifles pushed their way into the doorway.

"By God, it is Cornstalk," Captain John Hall said. And with that he leveled his rifle at the Shawnee chief and fired. The others took that as a signal and a symphony of shots rang out as the three prisoners crumpled to the floor. More shots were fired as the Indians lay there and by the time the murderers were finished, Cornstalk reportedly had between seven and nine bullets in his body.

The men who killed Cornstalk were arrested and tried, but they were freed after no witnesses came forward to testify against them. Meanwhile, Cornstalk's death became a rallying cry for Indians across the frontier to step up the fight, a sad irony for a chief who tried to make peace.

The Shawnee chief was buried outside of Fort Randolph, which was burned down by Indians after the soldiers abandoned it in 1779. Street-builders inadvertently unearthed Cornstalk's remains in 1840, and they were moved to the courthouse grounds, where they stayed until the construction of a new courthouse in 1954 meant they would have to be moved again.

This time they were taken to Tu-Endie-Wei State Park, site of Fort Randolph and likely part of the 1774 battlefield. In what was described as a lengthy ceremony, the old chief's last remains – three teeth and 15 bone fragments – were sealed in an aluminum box in the center of that four-ton stone monument to Cornstalk.

Impressive as the monument is, it shares the park with an 84-foot granite monument commemorating the frontiersmen who fought and died in the 1774 battle, the Mansion House log cabin/museum built as a tavern in 1796 and a tablet honoring "Mad" Anne Bailey, who joined the militia and became a frontier scout after husband Richard Trotter was killed in the battle. So I'm guessing that Cornstalk didn't get that much attention here after his remains were moved here from the courthouse grounds in the 1950s until that tragic bridge collapse.

Either way, at the end of the day we are left with this: Because of the influence of modern media, Cornstalk and the Mothman are the city's two most important figures. And one can't help but wonder how many curious visitors would know anything at all about the famous Shawnee chief were it not for an oversized creature that looks like it should be spending its time buzzing around streetlights at night.

Tourists now come to Tu-Endie-Wei State Park to pay their respect to Cornstalk, whose new-found fame might be compared to that of a researcher who cured cancer being famous for inventing the yo-yo.

But the old chief has never had anything to be ashamed of. This says more about us than it does about him.

6 YELLOW CREEK

In a rest area off Ohio Route 7 a few miles south of Wellsville, Ohio, and a few hundred yards from the Ohio River, an unobtrusive, two-foot high block of granite beckons visitors from several feet away. It sits there like a shy customer in a noisy pickup bar, receiving little notice from travelers who are in a hurry to exit their cars, do their business and be on their way.

If it were a bar patron, it would probably go home alone. Even for one who notices it, the small plaque almost apologizes for troubling you with its information:

Lest we forget
Chief Logan
"Tar-gah-jute"
A chief of the Mingoes
A friend of the whites

From near this place in 1774,
all of the family of Logan was
was lured across the Ohio River
and massacred by whites thus
sending Logan and Ohio Indian
nations on a path of war for
vengeance now known to history as Cresap's war.
"Who shall mourn"

For what it's worth, there a likeness of an Indian head to the left of the words which may or may not resemble Logan, Michael Cresap was cleared of any role in the ambush 200 years ago, and reducing Logan's eloquent speech under the Logan Elm to three words doesn't give the monument provider an "A" for credibility. But it's a nice little park with a shelter house, picnic tables and a wide expanse of grass and trees. It's a lovely spot for a picnic, or, if you were one of Logan's unfortunate family members, a pretty place to spend your last day on earth.

OK, the murders did take place on the other side of the Ohio River, which would probably be a more appropriate place for remembrance. And West Virginia does an even worse job of commemorating this horrific event than Ohio does. It placed a metal marker along the side of West Virginia Route 2, across the highway from the river-hugging Mountaineer Race Track and Casino complex, which isn't even where Logan's family and other members of the Mingo tribe were killed.

The West Virginia marker gets the name of the war right, calling it Dunmore's War, and mentions that Logan's family was killed "at this point. . . opposite their village at the mouth of Yellow Creek in Ohio."

The marker is probably over a half-mile from the spot on Baker's Bottom, where Logan's family was killed, on property that lies south of the racetrack and casino complex near the mouth of Dry Run. A Linde gas and engineering plant sits on property immediately south of the racetrack and north of Dry Run Road; a wooded area of tangled branches, weeds and uneven terrain lies on the other side of the road and the dry creek bed. The land immediately south of the forested creek bed is flat and open and could also be the site of Baker's cabin, which also served as a tavern. Signs are posted that indicate the property belongs to the racetrack and trespassers will be prosecuted.

If this is the actual location of Joshua Baker's cabin, in or near where the murders occurred, it would be a wonderful place for a park and exhibit – or even an unobtrusive, two-foot high block of granite -- to tell the story. The gas plant seems like an effective stop sign to development south of the casino, anyway. Regardless, the tale deserves a more complete airing than what it's getting today on both sides of the Ohio:

Logan was likely Talgahyeetah (Tah-gah-jute) when he was born near Auburn, New York, in 1726, and he had been a friend of the white man since he was a boy. His father Shikellamy was an Oneida chief and diplomat for the Iroquois confederacy and a friend of the white man and Christian missionaries. He worked closely with Pennsylvania colonial official James Logan to maintain the Covenant Chain trade relationship with the colony. Following a prevailing tribal practice, Talgahyeetah took the name "James Logan" out of admiration for his father's friend.

Logan spent most of his early life in New York and Pennsylvania. He had a village at the mouth of the Beaver River, twenty-five miles down the Ohio River from Fort Pitt and an equal distance upstream from the mouth of Yellow Creek until early 1774, when he moved his tribe because he thought the area was getting too crowded.

ROADSIDE PARK WHERE LOGAN'S VILLAGE STOOD

His new village contained about 60 members of the Mingo tribe and stood on a level bottom about half-mile from the actual mouth of Yellow Creek on the land now occupied by the rest area. It included several cabins including a small longhouse for councils. The village is sometimes referred to as Logan's "hunting camp" in accounts of the incident, which is misleading if technically accurate. Since moving from the mouth of the Beaver River, the Mingoes had lived there.

Cresap himself had visited with Logan there in late February, 1774, about two months before the incident. He was on his way down the Ohio and was about to make a stop at Baker's place when he noticed the budding Indian encampment on Yellow Creek. Logan had met him on occasion at both Fort Pitt and at the Mingoes' village on the Beaver River and flagged him down. Cresap told Logan that a party of rowdy soldiers had recently fired on some peaceful Shawnees at Fort Pitt. He spoke of increased white settlement on the Virginia side of the Ohio River and rumors of retaliatory Indian attacks. Logan knew of the incident at Fort Pitt, which caused hard feelings with the Shawnees even though none of them were seriously hurt. But he didn't buy the stories regarding recent Indian attacks on white settlers. He said he would have been aware of the attacks if they had happened.

About the same time a small group of Shawnees visited with Logan on their way to Fort Pitt. They were led by war chief Pucksinwah and intended to meet with George Croghan to make a final plea to keep white settlers out of Shawnee lands. Pucksinwah asked for Logan's support, as chief of the Mingoes. Logan told him that the Mingoes didn't have a chief. Pucksinwah said he knew that, but also knew that the Mingoes followed Logan's lead. Logan reaffirmed his neutrality in such matters and wished them well.

The Shawnee delegation stopped at Yellow Creek a few weeks later on their return trip to tell Logan of their frustration with the talks at Fort Pitt but he had gone on a hunting trip. Pucksinwah told Logan's brother Taylaynee that Croghan sympathized with them, but said there wasn't much he could do to stop the influx of white settlers. Taylaynee suggested that maybe the Shawnee should move farther west as Logan's tribe had done and Pucksinwah immediately rejected that thought. Taylaynee said he would tell Logan of the visit, but could do nothing more.

Future Shawnee war chief Blue Jacket and two fellow tribesmen were on a scouting mission for Pucksinwah along the Ohio a few days later when they came upon a party of white men along Pipe Creek about two miles downstream from today's Moundsville, W.Va., in Ohio's Belmont County. The group included Jacob Greathouse and George Rogers Clark. Blue Jacket wanted to pass by quietly without engaging them, but his companions wanted to greet them peacefully. They approached them with their hands out in friendship and some of the whites promptly fired at them. Blue Jacket's companions were killed and he escaped; in the confusion, he heard one of the men utter the words "Logan. . . Cresap. . . Yellow Creek. . . kill 'em all!"

When he got far enough away from his pursuers to stop his evasive actions, he headed straight for Logan's village on Yellow Creek to warn him.

He was glad to find Logan there when he arrived -- and frustrated by his response. It saddened Logan to hear what had happened to Blue Jacket's Shawnee brothers, but he believed Blue Jacket had misunderstood their intention to attack his village at Yellow Creek. He thanked Blue Jacket for his concern and told him that had always been a friend to the white man and couldn't imagine that he would be a target if a war started. An irritated Blue Jacket immediately left so he could tell Pucksinwah what had happened.

Even Blue Jacket didn't know the whole story, though. Fueled by rumors of impending war with the Indians, nervous white settlers met at Briscoe's Settlement (at the mouth of Briscoe Run just north of today's Vienna, West Virginia) and elected Cresap to lead a force against the Indians. Cresap accepted and advised caution, saying that it would be unwise to move in response to rumors. He suggested that all of the settlers return to Wheeling, where they would be safe and could better assess the situation.

A few days later, a messenger brought word from Major John Connally, the commander at Fort Pitt, that his scouts said the Indians were preparing for war and would strike as soon as they were ready. That was apparently enough for Cresap. He had heard that a party of two white men and two Indians were camped at Indian Short Creek, and he gathered a handful of volunteers and headed downstream. When they arrived, Cresap immediately shot and scalped the two Delawares, and shoved their bodies into the river. This surprised and upset the two white traders – the Indians were their friends -- and Cresap didn't care.

"We're at war with the tribes again," he said. "Any Indian we see is a dead one."

Word reached Wheeling of a hunting party of about 20 Mingoes at the mouth of Captina Creek (20 miles south of Wheeling at today's Powhatan Point, Ohio) a few days later, and Cresap quickly recruited 30 men and went there in hopes of a big score. They lost the element of surprise when one of his men's guns accidentally fired on their approach, but Cresap still managed to kill three Indians.

When they returned to Wheeling, the possible consequences of their unprovoked attacks sunk in and many of the locals began moving to the safety of Fort Pitt. With the town nearly evacuated, the Greathouse brothers – Daniel and Jacob – convinced Cresap to make one more strike, this one on the Mingoes at Yellow Creek, and he had reluctantly agreed. But five miles after the 11-canoe party left Wheeling, Cresap had second thoughts. Just past Upper Twin Island and still 35 miles from Yellow Creek, he angled the lead canoe toward the Virginia shore. He told the men that the more he thought about it, the more the attack on Logan's camp didn't make sense. Logan was a good man and he had always been a friend of whites. Maybe they could somehow smooth over relations with the tribes after their attack at Captiva Creek, but if they attacked Logan's camp, which included many women and children, nothing could prevent an all-out war with the Indians.

Surprisingly, most of the men agreed with him. The Greathouse brothers and about 30 men didn't. They told Cresap that they would honor his word not to attack, but they wouldn't return to Wheeling with him. They considered the retreating men cowards and said they were going to continue paddling upstream to Pittsburgh on their own.

As soon as Cresap and his men left, the Greathouse brothers told the group that they had no intention of giving up the attack on the Yellow Creek Mingoes. Plans would have to be changed because there were only 30 of them now, but because the Indians were friendly, killing them would be easy.

On April 29, 1774, the group arrived at Baker's Bottom, Virginia, a few hundred yards south of the mouth of Yellow Creek on the Ohio side. They stopped first at a cabin shared by James Chambers and Edwin King and tried to convince them to join them; Chambers declined, but King went along. They went to the Bakers' cabin next and explained their plan to Joshua and Sarah Baker. The Bakers gave them a jug of whiskey in support and the

Greathouse brothers headed across the river for Logan's village. Although Logan and some of the men had gone on a hunting trip, his older brother, Taylaynee, greeted them cordially. They presented him with the whiskey as a supposed act of friendship.

The Greathouses told him they were camped on the other side of the river with four of their friends. They said they had more whiskey there and invited the Indians to come across the river tomorrow afternoon and share it. They said that if the Mingoes would bring along some beaver skins, they could engage in some kind of sporting contest. If the Indians won, they would get another jug of whiskey. If they white men won, they would get the skins. Taylaynee agreed.

The ruse worked as planned. Two canoes of Indians bearing seven warriors and two women, one of them pregnant and also carrying a little girl of about two in a cradleboard on her back, came across the river and the Greathouse brothers greeted them warmly. The pregnant woman, Koonay, was Logan's sister. The other woman, Mellana, was his wife. Taylaynee was also there, and he introduced one of the young warriors as his son, Molnah.

From that point, the story has several variations. All say the Mingo men drank too much alcohol and were fired upon and murdered by the 26 members of the Greathouse party who had been hiding. Some say they engaged in a shooting contest in the woods and some believe the shooting occurred inside Baker's cabin. The horrific end is the same.

Mellana had been standing off the side when the shooting started and one of the white men ran up to her and put a gun to her temple. She raised her hand to stop him and he shot through her hand and killed her. Koonay ran for the canoes but one of the attackers tackled her and the crying infant rolled out onto the ground. A man scooped up the infant and tried to muffle her cries; another man announced that two more canoes were coming across the river bearing about 15 more Mingoes and some children.

One of the Greathouse brothers ordered the men to quiet both the baby and her mother, so that the two of them and Joseph Tomlinson could happily invite the next wave of Mingoes into their deadly ambush. All would probably have been killed if Koonay hadn't broken free and shrieked some kind of warning. Her screams alerted the Indians that something was amiss and caused the canoes to turn back; a barrage of shots rang out and possibly a dozen more Mingoes died before they made it out of rifle range.

Estimates of the number of Indians killed vary, but the best guess is about 21. With the exception of the two-year-old girl (who was spared because she was the daughter of white trader John Gibson), all of those in the initial party were killed, including Logan's sister, Koonay, whose baby was cut from her abdomen and scalped. This added to Logan's rage when he returned and learned of the tragedy. It also angered many whites already frightened by the prospects of retaliatory attacks.

Their fear had a face now. Logan vowed to kill 10 white men for every Mingo killed at Baker's Bottom and 20 for the life of his unborn nephew, who was torn from his mother's womb.

It's difficult to know how many whites he killed in revenge before the Camp Charlotte treaty ended Dunmore's War and Logan delivered his famous lament under the Logan Elm.

Whatever the number, it's hard to fault him.

7 MINGO JUNCTION

No one goes through Mingo Junction, Ohio, on purpose these days. A traveler hugging the Ohio River shoreline between East Liverpool and Martin's Ferry or Bridgeport breezes along Ohio Route 7 above the small steel town three miles south of Steubenville, bypassing a Commercial Street strip lined by dirty buildings that are the tired remnants of a once thriving business district.

Near the southern end of this strip, Conch's Avalon Bar called it quits in the summer of 2016. A 2013 Internet review on Yelp has somehow outlived the place, and its author fondly recalled its better days.

"This is a great place to stop in for a beer when out on the bike. This is a cool bar in an old industrial town. When steel was king, this place had standing room only. . ."

That vision stretches the imagination like a taut rubber band these days, but only until you glance over your shoulder at the massive size of the Wheeling-Pittsburgh Steel plant sitting beyond the structures on the other side of Commercial. It explains why scenes from The Deer Hunter starring Robert DeNiro and Meryl Streep were filmed here in the 1970s – released in 1978, it won five Academy Awards, including Best Picture -- and confirms the biker's memory that this weary little town was once a crowded place, its streets and its businesses throbbing with life.

In August of 2000, the Russia-based Severstal Corporation purchased the Wheeling-Pittsburgh Steel plant that had been in operation under several different companies since the late nineteenth century and shut down all production. JSW Steel USA, the American branch of an Indian conglomerate purchased the plant in 2018 and restarted the mill with about 250 workers that December. But it shut down the plant in July, 2020, due to a lack of demand for steel. It reopened in March, 2021, but the future of the massive plant that once employed thousands is still uncertain. Mingo Junction had 5,278 residents as recently as 1970. It is nearing 3,000 now.

If our wayward traveler ventures two blocks farther south, he is in for another surprise. Just beyond a two-story frame house on the west side of the street opposite a railroad underpass, an elaborate if overgrown rock garden surrounds a small pool of water. A sign identifies this as Potter Spring, a camping place for George Washington on October 22 and November 17, 1770. The sign, which some shrubbery is threatening to swallow, says that our future first president camped here on a trip to and from the Ohio country to select lands as payment to Virginia soldiers.

But why here? Given the surroundings it is certainly a question any sensible person might ask, especially since this was probably almost two centuries before they were packing in the crowds at Conch's Avalon.

The answer lies in those 18th century days when Washington passed through what was then called Mingo Bottom. Travelers came here then because it offered one of the easiest crossing places of the Ohio River. Long-gone Mingo Island divided the river at this point and crossings were usually made just above the head of the 20-acre land mass. The Ohio River was shallow enough there to be forded on horseback during dry times without the animal being forced to swim. Even when the river rose, the amount of swimming was limited.

In the days before bridges, this made Mingo Bottom an important location for all types of travelers, including Native Americans, adventurers, land grabbers, settlers and armies. It's the reason the Mingo tribe had a settlement at the mouth of Cross Creek at the southern end of Mingo Bottom as early as 1750. From that point forward, the broad, elevated 250 acres of bottomland located north of Cross Creek was a busy place.

In 1758, 30 soldiers from Fort Pitt led by Captain John Gibson, set out in pursuit of a Mingo party that had attacked and destroyed a settlement on the Monongahela River. The guilty warriors had too big of a head start for Gibson's troops, but the military men accidentally came across a party of seven or eight Mingoes led by Little Eagle at Cross Creek.

The Indians were sitting around a fire when they saw Gibson's soldiers approaching them. Little Eagle immediately let out a war whoop, grabbed his gun and fired at Gibson. The shot passed through a baggy part of the captain's shirt and struck a soldier behind him, at which point Gibson leaped forward, swung his sword and severed Little Eagle's head. Several Mingoes later reported that Gibson had cut off the chief's head with a long knife and the name stuck; to many Indians, Virginians became known as "the Long Knives."

The Mingoes frequently camped at Mingo Bottom and all of the Indian tribes crossed the Ohio here, but whites also recognized the value of the crossing. That explains Washington's visit here from Fort Pitt in October,

1770, with the intent of inspecting land for future claims. Two Mingoes guided his party from this point, and he stayed here for three days upon his return, while they waited for horses to be brought to them. In his writing, Washington praised both the commercial possibilities and the abundant nature in the area.

The site found a new use in May, 1782, when Colonel William Crawford sought to raise an army of settlers for an expedition against the tribes of the Sandusky Valley. He called for a rendezvous of all volunteer troops at Mingo Bottom on May 20. With his "troops" likely camped where the steel furnaces and rail yards of Mingo Junction stand today, Crawford waited four extra days for more volunteers to show up and finally left for the Sandusky Valley with 485 soldiers on May 24. Volunteers continued to show up at Mingo Bottom after he left and they hit the road to catch up with the army, which eventually reached 583 in number.

Unlike many others, Crawford didn't come back this way. When the Indians and their British allies at Fort Detroit learned of the troops' advance on the Sandusky, they confronted Crawford's army with almost 500 warriors of their own about a mile north of modern Upper Sandusky, Ohio. After over a day of fighting, the Americans found themselves surrounded and Crawford and some of his troops were taken prisoner. In the wake of a massacre of 96 peaceful Indians by company of Pennsylvania militia at Gnadenhutten in March, the Indians executed Crawford after hours of excruciating torture.

A small white settlement sprung up at Mingo Bottom and on December 7, 1788, a shooting competition here drew 150 men. One of them was famed Indian fighter Lewis Wetzel, who had escaped from jail at Fort Harmar in Marietta for the charge of murdering a friendly Seneca chief named Tegunteh. Tegunteh, nicknamed George Washington because of his exemplary character, had been killed by Wetzel as he approached Fort Harmar for treaty negotiations led by General Josiah Harmar.

Wetzel felt a deep hatred for Indians. A 13-year Wetzel and his 11-year-old brother Jacob had been captured by Indians in 1777 and managed to escape. Ten years later, his father (John Wetzel) and brother George were ambushed and killed by Indians while they were on a canoe trip. Lewis escaped, hating Indians even more than he had before. Since then, Lewis enjoyed hunting and killing Indians as other men hunted game and he became a hero to many settlers, who viewed him as a protector for their families.

Harmar didn't see him that way. Over two centuries later, it's difficult to know whether Harmar jailed Wetzel for killing a good guy like Tegunteh or whether he did it because the killing jeopardized his negotiations. But it is clear Harmar liked and respected Tegunteh and didn't intend to allow Wetzel to run free.

That was the situation when Wetzel arrived at Mingo Bottom for the shooting competition. A detachment of 30 soldiers from Fort Harmar under Captain Jacob Kingsbury showed up, and Kingsbury said they intended to take Wetzel back to the fort. The men there for the competition viewed Wetzel as a hero who had done nothing wrong in killing an Indian, and they made it clear that they would shoot Kingsbury and his troops if they tried to take Wetzel by force. Reluctantly, Kingsbury and the troops wisely left – without Wetzel.

His freedom didn't last. He left Mingo Bottom, presumably after the shooting completion finished, and was seen not long after that sitting in a bar in Limestone, Kentucky – today's Maysville – by a soldier who retrieved some of his men and arrested him. Wetzel was taken to Fort Washington (Cincinnati) and jailed again, before angry citizens again demanded his release. Judge John Cleves Symmes obliged.

With the area's Indian fighting days almost over, Wetzel eventually landed in New Orleans, where his arrests and Indian killing exploits weren't widely known. With his life's mission complete, he ended up serving considerable jail time in New Orleans for counterfeiting. He died at the home of a cousin in Mississippi in 1808 and his remains were eventually reburied in McCreary Cemetery in Moundsville, W.Va., near the family homestead.

If the events at Mingo Bottom seem like ancient history to the modern traveler, they probably seemed the same way to most of those who eventually settled in the town that became Mingo Junction as well. While nearby Steubenville was laid out and settlement begun in 1797, Mingo Bottom didn't become a community until 1869, when Lyman Potter sold the "lower locust grove" to capitalists for an iron works and another plot to Matthew Hodkinson for an oil refinery. These businesses created the need for a town and Mingo Junction was laid out three years later. Brickyards, oil refineries, copper mills, planing mills, coal shafts and coke ovens quickly followed.

The area of the river that had made Mingo Bottom such an important crossroads had already changed. Mingo Island, which in 1782 had supported a heavy growth of large maples on good, high ground, was gone. The great flood in 1832 cut the size of the island in half to about 10 acres, washing away much of that timber and leaving scrub willow to the part that remained. The doomed island gradually eroded and finally disappeared altogether about 1850, more than 20 years before Mingo Junction was born.

8 MARTINS FERRY

When you turn off Ohio Route 7 onto Hanover Street toward downtown Martins Ferry, a neatly carved wooden sign offers a friendly greeting and a subtle boast in painted white letters:

"Welcome to Martins Ferry, Ohio's First Settlement."

The average hungry motorist about to turn right into McDonald's for a Big Mac and fries has no reason to doubt this, of course, if he sees the sign at all. This is Martins Ferry and if this weren't Ohio's first settlement, someone certainly wouldn't have carved that into wood for the world to see, right?

Just about every community has something to brag about, so we naturally believe their prideful welcome-greetings. Can you imagine a town simply making up the name of, say, a state high school champion – Welcome to Blitzville, home of 1965 state champion golfer Larry Jones! --- for one of those sports-themed greeters? If you can't believe a "Welcome to Martins Ferry" sign, what can you believe?

And then again, a restless soul who has been welcomed into lots of Ohio towns might do a double take when he sees what seems like an indisputable fact. What did that official-looking sign say at Marietta's city limits?

"Marietta. First Organized Settlement of the Northwest Territory. 1788"

An "organized" settlement is different than a regular settlement apparently. But what to think of Gnadenhutten? Its sign doesn't make any claims. It just states one fact while conveniently omitting another, that a famous massacre wiped out the settlement and it took years for a new one to sprout in its place:

"Welcome to Historic Gnadenhutten. Founded October 9, 1772."

Just for the record, that is before the earliest record of settlement on land that became Martin's Ferry – 1779 – although it's doesn't take much digging to realize that on Martin Ferry's Wikipedia listing, it is called the "oldest European settlement in the state of Ohio." However, the city's own web page puts no such qualification on it, so obviously it stands by its sign.

The conflicting claims aren't so much nuanced lying as different interpretations of the word "settlement." In that way, this probably isn't much different than civic arguments over dozens of "firsts" for everything from double-decked hamburgers to automobiles to banana splits. If claims are subject to any interpretation at all, there is probably an argument over it

Martins Ferry was "settled' at least as early as 1779 as an extension of the budding Wheeling community on the Virginia (now West Virginia) side of the Ohio River. Settlement on the west bank of the Ohio wasn't legal – it was in violation of the treaties with the Indians -- which probably at least partially explains why those settlers didn't stay. At various times, squatters called their settlements there Hoglinstown, Mercertown and Norristown, all of which were apparently abandoned almost as quickly as they were settled. Various accounts say that the site has been continuously occupied since 1785.

But the questions linger: How many people constitute a "settlement"? And if a site is deserted for a few years, is the next settlement a continuation of the old one or a new settlement entirely? Was Hoglinstown really Martins Ferry?

Wheeling had been around since 1770, although it was initially called Zanesburg. After exploring the area and making tomahawk land claims in 1769, Ebenezer Zane came back with his wife Elizabeth and younger brothers Jonathan and Silas and established the first settlement in the area. As the number of settlers swelled and the desire to get to the other side of the river increased, Ebenezer and Jonathan answered the call by starting the first ferry between Wheeling and the Ohio side of the river. They established a tavern and a ferry house on land they owned on the south side of old County Road, today's Jefferson Street in Martins Ferry, and operated from the foot of First Street in Wheeling at a point even with the north tip of Wheeling Island. Strong men push-poled these early ferryboats back and forth across the river, it being extremely shallow north of the island.

The Zane ferry house stood in the vicinity of a long garage for Environmental Coordination Services & Recycling (ECS&R) at 604 South First Street. ECS&R provides environmental health and safety services to the industrial, academic and residential business sectors. There's no reason for an environmental health and safety services company to look like a ferry landing today and it doesn't at all. Trucks are parked there and storage containers are strewn about the lot. Some scrub trees line the river.

If there was a settlement on the land owned by Zane on the Ohio side no one is sure what it was called, although without any Martins to populate it, it definitely wasn't Martins Ferry. Captain Absalom Martin received a land grant in 1788 and settled upon his grant of one section -- 640 acres -- in 1789. He built a log cabin there near the Ohio River just north of present Hanover Street, and in December of that year applied for and received a license to operate a ferry between the Northwest Territory and the state of Virginia.

The presence of competing ferries shows how much Congress' passage of the Ordinance of 1785, written to raise revenue through land sales, had increased western traffic and made Wheeling a jumping off place for some of them. The ferries were so important to those early settlers that it seems fitting that "ferry" would eventually become a permanent part of the community's name.

Martin's original ferry stood on the north side of Center Street east of today's Martins Ferry Municipal Garage, on the site now occupied by the Martins Ferry Yacht Club. From a beach landing above his cabin on the north side of Hanover Street -- today's Center Street -- Martin would pole his ferry north along the Ohio shore to a bar just south of where Glenns Run entered on the Virginia side and pole the boat across the river.

It is easier to visualize Martin's ferry landing here at the yacht club than at a place crowded with trucks and storage containers, although neither spot bear much resemblance to the days when ferries were the preferred means of river-crossing.

Ebenezer Zane moved his ferry during the summer of 1789. He began operating a two-horse-propelled ferryboat from Beymer's landing at the west end of Ninth Street in Wheeling to Wheeling Island. This was to accommodate wagonloads of emigrants interested in settling on the Seven Ranges grant on the eastern edge of Ohio that was surveyed in 1787. From Wheeling Island, fording the river's back channel was easily accomplished during low-water summer months; during high water periods in the spring and late fall, those wagons had to be poled to the Ohio shore.

The ferry business must have been friendly; Absalom Martin married Ebenezer Zane's daughter, Catherine. They had five children including first son Ebenezer, born in 1791 near the site of his father's original log cabin.

Absalom laid out a town on his property in 1795 and called it Jefferson. But when he was unable to secure the town as the Belmont County seat, he vacated the infant town and bought back the lots that he had sold.

So it sounds as if Absalom's "settlement" became his farm again, the only difference being that he also ran a ferry to the other side of the Ohio from there. But because both the Martin and Zane ferries did a booming business, that probably changed quickly. New Ohio farms to the west of the river started producing more crops than could be consumed by the farm families themselves, and they used the ferries to get them to market in Wheeling. Large herds of cattle, sheep and hogs were also frequent passengers.

Again, how much of a "settlement" this was is debatable, but we do know that Absalom's son, Ebenezer, didn't lay out the town of Martinsville until 1835. When he requested that postal service be established there, he was told that the name Martinsville had already been taken. That's how he decided to name his town Martin's Ferry, which would eventually lose the apostrophe. His town didn't officially become a city until 1865.

If none of this makes Martins Ferry seem like Ohio's first settlement, European or otherwise, that doesn't make its early history any less intriguing.

Ebenezer Zane, the old ferryman who founded Wheeling and oversaw the construction of a frontier road from Wheeling to Maysville, Kentucky, in 1796-97 that became known as Zane's Trace, is buried in one-and-a-half-acre Walnut Grove Cemetery in Martins Ferry. But he isn't the star attraction of the little plot, which lies next to parking lots for the East Ohio Regional Hospital approximately six blocks west of the Absalom Martin's ferry. His younger sister Elizabeth "Betty" Zane has that honor.

Betty is known as the heroine of the battle for Fort Henry in Wheeling on September 11-13, 1782, commonly known as 'the last battle of the Revolutionary War." A statue of her stands upon a tall rock guarding the entrance to the cemetery at the end of North Fourth Street between the two parking lots. Her remarkable story explains why the statue depicts her clutching a folded apron of gun powder:

A force of about 300 Wyandot, Shawnee, Seneca, and Delaware Indians under George Girty accompanied by a force of 50 British Butler's Rangers under Captain Andrew Pratt laid siege to the American outpost, where downtown Wheeling now stands. A force of only 47 militiamen and several women and children including 23-year-old Elizabeth Zane occupied the fort, under the command of one of her brothers, either Ebenezer or Silas.

While the siege lasted three days, the settlers ran into trouble on the second day when their supply of gunpowder ran low and they realized they would not be able to defend the fort much longer if they lost use of the cannon and their rifles.

The Zanes remembered a store of powder in Ebenezer's nearby cabin, and Betty volunteered to retrieve it. While the others were reluctant to let her go at first, she reasoned that the Indians would be less inclined to shoot a woman. She argued that they couldn't take a chance of losing any of the men of fighting age. She said that she was young and strong and fast – and didn't mention that she had gone 40 hours without sleep as she molded bullets for the men. Given the desperation of their situation, the men grudgingly gave in to her request.

At noon, the front gate of Fort Henry opened and she bolted through it and ran 60 yards to Ebenezer's cabin. Enemy forces stopped shooting when they saw the young woman emerge and stared in awe as she disappeared into the cabin. Betty poured the gun powder into her apron, emerged from the cabin and sprinted back toward the fort. By this point, the attackers had realized the nature of her mission and opened fire. With the gunpowder clutched in her arms and bullets whizzing by her, the 60 yards up hill to the fort must have seemed like 600 on the return. Bullets pierced her clothes, but none struck her and she somehow made it safely inside the fort. The powder allowed the settlers to defend the fort until the next day when Captain John Boggs arrived with 70 American soldiers. The arrival of the reinforcements ended the siege.

It is a remarkable story, but one with credibility issues that may be even more serious than Martins Ferry's claim as Ohio's first settlement. Some historians question the veracity of the Betty Zane tale because no contemporary accounts from the time period mention her heroism, including the official report made by her brother Silas to General William Irvine. Her story's similarity to the account of Mad Anne Bailey's 100-mile dash for ammunition to save Fort Lee in Charleston, Virginia (W.Va.) in 1791 may have also added to the doubts.

It doesn't help that the story about Betty Zane's heroism was first published in Chronicles of Border Warfare in 1831 by Alexander S. Withers, eight years after her death in St. Clairsville, Ohio. By then, she had been married twice and had given birth to eight children.

It's certainly possible her brother didn't think his sister's act of courage belonged in a report to his commander, and that Betty and the other family members simply didn't make a big deal about it. They were used to overcoming difficult challenges, so this may have seemed like just another one.

Any chance that this would be merely regional legend changed when author Zane Grey, a distant relative, published a historical novel called Betty Zane in 1903 that focused on Betty's heroism in retrieving the vital gunpowder. At that point, she became one of the most famous pioneer women of the west.

Outside of the immediate area, her fame has faded a bit since then. The annual Betty Zane Days Festival in Martins Ferry keeps her name before the public and her statue, "erected by the school children of Martins Ferry" in 1923, still guards the entrance to the little cemetery, on the other side of a ridge of trees from whizzing traffic of Ohio 7.

If nothing else, the statue draws attention to the burial site of many members of the Zane and Martin families. All legends and civic claims aside, they deserve high praise for their role in the settlement of the Old Northwest.

9 FORT LAURENS

The average tourist doesn't spend much time looking for Revolutionary War sites while cruising Interstate 77 in eastern Ohio, so Fort Laurens is a revelation. A sign at the Bolivar exit ramp doesn't even hint at its status. This was the Old Northwest's Valley Forge.

Not as many soldiers of the Continental army suffered there during the winter of 1778-79 as they did under George Washington at their winter quarters the year before, but the hunger and cold were every bit as real. The men here were under-clothed, under-fed and under siege by British soldiers and their Indian allies. Some of them resorted to boiling their moccasins and eating shoe leather to stay alive.

If you don't live in the vicinity -- Canton is 13 miles north – there's a good chance you've never heard of Fort Laurens. But the site is commemorated by a park and a small museum, which is how it received part billing with the Atwood Lake Region and Zoar on the "next right" sign on I-77.

Because of the fort's history, it's ironic that its eastern bastions stood so close to all of those buzzing cars and trucks on the southbound lanes of the freeway. This was an isolated spot in the wilderness next to the Tuscarawas River when constructed in the fall of the 1778, which is what led to most of its problems.

George Washington ordered the campaign that created it, a march from Fort Pitt into the Ohio country. Colonial troops intended to attack Indian tribes friendly to the British along the Sandusky River and then attack and capture Fort Detroit.

The inability to secure the necessary number of men and supplies caused a reevaluation of the plans. The Continental Congress scaled back the mission, dropped Detroit from the plans and ordered the army to attack villages of hostile tribes along the Sandusky and the southwestern edge of Lake Erie.

Under the command of General Lachlan McIntosh, an American army of 1,200 men and its Delaware Indian guides marched west from Fort Pitt. It built a supply post 20 miles downriver at the present site of Beaver, Pennsylvania, that McIntosh called, uh, Fort McIntosh, and on November 4, McIntosh's troops headed west toward the Sandusky towns.

If McIntosh weren't a Georgia native with little experience in such matters, he might not have considered this to be such a grand idea. The weather worsened by the time the soldiers reached the Tuscarawas River in November and McIntosh decided to stop there and build a fort, 90 miles short of the Sandusky. He decided to leave a small garrison of 172 men and women at the fort under the command of Colonel John Gibson. He would return to the area with the rest of his army the following spring to continue his march toward Sandusky, Lake Erie and Detroit, if possible. Maybe because his own name was already taken, he named this fort after the president of the Continental Congress, Henry Laurens.

The wooden stockade on the west bank of the Tuscarawas River was a quadrangular-shaped structure with four bastions approximately 240 feet from the top of one bastion to another, approximately an acre in size. Storage buildings and barracks stood inside the walls.

Nothing about the operation went smoothly. Many of the men wore clothing too thin for work in this part of the Ohio country in late November, so the others were pressed to work harder to finish the structure. A shortage of supplies – food, clothing, nails, you name it – confronted the troops almost from the beginning, and many of the troops began openly calling the structure Fort Nonsense. The weather continued to grow worse. A fort deep in enemy territory, with no military support for more than 100 miles, made an inviting target for hostile tribes. The Indians frequently launched attacks, making outside forays for food and game dangerous.

A mutiny in December was quickly put down, but matters continued to worsen. The provisions brought from Fort McIntosh slowed to a trickle. Colonel Gibson tried another approach, sending Samuel Sample, a Pittsburgh merchant who served as Fort Laurens commissary, to the friendly Delaware village at Coshocton to buy goods. While Sample lodged there with a detachment of troops, a Delaware killed and scalped John Nash, the camp guard. This shocked the trader, who frequently dealt with these Delawares. Another incident followed where two warriors shot three of his horses, drove off two of the others and stole some of his goods. Delaware chief Gelelemend (also known as John Killbuck Jr.) apologized and sent a contingent of friendly Indians to escort Sample and his troops back to the fort. The supplies they brought with them provided temporarily relief to the beleaguered soldiers, but not much else.

Captain John Clark of the Eighth Pennsylvania arrived from Fort Pitt with a supply escort that carried shirts, shoes and clothing on January 21. His overnight stay enabled Gibson to write several letters for delivery to Fort Pitt. On their return, Clark and his escort had gone only three miles from Fort Laurens when a small group of Mingoes led by British sympathizer Simon Girty ambushed them. Two of Clark's men were killed, four were wounded and one was missing before the others returned to the fort. Unfortunately, the Mingoes captured the soldier who carried Colonel Gibson's letters.

Although Girty couldn't read, the British on the Sandusky River could. An interpreter read the letters to the Wyandots and then forwarded them to Fort Detroit and presented them to a joint Indian council. Now that the British and their Indian allies knew some of the details of the miserable conditions at the fort, they decided to attack.

Captain Henry Bird of the Eighth Regiment led a handful of British soldiers and probably 200 to 300 Wyandot, Mingo, Munsee, and Delaware warriors. They arrived on February 22, 1779, and surrounded the fort on three sides without being detected. Unaware of the enemy's presence, Colonel Gibson sent a wagoner and 18 soldiers out the following morning to gather horses that had strayed from the fort. The garrison needed the horses to bring wood into the fort, which had been cut earlier. The party was making it way across an open plain just to the south of the fort when the attackers opened fire and quickly cut down the surprised soldiers. Seventeen men were killed and scalped within sight of the helpless garrison. The other two were taken prisoner.

That evening, the soldiers inside the fort braced for another attack. Instead, the Indians paraded across the open plain in full war dress; one of the men in the fort counted 847, which must have terrified all of them. At that point, the fort held 172 soldiers, although only about 100 were fit for duty.

The Continental troops bought into a simple deception: The Indians moved in a large circle, which was partially hidden by a knoll. At dusk, it proved easy to for the Indians to pass behind the knoll and come back without being recognized, making their force appear much larger than it was.

In fact, the attackers must have believed that they didn't have enough men to take the fort without sustaining considerable losses and that it would be easier to force the starving soldiers to surrender with a prolonged siege. This may have worked if Gelelemend, the friendly Delaware chief, hadn't sent emissaries to the Indians and tried to talk them out of it. He told them that the Americans were about to grow stronger and more influential because the French had joined their side. Whatever the reason, after a few weeks, the Indians began to lose interest in the siege and many of them started to return home.

General McIntosh finally arrived with a relief force of 700 men from Fort Pitt on March 23 and the siege ended. The bodies of the ambush victims, decayed and gnawed by wolves, were picked up and buried in a mass grave in a rough cemetery 200 feet west of the fort near the graves of others who had died of various causes. Colonel Gibson and the men at the garrison were relieved of duty and permitted to return to Fort Pitt; General McIntosh wanted to press ahead with the others and attack the villages on the Sandusky River with an eye on Fort Detroit. But the other officers dissuaded him, both because the road to Sandusky was mostly under water and because they were short on provisions for such a mission. Consequently, McIntosh left 106 men under Major Frederick Vernon to man Fort Laurens and marched back to Fort Pitt with his troops.

For the next six months, Fort Laurens acted mostly as a decoy; the Americans had come to realize that its remote location rendered it mostly ineffective to their cause. The troops finally abandoned the fort on August 2. They arrived at Fort Pitt on August 7 and were subsequently dispatched to other campaigns.

The fort itself endured. In 1782, a young man from Washington County, Pa., named Carpenter escaped captivity on the Muskingum. He hid overnight in the abandoned fort and reported that it was still in good condition. It stood there like a silent ghost until construction of the Ohio and Erie Canal reached this spot in 1832. The canal ran just to the west of the Tuscarawas River and builders destroyed the two eastern bastions and the connecting wall. As late as 1850, the southern wall and southwestern bastion were "quite perfect" according to a geologist and historian who visited there. The site was farmed until the Ohio Historical Society acquired its 81 acres in 1917; at that point, little evidence of the fort remained.

The Fort Laurens State Memorial was born as little more than a remote park. Hedges marked the presumed outline of the fort, although the society admitted that the markings might be somewhat inaccurate. Nor until after Interstate 77 was built just west of the park in the 1960s and more visitors began to come here did anyone realize how inaccurate those markings were.

The society board of trustees proposed a bond issue to build a circular visitor center-museum on the site in 1968 and it opened in August, 1973. In the meantime, extensive excavation of the grounds had begun in 1972 under Michael Gramly, both to determine the exact boundaries of the fort and also to retrieve and restore artifacts. In the process, archaeologists discovered that what old timers had identified as the southern wall was in fact the northern wall. The fort had actually stood 200 feet south of where local tradition had put it, and at the edge of the already-constructed museum.

Today, the outline of the fort is cut out in the ground and filled with mulch, making it easy to walk along the walls that existed during the harsh winter in 1778-79. Hesitation and a few moments of silence allow the visitor to do a quick mental leap to the eighteenth century. The imaginary moans of sick, hungry soldier during the harsh winter of 1778-79 merge with the whines of speeding semis on I-77.

When you walk to the eastern edge of the park, you run into a wooded area with a deep trench next to the interstate, the bed of the long-gone Ohio and Erie Canal. The busy freeway occupies space once used by the Tuscarawas River; engineers moved the river to the east when the interstate was built.

The fort's story is told in markers placed strategically around the grounds. Low rock walls form a path near the woods to allow visitors to step up and peer down at the tangle of weeds, trees and brush that used to be the old canal and up at the cars and trucks passing on the freeway.

A tomb honors an unknown soldier from the massacre and rocks mark the site of the original burying ground of the fort. The bones of the others including the men killed in the raid were examined and placed in a crypt within the museum in 1992. All of the victims' skulls bore coarse legions that are signs of blunt force trauma and many had two or more, as well as fine legions that would have been created by scalping.

A huge rock of granite bearing information about the soldiers who died here sits on the edge of the grass plain, just south of the visitor center where the men presumably died.

"If you go (south) on that road toward a shelter house, there's a teardrop road where a dumpster is," Ohio History Connection archaeologist Bill Pickard said. "That's probably where the massacre happened, right there at the dumpster."

Because it is nearly at the end of an open space between the museum and the dumpster, it is easy to visualize the British and Indians surprising and killing the men within sight of the fort. When you look over that plain, it's possible to imagine the terror the men inside the fort must have felt for a month, every time they saw those decaying bodies lying there.

It is both a somber place and a pretty spot, but the ambience is mostly ruined by the noise from semis barreling by at 70 mph a little more than 100 yards away. The men who served and suffered here because of their remote location would doubtless be amazed by the irony.

That irony is apparently lost on some of the visitors.

"To show you how dumb people are," Pickard said, "I had people ask 'Why did they put the site next to the freeway? It's so noisy.'"

10 COSHOCTON

A young woman wearing a nineteenth-century style dress behind a Roscoe Village information desk in Coshocton, Ohio, laughed when I asked her how many visitors inquire about the name of the main street that runs through the restored canal town.

"A lot of them," she said.

The question was rhetorical. In the twenty-first century, "Whitewoman Street" seems like the creation of someone determined to challenge the laws of political correctness or at the very least try to provoke a reaction from those who find themselves there. Neither is the case, although the young woman said the latter is what usually happens.

"A lot people look at it and say 'Whitewoman Street'?" She punctuated her description with surprised look and raised eyebrows. "But when you explain it to them, they usually go 'Oh, OK."

"It" is the story of Mary Harris, a 10-year-old girl who was kidnapped along with about 100 others by a party of Indians and Frenchmen from Canada during a murderous raid on the frontier village of Deerfield, Massachusetts, on February 29, 1704.

The Indians were from an Iroquois tribe which had been converted to Christianity by Jesuit missionaries and made a permanent home at Caughnawaga (from which the sect took its name), about 10 miles above Montreal. Mary eventually took an Indian husband there, had three children including a son who became an officer in the French military, and moved to Ohio in 1750 as part of the French effort to increase its influence in a region also coveted by the British.

Harris is generally regarded as the first white woman to make her home within the confines of what later became the Buckeye State, although historians say that she was back in Caughnawaga by 1756. Even so, she lived in Ohio Valley long enough to make an impression on traders, explorer and

Native Americans who found the sight of a white woman on the Ohio frontier extraordinary. Today's Walhonding River, which converges with the Tuscarawas River at the site of modern-day Coshocton to form the Muskingum River, was known in those days at White Woman's Creek. The small settlement at mouth of Killbuck Creek five miles up the Walhonding where Harris and her husband lived became White Woman's Town. Both are listed that way on a 1755 map done by John Mitchell.

In Roscoe Village, Whitewoman Street came long after Mary Harris. It got its name because it led to and paralleled White Woman's Creek (the Walhonding). It struck a northwest path out of town (today's U.S. Route 36) and led past the first white woman's old settlement.

Mitchell's 1755 map places the settlement on the west side of the Walhonding and doesn't show Killbuck Creek, which enters the Walhonding from the north as the latter turns to the west. Lewis Evans' 1755 map places it on the east side of the Walhonding. In 1893, William Darlington's notes to Christopher Gist's Journals he used these maps and other writings to place what Gist called her "small Town" opposite the mouth of Killbuck Creek.

Regardless of which shore Mary Harris' "town" occupied, two of the three banks at the convergence of Killbuck Creek with the Walhonding are accessible by one lane roads. The drive back there feels like two centuries of travel rather than a mile of physical distance. The area's remoteness gives the modern visitor a feel for what it must have been like to settle here in 1750. The east side of the Walhonding and Killbuck (which continues north) is a narrow strip of land with a few small cabins, houses and trailers snuggled between the water and a small tree-covered mountain. They can be reached by going west from U.S. Route 36 (after crossing the Walhonding) on county road 28, then making a quick turn on Bethlehem Township road 29. The one-lane road crosses the Killbuck and runs along the east side of the river. There is also a chuck-hole happy one-lane public access road that runs behind the houses on U.S.36 and allows fishermen or curious historians to the point where Killbuck enters from the north and the Walhonding turns to the west. The flat, often muddy, semi-wooded ground there would be perfect for a small settlement, although the land on the south shore, which is covered by farm fields, would also fit the bill.

Mary Harris lived here for only a few years and is probably known today primarily because of Gist's journal, which aided the mapmakers of his time and was finally published years later.

Here is the sum of what Gist wrote on January 15, 1751:

"We left Muskingum and went W 5 M to White Woman's Creek, on which there is a small town; this White Woman was taken away from New England, when she was not above ten Years old, by the French Indians; She is now upwards of fifty, and has an Indian Husband and several Children – Her name is Mary Harris, she still remembers they used to be very religious

MARY HARRIS' SPOT ON WHITE WOMAN'S CREEK PROBABLY DOESN'T LOOK MUCH DIFFERENT THAN IT DID IN HER DAY.

in New England, and wonders how the White Men can be so wicked as she has seen them in these Woods."

If that doesn't seem like much to build what came to be known as the legend of the White Woman you're onto something. Mary Harris eventually became relatively well-known in the territory's lore because some so-called historians decided not let facts stands in the way of a good story. They took what Gist wrote, used some historical information that didn't apply to her and made up some on their own, adding lust and murder to a tale that helped make her famous over a century after she had gone.

Historian George F. Smythe wrote a piece for the Ohio Archaeological and Historical Society in 1924 that compared all of the known facts about Mary Harris with the things that were written about her in a number of books and county histories. "I will. . . show that in every instance where we are able to check up the statements of this "legend" by reference to history, they are absurdly un-true," Smythe wrote.

The earliest book that Smythe could find with references to the white woman "legend" was Charles H. Mitchener's *Historic Events in the Tuscarawas and Muskingum Valleys, and in Other Portions of the State of Ohio*, published in 1876. Here is Smythe's summary of it, including Mitchener's bestowing of the name of "Eagle Feather" on Mary's husband. Smythe writes that is no historical evidence of an Indian of that name:

."One day Eagle Feather came home from beyond the Ohio with another white woman whom he had captured, and who he intended should enjoy the felicities of Indian life on the Killbuck with Mary in her wigwam." Mary would not have this rival in her wigwam; so Eagle Feather, after threatening Mary's life, "took the new captive by the hand, and they departed to the forest to await the operation of his remarks on Mary's mind." At night they returned to the wigwam, and in the morning Eagle Feather "was found with his head split open, and the tomahawk remaining in the skull-crack, while the 'newcomer' had fled. Mary simulating, or being in ignorance of the murder, at once aroused 'The White Woman's Town' with her screams. The woman was pursued, brought back, and put to death as a murderer,"

Smythe points out that Eagle Feather could not have captured another white woman when there were none for hundreds of miles. He wrote it shows how Mitchener conflated a story that Gist wrote about a killing of a woman "who had long time been a prisoner, had deserted and had been retaken" at Muskingum (near present-day Coshocton) on December 26 with the legend of Eagle Feather's "newcomer" white woman. Smythe notes that if the Muskingum woman had been white, the killing would have a very big deal and Gist would have written about it; because he didn't, he concluded that she had to be an Indian. The killing also took place at Muskingum and not White Woman's Town, as it did in Mitchener's legend.

Smythe also pointed out that from all available evidence, Mary Harris was a respectable woman. The fact that she questioned the white man's wicked ways to Gist makes the murderous behavior assigned to her in the legend all the more suspect.

"To take a woman who, so far as we know, was respectable and humane -- to take her and make her out a blood-thirsty savage, is not legitimate," Smythe wrote.

Today, there is a "modern" version of Smythe's treatise that is distributed in pamphlet form to tourists who wander the shops and restaurants on Whitewoman Street in Roscoe Village, so attempts are being made to restore the reputation that nineteenth century writers stole from Mary Harris. But it apparently takes a while for the word to get out. While working on this book, I posted a photo of "White Woman Creek" on Facebook and gave a brief account of Mary Harris' story. It wasn't long before a newspaper friend commented "I think she killed her husband when he took a second and maybe younger wife." Ever after I told him that the story was fictionalized, he insisted that he had read in a couple of places, and finally grudgingly admitted "maybe it was just a story."

So the lascivious, bloody version of this white woman legend still commands attention long after it has been proven false, albeit in an area that has a fascinating eighteenth century history that is mostly ignored by outsiders.

The forks of the Muskingum were important in the early days, both to the Indian tribes who regularly settled here and to white frontiersmen such as Gist who often came this way, When Gist stopped in "Muskingum" on the way to White Woman's Town and other far flung parts of the Old Northwest, he did so because famed trader George Croghan had a trading post at a Wyandot village there. Gist came here on the orders of the governor of the colony of Virginia in quest for good land for the committee of the Ohio Company.

Croghan's trading post stood approximately one mile from modern Coshocton, and based on those two 1755 maps, it occupied a place on the north shore of the Walhonding above the forks. This could have been located almost any place along this stretch, much of which is flat, open ground to the east of today's U.S. 36. It is probably no more than a quarter of a mile from today's Whitewoman Street in Roscoe Village. Gist wrote in his journal that the town "consists of about one hundred families."

More consequential events were in store for other places in and around the modern city of Coshocton. During Pontiac's War in 1764, Fort Pitt commander Colonel Henry Bouquet marched 1,500 men into the Ohio country in an attempt to put down the Indians' uprising. On October 25, his troops reached the forks of the Muskingum and established a camp near the Walhonding River on a hill mile and a half north of the important Delaware village that occupied the site of modern downtown Coshocton.

Bouquet's army camped here in the heart of tribal lands until November 18, during which time he negotiated a peace with the Delawares that included the surrender of all of their white captives. When Bouquet and his men left for the east, 206 white men, women and children that had been captives – some willingly – went with them. A historical marker commemorates the event at the intersection of County Road 24 and Local Road 26. It sits at the bottom of the hill where the Bouquet and his men camped, a short distance north of Coshocton Lake Park.

The modern city takes its name from the Delaware village of Goschachgunk, which means "black bear" in their dialect. The Delaware or Lenape tribe moved to the area because of increasing pressure from European-American colonists on the other side of the Appalachian Mountains. By the late 1770s a Delaware chief named Newcomer first settled the tribe at a place to the east where the modern town of Newcomerstown grew up. Eventually he led 700 members of his tribe here and made this the principal Delaware village in the region.

On March 9, 1777, a great council of Delawares led by Chief White Eyes met in the Goschachgunk Council House, which stood on the parkway near the intersection of Second and Main streets in modern downtown Coshocton. A marker in the median on Main tells of this meeting, during which the Delawares decided "to refuse the hatchet from the British" and remain neutral in their war with the American colonists.

Unfortunately for the Delawares, their neutrality didn't stick. They eventually divided into two factions: those who supported the British and those who hoped to remain neutral. The Delawares who preferred neutrality lived primarily at Coshocton, but they began to fear that American settlers would flood the region if they were successful in their war with the British. More and more of them, including Captain Pipe, a Delaware chief at Coshocton, started to lean toward an alliance with the British. When this became apparent to the Americans, Colonel Andrew Broadhead of Virginia led a detachment of nearly three hundred American soldiers and militia to Coshocton in 1781 with the initial intent of securing an alliance with the turtle tribe of Delawares living there. But an increase in attacks on settlers by the wolf tribe of Delawares stirred anger and resentment among Broadhead's command. That became obvious when Broadhead approached the Delaware village of Gekelmukpechunk, current site of the town Newcomerstown, 14 miles east of Goschachgunk.

Broadhead requested a peaceful discussion between the main chiefs of the village and three were sent to meet him. Unfortunately, militiamen Lewis Wetzel attacked and killed one of the peaceful chiefs just as they had crossed the river to meet him. Sensing disaster, Brodhead retreated and decided to move on to Goschachgunk.

On April 20, Brodhead and his men reached the peaceful Moravian settlement of Lichtenau, located on east side of the Muskingum River a mile south of Goschachgunk. Seeing no difference between peaceful Christian Indians and those who killed white settlers, Broadhead and his men destroyed the village, which was never rebuilt. A stone marker in the front yard of a white house at the corner of Second Street and Clow Lane marks the site of the village today.

Goschachgunk was next. At the time, it consisted of 60 to 80 huts built of poles and bark, strung along in two rows with a street between, one corresponding with today's North Second Street. The council house stood near the center of village and it was much larger than any of the cabins.

Broadhead divided his troops into three regiments and attacked and destroyed the village. Twenty Delawares were killed and Broadhead's troops took 16 warriors and 20 others prisoner. The deaths apparently occurred near a spring east of the village. A limestone marker sitting in the grass easement in front of two houses at 1629 and 1635 Chestnut Street about a mile to the east marks the site of the "Broadhead Massacre" of 20 Indians "following destruction, the same day, of the two villages" of Goschachgunk and Lichtenau. A marker that looks like it belongs in a cemetery seems out of place in this residential neighborhood. It also doesn't explain why they were killed here and not closer to the center of the village.

That marked the end of this as an important Native American site. Almost 20 years passed before the Americans began building their own community at the site of the destroyed Delaware village. The white settlement that formed around 1802 was called Tuscarawas before residents changed the name to Coshocton in 1811.

Aside from the plaque marking the location of the Delaware council house at the base of a stone grinding wheel memorial in the median on Main Street, the most visible Indian presence within the confines of the old village today is the Cherokee Gift Shop on Main Street, a block north of the bronze marker. The strip where Delaware huts once rested boasts of a Tim Horton's donut shop, a cut-rate Valero gas station, a couple of auto repair shops and a Kentucky Fried Chicken restaurant.

If Colonel Broadhead had known what would come later, do you think he would have been so anxious to burn the village of Goschachgunk down?

11 GNADENHUTTEN

When you enter Gnadenhutten on Walnut Street off U.S. 36, it could be any of 100 pretty little Ohio towns. You pass two-story frame houses that have been around since William McKinley was president, an ice cream shop, a church and the Village Hardware. Off to the left is a white-painted two-story building with four columns at the entrance that might be the manor of a southern plantation if it weren't sitting where it is. It houses Gnadenhutten's village hall.

A sign at the intersection with East Main Street offers arrows to six different local "attractions" (Indian Valley HS, Industrial Park, Water and Street Department, etc.) "Museum-Cemetery" is third on the list. A right turn on East Main takes you past another block of old residences, where a green sign with a left-pointing arrow subtly announces "Historic Tour."

A quarter-mile drive on Cherry Street runs into a sign for "Gnadenhutten Historic Park," where the street makes a sharp right. The drive to the left of the sign goes straight into a modern cemetery, whose residents moved in long after "Gnadenhutten" became a name to remember. The sharp right is the beginning of a quick, hard left on County Road 10. The Tuscarawas River is on the right, and a park appears on the left. It has two log cabins, huge trees and almost a football field of grass in front of building emblazoned with the word "Museum."

It is a beautiful spot, a nice place for a family reunion, and maybe a little badminton or a Whiffle ball game. At least it seems that way until you turn left onto the little road that services more of that sprawling cemetery on the right and has a few parking spots on the left near the museum.

Suddenly, the pretty, green spot with those log cabins and a few towering sycamores in the center loses its innocence. This is the place where 96 peaceful, God-fearing Moravian Delaware Indians were bludgeoned to death with mallets and rifle butts by a troop of Pennsylvania militia led by Colonel David Williamson in 1782.

Lest we lose sight of that grisly image too quickly, words written in 1824 by noted Western Pennsylvania historian Reverend Joseph Doddridge, who may have known some of the participants, take your breath away:

"The particulars of this dreadful catastrophe are too horrid to relate. Suffice it to say that in a few minutes these two slaughter-houses, as they were then called, exhibited in their ghastly interior the mangled, bleeding remains of these poor unfortunate people, of all ages and sexes, from the aged grey headed parents down to the helpless infant at its mother's breast, dishonored by the fatal wounds of the tomahawk, mallet, war club, spear and scalping knife."

A MONUMENT WAS ERECTED A CENTURY AFTER THE MASSACRE.

The visitor doesn't make it more than a few steps from his car before he is confronted with a mound surrounded by white pickets and adorned by a simple slab of granite that reads: Burial Place of Remains of Indian Martyrs, 1783, 1798.

The mound seems too small for all of those remains without the full story: After those peace-living Indians were savagely beaten and scalped, their dead bodies were left in cabins that were burned down. When John Heckewelder, one of the missionaries who had lived in the village, returned to the site in 1798, he gathered all the remains he could find and buried them in that spot.

John Heil, site manager of the park and museum, drove up while I calculated the gruesome math: A raging fire and 16 years of decay equals what?

"The place had been abandoned, but when John Heckewelder came back, he knew where the place was," Heil said. "He found a chimney that was still standing. He started cleaning off the brush and finding all the remains that he could find and he gathered them all up and buried them in the mound. . . Shortly after that, 1799 to 1800, is when he came back and started rebuilding the white settlement."

It was June 1 and Heil probably wouldn't have been there if I hadn't sent a message to the park's Facebook page, asking if it would be open that afternoon. The Gnadenhutten Historical Society takes care of the museum and the cabins, which are open by appointment in the winter and staffed mostly by volunteers on summer afternoons. Heil and a small devoted group of local historians try to open the place whenever someone requests it; the good news/bad news situation is that outside of the summer months, interest isn't strong.

"We have phone numbers on the door," Heil said. "If people call the numbers, one of us will get out here and open it up, If I'm in town, I usually come over here and stay until they leave. We probably have 3,000 to 5,000 a year visit, but about 1,000 of those are in August."

Most who hear the story and spend an hour or so walking the grounds, viewing the cabins and touring the little museum of mostly Indian artifacts would probably agree that the number of visitors should be five or 10 times what it is.

This is a place every student of American history should visit, a place that delivers a sickening reminder that Native Americans weren't always the bad guys in the settlement of America, despite their depiction as such as in most movies and television shows.

The Gnadenhutten story begins in May, 1772, when missionary David Zeisberger led a band of Christian Delawares from eastern Pennsylvania to Ohio and founded a town named Schoenbrunn on the Tuscarawas River. The following spring John Heckewelder led another group to the Tuscarawas, and Schoenbrunn was so crowded that Zeisberger founded another settlement down river at Gnadenhutten. Heil said there may have been as many as 90 cabins on the site at one time, even some in the cemetery that lies adjacent to the village. Moravian villages were also settled a short time after that at Lichtenau and Salem.

While other Indians joined with the British during the American Revolution, those at the Moravian villages remained friendly and neutral.

Delawares at Coshocton eventually joined the war against the Americans, in part because of American raids against even their friendly bands. When Colonel Daniel Brodhead led an expedition of militia and regular soldiers out of Fort Pitt and destroyed that village and also the one at Lichtenau on April 19, 1781, he was able to convince the militia to leave the peaceful Delawares at the Moravian mission villages of Schoenbrunn, Gnadenhutten and Salem alone. If his own troops hadn't outnumbered the militiamen, he probably wouldn't have won that argument.

But Indian raids continued. In September, British-allied Wyandots and Delawares, believing that the Christian Indians and missionaries might be aiding the enemy, forced them from their villages. They took them northwest toward Lake Erie to a new village called "Captive Town" about 120 miles away. This was located near the Sandusky River about 10 miles southeast of Upper Sandusky, about a mile above Broken Sword Creek in Antrim Township. The British took the missionaries, David Zeisberger and John

Heckewelder, to Fort Detroit and tried the men for treason for allegedly providing military intelligence to the American garrison at Fort Pitt. The missionaries denied this and were eventually acquitted.

The Moravians arrived at their new home on October 11. They immediately started building huts and scrounging food for the winter, both for themselves and the livestock they had managed to drive from their village on the Tuscarawas River. The western Indians who brought them here had made no provision to feed or house them, and the Moravians found themselves facing the prospects of starvation over the winter.

For that reason, groups of these Delaware-Moravians returned to the towns they had abandoned to gather crops they had sown the previous spring. They collected corn in the fields and stored some of it underground in the nearby forest, where they could retrieve it when needed. But as the season progressed and Indian raids in the Ohio country increased, it became increasingly dangerous for the Christians to go there. Vengeful white troops became less inclined to differentiate between friendly and unfriendly tribes.

On a bitterly cold day in March, a group of almost 100 Christian Delaware Indians were gathering corn in the field near the old village of Gnadenhutten when a large group of Pennsylvania militia appeared on horseback. They hailed the Indians with a friendly wave, and after the two groups exchanged peaceful greetings, the soldiers told the Indians that they had been sent to rescue them from the approaching British troops and escort them to the safety of Fort Pitt.

With no reason to doubt their intentions, the Indians complied with the request to surrender their weapons. But as soon as they did, the militiamen surprised the Indians by turning their weapons on them. They marched their captives back to the deserted village and locked them in two cabins, women and children in one and the men in the other.

This didn't occur by happenstance. The 160 Pennsylvania militiamen had formally mustered at Mingo Bottom on the Ohio River under Colonel David Williamson a few days before for a campaign in retaliation for the deaths and kidnappings of several white Pennsylvanians by hostile tribes. They were angry over raids that had kidnapped and killed family, friends and neighbors, and set out to destroy the Moravian villages, which they saw as easy pickings among the Ohio tribes. The Moravians' religious beliefs didn't matter to them. Indians were Indians.

After imprisoning the peaceful Delawares, Williamson and his men held what amounted to a kangaroo court. They supposedly identified horses, farm implements and cooking utensils that had been obtained in Indian raids against the whites and declared them guilty. They ignored the Moravians' pleas of innocence, and Williamson decided to hold a vote among his soldiers about whether the guilty parties should be killed. Some historians believe he did that to deflect the blame, knowing how the vote would come out.

Williamson reportedly had the militia form a line and asked a direct question: "Shall the Moravian Indians be taken as prisoners to Fort Pitt or put to death here?"

He directed those in favor of sparing their lives to advance three paces to the front. Depending upon the source, only 16 or 18 of the 160 men did. Those courageous men left, spared the ignominy of participation in the gruesome scene that would follow.

With their doom sealed, the Indians asked to be spared until the next day so they could spend the night praying, singing hymns and preparing for their death. Some accounts have the Delawares returning each other's chants from one locked cabin to the other during the night. In the 1970s, the two cabins (the mission house and the cooper house) that are part of the park today were reconstructed on the foundations of the ones believed to have been used to imprison the Indians. Their closeness makes the chant story plausible.

The soldiers carried out the death sentences the next day. They entered the cabins and killed the Indians one by one with blows to the head with their mallets or their rifle butts as they kneeled and prayed. Those not killed by the hard blows likely died from the scalpings that occurred afterwards.

Obadiah Holmes Jr. was one of the militiamen who opposed the killing and he wrote later:

"One Nathan Rollins and brother (who) had had a father and uncle killed took the lead in murdering the Indians. . . Nathan Rollins tomahawked nineteen of the poor Moravians, and after it was over he sat down and cried, and said it was no satisfaction for the loss of his father and uncle after all."

When all of the Indians in both cabins were dead, the soldiers searched the village and took everything of value. The extent of the plunder – furs for trade, pewter, tea sets, clothing, etc., that the Indians had been unable to take with them to Captive Town -- took 80 horses to carry. Then the militia burned the cabins down and mounted their horses for Schoenbrunn, where they planned to do the same thing.

They arrived there to find an empty village, probably because word had been passed from two young men about 15 years of age who had escaped. One boy named Thomas reportedly survived his scalping, hid among the dead bodies, then crept away after dark and made his way to the Sandusky trail. A young boy imprisoned in the house with the women hid briefly in the cellar, then escaped through a window as the house burned around him. He said a young boy with him got stuck in the window and burned to death. Those two survivors are primarily responsible for reporting what happened in Gnadenhutten. Subsequent accounts of the massacre are mostly derived from the stories told by Heckewelder and Zeisberger, who got their information from the two boys.

Heil said "The mission house was the cabin where they held the women and children," and "they held the men in the cooper house." But the accounts seem to indicate that it may have been the other way around. When the Cooper House was excavated, the steps to a cellar were unearthed and visitors can peer down the stairwell and see where the surviving boy supposedly hid. Either way, the reconstructed cabins on their original sites allow the imagination to recreate this grisly scene in all of its horror and leave the visitor wondering how hatred of a people could ever reach such proportions.

After burning the cabins at Schoenbrunn, the militia returned to Pennsylvania. Although many settlers were outraged when they learned of the brutal killings of the peaceful Christian Indians, some frontier residents embittered by Indian attacks over the years probably supported the militia's actions. Despite talk of bringing the murderers to justice, the names of the participants were never made public and no criminal charges were ever filed. Williamson died in poverty in Washington, Pennsylvania, in 1814, 30 years after the massacre and was buried without a stone to mark his grave in the old cemetery on Washington's North Main Street.

Colonel William Crawford wasn't quite so fortunate. In retaliation for what had happened at Gnadenhutten, Crawford got tortured and executed by the angry western tribes after he was captured during another expedition against the Ohio tribes two months later. It didn't matter to them that he hadn't participated in the Gnadenhutten massacre.

The Indians never forgot what had happened here. In 1810, 28 years after the massacre, Shawnee war chief Tecumseh reminded then-Indiana Territory governor William Henry Harrison at Vincennes about the treachery of the white man. Tecumseh was building a confederation of Indians to try to win their lands back at the time:

"You recall the time when the Jesus Indians of the Delawares lived near the Americans, and had confidence in their promises of friendship, and thought they were secure, yet the Americans murdered all the men, women, and children, even as they prayed to Jesus?"

On June 5, 1872, 100 years after the tragedy, a 37-foot granite monument was erected in what had been the center of the original village with the inscription "Here triumphed in death ninety Christian Indians, March 8, 1782." It sits only a few feet from the front of the reconstructed mission house.

"The village was gone and there was absolutely nothing out here then," Heil said.

Thankfully, local historians cared more about accuracy with the cabin sites than the ascetic value of giving the monument space to breathe.

The only thing that could make this park better would be more excavation and the reconstruction of more cabins. Heil pointed to the spot where the schoolhouse had stood and said that when he learned the cost of rebuilding it – more than $200,000 – he knew that such a project was unrealistic.

"Our biggest problem is the lack of town cooperation," Heil said. "People in town just don't care about this place. I don't think people understand the amount of history that's here and what happened here. When you say 96 Indians were massacred here, they just don't seem to think that's important."

If it happened today, that would merit two weeks of non-stop coverage on cable television. Because the massacre happened when it did, it receives a collective shrug from our society and maybe 3,000 visitors a year.

II.

SHAWNEE TERRITORY

12 OLD CHILLICOTHE

An Ohio traveler on U.S. 68 between Yellow Springs and Xenia might zip through the tiny hamlet of Oldtown without noticing the limestone slabs in the small patch of grass in front of the Tecumseh Motel. A metal sign facing the driver announces this as "Old Chillicothe." But even if the driver sees it, his eyes are more apt to be drawn to the run-down 12-room motel behind it, a place that looks like a bedraggled refugee from the 1950s.

The two-story "office," painted yellow on the first floor and blue on the second likely more for economic than for artistic reasons, stands to the left, next to an L-shaped row of rooms. The office looks like it might have been a house before somebody got the brilliant idea of putting a motel here, three miles north of the Xenia city limits and maybe thirty years behind the times. But the "office" was in fact the Oldtown School in its former life and when viewed in that context, the row of memorials out near the road don't seem quite so out of place.

It's the tacky motel that doesn't belong. From a historical perspective, this town just east of the Little Miami River near the mouth of Massies Creek was one of the most important Indian settlements in the Old Northwest. It is a place where Tecumseh grew up, Daniel Boone was brought as a prisoner, Simon Kenton was forced to run the gauntlet and several important tribal war councils convened in the old council house.

Other than those markers there is no trace of any of that now, so it's ironic that the most noticeable remembrance is the rectangular sign that introduces the Tecumseh Motel. When I searched for the place on Google, up popped a 2006 YouTube video of three young guys who stopped here for the night on the way to a wedding in Xenia. They called it "quite possibly the worst hotel in America."

Even conceding that the video doesn't take in all of the marvelous improvements that have probably been made to the place in 14 years since, it's hard not to wonder if a charismatic Indian leader who united the tribes for a war against the white settlers wouldn't be appalled at how they have treated the village he called home. And then again, he might have issued a smug "I told you so" at seeing that this beautiful place near the scenic Little Miami River had been surrendered to enemies bearing, of all things, the Tecumseh Motel. As this book went to press, I learned that the state was negotiating to buy the property for possible use as a park, so maybe this saga will yet have a happy ending.

Tecumseh was actually born "three arrow flights" south of here in 1768, next to a spring in what is now a picturesque park called Oldtown Reserve. His mother, Methotasa, gave birth to him while she and her husband, Pucksinwah, were traveling from Kispoko Town on the Scioto River, where he served as the chief of the Kispokotha sept of the Shawnee tribe. His sept bore responsibility for all matters pertaining to warfare, including the training of warriors. In this instance, they were going to Chillicothe, then the largest of the Shawnee towns, for a council that would draw more than 5,000 Shawnee men including principal chief Cornstalk to discuss the encroachment of white settlers on their land.

Pucksinwah and Methotasa eventually had a wegiwa not far from the site of Tecumseh's birthplace for six years. That merits another marker along U.S. 68, a few hundred yards from Oldtown Reserve and maybe a half mile south of the short strip of houses and house trailers called Oldtown.

Black Fish was the chief of this Chalahgawtha village of the Shawnees. He ranked second only to Cornstalk among Shawnees when Thomas Bullitt came here in 1773 as an emissary of Virginia to inform the tribe that Virginians intended to settle in Kentucky. Indian tribes saw Kentucky as their sacred hunting grounds and were forbidden to settle there.

After the Indians lost at the Battle of Point Pleasant in 1774 and signed a peace accord at Camp Charlotte a few miles southeast of today's Circleville, another council was held at Old Chillicothe in 1775 because of the Shawnees' dissatisfaction with the peace treaty. This time, 350 chiefs and sub chiefs attended. Cornstalk spoke next to last. Black Fish, as the host chief, had the honor of being the final speaker.

Cornstalk cautioned that to make war could result in the destruction of the Shawnees. Black Fish, the "peace chief," proved more hostile.

"This is my memory," he said. "It tells me that no white man can be trusted as any time, any place."

The old bark council house where this took place was 120 feet long and 40 feet wide and lay on the ridge behind the Tecumseh Motel. It stood in the vicinity of a two-story white frame farm house that is flanked by a few trees

A ROW OF HISTORICAL MARKERS FLANKS THE SIGN FOR THE TECUMSEH MOTEL.

and surrounded by a wide expanse of cultivated fields that stretch to the Little Miami a quarter of a mile to the west.

Tecumseh was just a boy, but he had lived in the village since his father had been killed at Point Pleasant. When that happened, Kispoko Town became Black Snake's Town, and Methotasa and her children moved to Old Chillicothe, where Black Fish would serve as the kids' pseudo father. Tecumseh's older brother Chiksika taught him how to be Shawnee warrior and Tecumseh stood out, excelling in games and competitions with other boys, including the older ones.

He witnessed a lot of tribal history. After Cornstalk was killed at Fort Randolph (W.Va.) in 1777, Black Fish became the principal chief of the tribe. In February, 1778, Blue Jacket and his party captured 27 salt makers, including famed frontiersman Daniel Boone, at Blue Licks, Kentucky, and brought them here in preparation for their transportation to the British fort at Detroit. It had taken 10 days of hard travel in the dead of winter to reach here and they stayed a few weeks before going on to Detroit.

The others were sold to Governor Henry Hamilton, but Black Fish refused to sell Boone. The Kentuckian returned with the Shawnee chief to Chillicothe and Boone hunted with them frequently. As friendly as they were, Boone knew he would try to escape when the opportunity came, and he eventually did.

In September, the Shawnee captured Simon Kenton, another well-known frontiersman. They caught him while he and a party were "stealing" horses the Shawnees has supposedly stolen from them, and brought him here with the intention of killing him. Kenton ran a brutal gauntlet near the old council house and somehow survived. Like Boone, he eventually escaped.

A deep division existed among the Shawnees. One group wanted to continue the fight against the encroaching white troops and the other thought the time had come to move west. In March, 1779, the Shawnee met at Chillicothe again to decide for either war or peace. French trader Pierre-Louis de Lorimier (usually Anglicized as Peter Loramie) offered to guide those who voted for peace on a migration to a new home on the other side of the Mississippi River.

The majority of the members of three of the five Shawnee septs -- the Kispoko, the Peckuwe and the Thawegila – chose to leave and the Chalahgawthas and the Maykujays decided to stay. But the division was not that clear cut. A large number of the latter two septs also decided to join the migration. Kispoko chief Black Snake gave up leadership in his sept to Yellow Hawk in order to stay and fight, declaring that he would never make peace with the white man.

It proved to be an agonizing moment for Shawnee on both sides of the debate. In addition to leaving the land where they lived and family members were buried, the departing tribesmen knew they were probably leaving their Shawnee brothers to fight a war they couldn't win because of their diminished numbers. A few granite plaques in a narrow strip of grass cannot begin to convey the sorrow and heartache created by this council.

The pain was just beginning. Colonel John Bowman, looking for a little instant glory, led an army of 264 men here in July 1779. More than half of the warriors left from the split had gone to a tribal council at Wapatomica, leaving a total fighting force of 35 men and boys to defend the place. The inept Bowman dallied until he lost the element of surprise and found a nearly empty village when he got there; he ordered most of it burned before he departed. The Indians harassed the retreating troops all the way back to the Ohio River, killing 30 soldiers and wounding 60. The Shawnees suffered only two casualties but they were big ones; sub chief Red Pole died and Black Fish suffered a severe bullet wound that splintered his hip socket.

Black Fish finally died from the wound in October. Shawnee came from near and far to witness his burial. Many Shawnees had not been here since Bowman's attack and they found a shell of the great Shawnee center it had once been. Instead of a thousand or more wegiwas, only a few hundred had survived or been rebuilt and the ugly mounds of ash of those which had burned were a reminder of the attack.

Things would be no easier for Black Hoof, the new chief. On August 5, 1780, George and Simon Girty and a party of four Shawnees stopped beside at a spring about 20 miles south of Chillicothe. While they refreshed themselves, an army of 1,000 men following the Little Miami River appeared in the distance. The army stopped, apparently to make camp, and the Shawnee party correctly surmised that they planned to rest there and attack Chillicothe in the morning. The Girtys and Indians immediately rode off to the town to sound the alarm.

Black Hoof considered the circumstances – he had slightly more than 100 warriors – and decided the time had come to abandon the town and join their Shawnee brothers at Piqua town on the Mad River. It was already late in the afternoon and he called in his sub chiefs and told them what must be done; all of the tribe's valuable goods and treasures that they couldn't hope to carry with them must be hidden before they left.

With that, the women, warriors and children flew into action, carrying most of their possessions to the edge of a sharp slope behind the council house. Tools, pans, kettles, sealed bundles of clothing, ceremonial pipes, carved figures, knives, spare tomahawks and nearly a ton of items made of silver (bracelets, armbands, rings, necklaces, plates, etc.) that some believe the Shawnees mined in the great gorge of the Little Miami (now called Clifton Gorge) were brought here. They tied individual pieces securely in about 50 buckskin sacks and stacked them in a pile.

When they finished that part of the work, members of the tribe formed a line that stretched approximately 1000 feet down the incline and into a marshy area below, between the village and the river. Only a magnificent old oak tree grew in this marsh, and perhaps a dozen feet behind it, the line ended with Black Hoof himself. The Shawnees passed the items and sacks by hand down the line and when they reached the chief, he deposited them in a pool of black water, perhaps 15 or 20 feet in depth. All would remain here until the tribe could return and retrieve them at some time in the future.

At this point, even the most clueless twenty-first century observer can probably see where this is going. Black Hoof led his tribe back to the village, ordered everything set fire, including the council house, and led his people on the 13-mile trek to Piqua Town, where he hoped there would be enough warriors to make a stand against the advancing army led by George Rogers Clark now only five miles away.

After being routed at Piqua Town, the Shawnees moved on to the two established Piqua towns on the Great Miami River. While some tribesmen would eventually return here and try to resettle Chillicothe, the goods deposited in that black pool were supposedly never recovered.

In his notes to the 1967 book *The Frontiersman*, Allan W. Eckert writes: "This treasure, never recovered by the Shawnees, apparently still lies hidden somewhere in the marsh area, which has since been drained and is now cultivated. The old oak has long since disappeared and while certain marshy areas remain, the extensive bog is now gone. According to reports made to the author by present residents of the area, a deputation of Shawnees from Oklahoma returns to the area at irregular intervals to pay homage to the birthplace of the great chief, Tecumseh, and to once again walk in the fields of their ancestral homeland. Invariably, these parties are observed spending considerable time searching the old marsh site, allegedly for the unrecovered Shawnee deposit.

"One of the older Indians who comes has several maps which he consults frequently, but which he shows no one else. The author himself, with the aid of a mine detector, has gone over some of this ground, but has located only a scattering of artifacts and nothing of a spectacular nature."

So it ends there, right? Yeah, sure it does.

Catherine Wilson, executive director of Greene County Historical Society, said she used to work in the genealogy department of the local library. She said treasure hunters often showed up with metal detectors and asked her for directions to the "spot."

"We have a map that kind of shows where the trails were and approximately where Tecumseh was born – there's a marker by the spring," Wilson said. "So that's what I had and that's what I would show them and say "Go to it. If you think you can find it, go for it."

Were there a lot of them?

"There was at least one every spring," Wilson said. "Sometimes three, sometimes 10, sometimes one. . . I personally think (the Shawnee) came back and got it."

Either way, the story doesn't end there. Tecumseh loved it here, and long after the town had been abandoned by the Shawnees, he would return occasionally to walk the ground where he had grown up. In 1797, he returned and found a white man there with his family. James Galloway had been on George Rogers Clark's expedition 15 years before, remembered the beauty of the area and came here to show his family the site of Old Chillicothe. He told Tecumseh that he planned to build a house and settle here, and the Shawnee war chief was impressed by his love of the place and the two became good friends.

Galloway built a two-story log house that Tecumseh often visited, even when he had decided to bring all of the Indian tribes together and try to drive the white man from the territory that had become the state of Ohio in 1803. On one of his visits there in 1808, Tecumseh supposedly asked Galloway's 16-year-old daughter Rebecca to marry him, but after pondering this proposal for months, she finally declined.

The story is intriguing for a lot of reasons, not the least of which is the presence of the Galloway house on the north side of Church Street, between King and Detroit streets, in Xenia.

So this is the house where Tecumseh proposed to Rebecca Galloway?

"It's a good story, but I don't believe that," Wilson said. "For one thing, the ages don't match up (Tecumseh was 40, Galloway was 16), but this seems to go against everything that Tecumseh stood for. I think an old Galloway family member misinterpreted some of the things he heard or read. "

The cabin has probably had more trouble standing the test of time than the marriage tale. The Greene County Historical Society moved it from north of Old Chillicothe to the corner of Second and Monroe streets in Xenia in 1936; unfortunately, it was moved to its current location in 1965 and that was in the path of the famous Xenia tornado that killed 32 people and destroyed over 300 homes. The tornado partially destroyed the cabin. It has been rebuilt, but much of it is no longer original.

Nevertheless, it stands as a visible reminder of what it must have been like when memories of Old Chillicothe were still vivid in the minds of James Galloway and Tecumseh, images they recalled in the chief's visits here.

The house didn't suffer any additional damage when tornados also hit Xenia in 1989 and 2000, although in the process the Shawnees seemed to have gotten dragged into modern storms that weren't of their doing.

"Now we keep hearing that the Shawnee called this "the place of the devil winds," Wilson said. "When people write about Xenia, it's invariably mentioned. But I never heard that expression before the 2000 tornado and my predecessor in this job said she never heard it either. It drives me crazy. I've looked around and I can't find any reference to that before 2000. If the Shawnee had really said that, don't you think we would have known it before then?"

13 HANGING ROCK

When you first hear about it, Hanging Rock seems like it could be an intriguing, if minor, tourist attraction. A rock ledge protruding from an Ohio River hillside with a spectacular view of the river in both directions, one once used by Indians to scout and ambush oncoming white settlers and by a famous Shawnee chief to mourn his dead brother, could be the focus of a wonderful park.

It isn't, of course, but you would think that at least finding it would be a breeze. The little village of Hanging Rock (population 221) is snuggled against the western edge of the Ironton city limits in southern Ohio and squeezed between the river and a forested hill. A village visitor would logically assume that the famous rock would be peering down at him from that hill like one of those stone faces at Mount Rushmore. But while driving among the two dozen houses that lie just north and beneath the four-lane highway whose two-lane predecessor used to go directly through this place, no rock ledges are readily discernible on that hill or on a larger one that marks the western edge of the tiny village.

After a quick up and back tour of a residential strip offered no clues to the fabled rock's whereabouts, I spotted a middle-aged woman wobbling toward me on a middle-aged bike and hoped she knew more about local topography than she did bike-riding.

I called to her, explained who I am and what I was seeking and she looked as dumbfounded as if I had asked her for the square root of 600.

"I have no idea," she said without hesitation. "I've lived here for quite a while, but I didn't grow up here."

I didn't share my first thought: Not even once in "quite a while" did you think to ask how your town acquired its unusual name? The Indians would have made short work of this woman before she knew what hit her.

"Why don't you ask her?" she added, pointing to an older woman walking across a nearby yard.

I looked up and sure enough the "expert" I needed had slipped into view. After my brief explanation, she instantly tried to clear up the mystery.

"It's not here," she said. "I mean there are rocks on both of those hills there, but they aren't the hanging rock. The one I know is down (U.S. Route) 52 there, west of town. I don't know how to measure distance, but you can see it if you're looking. We used to go up there when I was younger, but I haven't been up there in years. Just head west on 52. Don't get off at the first exit. When you get to the electric plant, you've probably gone too far."

When I asked if there was a way to get to it, she frowned.

"We got there when I was younger, so there has to be a way. But I don't know how. You probably have to take some back roads."

The irony of her loose directions hit when I had driven about three miles west, saw and passed the bare rock she spoke of and turned off the highway. I made the first right possible in hope of somehow getting up there and looked at the sign.

Back Road.

A little southern Ohio humor? After about five minutes of driving along the road at the base of the hills without being able to see the rock in question, the joke seemed to be on me. I finally turned left onto Haverhill-Ohio Furnace Road and climbed into the trees. Ten more minutes into a ride to nowhere, I finally discovered a winding lane called Bonzo Road that surely got me as close to that rock as anyone could get in a car. It also occurred to me that there was no way to get there without a deep invasion into private property.

Given that this might not even be the rock in question, it seemed like a good idea to try to confirm it before embarking on an adventure that might end in the county jail. The next day, an email from the Ironton newspaper made it clear that Hanging Rock hasn't exactly been on the minds of area residents. The writer suggested that the rock might not be a ledge on the side of a mountain at all, but a rock in the Ohio where boats hung up when they were snagged there. That was the story that the reporter had heard from his uncle – the reporter even surmised that the rock may have broken off the side of a mountain and fallen into the river – and he suggested trying the library or the local history museum.

The ignorance of the subject didn't surprise me, even if it seemed that everyone should care about the old lookout more than they did. It was here that famous Shawnee chief Blue Jacket, whom legend says was a white man who was raised by the Indians, suffered a bullet wound to his side in 1788 from a lucky sharpshooter a half-mile away on a flatboat. It was also here that Blue Jacket supposedly brought the scalp of his brother, Charley Van Swearingen, after he had unknowingly killed and scalped him during Arthur

St. Clair's ignominious defeat at the place that came to be called Fort Recovery in 1791. With only a few words to his wife, Blue Jacket had abruptly left the Shawnee village on the Scioto River and was gone for more than a week. Traveling a hundred miles or more, he had come to Hanging Rock, gathered sticks and tinder and started a small fire on the rock ledge. He squatted there, cut his brother's scalp into small pieces and methodically tossed them one after another into the fire. While he did it, he remembered the Charley of his youth, the boy that he – Marmaduke Van Swearingen -- had known in Virginia before he had been captured by the Indians and adopted by the Shawnees.

Whether the story has been embellished through the years or not – many historians have argued that Blue Jacket wasn't Van Swearingen and recent DNA evidence would seem to confirm it -- it enhances the mystique of this place, a spot that apparently meant a great deal to Native Americans when the white man came here. Shouldn't everybody at least know that Hanging Rock was a flat ledge protruding from the side of a mountain and not a giant snag in the river?

The email to the Briggs Lawrence County Public Library in Ironton brought a phone call two days later from a helpful woman named Marta Ramey, who is in charge of the library's history and genealogy section. Like the woman in the village of Hanging Rock, she had a personal connection to that rock ledge – she had also been there during her high school days – but she wanted to talk to local historian Steve Shaffer before she returned my call.

"He said there are two stories," Ramey said. "One is that a piece of rock fell off there and ended up in the river where boats hung up on it, and the other, which is the consensus of most historians, is that it was a lookout that Blue Jacket and the Indians used to ambush whites who were coming down the river."

Just for the record, the story of a sneaky rock in the river may be true; it just appears to have no relation to the hanging rock that named the village. According to a description of the village of Hanging Rock in 1846, in volume two of Henry Howe's *Historical Collections of Ohio,* published in 1891, the origins of the name is pretty clear:

"The villages is named from a noted cliff of sandstone, about four hundred feet in heights, called the "Hanging Rock," the upper portion of which projects over, like the cornice of a house."

But is the rock three miles west of town definitely the rock?

"Oh, yeah," Ramey said. "When they were working on (U.S.) 52, they cut a lot of that hill away and you can tell a lot of that rock has been cut away. I think it was '57 or '58 when they did that, although you could probably find out for sure from the highway department. They probably have maps that show that."

But that rock isn't close to the river or the highway that supposedly caused its disfigurement. With so much uncertainty about that rock three miles to the west, I did a little digging with the Scioto County auditor's website – the rock is a short distance to the west of the Lawrence County line – and got the name of the property owner. Ironton accountant/rock owner Ed Rambacher was happy to let me visit the spot, but he kept referring to it as "High Rock" and said he has never known it as anything else.

"That's not Hanging Rock," he said. "It's called High Rock. I don't know where Hanging Rock is, but that's not it, at least as far as I know. Maybe you ought to go back to the village and ask at the police station."

Before I did that, I did another circuit on Bonzo Road, blew past a giant No Trespassing sign, took a quarter mile walk through the woods and visited his rock, which has an incredible view up the Ohio River and enough graffiti for two or three Manhattan subway stations. This has obviously been visited by dozens if not hundreds of kids over the years; a Marshall University student and his girlfriend visited it, posted pictures on Google and tagged it "Hanging Rock," which seemed to confirm what the woman in the village said. If you can't trust Google maps, who can you trust?

But U.S. 52 is four lanes now and lies a couple hundred yards from the river at that point and unless the river has shifted, always a possibility, this rock doesn't seem like one Indians used to spy oncoming settlers.

That meant that was time to go back to the village, which is much, much closer to the river. I stopped at the police station and municipal building and discovered only that it is closed on Friday. Secure in the knowledge that criminals took Fridays off, I went back to patrolling the village's three streets, looking for another "expert" when I noticed somebody standing on what appeared to be a rock at the top of the forested hill immediately behind the village.

I asked three women at a local child care if they knew anything about that rock or how to get there, got three "I don't knows" and was about to give up when I saw a man cutting his grass on a riding mower. I rolled down my car window and explained my mission.

"Do you want to go up there?" Mike Chatfield said. "I'll be glad to take you up there and introduce you to Chris, the guy who owns the property, but right now I'm a little busy. Can you make it in 45 minutes?"

When I returned, Chatfield graciously had his truck running and ready for me. We drove through what appeared to be a company parking lot and found a dirt path that took us up a house nestled next to the woods. Chris Hopper, a strapping guy in his late 30s, listened to my story and didn't crack a smile.

"Hanging Rock was in the river," he said. "Boats used to hang up on it. They blasted it out of there years ago."

I explained that there were two stories, told him about Blue Jacket and the Indian lookouts and said that maybe both stories were correct. He acknowledged that he had heard the Blue Jacket tale and said he'd be glad to take me up to there, even though he was certain that it's not Hanging Rock. With that, he invited me into his Honda UTV, and began a climb over terrain that would have been tough for a mountain goat to negotiate.

His rock also had a terrific view of the river, and it was much closer than "High Rock," the identity of which he also confirmed. It seemed like this could be Hanging Rock until I mentioned the story about part of the rock being blown away by the highway department when it was expanding U.S. 52.

"Oh, you're talking about that rock," Hopper said, pointing to the forested hill probably a quarter of a mile to the west. It stood taller than this one, marked the west end of the village and sat just behind the Hanging Rock Community Church.

"There's rock up there, too, you just can't see it. (U.S.) 52 used to go under it in a tunnel and the highway department blasted part of that hill away. The view up there is even better than this."

I asked him how to get there, and he finally smiled. "There aren't any roads, but I can get there in this. I own that property, too. I was getting ready to go the carryout and it's on the way, so I can take you right now if you want to go."

So began a wild ride in the UTV, sometimes almost straight up, sometimes with the vehicle learning over at a 45-degree angle, sometimes facing almost straight down. sometimes going through woods and hostile tree branches without any sign of a path. When we finally arrived, the view was partially obscured by trees but spectacular, and oh, so close to the river. It seemed almost certain that this was the spot, or at least close to a famous hanging ledge that had been blasted away by progress.

"I've always been interested in the story," Hopper said. "I used to come up here when I was a kid. I found a lot of Indian artifacts up here."

After a few minutes, we headed back through the woods, down through gullies and over sharp hills and places where the ground had been washed out by rain. While we bounced like a super ball, it finally made sense why questions about the real hanging rock drew so many blank stares; the actual rock had been gone for decades and may have even been obscured by trees and brush in its final years, the way the remaining rock is now.

Five minutes into a UTV ride that belonged in an amusement park, the Honda landed on a dirt road that took us into a parking on the other side of that hill, in front of Hop's Beer and Wine."

I laughed.

"So this is the way to the carryout?"

He nodded.

"It is for me."

14 LOGAN ELM-CAMP CHARLOTTE

The first time I drove south on U.S. Route 23 between Columbus and Portsmouth, a small sign along the highway five miles south of Circleville pointed the way to the Logan Elm. That must have been some time in the 1970s, and I passed it numerous times in the years after that. Sad as it is to say, I never took the bait.

Years later, I heard that the Logan Elm had died, and it bothered me that the ancient tree under which Chief Logan – Talgahyeetah -- delivered his famous lament in 1774 had passed without me ever taking time to pay my respects.

By the time I finally decided to visit the park where the Logan Elm had stood, that sign on US 23 was long gone. It surprised me to find that a) the old elm had died in 1964, long before I first spotted the sign directing me there, and b) the park where Logan had his camp was a picturesque spot surrounded by farm fields with no less than seven markers and/or monuments.

Expecting to find a 1950s-style roadside park with a plaque on a rock marking the site of the famous speech, I turned off Ohio 361 into a long, narrow park with monuments sprinkled about it like a mini-Gettysburg.

Like many historic eighteenth-century sites involving Native Americans, the relative isolation of the location emphasizes what a different world Talgahyeetah inhabited. In the more than an hour I spent at the park on a beautiful summer day, only one other visitor stopped by to pay his respects, a young man in his early 20s who wandered about for a few minutes while staring intently at his smart phone. He rarely looked up, and it finally struck me that he had come to this place not to make some spiritual contact with Logan or his ancestors but in hopes of "catching" some rare Pokemon while

LOGAN ELM STATE MEMORIAL CELEBRATION IN 1912

playing a game of Pokemon Go on his phone. He departed before I had a chance to ask.

As disrespectful as this seemed, Logan probably wouldn't have found it surprising. He had always been a friend to the white man since his birth near Auburn, New York, in 1726. He was the son of Shikellamy, an Oneida chief and diplomat for the Iroquois confederacy. In his position as chief and overseer, Shikellamy served as a supervisor for the Six Nations, overseeing the Shawnee and Lenape tribes in central Pennsylvania. He was a friend of the white man and Christian missionaries, which explains Logan's long-held desire to welcome white settlers and do his best to accommodate them.

That changed on April 30, 1774, when a group of 32 Virginians led by Daniel and Jacob Greathouse murdered 21 peaceful Mingoes, including Logan's older brother Taylaynee, wife Mellana, nephew Molnah and pregnant sister Koonay at his camp at Baker's Bottom, Virginia, in what became known as the Massacre of Yellow Creek.

It caused Logan to declare war on the whites and the Mingo chief and small parties of Shawnee and Mingo soon began striking at frontier settlers in revenge for the murders. When Lord Dunmore, the last colonial governor of Virginia, received notice of the fighting in May he asked the legislature to authorize general militia forces and to fund a volunteer expedition into the Ohio River valley.

This led to a relatively short conflict known as Dunmore's War, which counted the Battle of Point Pleasant as its only major battle. The Virginians under Andrew Lewis won that battle in October over Shawnee forces led by Cornstalk and Pucksinwah. Dunmore himself led another company of troops toward the Shawnee settlements on the Scioto. Cornstalk, who had counseled his Shawnee tribe against going to war against the whites in the first place, recognized the need to come to terms with the settlers.

Dunmore camped on Scippo Creek in a place he called Camp Charlotte (after the queen of England) with the intention of securing peace with the defeated chiefs of the Shawnee and Mingo tribes. He sent skilled interpreters Simon Girty and Joseph Nicholson and noted frontiersman Simon Kenton to Logan's camp on Congo Creek to request his attendance. Under a giant elm tree at Logan's camp, the Mingo chief turned them down in a speech that has become widely known as Logan's Lament.

The eloquent message was duly recorded and delivered to Dunmore at Camp Charlotte:

I appeal to any white man to say, if ever he entered Logan's cabin hungry, and he gave him not meat; if ever he came cold and naked, and he clothed him not. During the course of the last long and bloody war, Logan remained idle in his cabin, an advocate for peace. Such was my love for the whites that my countrymen pointed as they passed, and said Logan is the friend of the white men. I have even thought to live with you but for the injuries of one man. Colonel Cresap, the last spring, in cold blood, and unprovoked, murdered all the relations of Logan, not sparing even my women and children. There runs not a drop of my blood in the veins of any living creature. This has called on me for revenge. I have sought it: I have killed many: I have fully glutted my vengeance. For my country, I rejoice at the beams of peace. But do not harbor a thought that mine is the joy of fear. Logan never felt fear. He will not turn on his heel to save his life. Who is there to mourn for Logan? Not one.

Logan accompanied the three messengers most of the five miles to Camp Charlotte. They delivered his message to the Virginia governor while Logan joined John Gibson, who was talking with Cornstalk and other Shawnee chiefs in a nearby woods. It was here that Gibson, a prominent white trader who had a two-year-old child with Logan's murdered sister Koonay whom Logan assumed had also been killed, told the chief that his granddaughter had been taken hostage and was still alive. Gibson also told him that while Michael Cresap had been involved in the killing of Shawnees at Pipe Creek, of the Indians in the John Anderson trading party and also of a group of Mingoes at the mouth of Captina Creek, he had not been present when Logan's family had been murdered at Baker's Bottom. The Greathouse brothers had been responsible for that attack.

By that point, Logan's message had already been delivered to Lord Dunmore, so Logan's mention of Cresap in the speech was never changed. But in part because even the white community widely decried the murder of

Logan's family members and in part because the act precipitated a war with the Indian tribes on the western frontier, a campaign started to clear Cresap of involvement in this heinous incident.

In a sad stroke of irony, Cresap is also honored on one of the monuments in the Logan Elm Park, one placed here to correct the error in Logan's speech. Although Cresap counseled against the murder of Logan's family, his participation in other Indian-killing incidents would seem to disqualify him from a laudatory plaque near the spot where the Mingo chief made his famous speech. On this site, Cresap deserves a history-correcting asterisk, not a plaque.

The first marker placed on this site is the one that most visitors probably find curious: A stone pillar with an attached bronze plaque memorializes Captain John Boggs, the first American settler on the Pickaway Plains, upon whose property the Logan Elm once stood. The marker says that Boggs erected his cabin on this spot in 1782. Again, a park created to honor Chief Logan seems like a curious place to honor a white settler. On the other hand, the park might not be there were it not for the captain's grandson, also named John Boggs, who erected the monument in the 1880s.

One side of the monument reads: "Under the spreading branches of a magnificent elm tree nearby, is where Logan, the Mingo chief, made his celebrated speech and where Lord Dunmore concluded his treaty with the Indians in 1774 and thereby opened this country for the settlement of our fore fathers."

Well, OK, Mr. Boggs wasn't much of a historian: The treaty wasn't concluded here and it didn't actually open up this part of the country for settlement. But the monument he erected was the first to mark the location of the historic elm tree that stood a little to the west.

The Logan Historical Society had apparently planned to do that, or so it said in a resolution passed at its inaugural meeting at Westfall, Ohio, on June 23, 1841. It resolved to "erect a monument to the memory of Logan's worth, on or near the spot, (if ascertained,) where his celebrated speech was delivered, or as near as suitable a place can be procured." Maybe the well-meaning society never "ascertained" where the tree was located – in hindsight, the Boggs family sure seems like it would have been a good place to start – but the organization seems to have died without fulfilling its mission.

It's hard to believe that someone wouldn't have figured it out sooner or later. The giant elm was reputed to be one of the largest in the world when it died of tree blight and storm damage in 1964; it stood 65 feet tall with a trunk circumference of 24 feet and foliage spread of 180 feet.

The Ohio Archaeological and Historical Society apparently didn't have any problem confirming Boggs' claim, anyway. On October 2, 1912, the society took ownership of the property and dedicated the Logan Elm State

Memorial, which marked the first official recognition of it. In addition to Logan, Boggs and Cresap, markers now remember Dunmore's War, Cornstalk and his sister, Nonhelema, whom the Americans called "Grenadier Squaw." There is also a sign marking the spot once occupied by the Logan Elm, whose place has been taken by another American elm planted by the Ohio Historical Society in 2012.

The men present at signing of the peace treaty at Camp Charlotte are also given their due here; a plaque indicates that they were all present "on this spot" for the signing of the treaty. That could mean that the plate was placed there before someone realized that the treaty wasn't signed under the ancient elm and that Logan merely delivered his famous address there.

In fact, there is a memorial to Camp Charlotte itself in a pull off on Ohio 56 (also called Adelphi Pike) eight miles southeast of Circleville. A granite monument bearing a bronze tablet that tells of the treaty made between Lord Dunmore, Shawnee chief Cornstalk and allied tribes sits behind a black wrought iron fence. The Pickaway Plains chapter of the Daughters of the American Revolution erected it in 1928 and it was unveiled by Miss Ann Gill, youngest daughter of William Gill, whose family had owned the property for many years. Those looking for Camp Charlotte today will find a farmhouse and a few out buildings, one bearing a painted inscription that reads "Camp Charlotte Farm," but no sign of anything else other than farm fields.

The precise location of the conference between Cornstalk, Lord Dunmore and other dignitaries on those fields is lost to history; the contingent led by Dunmore included more than 1,200 men, so the camp doubtless covered a large area. The agreement demanded that the Indians cease further hostilities, give up prisoners, cease hunting south of the Ohio and stop attacking travelers on the Ohio River. Tribal leaders also agreed to appear at Fort Pitt the following spring with as many Indian chiefs as possible to meet the commissioners from Virginia and conclude and ratify the treaty.

As it turned out, the agreement between the tribes and the Virginians didn't accomplish much. Because Logan and the Mingoes didn't agree to terms, Colonel William Crawford slipped away from the camp with 240 troops and attacked and destroyed the Mingo village of Seekunk, located 30 minutes up the Scioto River. The village occupied an area near the river east of Neil Avenue and in the vicinity of Spring Street in the city of Columbus. And the following March, a band of Shawnees attacked Daniel Boone along a stretch of the Wilderness Road in Kentucky.

The agreement was never even formalized into a treaty. With the war between the colonies and the British impending, the general council at Fort Pitt was never held. No written copy of the agreement exists, and some historians believe the territorial aspects of the treaty were never agreed upon. The truce that started with the agreement didn't even last a full year.

The council at Camp Charlotte is still worth remembering though. Colonel Benjamin Wilson, an officer in Dunmore's army, sat immediately behind and close to Dunmore when the speeches were delivered. Wilson's description of Cornstalk, recorded by Alexander Scott Withers' Chronicles of Border Warfare, shows that Logan's speech wasn't the only one uttered by a native American during that period worth remembering:

"When he arose, he was in no (way) confused or daunted, but spoke in a distinct and audible voice, without stammering or repetition, and with peculiar emphasis. His looks, while addressing Dunmore, were truly grand and majestic, yet graceful and attractive. I have heard the first orators in Virginia, Patrick Henry and Richard Henry Lee, but never have I heard one whose powers of delivery surpassed those of Cornstalk on that occasion."

15 CHILLICOTHE

There have been at least six Shawnee towns called Chillicothe in the Old Northwest. In a quirk seemingly designed to foil shortcut-seeking students writing term papers, none of them were located on the site of the modern city of Chillicothe, Ohio.

Two were close. One stood where Paint Creek empties into the Scioto River three miles south of town and the other is three miles north of Chillicothe in an area called Hopetown. Today, the wooded area at the conjunction of Paint Creek south of the city is framed by farmland and not much else. Meanwhile, those farm fields north of town on the east side of the Scioto are more closely associated with mounds and earthworks that form the Hopewell Culture National Historic Park directly across the river from them than they are the city that became Ohio's first state capital.

Presumably, town founder Nathaniel Massie named his settlement Chillicothe to honor the Shawnees when he laid it out in what nineteenth century historian Henry Howe called "a dense forest" along the Scioto in August, 1796. And truthfully, there might be no better place for that today than this city of 21,000. Chillicothe wears its history with pride and it wears it well. Historic markers sprout like dandelions all over its surprisingly healthy downtown business district. The outdoor historical drama Tecumseh! plays in the nearby southern Ohio hills every summer. The city's replica of Ohio's first statehouse once housed the oldest continually operated newspaper west of the Appalachians. Even some of its current businesses weave the city's history into their advertisements.

On the first block of Paint Street, two blocks from the Ross County courthouse that sits on the site of that first state capital building, a restaurant called the Green Tree had poster-sized clippings from the July 1, 1799, edition of Cincinnati's Western Spy announcing the opening of The Green

Tree tavern by Thomas Gregg. Although the waitress seemed like one who would be more into hash browns than history, she welcomed a question about the restaurant's name.

"There has been a restaurant here for a long time, but it has only been the Green Tree since November," she said. "It used to be called Grinders. But the Green Tree was one of the first taverns in the county and it was located down on Water Street. It was called Green Tree because in those days most people couldn't read. The sign that hung outside was a sign with a green tree on it."

Sadly, the new Green Tree joined the original one in the graveyard of Chillicothe restaurants. The owners announced its closing on May 10, 2020, as an apparent victim of the coronavirus pandemic.

The original restaurant stood a half-block away at the corner of Paint and Water streets. It had a place in the history of the old Northwest Territory, of which Chillicothe served as capital from 1800 to 1802. At the time, territorial leaders divided into two groups. Federalists, under territorial governor Arthur St. Clair, wanted the territory cut into two parts with legislative capitals in Cincinnati and Marietta. That would keep it from reaching the 60,000-population threshold necessary for statehood. Jeffersonian Republicans, led by Thomas Worthington, Edward Tiffin, Michael Baldwin and Massie wanted it to remain the way it was. The others called them the "Chillicothe Junta."

The territorial legislature had been meeting in a two-story hewed log structure built by Basil Abrams that stood at the northwest corner of Second ant North Walnut Street. Lawmakers moved to the new two-story stone statehouse at the corner of Paint and Main Streets for the final session of 1801 in December and passed the Division Act that divided the territory. The move away from possible statehood – and Chillicothe -- outraged the local citizenry. On the night of December 23, Baldwin led an angry mob through the streets of Chillicothe that finally stopped at the Green Tree Tavern where St. Clair boarded. The crowd burned St. Clair in effigy in front of the building and prepared to enter the Green Tree when Worthington showed up with pistols in hand and stopped them. The chaotic scene was repeated the following night: this time Worthington and St. Clair appeared together and convinced the angry crowd to disperse.

The Division Act removed the territorial government from Chillicothe and St. Clair's followers must have happy to bid the unruly Scioto River settlement adieu. They didn't realize Congress would repeal the Division Act in the ensuing months and replace it with the Enabling Act, which allowed the citizens in the easternmost part of the territory to prepare for statehood. Its passage caused a legislative session meeting at Cincinnati in November 1802 to be cancelled. A constitutional convention -- at Chillicothe – to write a plan of government for the new state replaced it. When Ohio became a state in 1803, Chillicothe would again be the capital, probably to the consternation of St. Clair and his followers.

The area's historic roots are even deeper. The Scioto River connected the numerous Shawnee villages on the Pickaway Plains and the Scioto Trail also came through here. The Shawnee were divided into five septs or clans and their principal towns were generally named after the chiefs of those septs. The leader of the Chalahgawtha (or, in English, Chillicothe) sept served as the principal chief of the entire tribe and the town where he lived, the Shawnees' most important settlement, took the name of the sept. Its location sometimes changed because of lost battles, the invasive habits of white settlers and sometimes even when the leader of the tribe died and another chief took his place. If that chief lived in another Shawnee town that settlement might became Chillicothe.

In addition to the ones three miles north and south of the present city of Chillicothe, the other "Chillicothe" settlements were located three miles north of Xenia, Ohio, near the junction of Massies Creek and the Little Miami River (the subject of the "Old Chillicothe" chapter); on the north fork of Paint Creek ten miles northwest of Chillicothe on the site of Frankfort, Ohio; near the village of Westfall, Ohio, on the west bank of the Ohio River four miles south of Circleville, Ohio; and on the bank of the Great Miami River near the present site of Piqua, Ohio. Some historians believe an early Chillicothe may have also been located close to the mouth of the Scioto, near the current city of Portsmouth, Ohio. The Shawnee village of Sinioto or Lower Shawnee Town stood on west bank of the Scioto, and after a flood in 1758 wiped it out, it was reestablished on the east bank.

The Shawnees' Chillicothe had moved to the banks of the Great Miami by the time Nathaniel Massie founded his settlement of Chillicothe in 1796. Massie's town consisted of 456 lots and he promised to give away 100 lots to the first settlers. The burgeoning town's location is nearly equidistant between the early settlements of Cincinnati and Marietta -- it is 100 miles from Cincinnati and 115 miles from Marietta – which made it an important center of activity in the region.

For a modern visitor struggling to understand how this small city 45 miles from the region's primary highway (the Ohio River) might have become the legislative capital of the Old Northwest, he must think in the context of that time period. Cincinnati could boast of the region's most important military fortification (Fort Washington) but the town is itself was no larger than Chillicothe. The region's other important towns – Franklinton and Marietta – were both smaller. Columbus and Cleveland didn't exist.

Franklinton perched on the other side of the Scioto from the forest that would eventually become the state capital of Columbus, and when it got its first mail service, the mail was carried to Chillicothe. Massie's town was the only significant settlement for 100 miles in every direction, and many of the men who settled here – Massie, Worthington and Edward Tiffin -- were well-known by the settlers of other frontier hamlets in the territory. Tiffin would become Ohio's first governor, Worthington became one of Ohio's first U.S. senators and later became governor and Massie presided over the first Ohio Senate as president.

Because the city has remained relatively small, it's possible to walk the downtown streets and imagine what it must have been like when the territorial legislature met here. Many downtown buildings are old – not early state capital old, but nineteenth century old – and a visitor can complete a circuitous walk of most of most historic sites in about an hour.

Water Street fronts a beautiful city park (Yoctangee Park) that fronts the Scioto, and the buildings there are old one- and two- story structures that are the right size to be neighbors of the old Green Tree. Abrams' two-story log house, which came to be known as the Big House before it was torn down in 1840, has been replaced by a three-story, brick building that looks like it could have started life as a nineteenth century hotel. There is a historical marker on the Second Street side of the building partially obscured by trees and another larger marker on a pole that is more noticeable.

That one, titled "Abrams' Big House," includes a drawing of the structure with this description: "With the Division Act of 1800, the U.S. Congress divided the Northwest Territory at a line essentially the present boundary of Indiana and Ohio. The Indiana Territory stood west of the line. The name Northwest Territory was retained for the land east of the line and Chillicothe became its capital. The legislature for the territory convened in Chillicothe in November 1800. Since there were no public buildings in which the legislature could meet, its session was held in a two-story log house that stood on this site called Abrams' Big House. It was so called for its owner, Basil Abrams. During the War of 1812, the building became the barracks for the 19th U.S. Regiment of Infantry. Thereafter, it was known as the old barracks until it was razed circa 1840."

Behind the building, Second Street is a quiet, tree-lined, residential street that doesn't intrude on a time traveler's imagination, although the Carl's Townhouse diner across the street will do that to anyone who has the audacity to turn around. The Big House story speaks of a simpler time. It was built in 1798, two years after the city's first settlers arrived, and a hewed-log wing two stories in height was attached to the "main building," which extended along Walnut toward the Scioto. Colonel Thomas Gibson, the auditor of the Northwest Territory, had an office in the lower room of the addition, and a small family lived in the upper room. The upper room of the main building held a billiard table and "a place or resort for gamblers,' while the lower room was used by the legislature and as a court room, a church and for a "singing school."

The legislature only met there for two years but it's almost impossible to stand on this corner, a few feet and over 200 years away, and not think about what a different world the Big House occupied. A block-and-a-half away on Main Street, the replica of the first statehouse also adds to early nineteenth century atmosphere. Unfortunately, on the day I visited a "For Sale" sign in front of the building that had been home to the *Chillicothe Gazette* since 1941 partially destroyed the nostalgic mood.

That building never existed as the real legislative home of Ohio's government, either in location or stone, so jokes about the statehouse being for sale miss the mark. But the idea that a classy statehouse lookalike that includes two stones from the original structure could theoretically have a furniture store or Italian restaurant in its future is an affront to the senses. The oldest living newspaper west of the Alleghenies, the *Gazette* was born on April 25, 1800 as *Freeman's Journal and Chillicothe Advertiser* and became the *Scioto Gazette* in October of that year. It qualified as the ideal tenant for a building that offers the perfect window to the final days of the Northwest Territory and the earliest days of Ohio statehood. Let's hope future tenants don't close the blinds.

The real state capital building stood a half-block away and across Main at the corner of Paint Street, on the site of today's Ross County Courthouse. It hosted the constitutional convention that wrote the plan for government for Ohio in November, 1802, and then served as state's first capital building from 1803 until 1810, when the capital moved to Zanesville as part of a state legislative compromise to get a bill passed. Times may change, but politics doesn't.

The capital moved back to Chillicothe in 1812 and legislators continued to meet in the old statehouse until 1816, when the capital moved to Columbus. At that point, the historic old statehouse gracefully accepted a demotion and became the Ross County courthouse.

That building was razed in 1852 to make way for the present Ross County courthouse. Like the replica statehouse down the street, the "new" building also gives a nod to the old with a block from the old building as part of its Paint Street façade.

It is one more sign that Chillicothe remains the spiritual capital of the Northwest Territory, whether Arthur St. Clair likes it or not.

16 THREE ISLANDS

Manchester, Ohio, seems harmless enough to a modern traveler. It hugs the Ohio River like a poor soul who sees a rich relative as his only means of escaping poverty, while knowing deep down it is never going to happen. It is not unlike other small Ohio River communities in its obvious depression.

A row of attractive properties on the river seem detached from the run-down strip of businesses and boarded up structures only a street or two to the north. The entire community of 2.023 extends only six or seven blocks from the river. Most of those blocks are an unattractive mix of old buildings, empty lots and house trailers.

The economy obviously isn't booming here in the northernmost part of Appalachia. But this is small town Ohio. While there are times when you feel as if you have passed through a time warp to the 1960s or even the 1860s, the town is friendly and welcoming. It isn't threatening.

This stands in marked contrast to its ancient history. Before Manchester, there was Massie's Station, and before Massie's Station, there was Three Islands. The islands have always been there in the river just to the east of downtown Manchester; the only difference between now and the days of the Old Northwest is that the three islands are now two.

Well, that's not actually the only difference. In the days of Three Islands, their presence not only narrowed the river into smaller, narrower channels, as the two islands do now, but they made this a terrific place for angry Indian tribes to pick off prospective white settlers on flatboats.

Anyone who knows the history and views the biggest island from the Ohio shore – the U.S. Fish & Wildlife Service refers to it only as Manchester Island No. 2 – probably can't help but be a little unsettled by it. Imagine

THE SURVIVING ISLANDS ARE VISIBLE IN THIS 1930s PHOTO, LOOKING EAST.

yourself on a flatboat in the middle of that stretch of water and you immediately understand what the term "sitting duck" means.

Island No. 2 is four times larger than No. 1, which lies at the eastern end of it on the Kentucky side. The now submerged third island was even smaller and can be found on maps from the early nineteenth century, lying just west of No. 1 on the Kentucky side. The navigable channels on both sides of the islands are narrow enough that a major league pitcher with an accurate arm might be able to pick off a river traveler with a baseball. One can only imagine how easy it was for Indians with bows and guns.

Settled in 1790, Massie's Station is regarded as the fourth permanent white settlement in the Northwest Territory. Nathaniel Massie, a former Revolutionary War soldier and land speculator who helped survey the Virginia Military District, recruited men to help him build a fort there. They were required to sign a contract stating they would live in the fort for two years, and in return each man would be given one town in-lot, one town out-lot which consisted of four acres and 100 hundred acres located near a new town. Records show that 30 men took Massie's offer and he used the settlement as a base for his survey work. By the following year, with the settlement completely surrounded by a stockade to provide protection from the Indians, Massie named his town after Manchester, England.

But the Indians were in the area long before this and they had already made this a dreaded stretch of the river decades before anyone tried to settle in the vicinity.

The earliest would-be settlers often died here. Experienced backwoodsman Simon Kenton ordered a party of 14 doubting Virginia surveyors led by Dr. John Wood and Hancock Lee to beach their canoes and follow him around this site by land in 1773. They never doubted him again after he took them to a steep ridge and showed them the Indians clustered about this site, hiding their canoes and preparing to ambush them, both from the mainland and from the islands.

That same year, Captain Thomas Young and his crew sought what amounted to an Ohio River scouting report before they left Pittsburgh, and again they were warned to be careful near Three Islands. Report after report noted that the area was swarming with Indians. In 1775, Jacob Sodowsky reported that he and his company were "alarmed" by the signs of Indians at a crossing place near the mouth of Sycamore creek, a short distance above Three Islands.

White backwoodsmen also knew this place well. George Rogers Clark and John Gabriel Jones came through here late in 1776 with 500 pounds of gunpowder and lead issued by the Virginia assembly for support of Kentucky settlers being attacked by Indians. Under heavy pursuit by Indians, they stopped at Three Islands and buried the supplies in five different spots.

The Kentuckians desperately needed the ammo and a party of 30 men at McClelland's Station returned to the islands to retrieve it. But before they could leave, Indians killed Jones in a Christmas morning attack. Kenton eventually returned with Bates Collins and confirmed that the gunpowder was still there, and a 30-man contingent recovered the ammo in February.

Some of the most notorious killings at Three Islands occurred after unsuspecting river travelers were called to shore by Indians dressed as whites or by white prisoners who had been coerced into calling to the travelers for help.

One such incident occurred in 1791, when a militia of 200 men under Colonel Alexander Orr was traveling on the Kentucky side of the river and came across David Thomas and Peter Devine camped at a spot near Three Islands. In his jubilance at seeing the troops, Thomas wept uncontrollably, confessing that the Indians had forced them to lure the 14-member John May party ashore and all of them had been killed.

While some members of the militia were furious about what they had done, Orr kept his emotions under control and asked the two escapees if could show them the location of the Shawnees' camp. When they got there, they found the remains of the victims, 49 in all, most scalped and mutilated. The Indians were gone.

Although most of those killings had occurred up river, closer to the Indians' settlement of Sinioto at the mouth of the Scioto River, it is a graphic depiction of the horrors that occurred on this stretch of the river and the ultimate fate of many of the unknowing settlers ambushed near Three Islands.

In the 2013 book *Ohio River Trekking on a Small Budget: A 981-Mile Adventure* by Russell K. Tippett, the author commented on the emotions involved in passing the islands even as they exist today:

"Three Islands was one of those places where atrocities between the Indians and the white pioneers were committed with regularity. . .

"As Rio Trek '03 and crew passes between Two Islands, the hair on our necks virtually stand on end. We both believe it is because we know what occurred there historically. It is a very strange and emotional feeling. I wonder whether there is really such a thing as ghosts. Maybe. Hum-m-m. I wonder."

Today, the two islands are managed by the U.S. Fish & Wildlife Service as part of the Ohio River Islands National Wildlife Refuge. While the native trees on the islands were cut down early after the white man's settlement in these parts and some invasive species have probably changed the character of the forested property, it probably doesn't look a lot different today than it did in the eighteenth century.

After the signing of the Treaty of Greenville in 1795 ended the Indian threat in the region, settlement outside the fort in Manchester began in earnest. When French General Victor Collot visited the area in 1798, he noted that more than 100 houses had been constructed.

Massie had other ideas. He built a log cabin about four miles east of Manchester in 1791 on a ridge overlooking the Ohio and in 1797 he replaced it with a large frame structure that became known as Buckeye Station. It took that name because its timber came from a grove of Buckeye trees, which are still in abundance on the grounds of the overlook where it stood. Massie lived there until 1802, when he leased the 600-acre property to John Moore; Massie wanted to move closer to Chillicothe, another town he founded, which had eclipsed Manchester as the most important city in the region.

He eventually sold the property to Charles Willing Byrd, his brother-in-law and political ally, in 1807. Byrd had served as secretary of the Northwest Territory from 1799 to 1803 and as acting governor in 1802 and 1803, when Ohio became a state. Byrd lived in Cincinnati until he moved to Buckeye Station; with the arrival of statehood, Thomas Jefferson named Byrd the first judge of the Federal District Court of Ohio.

The house stood for decades and was still in use by a tenant family in the 1930s, when historian Morten Carlisle described it as "in very bad repair, filthy and dirty beyond description." Maybe with its impending demise in mind, the Adams County Historical Society erected a granite marker commemorating the site near U.S. 52, which can be noticed from a passing car if you're looking for it. It is a half mile south of the home site, located on that windy ridge known as Hurricane Hill.

Some crumbling ruins of the house still exist in a wooded area that is marked by a cell phone tower and a nearby farm field. A private property sign makes it clear that this is another one of those important Old Northwest places where visitors from the present aren't common -- or welcome.

17 FRANKLINTON

A conversation about Tommy's Diner with an Ohio State graduate from Cleveland sat in an undisturbed corner of my brain for years. He asked me where the popular Columbus restaurant was located, and when I told him he looked at me as if I had said "Swaziland."

"Franklinton?" he repeated.

"Yeah, you know. It's on West Broad Street on the other side of the river from downtown."

"Oh, yeah," he answered, in a dubious tone that said he didn't really mean it.

My friend hadn't lived in Ohio's capital city for a while, but I thought four or five years on campus might have given him at least a vague awareness of the oldest section of the city. That it didn't again confirmed my sad suspicion: before developers discovered the neighborhood in the last few years, it was possible to live in Columbus for years without even knowing of Franklinton's existence. At least from a historical perspective, it has always deserved better. The historic community that peers over at downtown's skyscrapers from the west side of the Scioto River preceded the city that swallowed it by 16 years.

Franklinton might have been Columbus instead of simply being part of it were it not for its low-lying location. When state legislators searched for a permanent capital for the infant state of Ohio in 1810, it was one of a handful of sites considered for it. The bustling trade center of 400 to 500 souls probably would have been an obvious choice if it weren't prone to flooding. Instead, the thick forest on the high bank on the east side of the Scioto proposed by four men (including one from Franklinton) who owned property became the legislators' choice.

In addition to a map of the 1200-acre site that showed how the streets and public square could be arranged, the four land speculators offered two 10-acre sites for a statehouse and state prison and willingness to build those official buildings and others. That probably doomed the area's first settlement to life in the slow lane, but the decision undoubtedly spared a handful of historic Franklinton properties that have survived.

In cities such as Cincinnati and Detroit, the area close to the river where the first settlers lived has been paved over by freeways or covered with skyscrapers. The heart of the old Franklinton sits far enough from the river and downtown Columbus to have mostly avoided those fates. The 315 interchange and freeway that replaced Sandusky Street in the 1950s split the heart of the old settlement, but the damage isn't as extensive as that done to the original plats of other cities perched on the banks of major rivers. Progress left Franklinton alone for decades.

Ironically, its location at the so-called forks of the Scioto is what captivated a Virginia-born Kentucky surveyor named Lucas Sullivant, who had been hired to help survey the northern part of the Virginia Military District between the Little Miami and Scioto rivers. He believed that the location near the confluence of the Scioto and Whetstone (now Olentangy) rivers would guarantee that his settlement became an important city. He drew up the original plat for his community in 1797, then saw it submerged in a major flood the following March after only a handful of cabins had risen there. That convinced him to move the plat a quarter of a mile west of the river to higher ground. The first lots sold that summer -- lots on Gift Street were given to those who settled there -- and within a few years, cabins and simple frame houses were scattered about an area that had previously been unoccupied forest.

In 1801, Sullivant erected the first brick house there and moved in with his wife, Sarah. The building, later expanded into the Order of the Good Shepherd convent, was torn down in 1964 for the construction of a car dealership that closed in 2008. The boarded-up dealership stood there until 2019, a visible reminder of the value of historic preservation and one that asked passersby a troubling question: Did Columbus civic leaders really see more value in a Ford dealership whose useful life lasted only 44 years than the centuries-old homestead of its community founder?

Fortunately, other historic Franklinton properties remain, starting with the Franklinton cemetery, which planted its first body in 1799. It lies a few blocks north of Broad Street on River Street and is nestled in a bend of the Scioto River. The dead don't complain about flooding, but sometimes their living relatives do; some of Franklinton's more prominent residents, including Lucas Sullivant and his wife Sarah, were originally buried there but were moved to Green Lawn Cemetery when it was founded in 1848.

THIS **1892** HARRISON HOUSE PHOTO OFFERS A TASTE OF EARLY FRANKLINTON.

A brick house believed to have been built in 1807 by Col. Robert Culbertson is another survivor. Some historians believe General William Henry Harrison used this house as his headquarters when Franklinton was a staging area for his American army during the War of 1812, the reason it became known as the Harrison house and probably one reason the city saved it when it was slated for demolition in 1975. But it is also possible that Harrison made his headquarters in a two-story log house at 762 West Broad that has long been among the dearly departed or even in another long dead log house that stood across the street from it. A frame house (the David Deardurff house) on Gift Street partially used as Franklinton first post office was built in 1807 and the Sullivant land office built in 1822 have also survived, although the latter was moved behind the Harrison house to keep it from ending up like so many of its long-forgotten neighbors.

The area has lost plenty of fights with progress. But if the little settlement had been on the other side of the river it's likely none of its historic structures would remain. None of the buildings from the capital city's first decade (1812-1822) made it through the buzz saw of progress, including the first state capital. Because of its location, at least a few scattered remnants of Lucas Sullivant's Franklinton have made it to the 21st century.

If he came back, it's doubtful the old surveyor would be pleased by much of what he saw, however. The little settlement he carved out of a forest bears no resemblance to the one Sullivant last saw on the day of his death in 1823, and to this point at least, progress hasn't been particularly kind. The area has been one of the poorest areas of Columbus for decades, a crime-infested, densely populated area of mostly old, dilapidated frame houses that survived the 1913 flood and empty lots for the ones that didn't.

This partly explains why so many people who should be aware of its existence aren't: for the longest time, a visit to historic Franklinton wasn't exactly like a sightseeing jaunt to Colonial Williamsburg. Unofficially, Columbus may have been born in Franklinton, but it mostly celebrates its history somewhere on the other side of the river. With the exception of Veterans Memorial, an auditorium that stood on Broad on the west banks of the Scioto from 1955 until it was torn down in 2016, Franklinton hasn't been much of a destination since the early days of the nineteenth century.

City fathers – and developers – are trying to change that. Old Central High School, which occupied an 18-acre campus on the Scioto riverfront until it closed in 1982, became the new home of the Center of Science and Industry (COSI) in 1999 and recently moved parking underground so that the lots surrounding it wouldn't have all of the scenic value of, well, parking lots. Across West Broad Street, Veterans Memorial came down for the construction of a memorial – the National Veterans Memorial and Museum -- that honors veterans better than an outdated building that saw big name entertainers go elsewhere and replaced them with more baseball card and travel shows. While it's true that the area that made up original Franklinton is almost a mile down the road, the revitalization of riverfront property that was a 150-acre prairie in Sullivant's day is the first step toward making old Franklinton a relevant part of the community again.

Old Franklinton still can use some work. The Harrison house is the only building on Broad that gives a visitor a sense of what it must have been like to have a row of old brick and frame buildings on both sides of the dirt street. Photos taken by historian Henry Howe in 1892 of the buildings once occupied by the stores of Sullivant (and later Lyne Starling) and Dr. Lincoln Goodale are of two-story buildings that look a lot like the Harrison House. Put aside thoughts of Target and Ikea; even the crude dry goods stores of the mid-19th century were generations away.

But if you know the Franklinton story and put your imagination to work, you can see what a vibrant place this was when Ohio became a state in 1803 and it became the seat of Franklin County. When James Kilbourn came east from New England to scout sites for the village of Worthington in the northern reaches of the county that year, he came to Franklinton first, for advice and supplies. Indians tribes came from as far away as Sandusky, more than 100 miles north, to trade in the Franklinton stores.

To truly appreciate Franklinton, a visitor has to think "frontier." One of the first laws passed by the county when it became the seat of Franklin County with Ohio statehood in 1803 concerned a two-dollar bounty paid for the scalps of wolves and panthers (one dollar for those less than a year old) which were a nuisance to those who lived here. Two prominent early settlers,

Jeremiah Armstrong and John Brickell, had both been kidnapped from their homes by Indian tribes when they were boys and had been released as a result of the Treaty of Greenville in 1794. Brickell helped supply the village with deer meat as a result of hunting tactics he learned during his time with the Wyandots.

The village had grown to 400 or 500 residents by the time staked-off tree-covered lots were put up for sale across the river in Columbus in 1812. That happened on the first day of the War of 1812, which launched a three-year period of prosperity for the prosperous little town doomed to wither in the shadow of the new capital. Harrison based his army here because of its central location, and for the next three years, supplies constantly moved in and out of Franklinton. At times 2,000 or 3,000 troops were camped here, many on Sullivant's lawn.

The most important moment in Franklinton's history occurred on that lawn on June 13, 1813. The war with England had been going poorly and Harrison called a meeting of fifty prominent Indian chiefs and made a speech seeking assurance that the Shawnee, Wyandot, Delaware and other tribes wouldn't fight on the British side. Some settlers came from great distances to view the proceedings, aware that Harrison's failure to convince the Native American leaders might threaten their own survival.

The future president spoke in what were described as calm, measured tones beneath a huge elm tree on Sullivant's lawn, surrounded by his officers in full military regalia. A tortured silence followed his remarks and finally Tarhe the Crane, a 72-year-old Wyandot chief who had assumed leadership of the assembled tribes, arose slowly, spoke a few words and then offered his hand in friendship. The other chiefs quickly joined him and cheers of joy erupted from the crowd of onlookers. Harrison's speech may have won the war and the elm tree where he spoke became a landmark to those who had gathered there. Predictably: it became known as the Harrison elm.

Harrison's triumph served as a kind of last hurrah for Franklinton, even though the little village prospered for the rest of the war. Sullivant obtained a charter from the state legislature to build a toll bridge across the Scioto in 1816 – it opened the same day the legislature met in Columbus for the first time. By then, there were already more than 700 people in the new capital, more than in Franklinton. By 1820, the Columbus population had doubled to 1,450 and many of Franklinton's more prominent settlers (including Armstrong, Brickell. Starling and Goodale) had moved to the other side of the Scioto.

Sullivant died in 1823, a year before Columbus built a new courthouse and the county seat followed the crowd across the river. By then, his little community of houses huddled near West Broad Street had already settled into a life as sleepy, rural town of 300 to 400 people, a corn field and a toll bridge away from the burgeoning capital city.

When it was absorbed by Columbus in 1870, it still retained those characteristics, as historian Henry Howe noted when he visited the place in 1886:

"Franklinton now is included in the city of Columbus. It has changed less than any part of the city so near the centre, and preservers to this day many of its old-style village features. It is a quiet spot, but cannot much longer so remain in the rapid progress of improvements."

Howe was right, of course. As the original settlers and their children died, memories of Franklinton's glory days faded and it became just another densely populated section of the growing state capital. Even memory of the Harrison elm faded. In 1902, the local chapter of the Daughters of the American Revolution wanted to mark the site with a memorial, but couldn't find anyone who knew where it was. Finally, someone suggested that they talk to an elderly physician – Dr. Starling Loving – who had come to the area in 1846 and remembered when Lucas Sullivant's son, Michael, had shown him the tree. When Loving conducted the DAR troupe to the site, they found the tree in the backyard of a house on Souder Avenue. Rather than having visitors ruin some poor sap's backyard barbeque, they placed their marker in a median on Martin Avenue, two blocks away but still in an area where desperate settlers and Indian braves gathered on that historic day.

The marker, a plaque on a huge rock, is still on Martin Avenue, which dressed for the occasion on dedication day with American flags on the porches of all of the houses. A Mount Carmel medical center parking lot that sits just south of West Broad Street and east of Souder Avenue occupies the real site of the Harrison elm today.

It is an improvement over a boarded-up Ford dealership, if only marginally.

18 LEATHERLIPS

Sometimes it seems as if the memory of an old Wyandot chief named Shateyahronya, whom the white man knew as Leatherlips, has been hijacked by the gods of golf.

Leatherlips is believed to be buried across the Scioto River and about a half-mile from the eastern boundary of the Muirfield Village Golf Club in Dublin, Ohio, the site of PGA's Memorial Tournament since the course designed by golfing legend Jack Nicklaus opened in 1977. The tournament has been plagued by rain over the years, which somehow turned into the curse of an old Indian chief who was angered that the golf course was built near his gravesite.

History sometimes takes its participants on a curious ride, and this is certainly one. Because the Memorial annually draws many of the world's top golfers, Leatherlips has been the topic of many a story in newspapers and on wire services and radio and television networks all over the world.

Shateyahronya was born in 1732 and lived most of a long life in the Old Northwest as a respected chief, probably in what is today northern Ohio. For many years, the Wyandots mostly lived in areas south of Lake Erie in the watershed of the Sandusky River. In 1795, he was one of many chiefs who put his scrawl on the Treaty of Greenville, in which beaten tribes acknowledged their defeat at the Battle of Fallen Timbers and recognized the white man's right to settle in what was then the Northwest Territory. Settlers had bestowed the name Leatherlips on him because of "his admirable trait of never breaking a promise."

Shateyahronya wasn't the principal leader of the Wyandots; that was his close friend Tarhe the Crane, who also signed the Greenville document. But he was a respected chief who built a reputation as being a friend of the white man. He maintained this stance in the years following the treaty, in the years before and after Ohio's achievement of statehood in 1803 and during the time when Shawnee war chief Tecumseh started building a coalition of tribes to try to drive the white man out of the lands that once belonged to the Indians.

For this, apparently, the man now called Leatherlips was executed 14 miles north of Columbus in a grove of sugar maples on the east side of the Scioto River in 1810. Witnesses said six Wyandot Indians traveled from Michigan to accomplish that mission. The visiting Indians charged him with witchcraft, held a brief mock trial where he was convicted and then marched him to his burial site, where one of the Wyandots buried a hatchet in his skull.

The witchcraft accusations were what we would call today a trumped up charge; the consensus of historians is that Leatherlips was executed for not joining with Tecumseh in what figured to be a last stand against the whites. Tecumseh and his brother Tenskwatawa (The Prophet) apparently realized that Leatherlips was well known enough for his death to cause other Indians to think twice about opposing the new coalition. They also may have figured that Leatherlips' lacked the power and prestige to generate the kind of backlash that would come from the execution of a chief such as Tarhe.

In and of itself, the Leatherlips story is fascinating. In an account by eyewitnesses printed in 1838, six Wyandots showed up at Benjamin Sells' house on the Scioto River on the evening of June 1, 1810, seeking the whereabouts of the old chief, whose camp was about two miles away. They were described as being "equipped in the most war-like manner" and exhibiting "an unusual degree of agitation," told Sells they intended to execute Leatherlips and immediately set off to do the job. Early the next morning, Sells sent word of this to his brother, John, who headed for Leatherlips' camp with brothers Peter and William.

When they arrived, they found the Wyandot chief seated in the middle of his six accusers, his arms bound by a small cord. A couple of neighboring white men were already there watching the proceedings, as was a sullen Indian who was a frequent companion of Leatherlips. He apparently knew that he best keep his mouth shut now. A charge of witchcraft had been made by some of his captors, who claimed he had destroyed their friends with his use of evil powers.

After a two-hour "trial" they announced their predetermined verdict – guilty – and indicated with a gesture toward the sun that the execution would take place at 1 o'clock. John Sells immediately approached the group and asked what the chief had done to merit his death.

"Very bad Indian," one of the accusers replied. "Make good Indian sick. Make horse sick. Make die. Very bad chief."

Sells tried to buy the old Indian's freedom with a fine horse that he said was valued at $300. After looking closely at the animal and a long consultation

THIS GRANITE MONUMENT WAS ERECTED IN 1889 WHERE A PILE OF ROCKS WAS BELIEVED TO HAVE MARKED LEATHERLIPS' GRAVE.

amongst themselves, the Indians declined the offer. Shortly after that, the leader of the group pointed to the sun and sky and indicated that four would be the new hour of execution, and Leatherlips slowly marched to his lodge, where he dined on jerked venison, washed and dressed in his best clothes and painted his face.

With the hour of execution near at hand, the aged chief shook hands in silence with the surrounding spectators. When he came to John Sells he appeared visibly moved, grasping his hands warmly and speaking for a few moments in the Wyandot language and pointing to the Heavens.

He then turned away from him, began chanting the death song and started a steady march to a place seventy or eighty yards from the camp, where the visitors had already dug a shallow grave. Leatherlips knelt down and in an elevated but solemn voice addressed his prayer to the Great Spirit. When he finished, the leader of the visiting Wyandots knelt next to him and said his own prayer. After the pair stood up, Sells again approached the visitor and this time objected to the old chief being executed so near the white settlement.

"No," the Indian said sternly and with obvious displeasure. "My friend, me tell you white man bad man, white man kill him, Indian say nothing."

Realizing the futility of his mission, Sells withdrew. After a short time, Leatherlips fell back to his knees and resume praying. When he finished, an awkward silence was interrupted when one of the visiting warriors burst from the crowd, swiftly walked up behind the old chief, drew a bright tomahawk from beneath the skirts of his jacket and held the weapon high for brief moment before burying it in Leatherlips' skull. The weapon landed directly upon the crown of his head and the old man immediately dropped to the ground. As he lay there dying, the six Wyandots rushed up and pointed to the drops of sweat that had formed on his face and neck, which they said proved his guilt. While the settlers contemplated the confounding logic of that, the executioner finished the job by forcefully striking two or three additional blows. Satisfied that Leatherlips was finally dead, the Wyandots tossed the lifeless body in the grave, covered it with dirt and rocks and mounted their horses and departed, their mission complete.

A small pile of rocks marked the grave for many years. The dense forest surrounding it was eventually cleared for the cultivation of crops and some have speculated that the rocks that marked the exact location of the burial may have been removed. In 1889, a group of 17 wealthy Columbus men who had organized as the Wyandot Club eight years before purchased the property and erected a granite monument to Leatherlips on the spot where they believed he had been buried.

William H. Davis, whose grandfather William Sells witnessed the execution and wrote an account of it later, said in 1904 that the monument stands a few rods farther north from a small ravine than was the pile of stones which once marked the grave. If the stones had been removed, that ravine and a spring that had once been close to the chief's dwelling that had stood approximately 70 yards to the west, would have been the only means of locating the gravesite.

Either way, the Wyandot Club was apparently convinced enough to buy a one-acre site there for its monument, which is located in a small park north of Dublin on the east side of Riverside Side, just to the south of Stratford Drive.

A few observations are in order: If the spirit of Shateyahronya were truly miffed that white men, whom he treated as his brothers, constructed a golf course across the Scioto River from his former camp and grave site, why wasn't he even more ticked a four-lane highway called Riverside Drive was constructed less than fifty yards to the west, probably right through the site where his dwelling stood? And what about that the Columbus Zoo, located about a quarter of a mile due north of his grave? Or those luxurious houses that lie on Stratford Drive and the other streets that feed it?

One of two entrances to the small park the Wyandot Club built around his grave, the one from the north or Stratford Drive side, has been walled off with trees, flowers and shrubs that mark the entrance to the Wedgewood community of houses. The main entrance to his grave site is still through a break in the west side of the stone wall that surrounds the little park, but a visitor has to walk within a few feet of the speeding cards on Riverside Drive to reach the entrance. Presumably that wasn't a problem in 1993, when Nicklaus' wife, Barbara, placed a shot of gin on Leatherlips' grave in an attempt to appease the old chief and secure better weather for the Memorial. It made for good story, but didn't do anything to clear the skies – or show respect to a peace-loving chief who was murdered because he was friend to the white man.

The city of Dublin partially rectified this by honoring his memory with 12-foot limestone sculpture of the chief's head less than two miles south on Riverside Drive in Scioto Park. The Dublin Arts Council commissioned Boston artist Ralph Helmick to create the striking sculpture in 1990 and place it on a hill overlooking the park and the river.

Leatherlips wasn't the only deceased Wyandot chief that the Wyandot Club honored. Its organization was founded on the west side of the Scioto River north of the Columbus suburb of Upper Arlington in an area called Walnut Grove, a spot reputed to have been the residence of Tarhe the Crane. The group purchased the 40-acre site from Joseph Sells in the 1890s and erected a stone and shingle clubhouse on a hill, high above the Scioto. The club held a party there annually with 100 or more guests and gave Tarhe (and probably even his old friend Leatherlips) his due until the club disbanded in 1924. One of the club members bought the property, which is located on what is now Carriage Lane.

The clubhouse burned on August 12, 1974, and a luxurious home is now located on the site. It is probably a good reason for Tarhe to curse a golf tournament, if one is ever held there.

19 WAPATOMICA

The night before I visited Wapatomica, the "most significant site of Shawnee history in Ohio," I actually dreamed that I had gone there and found a large museum and visitor center. Since the location was supposed to be in a forest marked only by a flagpole and a couple of small monuments, I wandered aimlessly around the parking lot surrounding this building, trying to figure out how this could have happened.

Finally, I entered a gift shop – I'm really not making this up – and they were selling souvenir plates with "Wapatomica" on them. While trying to comprehend this unfathomable development, I woke up.

That was the dream. This is the reality. The Wapatomica village site is located three miles south of the tiny village of Zanesfield on land owned by the Ohio History Connection, on high ground in the middle of the overgrown woods, surrounded by private property. The site is closed to the public, so there is no gift shop selling Wapatomica plates, bottle openers or coffee mugs. If you pick up anything on your visit here – and to do that you must have the permission of the OHC and the private property owner – it may be a case of poison ivy or a few hungry ticks.

It's not for me to determine the significance of this site related to others in Ohio; the Eastern Shawnee Tribe of Oklahoma inscribed the above designation on the new stone memorial they dedicated when they visited in 2010. But the spot's importance to the Shawnees is undeniable and it again underscores the different treatment Native American historic sites receive in comparison to those of their white counterparts.

Credit is due to what was then called the Ohio State Archaeological and Historical Society for having the foresight buy the property in 1947 (a granite marker has been on the site since 1922), even though this isn't the most convenient location for visitors to honor the Shawnee tribe. But as I slogged through the weeds and tried to imagine this spot in 1786 when Captain Benjamin Logan and his Kentucky militia destroyed the village (and several others in the vicinity), it occurred me that a white settlement of this importance probably would have developed into a great (or at least a not so great) city.

There is a Wapatomica historical marker that the public can see on County Road 5, a quarter of a mile east of the actual site, across another farm field and a more difficult climb (than I made) through the woods. Across the road, the Mad River lies less than a quarter of a mile away. This public marker is similar to one that marks the Shawnee village of Mackachak three miles south of here and a mile east of West Liberty, although that one is in the actual location of the settlement next to Macochee Creek.

The Wapatomica Trail ran past both villages and provided a convenient route from the Ohio River to Lake Erie. It connected with the Pickawillany and Miami trails south of modern Springfield, and with the Scioto Trail just south of today's Upper Sandusky. Thirty miles north of Wapatomica, where the trail (Ohio 265) crosses the small, winding Upper Scioto River at Pfeiffer Station, Dr. John Knight, the condemned friend of star-crossed Colonel William Crawford, escaped from his Indian captors following the defeat at Sandusky. From Rushsylvania through Zanesfield to Wapatomica, the trail follows County Road 5.

Wapatomica's historical cred stems from its status as the "principal Shawnee village from its founding. . . sometime before 1778 until October, 1786." (The Shawnee had another village named Wapatomica along the Muskingum River, near present-day Dresden, Ohio, earlier. It was one of five Shawnee villages destroyed by Virginia colonial militia led by Angus McDonald during Lord Dunmore's War.) Because of its elevation, it could be easily be seen from a considerable distance across the wide plain to the south and east. It hosted several important tribal councils in the tribe's bark council house, including the council of seven Indian nations in 1782. Notable Shawnee chief Black Hoof (Catahecassa), remembered as a fierce warrior, lived here.

Simon Kenton was forced to run a gauntlet here in 1778, one of nine including Mackachak the well-known frontiersman is known to have survived. His endurance here merely afforded him a chance to be burned at the stake, although renegade Simon Girty rescued him from this fate. Girty and Kenton knew each other from Fort Pitt. Over the years the Shawnees burned many of their prisoners at this stake, which supposedly stood at the site of the crumbling granite monument. That memorial served as the base for a flagpole that lightning struck at some point. Besides the burning of captives, the circle where the two monuments and a modern flagpole sit was used for war, religious and pleasure dances.

Today, the area near the circle is entangled with invasive amur honeysuckle bushes, upright non-native shrubs with long arching branches and tiny yellow flowers introduced in the United States from Europe and Asia in the mid-nineteenth century, a species that out-competes and shades out many more desirable native woodland species. Whether the "evil honeysuckle," as one of my friends call it, is really as bad as all that, it strikes me that Black Hoof and his Shawnee warriors wouldn't be pleased at having another European invader staking a claim on Wapatomica centuries later.

John Slover, a guide captured at the Battle of Sandusky (Battle Island) and brought here in 1782, is a source for some of the information we have about Wapatomica. Of the six white men captured by the Shawnee at the time, two were killed, one escaped and Slover and two others were brought here. Before they arrived, they came to a small Indian village a short distance away and the inhabitants emerged with tomahawks and clubs and beat the captives. The Indians stripped one of Slover's companions naked and painted him black with coal and water. He broke down and wept, having surmised that he would be the first to die.

When the trio arrived at Wapatomica, they had to run a gauntlet to the council house, a course described by Slover as about 300 yards. Beaten and wounded, Slover and the other man watched as their painted companion ran the gauntlet and then burned to death at the stake. While at Wapatomica, Slover saw a party of twelve captives brought to the council house and distributed among the Shawnee towns in the vicinity where they suffered the same fate.

Slover remained captive when the council of seven tribes – Ottawas, Chippewas, Wyandots, Delawares, Munsees, Mingoes and Shawnees – convened here. He recalled that Girty, Mathew Elliot and Alexander McKee all gave the tribes advice. The council investigated Slover and demanded information from him. When he told them that Cornwallis, the British general, had been captured at Yorktown, McKee branded this as a lie. The council broke up after 15 days and about 40 warriors accompanied by George Girty put a rope around his neck, tied his arms behind his back, stripped him naked and painted him black. They took him to Mackachak, tied him to a pole in the council house there and started a fire to burn him. But a heavy rain put the fire out, and Indians decided to wait until the following day to execute him. During the night, his three Indians guards fell asleep and he managed to slip out of his wrist bonds, steal a horse and make a wild escape – naked – while several warriors pursued him. After several days of riding, he found some of his companions camped near the site of modern Columbus. In 1786 George Rogers Clark got wind of a large assemblage of Indians and British agents planned for the upper Wabash region in September and October and decided to strike them in retaliation for recent attacks. Clark decided to lead a force against those on the Wabash and have Benjamin

THE OLD AND NEW MARKERS AT WAPATOMICA

Logan and fellow colonels Thomas Kennedy and Robert Trottier make a diversionary advance on the Shawnee towns on the Mad River. Daniel Boone, Simon Kenton and Robert Patterson served as advance scouts and also led units into battle.

Logan assembled his force of 790 Kentucky mounted militia at Limestone (modern Maysville, Kentucky) and proceeded to Mackachak. It was the first of the Shawnee settlements in this area including Wapatomica that the militia destroyed, a feat made easy because most of the warriors had left for the gathering on the Wabash.

The troops rode up on Mackachak with swords raised and guns blazing. With the warriors gone, only a dozen or so able-bodied men were left to defend the village and they did so furiously to buy time for the fleeing women and children. It was a futile effort, but one warrior killed Captain Christopher Irvine before he was riddled with bullets.

Colonel Kennedy chased down eight fleeing women with his sword high in the air. He drove it so deeply into the skull of a middle-aged woman that he nearly lost his balance as he tried to remove it. Then he chased down the others and killed six of them, including a 17-year-old who had been just been married to a young warrior who had gone to the Wabash with the other men. Of this group, only the sister of sub-chief Red Horse, who lost four fingers and suffered a severe cut to the head, survived Kennedy's relentless assault against the helpless women.

Across Ohio 245 and up a hill from the Mackachak marker a large boulder bears an old plaque that identifies it as the "Squaw Rock of Indian legend" and marks the site of the "Indian village of Mack-o-cheek home of Chief Moluntha." Legend says that a young woman hiding behind this rock was mistaken for a warrior and killed by soldier. A variation of it has her with a baby, who was raised by a white family after the killing. Whether the story is true or not, it probably started with Kennedy's murder of seven women during the attack.

Moluntha surrendered to Simon Kenton with his three wives, including the famous 6-foot-6 Grenadier Squaw (Nonhelema), sister of Cornstalk. The 94-year-old chief knew and respected Kenton from his time as a prisoner here, and Kenton promised him safety, ordering eight privates to form a ring of protection around him and his wives. Colonel Richard Butler also approached Moluntha, shook his hand and told him that he would not be harmed. After Butler and Kenton left to take care of other business, three men rode up on horseback, and forced their way into the circle. One was a hot–headed Indian hating captain named Hugh McGary, whom some blamed for causing the disaster at the brutal Battle of Blue Licks (Kentucky) four years before. Over eighty members of the militia had died there including one of his close relatives.

McGary stepped forward and confronted the old chief: "Were you at the defeat of the Blue Licks?"

Moluntha struggled to understand what he has been asked and finally answered, "Yes."

McGary instantly jerked out his tomahawk and buried it into the chief's skull to the handle and he fell dead on the ground. Logan and Kenton were furious when they learned what had happened -- McGary had been warned by Logan not to molest the prisoners -- and they had him arrested and held for murder. But when McGary was convicted upon his return to Kentucky, his sentence merely took away his command for one year.

After burning Mackachak, Logan's militia split up and burned and destroyed as many as ten other Shawnee towns in the vicinity, including Wapatomica, Moluntha's Town (in modern West Liberty), Blue Jacket's Town (Bellefontaine), Pigeon Town, McKee's Town, and Wapakoneta (near West Liberty). They also destroyed all of the crops near them. The other Shawnee towns were deserted when the soldiers arrived, all having been warned by those who escaped from Mackachak.

Over two days, Logan's force killed 22 Indians, took 33 prisoners (mostly women) and suffered three casualties. Logan and his men hoped that this raid would intimidate the Shawnee and possibly end their raids on white settlements in the region. Instead, the tribe became more aggressive and posed an even greater threat than before.

Most of the Shawnees moved to new villages in the Auglaize River region to the north, although a few of the Mad River towns were eventually re-settled. Some may have returned to Wapatomica, although a visitor to Logan County in 1800 reported that the site was deserted.

When I exited off U.S. 33 and headed toward Zanesfield on County Road 153, I was surprised to see a historical marker calling attention to a "Historical Home Site." A home of Simon Kenton had stood here, on or near a nondescript farm field on the way into the small town that stood on the site of an old Wyandot village.

"Here in a 20-foot square, one door, three window log cabin the old scout lived from 1819 to 1828. The home, built by his children, stood on a 65-acre tract of forest land."

I looked around at the drab surroundings, and thought of the impressive bronze statue of the frontiersman I had seen in Covington, Kentucky. I thought of the one that stands on Monument Square in Urbana, Ohio, and another one that stands atop his grave at Urbana's Oak Dale Cemetery.

Kenton ranged over hundreds of miles of unspoiled wilderness, fought numerous battles, survived nine gauntlets and probably escaped death on a dozen more occasions to end up in a 20-foot square log cabin here? The reality seemed incompatible with the legend until I thought about Wapatomica, a once-great Shawnee capital choked by weeds, trees and brush four miles away.

Time left both of them behind, and only one of them has since been celebrated.

III.

SOLDIERS AND SETTLERS

20 PICKAWILLANY

Pickawillany isn't on any list of Ohio attractions. Ask the first dozen Ohioans you meet about it and you're apt to get an answer similar to one I mined from a bored teenager:

"Isn't that the name of a circus?"

Uh, no, you're thinking of Piccadilly Circus.

"Oh, yeah . . .

I started to explain that the famous London intersection isn't actually a circus, but it seemed best not to stray too far from the original topic. Too late.

"I've never been to a circus."

It's a good bet he's never been to Pickawillany either. There was a time during the eighteenth century when it may have been the most important place in what became the modern state of Ohio, but today it doesn't even draw top historical billing around the city of Piqua.

A historical-minded visitor is directed north on Ohio Route 66 to Johnston Farm and Indian Agency, the 1815 home and farm of Indian agent John Johnston. Less than a mile from town, a brown sign with a right-pointing arrow beneath a generic "Piqua Historical Area" appears first, followed by a two-story Federal-style brick home across several hundred yards of farm fields, and then the intersection with Hardin Road on the right.

The road goes a short distance and turns toward the left past a pull off on the right side, which allows the visitor to view five markers/monuments lined up in a row in the grass probably 10 feet apart. The Johnston house lies dead ahead now, again a few hundred yards across a plowed field. A short distance down the road on the right, a large blue and white sign directs visitors to the turn for the "Johnston House & Indian Agency."

But the row of five markers is an unmistakable clue that this is more than just another picturesque Ohio farm photo for a state tourism calendar. Johnston, who had served as the Indian agent at Fort Wayne before he settled here in 1811, did operate an Indian agency here during the War of 1812 until 1829. But that doesn't begin to cover the history that occurred on this ground.

The historical marker for "The Battle of Pickawillany" and a large carved rock for Pickawillany" try to do that, although when you're staring at wide expanse of farm fields that back up to the Great Miami River, it's easy to wonder where you're supposed to be looking. The rock tells us that the "headquarters of the Miami tribes, the first English settlement and the most important trading post in the west 1748" was located one mile northeast of this memorial, which before a couple of short turns might have easy to locate. Before it occurred to me to check the compass on my cellphone – don't you wonder how Henry Hudson found the Hudson River without a cellphone? - - it struck me that Pickawillany supposedly stood near Loramie Creek's convergence with the Great Miami and both lay somewhere across the fields to the left (north) of the Johnston house.

Fortunately, the Ohio Historical Society (now the Ohio History Connection) purchased 37 acres west of the confluence of the creek and river and did excavations on the site from 2002 until 2013. So, the site of the small fort and trading post, the Pickawillany settlement and the famous "battle" where the French drove the English and Miamis out in 1752 is clearer today than it would have been fifty years ago.

It is difficult to definitively locate this important trading post 260 years later. But the concentration of artifacts, written descriptions and other evidence leads OHC archaeologist Bill Pickard to believe that the trading post was a short distance south of the confluence on the eastern edge of the 35-foot bluff closest to the river, approximately 350 yards northeast of the Johnston farmhouse.

Virginian Christopher Gist visited the site in 1751 and estimated the settlement at "400 families" and growing. That means it was large enough to have spread out over most of the fields visible from that five-marker location on the south side of Hardin Road. Pickard believes it could have swelled to 3,000 people at various times.

"This property we own now, I think that's kind of where Pickawillany was," Pickard said. "There are geographic features here. There's a ravine (to the south of the OHC property, north of the Johnson's farm), there's big glacier terrace at Hardin Road that's like a natural barrier. You can go up there, but all the flat land is between there and the river. And there are creeks and swamps up here (north) so there are natural limitations. This is 37 acres and it's about an eighth of it. People didn't live in cul-de-sacs and nice gridded neighborhoods; they were spread out over hell's half-acre."

Gist roamed the area, looking for sites for permanent English settlement, and he spent two weeks at the fort. On his first day there, he described the village in his journal: "This town is located on the northwest side of the Big Miamee River, about 150 miles from the mouth thereof: it consists of about 400 families, and daily increasing; it is accounted one of the strongest Indian towns upon this part of the continent."

Native people occupied this area long before the Miamis settled here in 1747. In addition to items found from Pickawillany days, artifacts have been found here from the Adena period, hundreds of years before. And even after the Miamis left, the Shawnee had a village called Upper Piqua south of Pickawillany on the spot that became Johnston farm, at a place General Anthony Wayne built a small fort during the winter of 1793-94 to support his northward march from Fort Greeneville.

Another Shawnee settlement south of here in what is now the heart of town was called Lower Piqua; the two nearby settlements form the basis of the city that exists as Piqua today.

Gary Meek, the man holding down the fort (sorry) in the History and Genealogy Department of the Piqua Public Library, said that Native Americans occupied spots all over the area at various times.

"There were a number of Indian encampments here, going back to prehistoric (times)," he said. "There was a big one out in the vicinity of the cemetery. That one was one they excavated and they documented it pretty well, and they basically took it off in layers. The rest of them were done by artifact hunters. Dig it up -- oh, that's neat."

The excavation at Pickawillany was done carefully on the ground that the OHS purchased for that purpose in 1999. But the archaeological work that was done here until 2013, coupled with the written history from various sources from the 1740s, show both how deep and how rich the history here is.

Recorded history tells us that Miami chief Memeskia (the French called him La Demoiselle and the British called him Old Briton, which we will use from here on out) rebelled against the French near his village of Kekionga, in today's Fort Wayne, Indiana. He was unhappy with the high prices and poor quality of the trade goods his tribe received from the French and during his earlier travels on the Ohio he had been impressed with the superiority and cheaper prices of the English.

When Nicolas, a pro-British Huron chief at Sandusky, came up with a plan to unite the western tribes against the French, Old Briton quickly joined the conspiracy. The plan had Nicolas attacking Detroit, the Ojibwa taking Michilimackinac and Old Briton attacking the French trading post at Fort Miamis near Kekionga. The Huron plot failed, but Old Briton's Miamis seized eight French soldiers and burned part of the stockade. After learning of the Hurons' failure to take Detroit and Nicholas' move to eastern Ohio to escape retribution from the French, Old Briton decided against killing the soldiers. Instead, during the fall of 1747, he moved his band of Miamis southeast and settled them at the bluff near the confluence of today's Loramie Creek (called Pickawillany Creek until the 1790s) and the Great Miami River in a village that came to be known as Pickawillany.

After working on the site there for several years, Pickard said that "there was almost certainly some sort of semi-permanent Native residency at that location that predates the traditional founding date of 1747 by many years if not decades."

How can he be so sure?

"Everything we found in the trash pits is French," he said. "Nobody was there after that, so that was before there was an English presence on site. This was a known location before Memeskia ever burned down the fort (at Kekionga); by the early 1740s, there were French traders there, guys who didn't have (French trading) licenses, who were trading with the Indians without a license.

"It's an important location. If you were going from the south to the upper great lakes, you just about have to come this way. There were no trails to speak of, so you followed the river valleys. So you jump off (at Pickawillany) and its 10 miles to the Auglaize, so many miles to the St. Mary's river, or whatever you're going. Pickawillany was the place to be. Memeskia didn't come here by accident. He knew where he was going."

The word Pickawillany itself seems to have Shawnee roots – the word roughly translates as "Place of the Ashes" – a sign that the Shawnees might have been there before the Miamis. But the Miamis move here is well-documented historically.

Old Briton believed his new village was far enough removed from the French military posts to be safe from French intervention and far enough west that he could attract other tribes interested in British trade goods. He asked Seneca and Shawnee tribesmen who had a trading relationship with the British in eastern Ohio to inform the traders of his interest, promising that he could easily free significant numbers of western tribes from their alliance with the French if there were an abundance of British trade goods here.

This excited traders and political figures in Pennsylvania and they urged Governor James Hamilton to appoint commissioners to meet with tribal leaders and conclude a formal treaty. Hamilton quickly followed up on that, sending a party to Pickawillany to accompany a Miami delegation to Lancaster, Pennsylvania, for a conference in July, 1748. After five days of negotiations (Old Briton stayed back at the village), the commissioners welcomed the Miamis into the realm of British "friendship and alliance," and promised that if the Miamis would have no more dealings with the French, the British would "give (them) assistance on all occasions."

British traders immediately made the trek to Pickawillany. George Croghan came here from Logstown (a settlement on the Ohio River west of today's Pittsburgh) and established a trading post with the chief's blessing that year. Old Briton sent runners to other tribes in the west, telling them of the new arrangement and urging them to come to Pickawillany and trade.

Naturally, the news of this alarmed the French. Back in Montreal, the acting governor-general of New France determined that he must reassert French influence in the Ohio country. In 1749, French military leader Celeron de Bienville led a force of 250 men down the Ohio River and planted lead plates at the mouths of the rivers entering the Ohio with inscriptions which claimed the land for France. After planting the plate at the mouth of the Great Miami, he followed the stream north to Pickawillany and arrived on September 13. Bienville had encountered English traders at several locations and demanded that they leave French territory but they mostly ignored him. The situation was no different here. He spent a week trying to convince the Miami chief to stop trading with the English and return his allegiance to the French and finally left after having no success.

He wrote in his journal: "All that I can say is that the tribes of these localities are very badly disposed toward the French and entirely devoted to the English. I do not know by what means they can be brought back."

Because France claimed the territory, the British convinced the Miami chief to allow them to build a stockade there for their protection. They built Fort Pickawillany in 1750 around a two-story main building with cabins for traders behind the high wall of split logs; other cabins were located outside.

Old Briton's attitude toward the French didn't improve. A party of French and Indians raided the town in 1751, killing two Miamis and capturing two British traders. Matters finally come to a head – and Pickawillany to an end – in 1752.

Charles Langlade, a mixed blood French-Ottawa leader from Michilimackinac, led a force of Ottawa and Ojibwa warriors and soldiers from Fort Detroit with orders to destroy the British fort and trading post and the Miami village which made it possible. They launched a surprise attack at nine in the morning on June 21, 1752, when they knew many of the warriors from the village were away.

The attackers captured Miami women working in the cornfields and came upon them so suddenly that the white men, who were in their houses outside the fort, had difficulty making it inside the stockade for safety. Three men didn't make it to the fort, shut themselves inside their houses and were soon captured. Old Briton sought refuge inside the fort, where he tried to rally the relatively small number of fighting men at his disposal – only about 20 men and boys including a handful of British traders.

They held off the French and Ottawas all morning, despite being outnumbered more than 10 to one. But the fort lacked water and it became clear that their resistance would ultimately prove futile. Late in the afternoon, Langlade called for a ceasefire. He offered to return his Miami captives, including Old Briton's wife and young son, and call off the attack if Old Briton would leave the fort and surrender all of the British traders.

Old Briton reluctantly surrendered five traders, including one who had already been wounded, but hid two others inside the stockade. When the Miami chief and the traders exited the fort, the Ottawas quickly seized the wounded trader and stabbed him death and cut out his heat and ate it. They discovered the hidden traders inside the fort and Langlade used that deception as justification for ordering Old Briton's execution. After the old chief died, the Ottawas threw his body in a boiling kettle of water and then ate it in front of the Miamis. The ghastly display convinced most of the Miamis to desert Pickawillany and return to the tribe's main settlement on the Wabash.

Captain William Trent left Logstown about the same time of the attack bearing gifts for the Miamis at Pickawillany. When news of the attack reached him, he diverted his troops to Lower Shawnee town at the mouth of the Scioto. Trent's journal, dated 15 days following the attack, tells of how his party went on to investigate Pickawillany after the battle. They found the deserted fort still standing, with two French flags flying. Trent and his party spent the night there, raised the English flag and then returned to Lower Shawnee Town.

Some of the Miamis may have eventually returned to the site. Pickawillany might have been the site of a 1763 battle during the war described by Shawnee chief Black Hoof, in which Miamis and Wyandots fortified themselves against Delaware and Shawnee warriors, who gave up a siege after seven days.

The area remained a beehive of Native American activity nonetheless. The Shawnee moved here and settled the Upper and Lower Piqua locations around 1780. The moves came after an expedition of frontiersmen and militia under the command of George Rogers Clark attacked and destroyed the Shawnee town of Piqua on the Mad River about five miles west of modern Springfield. The Shawnee brought the name Piqua with them in honor of their former home.

During the winter of 1793-94, Wayne built his small fort and supply depot west of the old Miami settlement. It was garrisoned through 1794 and 1795 and then abandoned. Today, a museum on the property has been constructed to resemble the small stockade that Wayne's troops built as a supply post.

"You know where the museum is?" Pickard said. "That's exactly where Fort Piqua was. Someone in their divine wisdom. . . put things on top of where other things were. Three hundred acres, and they had to put it there."

The museum holds some of the artifacts dug up at Pickawillany both by the OHS archaeologists and local treasurer hunters who scarfed the site in

1930s. For the tourist, it is nice complement to the house tours and restored section of the Miami and Erie Canal (Johnston was a canal commissioner), all of which make the Johnston farm site a historical treasure.

Still, a visitor to Piqua might be disappointed to find that there is little in the city of 20,522 that honors its native heritage. The area in Piqua east of the Great Miami is nicknamed Shawnee and there is a small playground on East Main Street that is called Shawnee Park, but that's about it.

It's not like Piqua isn't interested in history; the restored Fort Piqua Hotel building which is now home to the library, is gorgeous, and there are markers that celebrate other moments in the area's history.

After doing an hour-long walking tour of downtown Piqua that yielded no information on the tribes who once located here, I asked Meek if there were any monuments or markers in the area that mentioned the Indians tribes who meant to so much to the area. He had to confess that he didn't know of any.

"Uh. . . the only thing that we have is probably out at Johnston Park," he said. "There was an Indian village over on the flat ground by the river, but there is no marker to that."

And then again, there is doubtless more waiting to be discovered out at the Pickawillany site.

"We stopped in 2013 because we ran out of money," Pickard said. "And even if we knew everything that was out there, we didn't want to dig it all up. People 20 years ago didn't have near the technology that we do today, and what's it going to be like 20 years from now? So leave it alone and go back and investigate in 20 or 30 years when they have other machines that can see stuff differently.

"When (OHS) acquired the property in 1998 or 99, they hired a consultant to go out and see if he could make sense of it. They plowed it and nobody was allowed to walk on it. And they had to wait until the weather was just right and they got a hot day and then a cool night. They put an infrared camera on a balloon and tried to take a picture of it. It's easy sometimes to find sites because the soil is different. It promotes growth differently, it has different water retention.

"So, he tried to do that and a thunderstorm hit and one of the technicians had to chain himself to a tree to keep himself from being pulled away by this giant helium balloon. . . He tried, but it just didn't work out as well. He just dug a trench across God's knows where and I don't know why, looking for something he was hoping to find. He didn't have the luxury of all the data that we had."

21 LORAMIE'S TRADING POST

The 16-mile drive from Piqua to Fort Loramie on Ohio Route 66 takes the visitor past a barn-like wooden building called the Fort Loramie Trading Post. The modern structure is a dubious attempt to capitalize on the fame of the famous trading post and store that Pierre-Louis de Lorimier (often anglicized as Peter Loramie) started here in 1769.

One of the signs out front even advertises the sale of boots, a staple that actually might have been available for trade or sale inside the Frenchman's eighteenth-century store. But the rows of lawn ornaments this modern trading post is peddling probably wouldn't have been of much use to the Native Americans who lived in these parts, ancient customers who probably held higher expectations for Loramie's goods than a modern shopper might have for a place hawking concrete horses, chickens, lions and, God forbid, Indian chiefs.

Ironically, the Fort Loramie Trading Post is the most visible reminder of why this little western Ohio town of 1,478 is here today. Signs at the city limits note that this is the "site of Loramie's Trading Post and General Wayne's Fort Loramie 1795," but that pretty much covers it as far as visible evidence of the community's historic identity.

That might be a little confusing to an accidental visitor who passed the 'Welcome" sign and then found the modern trading post; truthfully, there aren't many accidental visitors here. Fort Loramie sits at a crossroads of two state routes that intersect 23 miles west of Interstate 75, which is to say that unless you live in Fort Loramie or one of the other small nearby communities – Minster, Newport, New Bremen or Maria Stein – your chances of inadvertently landing here are only marginally better than winning the Publisher's Clearing House sweepstakes.

So what brought Loramie here and why did his store do such a booming business?

As modern real estate agents are prone to call the three most important characteristics of a choice property: "Location, location, location."

This may seem odd given the previous description of modern Fort Loramie, but in fact, it is nothing of the sort. While this pleasant little village may not occupy an important place in today's geographical pecking order, Peter Loramie landed here because it is at the southern end of a portage between Pickawillany Creek (which was named for Loramie later) and the St. Mary's River, which connects to the Maumee, which flows into Lake Erie. The creek flows to the Great Miami, which flows into the Ohio, which flows into the Mississippi and so on. In other words, Loramie's trading post was on one end of a short portage that bridged a water route to most of the entire eastern half of North America.

The real Loramie trading post was located on the opposite (north) end of town. Loramie Creek crosses Ohio 66 there, and early chroniclers place both the store and Wayne's "fort" in that vicinity. According to an article in an Ohio Archaeological and Historical Society publication in 1908, Anthony Wayne's Fort Loramie "stood on the bank of the creek, one-half mile north of the present town and about where the Arkenberg house and farm buildings stand. This is also supposed to be the site of the Loramie store. . ."

The story-and-a-half Arkenberg house (which is pictured in that publication) is still there on the north side of the creek at the end of a lane that bisects several farm buildings, and the Fleckenstein family who own the farm today are part of the same family. That early photo includes a large stone in front of the house, which the cutline says "marks on of the corners of Loramie's Store." It may, in fact, mark one of the corner Wayne's "fort," but there will be more on that later.

Many early settlers in this area remembered Loramie as a French Jesuit missionary as well as a trader. Whether he viewed the tribes as converts, customers or both, by setting up shop near the banks of this creek he had come to the right place.

Loramie was born in Montreal in 1748 and came here from Quebec, by way of Vincennes. Various reports indicate that he was one of three Jesuit missionaries dispatched from Quebec "for the purpose of safeguarding the privileges accorded to the Catholics and Indians by the peace treaty signed after the Braddock (French and Indian) war at Paris in 1763." All of the Jesuit missions would subsequently be destroyed by the suppression of the Jesuit order by the Pope Clement XIV in 1773, so from that point Loramie could not publicly exercise any function as priest or Jesuit. That may explain why there is some confusion over whether he was a missionary.

There is no doubting Loramie's interest in trade and he saw this as a prime spot for his store. The Indians held an intense loyalty to him as they did many of the French traders. Loramie didn't like Americans and after the British gained control of the territory, he stood firmly on the Indians (and British) side. The Shawnee were frequent visitors to the outpost and during the Revolutionary War Indians loyal to the British used Loramie's store as a staging area for attacks against the colonists.

According to historian Louis Houck, Loramie joined 40 Shawnees and carried out a raid into Kentucky in 1778. The party kidnapped Daniel Boone in the process and took him to Old Chillicothe, a Shawnee village from which he later escaped.

This didn't set well with the Americans and General George Rogers Clark sent a force under Colonel Benjamin Logan to solve the Loramie problem in 1782. Logan's troops surprised the French trader and burned his trading post to the ground; historians estimate Loramie's losses at anywhere from $20,000 to $70,000. The loss ruined Loramie financially and he was lucky to escape with his life.

Loramie fled first to a Shawnee village at Wapakoneta and then to a tribal village in Indiana. He eventually moved with a colony of Shawnee to the Spanish territory west of the Mississippi, where the other parts of the Shawnee nation from Ohio joined them at different times. Loramie is credited with founding the town of Cape Girardeau, Missouri, where he died on June 26, 1812.

"Loramie was an interesting figure," said Tilda Philpot, director of the Shelby County Historical Society's Ross Center museum. "He had a pony tail long enough to whip horses. When he went west, the Indians saw him as one of their leaders."

His store site remained important geographically. General Josiah Harmar left Cincinnati on his failed expedition against the Indian tribes in October, 1792, and he reached the ruins of Loramie's store on October 10. He paused there briefly before continuing north toward his disastrous losses near modern-day Fort Wayne.

In 1794, after General Anthony Wayne defeated the Indians at Fallen Timbers and continued on to build Fort Wayne, he came back by way of Defiance and St. Marys (Girty's Town) and visited the store site. He examined the ruins and ordered a fort built on the site to provide protection to the settlers in the western areas of Ohio.

While Wayne initially intended this to be an actual stockade, he decided that with the Indian threat reduced it would best function as a supply depot for Fort Wayne, Fort Defiance and other points north. He determined that a blockhouse and several storage buildings would be more useful. He named the complex Fort Loramie, probably because by this point settlers in the area were calling the creek and other local landmarks after the departed French trader. Some modern historians have noted how unusual it is for a fort to be named for a vanquished enemy.

The post was occupied until 1812 when it was abandoned as a military garrison. At the time, James Furrow was one of the first settlers in the area. He told of how on the night when the trading post was burned, a high American officer was killed and buried not far from the ruins of the store. After the evacuation of the fort by military personnel in 1812, Furrow purchased the land there for farming. He tore down the main building of the fort and kept some of the minor ones for a country store and trading post of his own.

Furrow owned the farm until he died in 1842. He indicated in his will that he wished to be buried on his farm by the side of the American officer. Furrow, his wife and son are buried in a small family burial plot, a short distance north of the house and the farm buildings in what satellite images show as a clump of trees.

A modern curiosity seeker probably shouldn't linger too long on those satellite images, particularly on Google Maps. "Furrow Cemetery" appears over a small patch of green south of the creek and just west of Main Street, well south of the farm buildings. Early accounts indicate the fort and store site were located at or near the graveyard, so that immediately calls into question whether the accounts placing them near the Arkenberg farmhouse are correct.

Ken Sowards, a retired Fort Loramie teacher whom Philpot called "the historian for that area," quickly set the record straight.

"That's mislabeled," Sowards said. "That's just a little township cemetery. Now there may be some Furrows buried there, I don't know. But there is a cemetery site, an old family plot, on the Fleckenstein farm, 100 to 150 feet of so north of the house. That's where the Furrow family is buried. That's where Edward Butler's nine-year-old son was buried when (Butler) was the captain of the fort. The Furrow family, they bought the property from the U.S. government when they decommissioned the fort and they used that (burial site) as their family cemetery.

"We don't have any idea how many people are buried there, because when you walk around it after the grass is cut there are sunken places where it looks like graves have been added to that. It only makes sense that when there were soldiers stationed there for 20 years, there had to be soldiers who died on site and were buried on site, but we're not going to dig into that."

Sowards is part of a local archaeological group led by Greg Shipley which has been conducting meticulous digs on the Fleckenstein farm since 2014 in an attempt to definitively locate both the fort and the store site. They believe they have found both sites:

"Where the Fleckenstein farm is, there's a sewer pump house very close to the creek and very close to the bridge (over Ohio 66)," Sowards said. "The store site is probably 100 to 150 feet north of that. That's where we think the store was, where we found burnt material and the post mold holes. It is about 100 feet west of the road in that field.

"We know the store was burned to the ground in October 1782. And we found evidence of a hot fire in the burnt glass, the burnt gun flint and the post mold holes which had charcoal in them. And the ground leading up from the creek to the store site has a gentle slope that would have been perfect to drag canoes up the bank (to the store)."

And the fort?

"If you look where the old farm house is, that's where we think the fort was. The old homestead, the old farm house which somebody still lives in, we think the foundation of the (house) was the foundation to the fort. That site is on a high bank, and we found a trash pit back by the house. It would be just south of the house, literally within spitting distance. Because of the high bank, they were just throwing the trash over the side of the wall down onto the flood plain."

The group has put the dozens of items it has found on the property, including military buttons from Wayne's Legion, cannon ball fragments, gun parts, broken dishware and broken crockery on display to the public and plans to give all of the artifacts the group discovers to the Fleckenstein family.

"We've gotten a lot of grief from the professionals," Sowards said. "They think we're looting the site and we're not. We're putting on programs and what we haven't been doing is publishing, and we need to do that. This is a significant find."

On April 28, 2019, Shipley spoke and presented a slide show about their digs to a packed house of over 300 people at the Shelby County Bicentennial Celebration at Fort Loramie Elementary School and the group exhibited all of the items they had found at Fleckenstein farm. Afterwards, Shipley presented all of those artifacts to a beaming Ted Fleckenstein, who plans to keep and pass the items down in his family.

"Today, we are returning all of the artifacts back to the Fleckenstein family,' Shipley said. "It is time for this collection to go home, back to the farm property where these objects had been laying in the ground for the past 220-plus years."

While the concern of the "professionals" is understandable, it's difficult not be appreciative of the free work being done by a dedicated group of talented amateurs who appear to have discovered the locations of two important historical sites that no one else was looking for.

They have given meaning to a clump of farm buildings just north of town and a farm field west of Ohio 66 that looks like any other. A trading post that dates to the earliest settlement of the Old Northwest may have once located there, and the owner wasn't selling concrete chickens.

22 COLUMBIA

A quest for the frontier settlement of Columbia inevitably leads to Cincinnati's original commercial airport. Nearly every modern reference to the little community founded by Benjamin Stites in November, 1788, is accompanied by a simple description: Located where Lunken Airport is today.

Maybe this vague explanation is offered because it is a convenient way to take care of any and all questions; the city's old municipal airport covers so much ground west of the Little Miami River – 1,140 acres -- that there's not much room for argument. An armchair historian can take an inquisitive visitor onto the bike path/jogging trail that surrounds the airport, wave his hand in the direction of all of that open space, say "That's where Columbia was" and bring a tidy end to the discussion.

That is also the lazy way to do it. A better tour guide would take a visitor along Wilmer Road, north of Davis Lane and just to the west of the airport, where the only surviving part of Columbia awaits, often in solitude. Pioneer Cemetery sits atop a hill across Wilmer Avenue from several Signature Flight Service hangars, in a location that used to be the churchyard of the Columbia Baptist Church, organized in 1790 as the first Protestant church in the Northwest Territory.

The small parking lot near the road fronts a pretty 2.2-acre park with mature trees and a brick walk that leads to a concrete stairway. A tall Corinthian pillar that honors the "pioneers" stands at the end of the stairs. It sits atop a four-sided block of stone that lists the names of "the first boat-load" of 26 passengers who landed at Columbia and celebrates the "first Baptists" who erected their church here. The pillar was taken from an old Cincinnati post office that dates from 1856 and was placed here when it was razed in 1888. That seems a little odd (Hey, can anybody use this old pillar?)

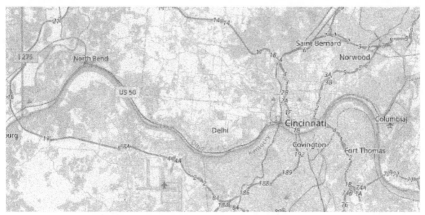

NORTH BEND, CINCINNATI AND COLUMBIA WERE SETTLED A FEW MONTHS APART.

but it looks like it belongs here, nonetheless. It lies on the location of the two-story church of hewn logs without weatherboarding or a fireplace that is depicted in a drawing on an information board at the site. One of those boards tells us that Reverend John Smith of Pennsylvania, who owned a farm and a small store, was the church's first pastor. The side story is that he became one of the first senators to represent Ohio in the United States Senate, but had to resign after being charged with treason because of his friendship with Aaron Burr.

In its quiet moments, this feels like the Columbia that Stites and his companions knew. In the tree-framed solitude of a cemetery over two hundred years old, it isn't difficult to imagine the crude wooden building that served as their first church occupying that spot overlooking the new settlement. The vision is sometimes marred by the sound of airplanes whose pilots apparently don't know they don't belong here and a yellow aluminum building across the fence south of the old church yard that is as unobtrusive as a yellow aluminum building can be. But the area still feels isolated, even with people on the other side of that aluminum and an airport down the hill and across the street.

Even when the area was isolated, that didn't always mean it was serene and peaceful. Forty-four years after Indians abducted him on his return here from Cincinnati as an 11-year-old boy, Oliver M. Spencer recalled attending services in that little church shortly after its construction. His memories remind the visitor that this may not have always been quite the paradise we imagine:

"Fresh in my remembrance is the rude log house, the first humble sanctuary of the first settlers of Columbia, standing amidst the tall forest trees on the beautiful knoll where now may be seen a graveyard and the ruins of a Baptist meeting house of later years. There on the holy Sabbath, we were wont to assemble to hear the word of life; but our fathers met with their muskets and rifles, prepared for action and ready to repel any attack of the enemy. And while the watchman on the walls of Zion was uttering his faithful and pathetic warning, the sentinels without, at a few rods distance, with measured step were now pacing their walks, and now standing with strained eyes endeavoring to pierce through the distance, carefully scanning every object that seemed to have life or motion."

Most of the ancient gravestones in the former churchyard lie to the north of the church site and include many familiar names, including several members of the Stites' family. Benjamin Stites' marker is prominent, in part because he was a major during the war for independence and the Daughters of the American Revolution erected it in 1923. He died in 1804, and it seems likely that one of the worn stones that lay nearby also belonged to him. The oldest readable stone in the cemetery is that of five months old Phebe Stites, daughter of Captain Hezekiah Stites. Phebe died on March 14, 1797. Given the short life span of the era and the hardship the settlers endured, it seems unlikely that little Phebe was the first burial there. Some relatively recent graves are scattered around the grounds – a few veterans of the Civil War, for example -- but it is clear from the dates on most of the gravestones that many of the dead were among Columbia's early settlers.

It is fitting that this is Stites' final resting place because he is at least partially responsible for the white migration into the entire Miami region, including the settlements at Cincinnati and North Bend that began within about two months of that of Columbia. Stites came here first, not with the first "boat-load" of settlers but in the spring of 1786 while leading a party in pursuit of a band of Indians who had stolen horses in Kentucky.

At the time, Stites lived in Redstone, a settlement on the Monongahela River in western Pennsylvania and he was on a trading expedition in Kentucky. He and his men pursued the horse thieves across the Ohio River and chased the Indians up the Little Miami River all the way to the site of present-day Xenia, Ohio. They never recovered the stolen horses but Stites returned with something better: a vision of land near the Little Miami that he thought would be the ideal settlement.

After returning home, he went to New York to convince members of the Continental Congress to open up the region for settlement so he could purchase the lands he had explored. He found a willing listener in John Cleves Symmes of Trenton, N.J., a member of Congress and a former judge of the state's Supreme Court. Symmes already had an interest in western settlement, possibly because of his awareness of the Ohio Company's efforts, and Stites' enthusiastic sales pitch spurred him into action. After a scouting trip down the Ohio in 1787 that went as far as the Wabash River, Symmes decided to petition Congress for a grant of 1,000,000 acres that bordered on the Ohio

River between two Miamis. Of this, he sold 20,000 acres to Stites at his dream site east of the mouth of the Little Miami.

Symmes' planned his own development (which became North Bend) near the mouth of the Great Miami and sold Matthew Denman 600 acres on the Ohio shore across from the mouth of the Licking River at the site of Cincinnati. All three led groups of settlers west in the summer of 1789 with the idea of setting up camp before the winter set in.

Limestone – today's Maysville, Kentucky – was the jumping off point for the groups, 52 miles by river from today's downtown Cincinnati. Of three groups, Stites' party left first, leaving Limestone by flatboat on November 16. Because they heard that a party of 500 Indians might be waiting to ambush them, they slowed down as they approached the mouth of the Little Miami and timed their landing for sunrise on November 18. They landed on the first high bank, about a half mile west of the mouth of the Little Miami. This was probably in the general area west of Pioneer Cemetery; Kellogg Avenue (U.S. 52) splits this mostly industrial area today. A clearing was made in a thicket of paw-paws and sentinels were posted. Thomas Wade led the singing of a hymn and a thanksgiving prayer followed. Then

A MONUMENT IN PIONEER CEMETERY

the nervous settlers immediately began building a blockhouse for their protection.

Stites' experience with the Indians had blessed him with a sense of urgency about providing protection for the travelers, so they came with lumber prepared so that construction could begin immediately. One report even indicated that Stites and his son Benjamin came to Columbia with doors that had hinges attached.

After work on the first blockhouse was finished on November 24, work began on three more which were eventually connected by palisades that formed a crude fortification they called Fort Miami. The fast work shows that all recognized the danger they had undertaken by settling here.

Only five of men – Stites, Elijah Stites, Greenbright Bailey, Abel Cook and Jacob Mills -- brought their families along in that first group of settlers. The others were unmarried or planned to bring their wives and children later when the settlement was .secure. Wade, Hezekiah Stites, John S. Gano, Ephraim Kibby, Benjamin Cox, Joseph Cox, Hampton Woodruff, Evan Shelby, Daniel Shoemaker, Edmund Buxton, Elijah Mills and a man named Hempstead were among this group.

The settlers initially built on a low plain because its rich soil made it an ideal for cultivating corn, which it also supplied to Denman's village at Losantiville (Cincinnati). They also discovered a clearing a mile and a half up the Little Miami called Turkey Bottom that had long been cultivated by Indians. From nine acres there, the new settlers supposedly reaped an enormous crop of 963 bushels of corn the first season.

By the end of 1790, the settlement already consisted of 50 cabins, a mill and a school. Because of its early start and quick development, at first it seemed like the most likely of the three Miami settlements to succeed. Cincinnati won that competition, primarily because the construction of Fort Washington offered settlers more safety from hostile Indian tribes. But the original settlements of Columbia and North Bend also suffered flooding problems that stunted their growth.

Probably the most important event in the frontier settlement's history occurred on July 7, 1792, when Indians captured Oliver M. Spencer (the 11-year-old Columbia boy we met earlier) on his return from a Fourth of July visit to Cincinnati. Spencer was the son of Colonel Oliver Spencer, a prominent New Jersey officer during the Revolutionary War who had brought his family west after British forces destroyed his home and tannery and he lost his fortune with the devaluation of Continental currency.

But the real reason that his son's seven and a half months captivity and more than two years away from Columbia is so important is because he eventually wrote a long narrative about it that became a widely-read book. Young Oliver became an Episcopal minister and a resident of Cincinnati as an adult, and he wrote *The Indian Captivity of O.M. Spencer* for an edition of the *Western Christian Advocate* dated December 1, 1834. It was copied into the *Christian Advocate and Journal*, which led to its publication in several other papers. It first appeared in book form in 1835 and is still reprinted today.

In it, Spencer described Columbia as it was when his family arrived there in December, 1790:

"It is, perhaps, unknown to many that the broad and extensive plain stretching along the Ohio from the Crawfish to the mouth, and for three miles up the Little Miami, and now divided into farms, highly cultivated, was the ancient site of Columbia, a town laid out by Major Benjamin Stites, its original proprietor; and by him and others once expected to become a large city, the great capital of the West. From Crawfish, the small creek forming its northwestern boundary, more than one mile up the Ohio, and extending back about three-fourths of a mile, and half way up the high hill, which formed part of its eastern and northern limits, the ground was laid off in blocks containing each eight lots of half an acre, bounded by streets intersecting at right angles. The residue of the plain was divided into lots of four and five acres for the accommodation of the town. Over this plain, on our arrival, we found scattered about fifty cabins, flanked by a small stockade nearly half a mile below the mouth of the Miami, together with a few blockhouses for the protection of the inhabitants, at suitable distances along the bank of the Ohio."

The description is a little confusing; Crawfish Creek is long gone, although Delta Avenue, once Crawfish Road and curvier and narrower than it is today, was close to the creek and provides a decent guide. Delta Avenue ends at a baseball diamond in Turkey Ridge Park on the Ohio about a half-mile north of the airport. But Spencer's description does give the image of 50 cabins scattered along the river and across the plain that is now consumed primarily by Lunken Airport. His description of the area also tells us that by 1834 it was now divided into "highly cultivated" farms, an indication that in 44 years, Stites' dreams of a great city had already been doused by frequent floods.

Columbia survived as its own village until Cincinnati absorbed it in 1873 and today the Columbia Tusculum neighborhood is regarded as the oldest in the city. But today's Columbia is mostly northwest of the original settlement, founded by Stites. The Morris house at 3644 Eastern Avenue is considered the oldest continually inhabited house in Hamilton County and is thought to have been built in 1804, the year of Stites' death and 16 years after he arrived. That was already long enough for settlers to have realized that the ground near the rivers wasn't as good for living as it was for growing.

In 1815, the last of the log cabins built in 1790 washed away and those who remained from the original settlement moved to its present location at the foot of Tusculum Hill. The last blockhouse collapsed in 1838 when a large wake created by two passing steamboats washed out the base of the bank which had been supporting it. One of the oldest surviving houses in this area at 315 Stites Avenue was built by Hezekiah Stites, Jr. in the 1830's.

By then the old Columbia Baptist Church had built a second meeting house at Duck Creek. After several years of coexistence, it changed its name to the Duck Creek Baptist Church and closed the historic one in old Columbia. The Columbia Baptist Church that exists in the neighborhood today was organized in 1865.

The area's original settlers might find it confusing to know that their church isn't the one in Columbia with the same name, but I'm guessing that the airport that has devoured the settlement might be more problematic to them. Airplanes would probably seem like fantasy to people who came here on flatboats.

23 NORTH BEND

On a nice day with moderate traffic, you can make the drive from Columbia to North Bend in about 30 minutes. The drive over U.S. 50 slips past downtown Cincinnati less than a quarter mile from where the first pioneers landed, so it effectively takes in the three Ohio River communities settled within a few months of each other during the winter of 1788-89.

Benjamin Stites brought his family and friends to Columbia, where the Little Miami River empties into the Ohio. Matthew Denman founded a town called Losantiville (that was soon called Cincinnati) opposite the mouth of Licking River. And John Cleves Symmes landed his group at a spot near where the Great Miami River enters the Ohio.

All three had visions of success for their little communities. But Symmes, a former colonel in the state militia during the Revolutionary War, a member of the Continental Congress and a justice of the Supreme Court for the state of New Jersey, had more than that. He had secured the land grant that encompassed all three communities, having petitioned the federal government for one million acres between from the Ohio River north between the two Miamis for sale and settlement. He chose the flat ground just to the east of the Great Miami because he thought that would be the best location in the grant for a grand city. For that reason, the location for "Symmes City" as he planned to call it would have been the prohibitive favorite to become the metropolis that Cincinnati is today. Instead, North Bend, named because of its location as "the most northerly bend in the Ohio River from the Muskingum River to the Mississippi," is the smallest and most rural of the three, a village of about 800 that has little in common with the other two.

An aside: A company of soldiers from Fort Pitt landed at the actual mouth of the Great Miami about three miles from North Bend on October 28, 1785, and began construction of a structure they called Fort Finney at the site. Its purpose was to provide a location for negotiation with the Shawnee Indians for lands in the region. About 450 Indians attended a conference there during January, 1786, and agreed to a treaty, which accomplished little. The fort had been abandoned before John Cleves Symmes arrived. Today, that spot is occupied by the Miami Fort Power Station.

North Bend's defining feature today is the tomb of President William Henry Harrison, the army lieutenant who served as Anthony Wayne's aide-de-camp during his triumphant campaign against the combined Indian forces in 1794 and eventually met and proposed to Symmes' daughter, Anna. When Symmes wouldn't give his consent for the then-army captain to marry his daughter, they were married at his North Bend home while he was away.

Symmes eventually realized that his new son-in-law was no ordinary soldier. Harrison became secretary of the Northwest Territory, the first Congressional delegate for the territory, governor of the Indiana Territory, military hero of the War of 1812 and finally president. When he died of pneumonia just 31 days into his term in 1841, he was buried here not far from his home – nothing is far away from anything else in little North Bend and neighboring Cleves – in a tomb that sits on top of a hill that overlooks the Ohio. Today that tomb is at the bottom of a towering, 60-foot granite monument.

On this day, Rick Hill, the volunteer for the local Harrison-Symmes Memorial Foundation who unlocks the outer gate of the tomb for visitors daily, took in the view and marveled.

"I love coming up here," Hill said. "It's so peaceful."

The thought summoned a soft chuckle from his visitor.

"If Symmes had had his way, it wouldn't be like this,' I said. "This would have been Cincinnati and we would have been standing in the middle of a huge city. There would cars and concrete, buildings and people all over the place."

Now Hill was the one who laughed.

"Exactly," he said. "There would probably be a bridge to Northern Kentucky here and so forth. It would have been terrible."

In fact, if you walk a short distance up Cliff Road from where the stairs to the tomb begin, a display of information boards across from Congress Green Cemetery where John Cleves Symmes and his relatives are buried springs a delightful surprise: If Symmes' vision had come to fruition, the central square of his so-called Symmes City would have been in that very spot. He apparently drew map of his city that stretched from the village of North Bend, which he founded first, to the mouth of the Great Miami River three miles to the west.

Symmes' plans for a great city ran into an immediate problem when his party arrived; the low-lying location he had selected near the mouth of the Great Miami was under water. After a careful examination of the tract, he decided that it would be a mistake to locate his city there and that it would have to be placed either a couple of miles up the Miami or stretched out to the east along the Ohio.

In the meantime, he laid out 48 one-acre lots, 24 of which were "donation" lots he gave to those who would immediately build cabins on the sites in what is modern North Bend. He expanded that to one hundred lots that extended the village up and down the Ohio for a mile and a half. He also laid out a village called South Bend seven miles to the east, on ground where the Anderson Ferry to Kentucky operates today. Younger brother Timothy Symmes, a judge from Sussex County, N.J., who came with him from the East with sons Daniel and Celadon, was one of the first to locate there.

It would be fascinating to see Symmes' grand vision for this entire area. His' map of his great city may have burned with his other papers when his house burned down in 1811.

"There's a map upstairs in the museum, but I don't think that's what it is," Beverly Meyers said. Meyers is the president and founder of the memorial society and, like Hill, a lifelong resident of the area. "I don't know if any of the streets in North Bend follow his map. . . the streets in Cleves, (Symmes) did not plat Cleves. It was William Henry Harrison who platted Cleves and he named it in honor of his father-in-law."

The museum Meyers spoke of is in Cleves, which had 3,234 residents in the 2010 census and has more of a small town feel than neighboring North Bend. North Bend is essentially six or eight cross streets of widely spaced houses and a couple of churches. Down on Symmes Street, a historical marker sits in front of a little yellow house that is fronted by an old stone wall that stands about a foot high. The marker says the Benjamin Harrison, William Henry Harrison's grandson and a president himself, was born here on the farm established by his grandfather.

Hill told me that he had heard that the wall, which extends beyond the little yellow house past another old house next door, was once the foundation of the William Henry Harrison house, which burned down in 1858. It's an intriguing story, but one that was disputed by Meyers later. She said she was involved with the Ohio bicentennial in 2003 and was on a committee that had permission to erect a historical marker. She had heard that the Harrisons' sprawling house had stood near the old Catholic church two blocks north at the corner of Symmes and Taylor Avenues, but because she is an artist who has studied the hills and has seen old drawings of the house, she believed it was closer to the river and hence near the yellow house.

"I went to the United Methodist Church there (on Symmes, across the street and just north of the yellow house) that was 110 years old and I was reading some of their early minutes," she said. "It said that they dug the foundation for what I believe was the front wall of the church and they put the foundation where Harrison's home was. The men worked all day and then they would come home and go back out and hand-dig the foundation for the church by the moonlight on the site of William Henry Harrison's home. So I was pretty close with that marker; it is only about 50 feet away."

Harrison's house had white clapboard over logs and faced the Ohio, which lies about 300 yards to the south. In 1796, Harrison had purchased 160 acres at North Bend from Jonathan Dayton (one of Symmes' partners in his Miami land ventures), and he purchased a four-room cabin on the edge of the property the following year that would expand into his sprawling house.

After the hero of the Battle of Tippecanoe died after only a month in office in 1841, his widow Anna lived in the house until it burned to the ground. It had apparently been set on fire by a girl who has been fired as one of the Harrisons' servants.

North Bend's fate had been sealed long before that, shortly after the Symmes' party landed there on February 2, 1789. Stites' group had landed at Columbia in November, 1788, and Denman's group reached Cincinnati on December 24. Stites, who had tipped off Symmes about the potential of the land between the Miamis after a visit here in 1787, purchased 10,000 acres there from Symmes; Denman had secured 800 acres across from the Licking.

The three little settlements had similar ambitions, shared a need for military protection and felt a strong kinship to each other. Because Stites' group landed first and had the benefit of better weather for building, Columbia got a head start as the business center of the little colony. It had more settlers and was closer to Limestone (now Maysville, Kentucky) and points east. But because of Symmes' influence, troops sent west by General Josiah Harmar for the protection of these western villages were drawn to North Bend and his great city was on its way.

No one today cheers for the Symmes City Reds or Symmes City Bengals, so we know that never happened. Symmes' dream actually unraveled pretty quickly.

Most of the troops that had landed there moved on to Louisville. The commanding officer of those who remained found the location unsuitable for a permanent fort and moved the troops to Cincinnati. When Major John Doughty arrived during the summer months with more troops from Fort Harmar and agreed that Denman's settlement would be the best location for a fortification that sealed the deal. The troops commenced building Fort Washington.

There is a story that the commanding officer had fallen for "a beautiful, black-eyed female" who was the wife of one of the North Bend settlers. When her husband discovered this, he packed up and moved to Cincinnati with his wife; this in turn caused the officer to lose interest in North Bend as a military post and move the troops to Cincinnati.

Regardless of the reason, having the military installation at Cincinnati doomed Symmes' plans for a marvelous city in North Bend. Settlers were more interested in living in safety than being part of Symmes' grandiose plans for a metropolis. The small detachment of troops stationed at the fort provided all of the military support for the entire region and in the mind of a nervous settler the 15 miles between Cincinnati and North Bend might just as well be a thousand.

As Cincinnati grew as a commercial and governmental center, Symmes spent more and more time there. A few months before he secured his grant, the former justice of the New Jersey Supreme Court received an appointment as judge for the Northwest Territory, a job that required him to spend considerable time traveling between far-flung outposts.

Many of those who bought property from him probably wished he had spent more time on his land business. Symmes assumed that he would receive the grant for the one million acres that he had requested and Congress granted him only 350,000. He sold land that didn't belong to him and continued to do that even after he learned of the actual grant, thinking that Congress would eventually give it to him. That and sloppy record-keeping caused him to face countless lawsuits that would eventually drain him of nearly all of his land and fortune.

Between his work on his North Bend farm, his judgeship and his massive land business, Symmes probably tried to do too much. Anxious to please his third wife, Susan Livingston, the eldest daughter of the governor of New Jersey, he built a house that one of his biographers described as "quite elaborate for the time and place."

An English traveler named Thomas Ashe who stopped to have breakfast with Symmes on his trip down the Ohio in 1806 wrote that the "noble stone mansion" was set amidst a "pastoral scene" of woods, orchards, cornfields and pastures, overlooking the river.

Symmes maintained his residence near the banks of the Great Miami until the house burned down during one of extended absences in March, 1811. The fire was supposedly the work of a man angry with him for failing to appoint him as a justice of the peace. By then, his third wife had moved to New York, having decided that frontier life didn't suit her; she had opted for an amicable separation in 1808. After the fire, Symmes moved in with Harrison and his daughter in their Front Street home in Cincinnati. He died there of cancer on February 26, 1814.

There are no markers to offer a clue to the location of his North Bend house, even though the ruins of it were apparently still standing when Henry Howe came through here in 1846 in preparation of his remarkable *Historical*

Collections of Ohio. Howe visited the site, which he described as being "about a mile northwest of his grave."

This would seemingly place the home site on or near Miamiview Road, although Meyers said that a historical marker which claimed to be on the site of Symmes' house had once been placed in the yard of a two-story house a block west of US Route 50 on Mount Nebo Road.

"As you go south or west on Mt. Nebo Road there one's house on Bassett Street and then there's kind of like an alley and then there is another big two-story house on the right-hand side," Meyers said. "That's where the marker was for John Cleves Symmes house that burned down, but I don't know how they knew that. I don't think that's where it was. It was probably down that road or Lower River Road or Miamiview."

The house where the marker had once stood isn't remotely close to the river, which is counter to everything that has been written about it. Like Howe, Benson John Lossing, author of the *Pictorial Field Book of the War of 1812*, visited the ruins of the house on September 18, 1860, and wrote that "about a quarter of a mile above the present railway station, on the bank of the river, Judge Symmes had erected quite a commodious house for himself, the ruins of whose chimney and fire-place might yet be seen in 1860."

Meyers said her father worked for the B&O railroad and its station "was right below Harrison's tomb," so if that was depot in question (apparently there was also a depot for the Big Four line), it suggests that Symmes' home might have been directly north, somewhere on Miamiview Road near Gulf Community Park.

The idea that no one in either North Bend or Cleves apparently knows the location of it today seems a little odd given the size of the two communities and its importance to both of them. But then Meyers said that the home of John Scott Harrison, the only man to ever be both the son and the father of a president, a house that served as the residence of Anna Symmes Harrison after the Harrison family home burned, was torn down in 1958 with little or no remorse.

John Scott Harrison has suffered worse indignities. He was originally buried in Congress Green Cemetery but his body was stolen by grave robbers who sold corpses to Ohio Medical College in Cincinnati. When the body was recovered, it was reburied in his father's tomb, which now holds 12 bodies.

William Henry Harrison's North Bend house enjoyed a rebirth of sorts. On the 100th anniversary of his death, a replica of his house was erected on the Ohio State Fairgrounds in Columbus. It stood for several years and was finally torn down, apparently because of the need for more fair space.

One can only hope that the "need" didn't involve more room for stands selling deep fried Snickers, Frito pie or chocolate-covered bacon on a stick.

24 FORT WASHINGTON

A security guard from the nearby Western and Southern parking garage in downtown Cincinnati was drawn to the stranger wandering an empty lot east of the building and snapping photos with his phone.

"What are you doing, trying to get a good shot of US Bank Arena?" His friendly inquiry helped disguise his subtle attempt to fulfill his duties.

I shook my head and smiled. "No . . . Fort Washington."

Surprisingly, the answer didn't seem to surprise him. Maybe he had already decided that anyone snapping iPhone photos in a weed patch behind a downtown parking garage probably isn't playing with a full deck. Or maybe he had read nearby plaques that identified the site of the Fort Washington powder magazine, now the location of the five-story garage he was hired to protect on the southwest corner of Third and Broadway.

It didn't really matter. My subsequent two-sentence explanation about this book signaled the end of further communication on the matter.

"Well, good luck with that," he said, flashing a plastic smile and disappearing as quickly as he came.

Any twenty-first century visitor in search of a fort considered the most important military outpost in the Northwest Territory for most of its life could use some luck, even if a 150-year debate over the exact location of it apparently ended in the 1950s.

When brevet Brigadier General Josiah Harmar dispatched a company of men from Fort Harmar (Marietta), down the Ohio River in August, 1789, to find a suitable site to construct a fortification for the protection of three new frontier settlements between the Great and Little Miami Rivers, it was by no means certain where it would be located.

Be it for strategic or personal reasons, Major John Doughty chose to locate the fort here, opposite the mouth of the Licking River and above the tiny settlement of Losantiville (Cincinnati) that lay between new outposts at Columbia (six miles east) and North Bend (16 miles west).

The site lay on a ridge about 550 feet back from the river, above and behind the scattered houses and cabins that made up Losantiville. Surrounding woods thick with black and red oak, beech, ash, hickory and black walnut trees offered plenty of wood for the fort's construction.

Good luck finding any trees within the boundaries of Fort Washington's walls today. We know now that the fort stood just north of Third – and didn't straddle Third as had been thought when Robert Ralston Jones wrote a book about the garrison in 1902 – and that the east wall stood near what is today's Ludlow Street. At the time of its construction, the square structure had walls 180 feet in length between the corner blockhouses and sat at a slight angle to the east. Part of it straddled Arch Street, which lies midway through Third and Fourth on the north side of the parking garage. Barracks for the soldiers served as the south wall, which featured the main gate in the center.

A triangular extension was added on the western side of the fort in 1791. It contained the artificer's yard with blacksmith, carpenter, armorer and wheelwright shops and a fifth blockhouse at its tip. A similar triangular extension was added to the northern side later that year to house the wounded men from General Harmar's military campaign.

When Israel Ludlow platted the grounds for proprietor John Cleves Symmes, he placed the fort within a 15-acre military reservation that stretched from north of the fort (where Fourth Street now stands) to the river. Symmes deeded property around the reservation but not within it. After Harmar officially took command of the still unfinished structure and its 300-man garrison on December 29, 1789, he asked Symmes for an acre on which to keep a vegetable garden. The fact that Symmes readily sold it to him -- and some of it ended up being within the reservation because of conflicting land surveys -- says a lot about the Ohio wilderness they found there and why we have trouble finding a fort in this concrete jungle now.

You can face south from that empty lot on Arch Street next to the Western and Southern garage all day and not conjure an image of General Harmar's vegetable garden. There is nothing bucolic about staring into the spaghetti-like tangle at least seven freeway lanes between there and US Bank Arena, nothing that makes you think about Harmar's green beans or carrots. The lots Symmes sold him helped tangle some of the land ownership records after both Harmar and the old fort had been swept into the dust bin of history, but their images died beneath the hungry scoops of backhoes and landscape-altering bulldozers long before we tried to visualize them in all that concrete and whizzing traffic.

Maybe the most difficult concept for the modern visitor to grasp is Fort Washington's relatively remote location relative to the fledgling town of Cincinnati. A drawing of "Cincinnati in 1802" shows the fort off in the

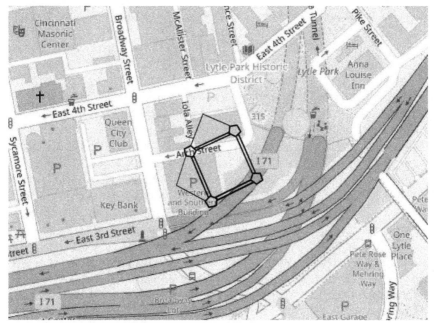

FORT WASHINGTON ON A MODERN MAP OF CINCINNATI

distance, sitting well to the north of most of the scattered buildings in the riverfront village. Most of the original buildings of the town were located in what is now that wide corridor of freeways. It makes the frontier settlement difficult to visualize; what many of today's residents probably think of as the southern edge of downtown – Third Street – was the northern edge of the city in 1802.

It was even smaller in 1789 when Harmar arrived. Outside of the fort, the little village of what was then called Losantiville consisted of 11 families and 22 single men. It had been settled only one year and one day before. Arthur St. Clair, the governor of the Northwest Territory, arrived from Fort Harmar on January 2, 1790, to inspect the fortification, the largest in the West at the time. He was pleased, but stayed only three days before continuing west on other territory business.

He made a couple of things clear before he left however. The name Losantiville, a jumble of French and Latin meaning "town opposite the Licking River," was history. St. Clair decided that the village would be named "Cincinnati," in honor of the Society of the Cincinnati, a hereditary organization of American and French military officers of which he was a member. Fort Washington would also be the new center of territorial government. As settlers moved westward, Fort Harmar quickly became too far removed from the western regions for effective government. St. Clair would henceforth conduct the territory's business from his office in the blockhouse at the southeastern corner of the fort. Later maps put that blockhouse on the west side of Ludlow Street just north of Third, which today places it in the vicinity of the southbound lanes of Interstate 71 and the Third Street entrance ramp. It is the only part of the old fort has been swallowed up by modern freeways.

Three treaties had opened up the area north of the Ohio River for settlement. Unfortunately, the tribes who had signed the treaties didn't live on the lands they ceded. So it came as no surprise that those that did – the Shawnee, the Miami, the Delaware, the Wyandot and the Maumee – didn't find the new incursions into their territory acceptable and they launched a series of raids on the white settlers in the spring of 1790. They ambushed and killed an increasing number of settlers on the Ohio, and in one raid on a small settlement called Kenton Station near today's Maysville, Kentucky, about 65 miles upriver from Cincinnati, a dozen settlers were killed.

Those raids led to three military campaigns launched from Fort Washington against the western tribes, the first two of which ended in defeats that rank among America's biggest military disasters.

Harmar's came first. With orders from President George Washington and Secretary of War Henry Knox to punish the Shawnee and Miami tribes for their att acks, he gathered an army of 320 regular troops of the First American Regiment and 1,133 militia from Kentucky and Pennsylvania at Fort Washington. On October 7, 1790, the 1,453 troops and three 6-pounder cannons drawn by horses began a northward march toward the main Miami village of Kekionga, part of today's Fort Wayne, Indiana.

Primarily because of inexperienced troops and poor weaponry, the campaign proved to be a disaster. In three battles near Kekionga, Harmar's army suffered the loss of 262 men and reported 106 wounded, the worst defeat of U.S. forces to Indians to that point. When the retreating force reached Fort Washington on November 3, Harmar tried to claim that his troops had achieved a great victory. But surviving militiamen who gave interviews to the press quickly exposed the lie, accusing Harmar of alcoholism, incompetence and cowardice. In an attempt to clear his name, Harmar was subsequently court-martialed at his own request. A court of inquiry overseen by Major General Richard Butler, Lieutenant-Colonel George Gibson and Lieutenant-Colonel William Darke in Fort Washington's southeast blockhouse exonerated him, but he was relieved of his command and replaced by Governor St. Clair in March, 1791.

St. Clair had been a brigadier general and aide-de-camp to Washington during the Revolutionary War. Commissioned as a major-general, he immediately began preparing for another "punitive" expedition against the Indians. He raised a larger and more experienced army than Harmar's and took more than 3,000 men with him when they departed Fort Washington in October. St. Clair had his troops build three forts at intervals on the march north. But the fort-building slowed the pace and reduced his numbers as he left a contingent of soldiers to man each new post. On the morning of November 4, 1791, a large Indian force led by Little Turtle surprised his troops at what later became Fort Recovery, Ohio, resulting in a devastating massacre that made Harmar look like a military genius. Many of the panicked soldiers turned and ran as the rout began and when the survivors reached Fort Washington, they brought bad news: St. Clair's campaign had lost 623 men and officers, including Major General Butler, compared to about 50 Native Americans killed. It was clear who ruled the Old Northwest and it wasn't Governor St. Clair. Many terrified settlers from outlying areas fled to the safety of the fort, which must have been a crowded, tense and anxious place. Christmas in Cincinnati was described as "a gloomy affair" that year.

St. Clair resigned his commission in March, 1792, at the request of President Washington, although he continued to serve as governor. In his place, Washington named Anthony Wayne, who had become a brigadier general during the Revolutionary War and achieved a key victory at Stony Point, New York. Wayne assembled another American force at a camp he called Legionville, 22 miles west of Pittsburgh on the site of an old Indian trading post called Logstown.

He earned the nickname "Mad Anthony" because of his tactics, but he wasn't crazy. Unlike Harmar and St. Clair, he refused to march until his troops were ready. The troops underwent extensive training at Legionville from the fall of 1792 until the following spring. On April 30, Wayne led a flotilla of his troops down the Ohio to Fort Washington. Wayne didn't care much for the fort or for Cincinnati, which he thought was dirty – uh, this was a four-year old settlement carved out of the wilderness, right? -- and provided too many distractions for his troops. He complained of "wenches" who sold whiskey to his soldiers and believed his attempts at instilling discipline were being compromised.

It is worth noting that a distillery that stood off by itself in the narrow Deer Creek valley east of town was at the end of two well-worn paths, one that led from the small village near the river and one from Fort Washington. The "wenches" apparently weren't the only ones who knew the way.

Late in 1793, Wayne ordered the quartermaster and a few other officers to examine the grounds surrounding the town to find a site for an encampment and training site where he could move his army. The site they found, a plain near the river west of town (between Interstate 75 and Mill Creek), was nicknamed "Hobson's Choice." When viewed today from Paul Brown Stadium on the downtown riverfront, it's difficult to believe that such a nearby site could have solved St. Clair's distraction problems. But viewed within the context of the times -- the entire settlement lay within a few blocks of the river east of Vine Street -- the two-mile buffer seems more logical.

Wayne drilled his troops there until October 7, when he finally broke camp and headed north. The army of almost 4,000 camped the first night near the present city of Elmwood and the second night at Fort Hamilton (the present site of Hamilton, Ohio), one of the fortifications St. Clair had constructed 25 miles north of Fort Washington. It continued north another 50 miles to the current site of Greenville, Ohio, where Wayne built Fort Greeneville, named for Nathaniel Greene, his friend and comrade in the American Revolution. Wayne's army spent the winter there and began its northern march the following summer. On August 15, 1794, it won the Battle of Fallen Timbers, which avenged the defeats of Harmar and St. Clair and effectively ended the Indian threat in the Ohio country.

The Treaty of Greenville that the Indian tribes signed during the summer of 1795 marked the beginning of the end for Fort Washington. With the Indian threat diminished, settlers had less need of the army for protection. The number of soldiers stationed there fell sharply in coming years and a fort designed to house more than 1,500 men seemed empty.

The fort still functioned as an important political center until the division of the territory in 1800 in anticipation of Ohio's coming statehood status. Future president William Henry Harrison, aide-de-camp to Wayne, succeeded Winthrop Sargent as secretary of the Northwest Territory in 1798. He kept an office in the fort and frequently served as acting governor during St. Clair's absences. But when the territory became eligible for a non-voting representative in Congress, Harrison defeated Arthur St. Clair Jr. for the position and took his seat in 1799. When the territory was divided in 1800, Harrison became governor of the Indiana Territory, Chillicothe became the territorial capital of the old Northwest Territory and Fort Washington's status fell even further.

The old fort was on its deathbed. In 1802, Fort Pitt and Fort Washington shared one company of infantry troops, so that year only 35 soldiers were stationed there. In 1803, the federal government acquired six acres of ground for a new garrison across the river in Newport, Kentucky. When the remaining troops moved there with the completion of the facility in 1804. the American flag was lowered and the old fort was abandoned.

Fort Washington sat empty, like an old monarch waiting to be restored to its throne, but its useful life had ended. As the little town grew, the property had become prime real estate. At some point, probably in 1805 or 1806, most of the structures were torn down and the palisades were bought and sold as firewood by John Miller.

Jared Mansfield surveyed the military reservation in 1807 at the request of the federal government, which was anxious to sell it. He staked out 15 lots within the 15 acres. No references to the fort are found in this survey; some researchers take this as evidence that the fort had been completely dismantled and no landmarks had been left that a surveyor might use as a reference point.

The fort and military reservation property was sold at a public auction on March 17, 1808. But it didn't take long for it to become apparent that the survey Israel Ludlow completed in 1790 and the one Mansfield did in 1807 were in conflict.

On May 6, 1791, John Cleves Symmes had sold eight lots of 60 square rods each to General Harmar, the deed to which was confirmed in lawsuits in 1809 and 1829. Based on a plat map ("In the Eastern Part of Cincinnati") created by Ludlow in 1790, four of Harmar's lots were on the north side of Second Street and bounded by Lawrence Street to the west, which would place them opposite modern US Bank Arena. General Arthur St. Clair had four lots on the south side of Second (between Second and Front) opposite Harmar's. That places them on the eastern side of U.S. Bank Arena and in part of the roadway that turns into the Taylor Southgate Bridge. All of these lots were described as "lying directly in front of Fort Washington." Interpreting this phrase became the lingering controversy of the 1829 trial.

The conflicting surveys created problems both for the alleged owners of the property and historians who wanted to know precisely where the walls and blockhouses of the old fort stood. Mansfield's survey put Harmar's upper two lots across the southwest corner of Third and Ludlow (which

DANIEL DRAKE'S HOUSE WITH NEW FORT MARKER IN THIRD STREET IN 1902

also took up Dr. Daniel Drake's property on the south side of Third) and in both streets.

Drake's house at 429 East Third Street, which stood on the south side of the street near Ludlow, was torn down in 1956 for construction of the Third Street freeway ramp of Fort Washington Way. He testified in the 1829 trial that it was within the walls of the fort and that his property was the site of the southeast blockhouse.

Jesse Hunt, who described himself as Harmar's agent from 1801 or 1802 until 1821, testified that "two lots of Harmar's were lost to the Garrison Reservation." When asked if he understood that the lost Harmar lots "could have enclosed the ground on a part of which Dr. Drake's house now stands" he answered in the affirmative.

Drake's testimony in that trial seemed like strong evidence the fort straddled Third Street, a proposition difficult to dispute at the time. Drake was a leading citizen of early Cincinnati and he sounded convincing in his testimony about the location of the old fort. A few of the city's early citizens even agreed with his assessment at the 1829 trial.

"I once lived in the rooms that were occupied by the Commander of the Garrison," Drake said. "This was in 1802 or 3, and afterward in 1808 when the reserve was sold by the government, I purchased several lots which included the Southeast Angle and blockhouse and built upon the same, where I resided from 1812 to 1823, during which period the foundations of the fort were everywhere to be seen and could be compared to the lines and corners of the lots and streets, finally in preparing for a plat of the town, for the Picture of Cincinnati in 1814 (a book written by Drake). I took great care and pains to lay down the site of the fort correctly and find that the plat laid down by Mr. (city surveyor Joseph) Gest corresponds almost exactly with it."

That seemed to settle any arguments. Drake was a community leader, he had lived in the fort, bought property within the fort after its demise and seemed to remember very clearly where everything was. So when Jones wrote his book in 1902 and used Drake's testimony as proof of the fort's location, the decision was made to put up a monument in the middle of Third Street (near Broadway) with a small map in bronze showing the precise location of the fort in relation to the city's streets. It showed that the fort straddled Third Street and its northern edge lay south of Arch Street.

The monument remained there until the excavation of the old powder magazine during the construction of the Western and Southern parking facility in 1952. Ancient maps of the old fort showed precisely where that powder magazine stood in relation to the fort's walls (49 feet north of Third Street and 204 feet east of Broadway near the southwest blockhouse), and the location and angle of the structure indicated that the fort apparently didn't straddle Third Street after all.

Whether Drake's memory played tricks on him or whether he played tricks on the jury to protect his own property interests doesn't matter much 200 years later. But it did make a difference to historians who wanted to know precisely where the old fort stood.

So in 1952 historians went to work deciphering all of the facts and came up with two different, but similar configurations of the fort, both north of Third, and wrote about it in the *Bulletin of the Historical and Philosophical Society of Ohio* in 1953.

In "The Re-Discovery of Fort Washington," Richard C. Knopf, Raymond S. Baby and Dwight L Smith describe the excavation of the fort's power magazine in detail, dispute Drake's testimony, provide maps of the old fort and apparently misinterpret Drake's description of it as lying at angle, "south by east," which they claimed the 1789 plan showed was actually "west of south."

It got most of the fort out of today's Third Street and the freeways and ramps running south of it, but apparently got the angle – and hence, the exact location – wrong.

In the next issue of the *Bulletin*, Arthur G. King corrected that in piece titled "The Exact Location of Fort Washington and Daniel Drake's Error." King presents lots of mathematical evidence to show how both Drake and the "re-discovery" trio got it wrong. It is an impressive case but frankly doesn't make for compelling reading for anyone who used to fall asleep in math class.

Still, it made a convincing enough case that his map of the fort superimposed on a map of current streets is now the one cast in bronze on that old Fort Washington monument, which now stands north of the fort. The monument in the form of a blockhouse is situated just off the sidewalk on Ludlow, north of Arch Street and next to the parking lot in front of the Guilford School. The Cincinnati Chapter of the DAR presented the small plaque of the second map revision in 1963.

More interesting than King's calculations is his dissection of Drake's testimony about the fort itself standing on his property (south of Third). Right up front, King hints that he is skeptical of Drake's motives. He prefaced his analysis with the phrase "whether due to faulty memory or wishful thinking" and eventually noted – in italics – that the net effect was to exclude his property from the disputed 'lands lying directly in front of the Garrison.'"

In other words, Drake, legendary figure or not, might have, uh, conveniently forgotten where the south wall of the fort was in order to make sure that his property was clear of the claims in question.

It makes it clear that a debate two centuries old could have been caused by something as simple as a respected Cincinnati citizen looking out for his own self-interest.

More confusing are the twenty-first century conspiracy theorists at a Ohio tourism website, who questioned whether the new location of the fort was determined by the excavations of the powder magazine or whether it was moved back "to make room for progress," i.e., to keep most or all of it out of the Fort Washington Way freeway and the interstate highways that came later.

Even Daniel Drake would probably get a good chuckle out of that.

25 FORT HAMILTON

Fort Hamilton's final chapter might be its most intriguing.

One hundred and seventeen years after the old fort of Arthur St. Clair, James Wilkinson and Anthony Wayne had been dismantled and used in the construction of the fledgling town of Hamilton, Ohio, its powder magazine still stood proudly on the banks of the Great Miami River.

It wasn't in its original location; the 12-foot square log structure found itself in the way of progress and had to be rescued and moved by the local chapter of the Daughters of the American Revolution in 1901. But it occupied a place that would have put it safely within the walls of the old fort. Unfortunately, that spot was on the riverfront, just north of the High Street Bridge, when the angry flood waters of the Great Miami came roaring through here in March of 1913.

It should probably go without saying that a building constructed in 1791 and sitting directly in an angry river's path wouldn't be able to withstand waters that tore 290 Hamilton houses off their foundations. But there's a postcard out there that shows the bridge just before it washed away and the little powder magazine is still perched to the right of it like a sea gull holding onto the fronds of a palm tree during a hurricane.

Of course, the raging waters subsequently carried away both the bridge and the powder magazine, a sad circumstance for obvious reasons and one less than obvious one: the magazine was being used by the John Reily chapter of the D.A.R. for meetings and had also become a repository for its artifacts, records and other valuable objects.

Given that 85 people in Hamilton died in those same rushing waters, it's difficult to get overly maudlin about the loss of an old wooden building, no matter how historic. Well, at least it would have been if I hadn't stumbled across two news stories in the *Hamilton Evening Journal.* On Friday, April 18,

1913, the paper had a story at the top of page four with the headline: "Power Magazine Landed Safely South of Town". One of the two deck headlines beneath it noted that "It Will Be Brought Back to Hamilton Soon." The story indicated that an unnamed farmer showed up at the Butler County Soldiers, Sailors and Pioneers monument building across the High Street from the spot where the powder magazine had been standing and informed janitor Jacob Jackson that the log structure had landed on his farm on the west bank of the river, four miles south of the city. He said that it was in good shape and that it could be moved back to the city.

The next day, the same paper ran a story, with a photo of the powder magazine before the river got ahold of it, with the headline "Only Portico and Cupola of the Old Powder Magazine Damaged by its Wild Ride Down the Flooded Miami." That story also tells us that it "rests on Charles Sohngen's farm near Venice on the east bank of Indian Creek." The final paragraph of that story concludes: "There is no doubt that public sentiment is strong enough to raise sufficient funds to bring the house back in Hamilton, where it can take its place in a new river center."

Seems pretty definite, right? Well, that appears to be the last time the newspaper mentioned the possibility of saving the old powder magazine. A close search of the paper for the next month and a half turned up no more mentions of the historic structure. Digital searches on the Internet show that the when the paper wrote about Fort Hamilton in the 1950s and beyond, mentions of the old powder magazine always indicate that it had been swept away by the 1913 flood.

It's easy to come up with theories as to why this curious story may have died late in April, 1913. Maybe the money couldn't be raised to move it; after all, in the aftermath of a deadly flood that killed and displaced so many local residents, a log building that might have been destroyed 12 years earlier on purpose if the D.A.R. hadn't saved it probably didn't rank near the top of everybody's priority list. Or maybe someone tried to move it and it collapsed in pieces, and the poor unfortunates who authorized its move didn't rush to the newspapers and alert them to avoid embarrassment. Or maybe that little log house they found on Charles Sohngen's farm wasn't the same log house that once served soldiers at Fort Hamilton, and the realization of that was even more embarrassing to the discoverers of if (and the newspaper) than it would have been to the hypothetical movers who may have seen it crumble before their eyes.

The possibilities are fascinating and made all the more so by the ready availability of postcards of the old powder magazine, which were apparently quite popular before the Great Miami flushed it down the river in 1913. They can easily be found at antiques shows and are readily available on eBay. They are the only photographic evidence that Fort Hamilton existed, although memory of the old fort has actually been better served than many

HIGH STREET BRIDGE, OLD FORT HAMILTON POWER MAGAZINE, RIGHT, MINUTES
BEFORE BOTH WERE SWEPT AWAY IN THE 1913 FLOOD

of its counterparts from Northwest Territory days. Two granite memorial blockhouses stand on the Great Miami riverfront south of High Street in downtown Hamilton guarding the Butler County Soldiers, Sailors and Pioneers monument that sits behind them on land that once held the frontier garrison. A drawing of the fort was part of the masthead of the *Hamilton Evening Journal,* and its successor the *Hamilton Journal-News* for decades until it died in a redesign of the paper in the 1970s. But when that "new look" paper began sponsoring a city-wide summer event in the ensuing years, it was called "Fort Hamilton Days" and a drawing of a blockhouse became part of the event's logo. There is no doubting that the fort is a recognizable symbol in the city even today, more than 220 years after it has gone.

The first of two fortifications that General Arthur St. Clair had constructed to provide both a supply chain and security for his army on its campaign against the western tribes, it occupied an area that had been a hotbed of Indian activity. It also provided a brief stopping off place for St. Clair's terrified, wounded soldiers on their return to Fort Washington from the greatest defeat to the Indians in American history at what is now Fort Recovery, Ohio.

Probably because General Anthony Wayne's army also stopped here during his successful campaign against the tribes in 1794, his name is better known in Hamilton than the predecessor who had the fort built. Across Monument Street from those granite blockhouses and the county memorial that honors soldiers including those on the St. Clair and Wayne campaigns, an eight-story seniors apartment building that opened as a hotel in 1926 bears the name of Anthony Wayne. At least part of that building would have been inside the fort, which (after being expanded by Wayne in 1793) would have straddled modern Monument Avenue from Market Street (north of High) to a short distance south of Court Street (south of High) and the beginnings of Neilan Boulevard.

In following the river bank, the fort lay on a slant to the east, so that its southeast corner touched Front Street, but the rest of it stood west of Front. In its entirety, the fort covered an area slightly smaller than a football field. An advance unit of St. Clair's army of 300 men under the supervision of General Richard Butler and Colonels William Darke and Alexander Gibson started construction of the fort on September 17, 1791 and finished it in two weeks.

Because there was a second, higher bank where the Butler County Courthouse now stands, the pickets on the land side of the structure were higher than those on the river side to make it more difficult for attacking enemies to fire into it. Three blockhouses were located on the east (courthouse) side of the fort. A barracks for 100 men, a guard room, two attachments for provisions and the powder magazine were all built within that two-week period.

The bulk of St. Clair's army of 2,300 men arrived at Fort Hamilton on September 30 and stayed only until October 4, when they resumed their northward march to disaster. Captain John Armstrong was left in charge of a small detachment of men. After the Indians ambushed St. Clair's troops at Fort Recovery on November 4 with a loss of more than 600 soldiers and officers and possibly several hundred camp followers (teamsters, pack horse drives, wives and children), the retreating made it back to Fort Hamilton on November 6. Some of the wounded were transported from there back to Fort Washington on the river.

St. Clair returned to the east to try to repair his reputation and James Wilkinson assumed command at Fort Washington. Wilkinson is a notorious figure in American history who would later become mired in controversy after he was discovered to be a paid agent of the Spanish crown. At the request of the president, St. Clair resigned as the commander of the U.S. Army in March of 1792 and Wayne took his place. Wilkinson remained in charge of the post at Cincinnati until Wayne arrived.

Wilkinson often corresponded with and sometimes visited Captain Armstrong at Fort Hamilton. During the winter of 1792, Wilkinson and Armstrong had a falling out – Wilkinson thought Armstrong guilty of using sick leave when healthy – and Armstrong resigned from service early in 1793.

Wayne would soon transfer his army from its training camp at Legionville, Pennsylvania, to Fort Washington; Wilkinson, knowing that he could no longer do as he pleased once Wayne arrived, planned to transfer his base of operations to Fort Hamilton when that happened.

Wilkinson loved the area around Fort Hamilton. He called it an "interesting, captivating" place, acknowledged its "abundant sport for dog and gun" and noted that it offered a plentiful supply of "fish, fowl and wild meats." He relished a piece of venison washed down with a cool Madeira, or made piquant with "tomato essence" furnished by his friend, Winthrop Sargent. secretary of the Northwest Territory. Sargent's office at Fort Washington was a mere six hours away.

Wayne spent most of the spring and summer of 1793 at Hobson's Choice west of Fort Washington drilling his troops, waiting for the expected failure of peace talks to afford him the go ahead to advance. Meanwhile, Wilkinson and his wife, Ann, spent the summer at Fort Hamilton. Wayne visited in July to oversee an expansion of the fort on the north side, but otherwise he remained near Fort Washington, awaiting word to move. Wilkinson was happy at his frontier outpost, and when Wayne finally received permission to head north in September, he didn't greet the news with joy. Three-quarters of Wilkinson's men at Fort Hamilton were sick and he was in bed with colic when the news arrived.

Wayne's army left Fort Washington on October 6 and reached Fort Hamilton on October 8. It camped on the edge of a prairie about a half mile south of the fort, but was merely passing through. Wilkinson assumed command of the right wing of the advancing army, which continued north on October 9. On October 13, it stopped and built Fort Greeneville, six miles north of Fort Jefferson, where it would spend the winter.

Wilkinson didn't enjoy his role as a subordinate to Wayne and criticized nearly everything he did behind his back. This didn't play well after Wayne achieved his great victory over the Indians at Fallen Timbers on August 7, 1794; it also didn't stop Wilkinson from sniping at him.

Wayne had appointed Major Jonathan Cass as commanding officer at Fort Hamilton after Wilkinson's departure, and Cass remained in charge until after the Treaty of Greenville ended the war with the Indians in August of 1795. With no more battles to win, Wayne ordered Fort Hamilton abandoned. The public property and stores were sold at public auction during the summer of 1796. Israel Ludlow bought the land occupied by and surrounding the fort from Jonathan Dayton and laid out a town that would become Hamilton. Darrius C. Orcutt, a soldier in St. Clair's and Wayne's armies, erected the first log cabin beyond the confines of the fort just to the north; Dayton directed him to contract with purchasers for his other property.

Some of the buildings once inside the old fort began civilian life. Two storehouses built by Wilkinson to accommodate his officers and the stables to the north were sold to William McClellan, who opened a tavern in them. One of the buildings housed the clerk's office after the formation of Butler

County. The mess room became a court room until 1810, when it housed a school and a church.

All of the buildings of the fort consisted of hickory logs with the bark peeled except for the powder magazine, whose logs were hewed square and set close together. In its original location, it sat next to the south wall of the fort, on or near the current site of the Presbyterian Church at the corner of Court Street and Monument Avenue. In 1803, the magazine became a jail. It became a church in 1810, a schoolhouse in 1812 and alternated between the two uses for decades until both parties used it for political rallies in 1840.

It moved in 1849 and became an individual dwelling until the property was sold and was about to be torn down in 1902 when the D.A. R. saved it.

No one could save it from the 1913 flood, although what happened to it afterwards is a mystery, even to the D.A.R. Valerie Elliott, manager of the Smith Library of Regional History in Oxford, Ohio, found an article in the *Hamilton Journal-News* in 1997 in which local D.A.R. officials, who seemed to have no knowledge of the damage the flood had wrought, sought the whereabouts of the building. The library also produced an article in a December, 1994 Butler County Historical Society Newsletter, quoting one of the newspaper accounts from 1913 and asking readers if the building were ever brought back to Hamilton. Obviously, nothing came of it.

"I ran into the Butler County historian on Saturday who said he had a vague memory of a one-story building near Ross (maybe in the 1950s?) that was used for a fishing camp and later burned," Elliott wrote in an email. "He wonders now if that could have been the Powder Magazine."

26. FORT JEFFERSON

When General Arthur St. Clair's troops built Fort Jefferson in 1791, it was a forlorn frontier outpost surrounded by woods, wildlife and Native Americans who didn't want it there. The 6 ½ acre park that has replaced it makes it seem as though not a lot has changed.

This is one of those places where you can almost imagine Indian warriors peeking around mature trees or crouched in the tall grass in the wide expanse beyond here. Within the field of view, there are fields and trees and not much else, which makes it easy for the visitor to pause and reflect on life here back in the day when Little Turtle and Blue Jacket called the shots in the rest of the neighborhood.

The tiny village of Fort Jefferson is back there somewhere, but you don't notice it while engaged in a little time travel within the now-imaginary walls of the frontier fortification that gave it its name. This was the second of two forts General Arthur St. Clair had constructed to provide a supply chain and security for his advancing army on its campaign against the western tribes. The first, Fort Hamilton, was constructed 25 miles north of Fort Washington in October, 1791. After it completed that one completed, St. Clair's army marched north and chose one of the gravel knolls in a picturesque area of rolling hills for his second one. His troops immediately started construction of a square fort with four 100-foot walls and four corner blockhouses. Poor weather slowed the work on the structure called Fort Deposit, because of its intended purpose as a depository of weapons, ammunition and provisions for St. Clair's army. By the time soldiers finished, it had been named for Secretary of State Thomas Jefferson.

With the fort completed, St. Clair's army of more than 1,600 troops (and the hundreds of support personnel, wives, children and girlfriends who had been following them) resumed its northern march on October 24, en route to the greatest defeat ever suffered by an American army at the hands of Native Americans.

Over half of St. Clair's army was lost in a "battle" at the site of today's Fort Recovery, Ohio, on November 4. Many of the terrified survivors ran for almost the entire 29-mile distance back to the safety of Fort Jefferson, which had neither the medical supplies nor the provisions to accommodate all of them.

St. Clair arrived at the fort a little after dusk. He convened a war council there and decided to leave about 300 sick and wounded soldiers at Fort Jefferson with a small detachment under Captain Joseph Shaylor. St. Clair left with the rest of his emotionally-scarred army the next day and arrived at Fort Washington on November 8.

It's difficult to imagine a more miserable assignment than the one Shaylor drew – an isolated fort teeming with sick and wounded soldiers sitting in the middle of country occupied by hostile tribes flush with a magnificent victory. Supplies were scant and Fort Hamilton, the post Fort Jefferson depended upon for them, was 42 miles away.

The soldiers stationed there also knew that the bodies of many of their friends had been left on the battlefield and some were determined to return there and take inventory on what remained. So on January 5, 1792, five soldiers followed the buzzards from Fort Jefferson to the scene of the battle. They counted 538 bodies during their brief time there, always on the lookout for Indians ready to add them to the frozen dead.

After James Wilkinson assumed command of the western army a few days later he issued an appeal to the militia in the areas north of Fort Washington to join him and his 150 troops in a northward march to the battle site. The purpose of the mission: bury the dead and recover any cannons and weaponry that had been left there.

Wilkinson and his troops left Fort Washington on January 24 for Fort Jefferson. One hundred thirty mounted militia embarked the following day. Heavy snow slowed, but didn't stop them. They dropped off supplies at Fort Jefferson and continued their depressing march, finally reaching the desolate battlefield on February 1. A member of the militia said that he counted 78 bodies along the route to the battle site.

Wilkinson's troops buried more 600 frozen bodies, many mutilated beyond description, then made the 67-mile march back to Fort Washington. He dismissed and thanked the volunteers when they arrived on February 5; the dismissal couldn't erase the memories of what they had seen. Many of those who made this journey probably didn't get a good night's sleep for weeks afterwards.

The men stationed at Fort Jefferson endured their own nightmare. Six days after Wilkinson's troops arrived safely at Fort Washington, Captain

Shaylor left Fort Jefferson with a small hunting party that included his son, Joseph. Four Shawnee warriors ambushed the party, killing Joseph and nearly killing his father. Shaylor's son was buried with military honors, but the captain himself was court-martialed. He was relieved of his command for leaving the fort and "hazarding the immediate safety of the garrison." He was also charged with making an "uncandid report" to Wilkinson.

Captain Joseph Monfort succeeded Shaylor as commander of the post and he was killed on April 27 by Indians who made turkey calls and lured him outside of the fort. While he probably should have learned a lesson by what happened with Shaylor and his son, it says a lot about how difficult it must have been to be cooped up in a 100-foot square fort in the middle of nowhere in the dead of winter with scant supplies and 300 sick and wounded soldiers. After a while, the threat of death might seem like a reasonable tradeoff for some time spent outside the fort.

Wilkinson's trek through here on the way to the battlefield did bring one measure of relief for the isolated outpost: when he realized that it took supply convoys two days to cover the distance between Fort Hamilton and Fort Jefferson, he ordered his troops to erect a new post halfway between the two. He named the new fort, erected near the site of today's Eaton, Ohio, Fort St. Clair.

It made it easier to get supplies to Fort Jefferson, but it didn't make life any easier there. On June 25, soldiers were cutting hay for the animals outside of the fort when a party of over 100 warriors under the command of Simon Girty attacked. Sixteen men from the fort were killed or wounded.

Following St. Clair's defeat the previous November, Wayne took his place as the commander of the army. He trained his Legion of the United States at Legionville, Pennsylvania, and just west of Fort Washington, and led the army north in October, 1793. It marched six miles past Fort Jefferson and camped, with the intention of advancing to the scene of St. Clair's retreat and building a fort there. But cold weather accompanied by snow and high winds now confronted the army. The brutal conditions continued for several days and were followed by hard rain. With miserable weather and no Indians to fight, many members of the Kentucky militia that accompanied Wayne's army wanted to return home.

On October 31, Wayne convened a council of war that consisted of five generals including Wilkinson and asked whether they believed it was in the army's best interest to continue. The answers convinced him to stay here for the winter and build a fortification that became Fort Greeneville. With that, nearby Fort Jefferson lost its place as a strategic post deep in Indian country and became just another supply post near Fort Greeneville.

After Wayne's army defeated the Indians at Fallen Timbers and the Treaty of Greenville was signed, Fort Jefferson was abandoned in 1796. White settlers subsequently started to take up residence in the vicinity of the abandoned fort, which became the tiny community of Fort Jefferson.

No trace of the fort was visible when the Greenville Historical Society dedicated a memorial obelisk of granite boulders in the fall of 1907 on the site of the structure. That monument is still the primary marker on the site, acquired by the Ohio Historical Society between 1928 and 1931. Excavations conducted by the two organizations in 1930 determined the exact location of it. It unearthed clues on the fortification's blockhouse, stockade, magazine and water source, as well as a tunnel that ran from the fort to the well and magazine. As a part of the Ohio History Connection's Ohio Memory project, virtual visitors can view a fascinating 50-photograph album of that excavation at the "Seeking Site of Fort Jefferson" webpage.

The excavation has allowed the park's visitors to see the location of the wells, the magazine and the even the walls of the long-departed fort.

With a little imagination, they can see a lot more.

27 FORT ST. CLAIR

Cold rain and mule gray skies greeted me on the Sunday morning I visited the site of Fort St. Clair. Temperatures crept into the upper 30s, accompanied by a biting wind. Soggy grounds sometimes made walking difficult. Given the capricious nature of Ohio weather, no one in their right mind would pick this late April day to visit when in a few days it might be sunny, warm and dry. For my purposes, that made it just about the perfect day to be here.

The 76-acre park on the western doorstop of Eaton, Ohio, may have been as quiet as the day in March, 1792, when General James Wilkinson and his troops arrived here with the intention of building a supply post that would sit halfway between Fort Hamilton and Fort Jefferson.

If the centuries old "whispering oak" on the site whispered any late eighteenth century secrets to its solitary visitor, I couldn't hear them because of the rain. For the hour and a half that I visited, it seemed like this really could be the desolate Ohio frontier.

Like Fort Jefferson, 21 miles to the north, Fort St. Clair has been commemorated better than many of its more important counterparts because of its location. Eaton is a small city of 8,400 and the fort site is a mile to the west on the fringe of the city. There are houses and a cemetery north of the park and few houses to the east. Farmland lies to the south and west, so the property might still be part of a family farm if it weren't for the history. That's what it was when the property became a park in 1923.

Other fort sites with stronger historical pedigrees – Fort Washington, Fort Greeneville and Fort Wayne, for example – have had to settle for a historical marker, plaque or a similar remembrance because their location has been buried beneath streets, buildings and houses. But the outline of Fort St. Clair is marked off with a hewn log fence within the confines of Fort St. Clair

State Park, on the exact spot where Wilkinson, young lieutenant William Henry Harrison and their men built it, proof positive that all frontier sites are not treated the same in their afterlives. Historical significance sometimes has little impact on how a site is commemorated today.

The 120-foot square fort with arrow-shaped bastions on each corner was small in comparison to most of its contemporaries. Its role in the settling of the Ohio frontier is also relatively minor when compared with the importance of many sites which receive far less visual treatment. A small battle was fought here in 1792, so it does have that. Miami chief Little Turtle called off a planned attack of Fort Hamilton on November 3 (he had already taken two prisoners near the fort) when he heard that a convoy of packhorses had left for Fort Jefferson and was due back in a matter of days.

Little Turtle led nearly 200 warriors north from Fort Hamilton, found the convoy of nearly 100 horses and 100 Kentucky militia camped just outside Fort St. Clair and attacked them at dawn.

The visitor who enters the site off Camden Road/Ohio Route 355 first encounters the battle site on the left. A field of grass rimmed by woods marks the spot where Major John Adair and his men were camped when the Little Turtle and his warriors surprised them. The fort site is maybe 60 yards away and on the opposite side of the road from the battlefield. Several parking spaces and a roofed bulletin board stand between the road and the fort site, which has a bronze historical marker that tells Fort St. Clair's story.

That giant "whispering" oak and a small fenced burial plot lies about 100 feet southwest of the fort.

The six soldiers killed by Little Turtle's forces -- Lieutenant John Hale, Sergeant Matthew English, Robert Bowling, Joseph Clinton, Isaac Jett and John Williams -- are buried here beneath the "whispering oak," so named because over the years many have claimed to have heard voices coming from near the tree. Paranormal investigators say the site is haunted, be it by ghosts of dead soldiers or, uh, a talking tree. Sorry to say that I can't confirm that. The soldiers' graves are marked by small granite markers etched with their vital info. On the day of my visit, a small American flag flew over each grave.

Again, on a cold, rainy day surrounded by mature trees and empty fields and not a living soul in sight, it's easy to put yourself in that field with these men and imagine the fear and anxiety created by that surprise attack by the Indians.

It's also easy to assume the role of armchair general and wonder why a garrison was built here, even if the nearby ravine did hold "a fine spring gushing out of the bank." The decision came in the wake of General Arthur St. Clair's disastrous defeat on the later site of Fort Recovery in November, 1791, when some of the retreating wounded reached Fort Jefferson and were forced to remain at the overcrowded fort because of the two days travel to Fort Hamilton, the next safe stop on the way back to Fort Washington.

When St. Clair left Cincinnati for Philadelphia in an attempt to salvage his reputation in January, 1792, Wilkinson assumed command of Fort Washington and decided that a post between Fort Hamilton and Fort Jefferson would strengthen the supply chain and eliminate the unnecessary suffering experienced by the wounded who had been confined to Fort Jefferson. He named the new post for his soon-to-be ex-commanding officer and still governor of the Northwest Territory.

It didn't take long for the fort's remote location to claim an unlikely victim, commanding officer Major John Smith. Smith's subordinates believed he was cracking up after less than six months on the job. Smith brought a

THE WHISPERING OAK, WITH GRAVES OF SIX SOLDIERS BENEATH IT

reputation as a habitual drunkard to the position – probably not the best resume for a job commanding a far-flung post in the middle of territory controlled by Indians – and in late October, 1792, he began to imagine that Lieutenant Daniel Tilton, Ensign Jacob Kreemer and Surgeon Mate Samuel Boyd had entered into a conspiracy to kill him.

The problem began when Smith asked Boyd for a prescription because of his "bad state of health," doubtless caused in part by the pressure of his position as fort commander. The drug Boyd administered constipated Smith and opium was the only relief Boyd could provide. This kept Smith from sleeping, and possibility because of his dependence on alcohol (or the combination of opium and alcohol), he fell into a state of exhaustion and imagined being targeted by Kreemer," who frequently threatened to blow my brains out." When a delirious Smith ordered a guard to protect him from his stalkers, Captain Daniel Bradley removed the guard, disarmed the patient and assumed command of Fort St. Clair. Bradley told General Wilkinson that Smith had been "deranged" for the past four days.

Bradley had command of the fort when Little Turtle attacked Major Adair and his forces outside the fort. If Miami leader had had his way, the fight with Major Adair's forces wouldn't have taken place here. Little Turtle had expected to find the convoy camped in some remote spot along the way and that might have happened if Adair's troops hadn't been delayed a day at Fort Jefferson after delivering its goods.

When Little Turtle realized this, he had his warriors quietly closed in on Fort St. Clair on the southeast and north, and attacked Adair's attachment just before daybreak. Though surprised initially, many of the Kentuckians fought with fury.

In his report to Wilkinson, Adair told of how men retreated to nearby stables and made a stand.

"We made a manly push, and the enemy retreated, taking all our horses, except five or six," Adair wrote. "We drove them about six hundred yards, through our camp, when they made a stand, and we fought them some time; two of my men were here shot dead."

The Indians drove the soldiers back and the point of attack moved back and forth until the militia's ammunition's supply began to dwindle and some of the soldiers retreated to the safety of the fort.

"I had six men killed and five wounded; four men are missing," Adair wrote. "I think they went off early in the action on horseback and are, I suppose, by this time at Fort Hamilton. My officers and a number of my men distinguished themselves greatly.

"Poor (Lieutenant Job) Hale died calling to his men to advance. (Lieutenant George) Madison's bravery and conduct need no comment; they are well known. Florin and (Ensign James) Buchanan acted with a coolness and courage that do them much honor; Buchanan, after firing his gun, knocked an Indian down with the barrel. They have killed and taken a great number of the pack horses.

"I can, with propriety, say that about fifty of my men fought with a bravery equal to any men in the world; and had the garrison not been so nigh, as a place of safety for the bashful, I think many more would have fought well. The enemy have, no doubt, as many men killed as myself; they left two dead on the ground, and I saw two carried off. The only advantage they have gained is our horses, which is a capital one, as it disables me from bringing the interview to a more certain and satisfactory conclusion."

In the aftermath of the battle, Adair strongly criticized Captain Bradley for doing nothing to assist his troops other than by re-supplying them ammunition. And at least one lieutenant in the fort apparently agreed with the major, whom he told "I went on my knees and begged him to let me take fifty men to your assistance, but he refused and said it would be sending them to be murdered." But in Bradley's defense, General Wilkinson had sent out an order in February that prohibited the commanding officers of the forts from leaving the walls beyond musket shot. He said the garrisons had been posted "for defence, not offence," which seemed to indicate that Bradley was only following orders.

That would prove to be the only actual battle at the Fort St. Clair site, although things heated up there again in October, 1793. First, Anthony Wayne and his army came this way on their march north, on the beginning of a campaign that would eventually conclude with the war-ending victory at Fallen Timbers in 1794. Wayne's army would stop on October 13 six miles north of Fort Jefferson and erect Fort Greeneville, where it would winter before continuing north.

Less than a week after Wayne's troops passed by here Lieutenant John Lowery and his command of 90 men with 20 wagons of supplies for Wayne's army passed through here. On the evening of October 16, probably later on the same day they passed Fort St. Clair, they camped on the bank next to Lowry's Run at Ludlow's Spring, four miles north of the garrison. This is a short distance to south of the Zion Cemetery on the east side of U.S. 127.

In what amounted to a replay of the surprise attack on Major Adair's troops the year before, Little Turtle and his force of two hundred fifty Indians surrounded the camp during the night and attacked early the next morning. During a fierce but relatively brief battle, Lowery, Ensign Samuel Boyd and 13 of their men were killed and the rest of the troops fled to the north, leaving their attackers to gather up their horses, guns and ammunition. Fearing that Wayne would hear what had happened and return this way to take revenge, wagon loads of provisions were left standing in the road, which Wayne's troops recovered when they made it here. The Indians did abscond with about seventy horses.

Lowery and the other victims were taken to Fort St. Clair and buried, an unpleasant reminder to the garrison's inhabitants that there were better places to be stationed. It seems unlikely that any of them needed it.

The remains of Lowery and his troops were subsequently removed to Eaton cemetery in 1822, and in 1847 a public subscription raised enough to move them again, this time to part of a mound in Mound Hill Union Cemetery. There a slab of Rutland marble tells the story of the brief skirmish that claimed their lives.

Fort St. Clair was long gone by then, having been abandoned in 1796, not long after the Treaty of Greenville brought peace that rendered the supply post unnecessary.

The fort site received scant attention until the early twentieth century. It was farmland until the Preble County Historical Society organized in 1921 and began to petition the state to purchase the property and commemorate the fort with a park. During the winter of 1922-23, the Ohio legislature appropriated the money for it and 76 acres were purchased for $10,000.

Since then, the park has become more than a historical memorial, sprouting picnic tables, shelter houses, cabins and a playground in areas away from the fort, battlefield and gravesite. A recent Internet reviewer on Tripadvisor offered this criticism: "we enjoyed the pleasant loop drive through the park that seems to appeal mostly to runners, walkers, and picnickers. It seems that its significance in the westward expansion against Native Americans is largely overlooked."

This beautiful park is here for the enjoyment of picnickers and joggers because of the poor beleaguered soldiers who put their lives in jeopardy here in what was then a dangerous, isolated place. At least some of them would probably be pleased to know that if their time here didn't have a significant impact during the campaign against the Indians, it at least resulted in a pretty park that visitors can enjoy without fear.

Those soldiers could appreciate the difference, even if we can't.

28 FORT RECOVERY

From a seat at a table in the North End Bar and Grill in Fort Recovery, Ohio, the smell of ancient gunpowder is almost perceptible. My mind is playing tricks on me, I know.

My eyes stain to focus on a vision they can't see, a gruesome, horrible 220-year-old scene of desperate, frightened soldiers frantically running in every direction, stepping over bloody bodies of other soldiers, and in many cases joining them in a lifeless heap.

I close my eyes, listen for the anguished wails of the dying, and open them. None of this is happening. The bar is to my left. There is drab, brown paneling on the wall behind it and a rack with bags of snacks meant to comfort a modern "soldier" who is having a tough day. The windows to Wayne Street, one dressed in a neon Miller Lite sign and another advertising Bud Light, lie straight ahead. One of the two men seated at the bar is talking about how he just drove across the state of Iowa yesterday and the temperature never dipped below 90, and the other man is muttering his sympathy, saying that it should never be this hot in Ohio in June. There are eggs, sausage, hash browns and two neatly-sliced triangles of wheat toast on my plate.

This is my second breakfast here over a period of several years and both came with a side order of uneasiness. The little timeworn place of dirty yellow brick in a two-story building where the brick is mostly blood red stands at 129 Wayne Street, in the center of a long-ago battlefield where U.S. troops suffered their worst defeat to Native Americans in history.

My table sits in the middle of the eastern or rear line of the army's main camp, probably on the edge of where Major Henry Gaither's Maryland

Battalion camped and about in the middle of a battle that became an unspeakable horror for the participants.

This grisly massacre saw 632 soldiers and an undermined number of the 200 to 250 camp followers – mostly women and children – killed or captured. (Some accounts indicate nearly all of the camp followers killed.) Twenty-four "workers" were also reported killed. Another 264 soldiers were wounded, and the remainder of General Arthur St. Clair's army of about 1,100 ran from this place like frightened jackrabbits, some not stopping until they reached Fort Jefferson, 29 miles away. The losses of the 1,500 "confederacy" Indian forces led by Miami chief Little Turtle with assistance from Shawnee chief Blue Jacket, Delaware chief Buckongahelas and Wyandot chief Tarhe the Crane range from 35 to 70.

That the "battle" has been called many things – St. Clair's Defeat, the Battle of the Wabash, the Battle of a Thousand Slain and even, as is the title of relatively recent book, The Victory with No Name – probably says something about how this horrendous defeat has mostly slipped through the cracks of American history.

People remember George Armstrong Custer and his loss of 268 men to the Indians near the Little Bighorn River in Montana in 1876; St. Clair's horrific defeat was so long ago that it has mostly escaped notice of the masses. But the small town of Fort Recovery eventually grew up on the site of a fort built on the site of the battlefield, so it can't help but notice, even if only subconsciously.

"Older people probably think about it," said a perky teenaged girl with a welcoming smile, while she manned the counter at Kaup Pharmacy on Wayne Street. "But I don't think teenagers do."

Her answer isn't surprising, although ignoring the past here is anything but easy. A large brown historical marker stands near the sidewalk in front of the insurance building next to the pharmacy. It reads:

GEN. RICHARD BUTLER
WAS KILLED BY INDIANS
beneath a tree which stood
on the site of this building
IN
ST. CLAIR'S DEFEAT
November 4, 1791

Butler probably has his own sign not only because he served as St. Clair's second in command but also because his is a compelling story; he was wounded twice, the second time so badly that his retreating soldiers couldn't carry him to safety. So they propped him up against a tree and gave him a loaded pistol to defend himself when the Indians came for him. Warriors who swarmed the site killed and scalped the wounded wherever they found them, so historians doubt Butler stayed alive even five minutes after his comrades left him there.

All of the dead have a 101-foot, 4-inch limestone obelisk in a park two blocks to the east that was dedicated in 1913 on the spot where many of the victims, both of this battle and of the Siege of Fort Recovery seven and a half months later, were eventually buried. Some doubtless lie elsewhere. While hundreds were killed when the soldiers were surrounded by the attackers in what now is the heart of the today's Fort Recovery, many also died while fleeing the carnage, in a desperate attempt to get to Fort Jefferson. Indians mutilated just about all of the bodies and left them where they died, and none of them were buried immediately. More on that later.

A survey of the site done by Ball State University researchers in 2011 expanded the site of the battlefield from 97 to 630 acres, an area that encompasses nearly the entire town of Fort Recovery. But a modern time traveler can closely follow the footsteps of Wayne's army all the way from Fort Jefferson to the scene of the disaster and back, which makes the tragedy seem all the more real.

The backstory: St. Clair's army had been raised after General Josiah Harmar's 1790 campaign to drive out the Indians and open up the Old Northwest to settlement ended in defeat – and retreat – near Kekionga, the modern city of Fort Wayne, Indiana. George Washington promoted St. Clair, a Revolutionary War general and governor of the Northwest Territory, to Harmar's position and wanted him to move north toward Kekionga and the same Miami villages during the summer months, but problems plagued the campaign from the beginning. St. Clair's new recruits were poorly trained and disciplined. Repeated logistics and supply difficulties slowed his preparations. The food furnished to the men was substandard and the horses were of poor quality.

For all of these reasons, St. Clair's army didn't leave Fort Washington (Cincinnati) until October. St. Clair had his troops pause and build supply posts at Fort Hamilton and Fort Jefferson as it advanced, which slowed the march further. Many of his troops battled illnesses and St. Clair himself suffered from gout and arthritis, which made the journey all the more difficult. After building Fort Jefferson, St. Clair's army lingered there in late October, awaiting supplies. Finally, on October 30 the army resumed its northward march on what was known as the Wabash Trail; it made it seven miles, but it was hard going.

Today, the army's path is Ohio Route 49. A boulder that holds a large greenish plaque on the west side of the road in front of a two-story brick farmhouse identifies this as Camp Sulphur Springs. It says that St. Clair's army camped on the ridge to the east "from Sunday evening, October 30, to the morning of November 2nd, 1791, awaiting the forwarding of flower, tents and heavy baggage." Major Ebenezer Denny described the three nights here as "a very unpleasant camp in the woods." The first night came with a violent thunderstorm that brought down numerous tree branches, heightened the men's anxiety and robbed them of some sleep. While the army continued to wait for packhorses, sixty hungry militiamen deserted. St. Clair worried that they would plunder the oncoming supply train and ordered Major Hamtramck and three hundred men of the First Regiment to go after them. Considering the disasters that lay just ahead for St. Clair's army, it's hard not to look at that ridge and wonder how many of the deserters were saved from death by their hunger, and whether those three hundred soldiers might have made a difference in the battle that lay ahead.

On November 2, the army marched eight miles north in a light snow and encamped again. A marker that sits on the east side of Ohio 49, this one in front of a modern brick house, pegs this as Camp Mississinewa, the final stop before the troops faced the Indians on the bank of the creek known as the Upper Wabash River. The marker notes that at this camp "the troops were drawn up in two parallel lines facing the creek, with the artillery in the center," the same formation they used when they camped in Fort Recovery. In the pleasant rural atmosphere of a modern brick home and the lush, green fields surrounding it, it's difficult to believe that hundreds of men, women and children once camped here not knowing that they didn't have forty-eight hours to live.

St. Clair's army of about 1,100 soldiers marched nine miles the next day and camped in two parallel lines, about 70 yards apart, on elevated ground surrounded by woods and overlooking the Wabash River, an area barely large enough to contain them. In today's Fort Recovery, this places the far western front line of the troops in a residential area near the corner of Butler and George streets, and the far eastern front in the backyards of houses on Wayne Street north of the business district just north of the East Broadway Street. The Kentucky militia had to bivouac 300 yards across the river.

When he viewed the area later, Winthrop Sargent called it "a death trap." The men were cramped together; Sargent wrote in his diary "lines rather contracted" and said that rather than making any defensive formations that night, a plan "was agreed on intended to be commenced early tomorrow." That, of course, would be too late.

St. Clair and his fellow officers didn't know exactly where they were, but they thought they were on the St. Mary's River. They knew there were Indians in the vicinity – they had no idea there might be more than 1,000 -- and thought they were about 15 miles from the Miami towns. They didn't expect an attack.

The soldiers paraded at the usual time on the morning of November 4, before sunrise. "The men suffered from the cold," so Lieutenant Colonel Darke ordered the officer of the day to dismiss them. A few minutes later,

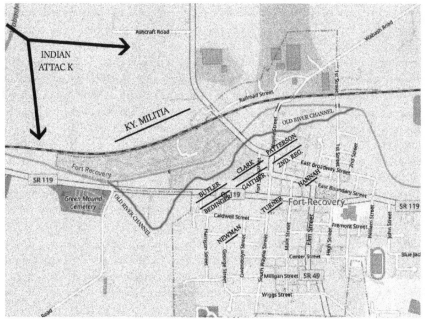

ST. CLAIR'S SOLDIERS CAMPED IN PARALLEL LINES, 70 YARDS APART, OVERLOOKING THE RIVER WHEN THE INDIANS ATTACKED, FROM UPPER LEFT, BEFORE DAWN.

the woods erupted with the yells of Indians, an unusual sound that some described like howling wolves and others said sounded like packhorse bells. This noise preceded the first firing on the militia by about five minutes; the militiamen barely had time to return a shot before they turned and ran, with the Indians right behind them.

When they ran "helter-skelter" into the main camp, confusion and disorder reigned. The militia commander, Lieutenant Colonel William Oldham, was killed trying to stop his troops' mad retreat; a few of Major Gaither's levies joined them in their flight, but were repulsed by the Indians concealed in the woods on the back side. Butler's troops, on the left end of front (western) line, stiffened and checked the Indians' attack, but the halt proved temporary; a red-coated chief who may have been Wapacomegat, a Mississauga Ojibway chief, rallied the warriors on horseback. Meanwhile, parts of the attacking force peeled off to the left and right with what wagoner Thomas Irwin called "a view to surround the army, which they done in a very short time." Irwin said that the "battle always reminded me of one of those thunder storms that comes up quickly and rapidly."

It must have felt that way to all of the soldiers. St. Clair recalled that "in a few minutes, our whole camp, which extended above three hundred and fifty yards in length, was entirely surrounded and attacked on all quarters."

The artillery lines, near the center of the lines of the main camp, were mostly ineffective. Because the camp sat at a higher elevation than the attackers, the initial shots fired into tree tops, and the Indian sharpshooters first focused on killing artillery men and officers. In fewer than 90 minutes, a badly-wounded Captain Mahlon Ford was the only artillery man alive and the cannons fell silent.

The battle started before St. Clair had time to put on his dress uniform, so he wore an old, hooded cloak and a three-cornered hat. That plain outfit made his less conspicuous and probably saved his life. Luck helped, too. Two of his horses were killed before he could mount them and he charged into battle on foot, a triumph of adrenaline over pain from gout and arthritis.

After the battle, St. Clair wrote his assessment of the dire situation: "Finding no great effect from our fire, and confusion beginning to spread from the great number of men who were falling in all quarters, it became necessary to try what could be done with the bayonet."

It seemed like a good idea, anyway. St. Clair led one bayonet charge and Darke led two, and each time the Indians fell back and then resumed fire as the attacking Americans lost their momentum.

While the fighting raged and men fell, chaos swept through the middle of the camp where the non-military personnel had collected in the wide gap between the two American lines. Terrified women and children found themselves caught between violence and carnage on all sides. Some women hid beneath wagons and some knelt and prayed for their safety, while others "were running to and fro, wringing their hands and shrieking out their terrors."

Some of the wounded soldiers were taken to the center of the camp to keep them from being scalped and killed, but it was anything but safe. With the American lines crumbling and the Indians advancing, the line squeezed closer and closer together, leaving many of the soldiers in a dangerous crossfire. Dead bodies were everywhere, which intensified the fear and hysteria.

Major Jacob Fowler offered a personal recollection of the battle in Charles Cist's *Western Weekly Advertiser* in 1844 that gives a customer sitting inside the North End Bar and Grill, a clerk at a teller's window in the Second National Bank or anyone strolling down modern Fort or Wayne streets an idea of just how horrifying the now tranquil scene around them had once been: "Even during the last charge of Colonel Darke, the bodies of the dead and dying were all around us. And the freshly scalped heads were reeking with smoke, and in the heavy morning frost looked like so many pumpkins through a cornfield in December."

As his men continued to fall and the panic and confusion spread, it became obvious to St. Clair that the remainder of his army could only be saved by retreat. Captain Alexander Truman, who commanded the mounted dragoons, made a charge at the Indians with his surviving horsemen as if they were attempting to turn the right flank, then shifted suddenly toward the route that brought them there from Fort Jefferson. The frightened soldiers rushed to follow, while the Indians hesitated, as if taken by surprise. It didn't take long for them to figure out the soldiers' tactics, though. Major Clark's battalion tried to cover the army's rear, but as the Indians picked them off, it quickly became a wild, every-man-for-himself scramble for safety.

As the army retreated, it left most of the wounded to the attackers, who killed and scalped them as they advanced. Sargent later said he believed the Indians could have caught and killed them all had they not been concerned with killing and scalping the wounded and collecting the plunder that had been left behind. When the Indians left the battlefield, many were leading packhorses piled high with scalps and goods. Sargent's list of the materials lost – 1,200 muskets and bayonets, 316 fully-furnished packhorses, 384 common tents and eleven marquees, six cannons, four ox teams, 163 felling axes, etc. – shows that for the beleaguered military, the disaster extended even beyond the lives lost.

The retreat began around 9:30 a.m. and some of the soldiers reached Fort Jefferson, a distance of twenty-nine miles, around sunset. When they were about nine miles from the fort, the retreating soldiers were met by Major Hamtramck and the First Regiment, who had started to advance at the report of gunfire. When told of the retreat, Hamtramck ordered his force to return to the Fort Jefferson and prepare to defend it against the victorious Indians. St. Clair found no reason to criticize that decision later and admitted that if the First Regiment had been at the scene of the battle it probably wouldn't have mattered, the Indians' victory might have been even more complete and had longer term ramifications.

Wounded soldiers in need of immediate medical attention remained at Fort Jefferson; the rest continued on to Fort Washington, where they started arriving on November 8. After St. Clair headed east to salvage his reputation, Lieutenant Colonel James Wilkinson assumed command. He appealed to settlements north of the Ohio River to join an expedition to St. Clair's battlefield, to bury troops and salvage cannons. Wilkinson led a detachment of 150 troops with supplies for Fort Jefferson on January 24 and 130 mounted militia left for the battlefield on February 1, almost three months after the battle. A volunteer with that force counted 78 bodies along the way.

When they arrived, one officer described the gruesome scene: "Upwards of six hundred bodies, horribly mangled with tomahawks and scalping knives, and by wild beasts, lay on the ground, and presented a spectacle too horrible for description." Sargent said that although the field was covered with snow, "at every tread of the horse's feed, dead bodies were exposed to view, mutilated, mangled and butchered with the most savage barbarity, and indeed, there seems to have been left no act of indecent cruelty or torture which was not practiced on this occasion, to the women as well as the men."

Not all of the bodies could be buried, in part because the job was too large for the assembled force and in part because many were frozen to the ground. The rest of that grim task was left to the unit that Anthony Wayne sent there in December, 1793, almost two years later.

"When the men went to lie down in the tents at night they had to scrape the bones together and carry them out to make their own beds," soldier Samuel McDowell wrote later. "The next day holes were dug and the bones remaining above ground were buried, six hundred skulls being found among them."

Wayne ordered those soldiers to build Fort Recovery on the site of the battlefield. The size and exact location of the fort have not been determined, even though a 1956 recreation of a wall and two of the blockhouses stands on Fort Street, at the edge of a large park with a museum and a baseball field. At the time of the battle most of that park lay west of the river; the channel has since changed and is now a couple hundred yards west, on the other side of the ballfield.

On June 30, 1794, a combined force of 2,000 Indians, Canadian militiamen and British officers under Little Turtle attacked a supply convoy near the fort. The convoy lost its commander, Major William McMahon, and retreated within the structure. The Indians' assault continued into the following day but the 250 soldiers inside the fort finally drove the attackers off. Twenty-two soldiers died in the battle, while the Indian groups suffered 40 dead; the discouraging defeat caused most of the Ottawa and many of the Ojibwa and Potawatomi to return to their homes in the North. The now weakened Indian army would find itself in trouble when it fought Wayne at Fallen Timbers.

The soldiers' triumph in the Battle of Fort Recovery helped set up Wayne's win on the Maumee River. But it will never erase the memories of the original battle that may have seen as many as 900 soldiers, workers and camp followers die.

"You don't think much about it when you live here," said a male teenager working at the Fort Recovery museum gift shop. "But when they were re-doing our (high school) gym, some people who worked there said they heard a lot of strange sounds. . ."

When I asked him where the school is, he smiled.

"The high school is right by the monument where all the soldiers are buried."

29 FORT GREENEVILLE

On a June afternoon so hot that kids wanted nothing to do with the playground behind St. Mary's School in Greenville, Ohio, a guy about 50 years too old to be there drew some quizzical looks from drivers in passing cars.

My cellphone photo snapping may have allayed fears that I was about to take a stab at a bright blue slide, but that still didn't make me look any less out of place. A woman crossed the parking lot to the south of the playground equipment and didn't look up. She unlocked the side door to the school and didn't look up. Her behavior reminded me of subway riders in New York who won't look at another rider they're pretty sure is crazy.

After she disappeared into the building, I escaped the magnetic pull of the playground equipment to wander that deserted parking lot. A car passed on the street to the south and an elderly man gave me a skeptical glance, as if to say "Who are you, a blacktop salesman?"

But, hey, even if he knew of my interest in the Treaty of Greenville, that wouldn't explain why I was here. There is a beautiful marble sign that sort of marks the spot of the signing of the famous treaty and it lies almost a block away. It sits at the front of an empty lot at the southeast corner of West Main and Elm streets that occupies the half-block in front of the playground, school and the parking lot that sits behind them. There is nothing to connect the sign, which most Greenville residents have probably passed a thousand times without looking at it, and anything else that is part of the here and now.

I had just come from the city's Garst Museum, so visualizing that moment in 1795 when 1,100 Indians of various tribes signed away ownership rights to most of the land that became Ohio was relatively easy for me. The Garst

Museum has an amazing model of the 50-acre fortification called Fort Greeneville where the agreement was signed, one that provides a detailed roadmap to the past.

"We think they signed (the treaty) in (Anthony Wayne's) garden." Nancy Stump, longtime member of the Greenville Historical Society and one of the museum's experts, seemed happy to honestly share her knowledge about the momentous event. "It was in a cool place and we think that's where it was. We put a stone on Main Street and said it was signed 'near' this spot. . .' Nobody really knows exactly where. The things we read said it was in an orchard."

Commanding General Anthony Wayne's orchard? Makes sense. The scale model of Fort Greeneville, under glass in the middle of a room at the Garst Museum, shows Wayne's headquarters on a corner of two streets that are a tad east and south of modern Main and Elm streets, which are pretty much in the middle of the sprawling camp.

There is a lighted map of Fort Greeneville's "streets" on the wall that is placed over an aerial photo of modern Greenville, so if the maps are accurate, you can see right where Wayne's headquarters would be today. That little playground marks the spot, or at least it did on the day I made my visit. But a recently discovered drawing with the exact dimensions of the fort shifted the fort's streets ever-so-slightly, landing the playground in the middle of the intersection at the center of the camp and Wayne's headquarters on the north end of the parking lot behind it. And yes, the orchard that lies behind Wayne's place on the model also falls on that not-so-cool sea of blacktop that wouldn't grow a blade of grass today.

"The map's accurate," Stump said. "The men who researched this did a great job."

There is no doubting that Dr. David Cox, David Heckaman and Floyd Barmann did a remarkable job; they're also the ones who adjusted and published the new map in the *Ohio Archaeologist*. The shift doesn't affect the model of the fort that Andrew S. Janicki took 15 months to construct, which is mesmerizing. The scale for the model is 1/64 of an inch to one foot. The picket walls consist of approximately 3000 logs, and the eight redoubts away from the fort consist of 1500 logs. The model includes 240 privates' huts, camp kitchens, stables, bake houses and bread ovens, granaries, saddlery and blacksmith shops, the private residences and gardens of Wayne, General James Wilkinson and Lieutenant Colonel John Hamtramck and so on, which hints at why a four- by six-foot model was required to accurately portray a fort that was the largest wooden fortification in the United States.

The model offers the historian a chance to wander the roughly 12 city blocks of modern Greenville that Wayne's fortification occupied – Water the south and Mud Creek (a block past Vine) on the west – and have at least a rudimentary knowledge of what was there over 220 years ago.

As fascinating as it to know that Broadway between Water and Third, including Public Square, was occupied by rows of privates' huts or that General Wilkinson's residence probably stood near a parking lot off Sycamore in the rear of a Main Street building occupied by Tree of Life Health Care Solutions, the treaty site is the star or the show. The model has

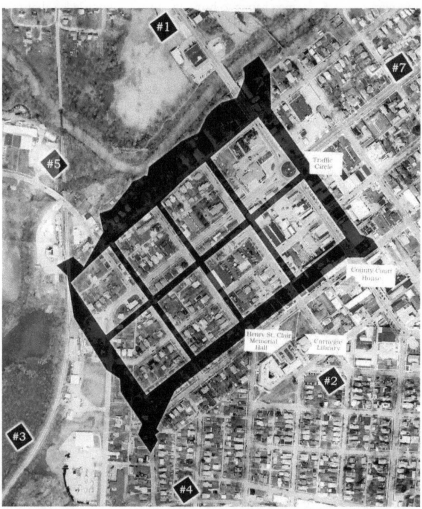

THIS GARST MUSEUM OVERLAY SHOWS HOW SOME OF FORT GREENEVILLE'S STREETS RAN NEARLY PARALLEL TO MODERN ONES. MODERN MAIN STREET LIES JUST NORTH OF THE FORT'S MAIN STREET (IN BLACK). VINE, ELM AND SYCAMORE LINE UP WITH THE FORT'S CROSS STREETS. BROADWAY(EAST) AND WATER (NORTH) LIE CLOSE TO THE FORT'S WALLS. THIS HASN'T BEEN UPDATED TO SHOW A WIDENING GAP BETWEEN THE TWO MAIN STREETS. NUMBERED BOXES SHOW REDOUBT LOCATIONS.

Wayne's gardens to the immediate south and east of his headquarters and a council house to the immediate east of the arbor house or orchard, which a pamphlet of the model says is the "treaty site."

A 1945 edition of Robert E. Perry's self-published book *Treaty City, A Story of old Fort Greeneville* locates Wayne's headquarters in "the formal garden of Howard Hoel," a prominent Greenville resident who lived at 214 West Main Street. That address is a parking lot today; it is also on the north side of Main more than a half block to the east of the location of the marker, although the address doesn't necessarily describe the site of Hoel's gardens.

Since we can't be absolutely certain where Wayne and the Indian chiefs signed it, that pretty marble stone etched with an outline of the famous painting of the signing done by Howard Christy is probably best served by its description of the treaty being signed "near" here.

To those unfamiliar with the history of this part of the country the exact location of the signing might seem like a small matter. In fact, the Treaty of Greenville is probably the second most important document in the history of the Old Northwest, second only to the Northwest Ordinance of 1787 that created the Northwest Territory and allowed for the creation of states that became Ohio, Indiana, Illinois, Michigan, Wisconsin and Minnesota.

Wayne didn't build a massive fort in this location so he would have a nice place for a treaty signing. The first part of his army arrived here on October 14, 1793, while it was on its way north to avenge St. Clair's embarrassing defeat in 1791 at a location that became Fort Recovery. The soldiers marched six miles past Fort Jefferson and established a camp on a slight hill "near the edge of a large, extensive, verdant prairie, or natural meadow, covered with grass and innumerable flowers." The prairie extended for miles to the south, while land on the north, west and east offered a thick forest of beech, maple, oak, ash, hickory, magnolia, sycamore and walnut trees. One of the soldiers called the spot a "terrestrial paradise."

The army waited for the rest of Wayne's legion, supply train and volunteer units to join it there and after several days of frigid temperatures, snow and high winds, Wayne convened a council of war consisting of Generals Wilkinson, Scott, Posey, Todd and Barbee, read them his instructions from Secretary of War Knox and intelligence from his scouts, and asked their opinions on whether it made sense to move forward at this time and whether they should continue 23 miles north to site of St. Clair's defeat on November 4, 1791. Wilkinson and Posey answered with "no's" and the Kentucky generals didn't feel qualified to answer. Wayne then reported the results of his council to Knox, and unhappily explained that he had no choice but to "halt & Hut at this place for the present." This was the beginnings of Fort Greeneville.

With winter approaching and no Indians to fight, the Kentucky volunteers under General Scott returned to their farms and on November 3,

Generals Wilkinson and Posey directed their soldiers to begin cutting pieces of timber 10 feet high for the construction of a stockade. Quartermaster James O'Hara began working on the layout of the structure and the huts for the soldiers were constructed first. On November 21, General Wayne announced to his legion: "This encampment shall in future be known and distinguished by the name of Greeneville," in honor of his old friend General from the American Revolution, who had died in 1786.

A month later, Wayne assembled a company of 300 soldiers under Major Henry Burbeck and sent them 28 miles north on December 23 to reclaim the St. Clair battlefield, finish burying bodies that were still rotting there and build a fort on the site. When it was finished, Wayne put Captain Alexander Gibson in command there. Wayne devoted a great deal of time that winter in assuring that the new post he called Fort Recovery could withstand an Indian attack. (The attack finally came in June; Gibson's troops repelled it.)

After a winter and spring spent preparing for a resumption of the march north and a general review of his legion on July 13, Wayne called his officers together and told them to be ready for a campaign "at a moment's warning." Between seven and eight in the morning of July 28, a canon fired from the east bastion of Fort Greeneville, telling the troops that the campaign to determine the destiny of the Northwest Territory had begun. Wayne's force consisted of approximately 2,000 regular troops of the legion and 720 mounted volunteers. At least 800 of the Kentucky troops were left behind to escort supply convoys.

When Wayne and his troops finally returned to Fort Greeneville on November 2 after a campaign that included his momentous victory at Fallen Timbers and construction of both Fort Defiance (before the battle) and Fort Wayne (after it), the hostile environs the legion had left in July had changed.

During the winter months, all of the nations of the Indian confederacy sent delegations to either Fort Wayne or Fort Greeneville seeking peace, the last of which were the reluctant Delawares and Shawnees. On February 7, 1795, a delegation from the two tribes led by war chief Blue Jacket visited Wayne and signed a preliminary treaty that established a truce on the Ohio frontier. They also agreed, as other tribes had, to come to Fort Greeneville on June 15 to negotiate and sign an overarching treaty between the U.S. government and all of the tribes north of the Ohio River.

Because of the late arrival of some tribes, Wayne had to push back the opening of the conference for about a month. In the meantime, the Army distributed rations to those delegations that had arrived and camped in land surrounding the fort. Future president William Henry Harrison served as Wayne's aide-de-camp, and autograph dealers frequently offer ancient slips of paper signed by Harrison from Fort Greeneville that passed for requisition

orders for rations, whiskey, etc. for various Indian tribes during this period. When the terms were finally negotiated, the Indians tribes received relatively little in exchange for the ceding of the southern and eastern two-thirds of the state of Ohio, smaller tracts of land of Indiana, the posts at Fort Detroit and Fort Michilimackinac and an area of Illinois that became the future site of the city of Chicago.

In return, the United States agreed to deliver a quantity of goods valued at $20,000 and annually deliver another shipment of goods worth $9,500, as well as one-time cash payments of $1,000 to the Wyandots, Delawares, Shawnees, Miamis, Ottawas, Chippewas and Potawatomis, and $500 to the Kickapoo, Wea, Eel River, Piankeshaw and Kaskaskia tribes.

Among other terms in the document, an "exchange of prisoners" may have been the most notable. As news of this spread, dozens of citizens looking for friends and family members who had been captured or gone missing traveled to Wayne's headquarters hoping for some word of their lost loved ones. Others sent letters to him describing individuals who had presumably been kidnapped by Indians in Pennsylvania, Virginia, Kentucky and all parts of the Northwest Territory. This resulted in some emotional reunions and separations at Fort Greeneville that seem unimaginable today. An American officer living in the fort described what he saw there in an October 31, 1795, letter to a friend in Massachusetts that was printed in the *Windham (Conn.) Herald*:

"A peace is concluded with the Indians, and, I believe, the best that has ever been made. I think they will go away better satisfied than they have at any former treaty. It was signed the 3d inst. It has been a pleasing scene to me. I have been a witness to parents receiving their children, who have been absent for 15 or 16 years and had grown to an adult state, but could not speak one word of English and likewise some of the Indians who had been with our people, and totally lost their mother tongue. Husbands meeting their wives and wives their husbands on both sides. The other day a beautiful girl came in who was married to an Indian. Her father came here in quest of her; she had been gone about 12 years, and was seven years old when she was taken. Her father despairs of having her restored to him again; she appears quite afraid of him. One respectable old man from Kentucky, had two sons, whom he met there, the oldest could speak a little English, and remembered the time of his capture. The father took them both home; they stayed with him but a few days, then stole two of his best horses and left him. I believe white savages are harder to be civilized than Indians."

The description reminds us that the roughly eight blocks of homes and businesses in modern Greenville where Wayne's fort stood saw more than just Wayne's legendary drilling of his troops before sunup, the monotonous grind of daily chores and the pomp and circumstance of a ceremonial treaty signing.

The "signatures" on that treaty are a practically a who's who of Indian chiefs of that era, including Little Turtle (of the Miami tribe), Tarhe the Crane, Roundhead and Leatherlips (Wyandot), Blue Jacket, Black Hoof and Red Pole (Shawnee) and Buckongahelas (Delaware) among others. The notable missing name is that of Tecumseh, who refused to attend. Blue Jacket subsequently paid him a visit to his camp on Deer Creek and relayed the terms on which the peace had been concluded.

Meriwether Lewis and William Clark, partners in the famed Lewis and Clark expedition to the West, were both present at the signing ceremony. Clark had been a lieutenant in Wayne's legion from the beginning; Lewis joined the Army in 1795 and held the rank of ensign (equivalent to today's second lieutenant) and met Clark here for the first time. Clark later met one of the Delaware chiefs from the peace conference at Camp Dubois (starting point for the expedition), and mentioned it in his journal for December 23, 1803: "a raney day... several Deleaway pass, a chief whome I saw at Greenville Treaty, I gave him a bottle of whiskey."

With the war over and peace negotiations concluded, the troops evacuated Fort Greeneville in spring of 1796. Later that year, some of its buildings were burned to obtain nails and other material for use in the construction of the first buildings in Dayton. For several years after that a few Indians used what remained of the structures, although most of the buildings that hadn't burned began to rot.

Stump said that "Abraham Scribner lived in the (headquarters) house after Anthony Wayne was gone" and that "he had a little shop and he sold all kinds of things to the settlers when they came out." But a nineteenth century history of Darke County makes no mention of this. It notes that Abraham's brother Azor came here in 1806-07 with a load of Indian goods and occupied the empty log house of a Frenchman who had built it on the west side of the creek, opposite the site of the burned fort. The book reports that Abraham came to the area in 1811 but doesn't connect him to the fort or Wayne's headquarters.

Even after the treaty signing and the fort's abandonment, the area remained a focal point of Indian activity. Tecumseh and his brother Tenskwatawa established a camp across Mud Creek from the site of the fort in 1805, in a location today known as Tecumseh's Point. It was apparently here that Tenskwatawa began to see visions and became The Prophet, after the death of an elderly Shawnee prophet named Penagashega. Tenskwatawa denounced the American settlers, calling them offspring of the Evil Spirit, and led a purification movement that promoted unity among Native Americans, rejected alcohol and encouraged his followers to pursue traditional ways.

Throughout 1806, many Indians from different tribes visited the brothers at their village and some became their followers. By April, 1807, about 400 Indians, most of them gripped by religious fanaticism, had assembled there and the number almost doubled by the fall. After expressing their peaceful intentions in a visit by delegations from the governor of Ohio, the brothers moved their village west to a spot near Lafayette, Indiana, in 1808 that came to be known as Prophetstown.

Today, Tecumseh Point is a rough, wooded, rocky area near a railroad trestle that isn't easily accessible.

"You can't even get to it, really," Stump said. "The only way you can get to it is come over the bridge (from Vine Street) and then walk down in there. All you can do is stand there on a lookout and look over. We don't let people down in there. They'll get you killed. It's rough down in there.

"The rocks they used for steps are (huge). I've been down there once and I won't go down there again. I think they put the steps in when they put the railroad in because they needed all of this area not to cave in. They dug out a lot of dirt to put the railroad in. They put in big rocks to keep that dirt there."

Tecumseh eventually led an alliance of Indian tribes that fought with the British against the Americans during the War of 1812. He died at the Battle of the Thames in Upper Canada in 1813. When General William Henry Harrison sought to sign a treaty with the Indians in 1814 that would bring their support in the war, he thought it would be appropriate to do it in the same place that the Treaty of Greenville was signed in 1795.

It was just 19 years later, but the area had clearly changed. The arbor that the soldiers put up over the spot had to be taken down because it was in the wrong location. Because Harrison was part of the ceremony, the confusion over the site stands as strong circumstantial evidence that the house that served as Wayne's headquarters and the orchard or garden where the famous 1795 treaty had been signed were either torn down, overgrown or both.

Whether the treaty signed by Harrison and Michigan Territory Governor Lewis Cass with the Wyandot, Delaware, Shawnee, Seneca, Miami and Potawatomi tribes on July 22, 1814, was in the same exact location is lost to history, as was most of Fort Greeneville by that point. Excavations over the years would reveal precisely where just about everything was, although only one of the eight exterior redoubts, built to give the fort added protection and advance warning in case of attack, has been uncovered. It stood on the other side of Mud Creek, west of Tecumseh Point,

"We've only found one of the out places and that was No. 8," Stump said. "They found it in the park district. To find the others ones, we'd probably have to dig up somebody's yard."

IV.

CONTESTED GROUND

30 FORT ST. JOSEPH

A giant boulder atop a small forested hill behind a set of concrete steps on Bond Street in Niles, Michigan, is inscribed with the words "Fort St. Joseph 1691-1781." Because of its massive size and its simple message, it clearly predates the historical marker beside the steps that briefly tells the fort's story. It also offers a weighty argument – written accounts tell us the 12-foot boulder weighs 70 tons – that the French fort, trading post and mission near the St. Joseph River stood on the spot of that massive rock.

Presumably, Jesuit missionary Claude-Jean Allouez saw the rock, interpreted it as a message from God and decided to establish the Mission de Saint-Joseph on that very spot in the 1680s. The fort followed and when the site went back to nature after being abandoned for good in the 1790s, area settlers made annual treks to the giant stone and finally chiseled the words in granite so they would never forget what had occurred there.

That isn't what happened, of course. The Fort St. Joseph Historical Society actually moved the boulder there from three miles away in 1913, when historians still weren't sure of the precise location of the fort. Some historians even supported the hypothesis that the fort had been located on the other side of the river. There were compelling reasons to believe the society had put the rock in the vicinity of the fort and mission site (the fort site is actually several hundred feet away near the river), but archaeologists had taken several unsuccessful stabs at finding it until a team from Western Michigan University led by anthropology professor Michael S. Nassaney began doing extensive digs in the summer of 1998 that have continued almost annually.

To be clear, this isn't your ordinary "we lost the fort" story. For one thing, the good citizens of Niles didn't turn a blind eye to their history; the structure was long gone when the first permanent settlers came here. Esquire Thomson settled on the property in 1823 or 1824 and when he planted corn

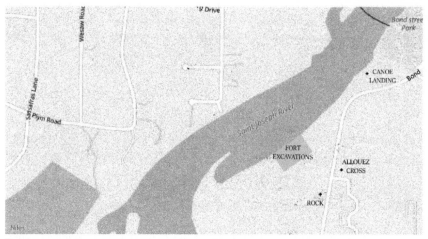

EARLY ARCHAEOLOGICAL EXCAVATIONS WERE DONE ON THE HIGHER GROUND, NEAR THE FORT ST. JOSEPH ROCK THAT WAS PUT THERE IN 1913.

along the river, he plowed up many old relics – sword blades, flints, musket balls, screws and springs and gun lock plates -- of both French and English occupancy that he probably saw as evidence that the fort has been located there.

Decades later local collectors, notably E.H. Crane and L.H. Beeson, frequently searched and recovered what was called "thousands" of copper, brass, silver and iron articles in the mold and the clay of the property. (Many of those artifacts are now displayed in the Fort St. Joseph Museum in Niles). In 1900, Beeson wrote an article for the Michigan Pioneer and Historical Society on the history of the fort and trading post. Based on both his collections and various maps and research, he described what he believed to be its precise location.

A couple of similar articles followed, one in 1900 and another in 1914, which disputed earlier accounts that had placed the fort several miles south or across the river. That is presumably why that massive boulder landed there above those concrete steps.

The story takes another sharp turn – or dive – here. In 1876, the Niles Water Power company completed a dam across the river that raised the water level 10 to 12 feet and submerged at least part of the site. When the elevation of the dam increased in the 1930s, it submerged even more ground and made other parts of the property swampy. Under the circumstances, the city decided that the useless ground at the far south end of town would make the perfect place for a dump.

So, you begin to understand how easy it was to lose evidence of an old fort's location that had never been a sure thing to begin with, especially after researchers from the University of Michigan, Notre Dame and Michigan State all tried to locate it over the years and failed.

A local group called "Support the Fort" raised money in the 1990s to try to find it and contacted archaeologists at Western Michigan to do the work, which is why we now know that the fort site stood on the low, swampy ground near or even under the modern river and not on the high ground near the rock where everyone had been looking.

"We started our survey in 1998 near the rock," said Nassaney, whose 2020 retirement hasn't stopped his work or interest in the project. "We dug shovel test pits a couple of feet deep, dug them in a line on a transect every 10 meters. . . We went all the way to the river. We dug 350 holes. Nobody had ever done anything as systematic as that. They had only dug near the rock.

"We found some artifacts, but not that many. But what was useful about that survey, the work had been so intensive that there's no way the site could have been in the area that we looked."

That area – the high ground – was where you would expect to find a fort used for defensive purposes.

"We thought a fort would be on the defensive, high ground," Nassaney said. "We weren't really thinking commercial center. We weren't really thinking trading. So fort's a bit of a misnomer. Yeah, it was a fort, but it wasn't defensive.

THE ROCK WAS PLACED AT SITE IN 1913.

In 1762, there were a thousand native people living across the river. A little palisaded area with 12 soldiers? It wasn't going to defend anyone. If they wanted in, they're in. They had an amicable relationship, so it was more of a symbolic place."

After Allouez established his mission here among the Miamis in the 1680s, New France governor-general Louis de Buade, Comte de Frontenac sent Augustin le Gardeur de Courtemanche and a small detachment of soldiers to construct a fort near the mission to protect French trade interests in 1691. Allouez likely didn't land here by accident: His put his mission at or just north of the place where the east-west Great Sauk Trail and a north-south, southern branch of the St. Joseph Trail combine and cross the river.

By the early eighteenth century, the fort/trading post supported eight officers, 10 enlisted men, a priest, an interpreter, a blacksmith, and about 15 fur traders and their wives. By 1750, it ranked fourth among New France posts in terms of volume of furs traded.

But it's clear from the history that it was never an impregnable fortress. Father Pierre François Xavier de Charlevoix visited here in 1721 and gave the place the eighteenth century equivalent of a one-star rating:

"There is a commandant here with a small garrison. His house, which is but a sorry one, is called the Fort, from its being surrounded with an indifferent palisade. We have here two villages of Indians, one of the Miamis and the other of the Potawatomis, both of them mostly Christians, but they have been for a long time without any pastor. The missionary who has been lately sent to them will have no small difficulty in bringing them back to the exercise of their religion."

The British took over the fort in 1761. During Pontiac's rebellion seventeen Potawatomi warriors entered Ensign Francis Schlosser's quarters at Fort St. Joseph on May 25, 1763, on pretense of holding a council. They seized the unsuspecting Schlosser and killed ten of his soldiers. They captured three others prisoners and took them and the commandant at Fort Detroit, where they were exchanged for Indian prisoners.

Richard Winston, a British trader at Fort St. Joseph, wrote that he "escaped being killed when the unfortunate garrison was massacred" with the help of M. Louison Chevalier, who hid him and "Mr. Hambough" in his house for four days and nights.

The British eventually reclaimed Fort St. Joseph, but never permanently garrisoned it again. So French trappers used the fort to trade with local Indians, and in 1780, Patrick Sinclair, British commander at Fort Michilimackinac, decided he wanted them out of there and easily captured the fort.

On January 2, 1781, the fort was attacked and plundered again -- beginning to see a pattern here? -- this time by a force of French and Indians from St. Louis. The attack had been authorized by Spanish Governor Francisco Cruzat, who thought control of the fort would diminish British control in the region.

The troops overwhelmed the little fort, flew the Spanish flag and looted it of supplies, which they were forced to split with the Potawatomis as a condition of them failing to come to the aid of the occupants. Satisfied with their plunders, the invaders abandoned the fort the next day and returned to St. Louis. Today, we know this one-day occupation as more of a marketing success than a military one: The modern city of Niles claims to be the only town in Michigan to have lived under the flags of four nations (France, Great Britain, the United States and Spain), giving rise to its self-proclaimed title as the City of Four Flags. (In his 2015 book *The Archaeology of the North American*

Fur Trade, Nassaney wryly noted that "the Potawatomi takeover of 1763 was not accorded a 'flag.'")

Fort St. Joseph was never officially occupied again, although a small French population and a few traders lingered in the vicinity and the Potawatomi tribe remained nearby. During the early nineteenth century, census takers reported six to 10 Potawatomi villages along the St. Joseph River in various locations.

The absence of a military presence doesn't seem to have mattered much to the traders. In 1796, William Burnett's ledger shows that he sold 99 packs of furs from a take of "5 bears, 5 pound beaver, 10 fishers, 58 cats, 74 doe, 78 foxes, 198 wolves, 117 otters, 183 minks, 557 bucks, 1,231 deer, 1,340 muskrats and 5,587 raccoons."

But it's unclear how much of the fort/old trading post still existed at that point, if any at all. In 1831, a visitor to Niles described his visit to the site:

"We put up at a small and comfortable inn, and after supper strolled up the river along its banks in search of those antiquated remains of the ancient race that once was supposed to have peopled the western part of the continent. We had not rambled far before we came across the remains of an old fort, the appearance of which indicated that it was near a century and a half old. Upon the higher bank on the opposite side of the river were to be seen several mounds, apparently the burial place of our red brethren. A few rods from the fort, and higher up the bank, we found one solitary mound, surmounted with a rude cross bearing no inscription."

Allouez died here in 1691 and the cross is presumed to have marked Allouez' burial place. The decaying wooden cross was eventually replaced with another wooden one -- replacing it when needed apparently became a local tradition -- and in 1918 the Women's Progressive League of Niles replaced the latest rotting cross with one made of granite that still stands in honor of Father Allouez. It sits atop a hill about 100 yards north and on the opposite side of Bond Street from the giant boulder.

All this points to this as the general vicinity of the old fort (as opposed to, say, on the other side of the river), but it didn't offer the proof that researchers coveted. That proof had also eluded the Western Michigan team after it had conducted the most extensive digs yet in 1998 on the higher ground where others had looked.

What changed?

"After we did that work in the fall of 1998, a local collector came by and he had been working by the bank of the river with his metal detector and he showed us a box of artifacts," Nassaney said. "Among them were hand wrought nails, nails made by a blacksmith. There hasn't been a blacksmith making nails here for maybe 250 years. And a piece of pottery that we could identify as having come from France. He had gunflints from flintlock muskets, those went out of style basically at the end of the eighteenth century.

And then we had these knife blades and on them were stamped the names of French couples. That was a start.

"He showed us where it was, we dug about 80 holes in that wet ground down there and we found artifacts in about 20 of them. And we hit the water table. So that's a problem. Archaeologists can't dig in muddy water because we can't see the spatial relationships. Is that gun flint next to a foundation wall? You couldn't tell. So it took us four years to figure out what to do."

What they did was hire a company from the Netherlands that installed a series of inch and a half PVC tubes about 12 feet deep along the margins of the site, connect them to a pump "the size of a Volkswagen" and lower the water table by pumping the water out faster than it could go back in. The research team has done this about every summer since (the old diesel fuel pump has been replaced by electric pumps), temporarily creating dry ground so they can dig. They have identified the remains of six buildings in the process.

"The width of the river as it appears today is probably twice as wide as it was when the fort was occupied," Nassaney said. "The deep part of the river, the river channel, is on the opposite side of the river from us. The river where we are, nearest where the fort was, is very shallow. We don't think there was a lot of activity there. Because we did a geophysical survey when the river was frozen and we didn't find many targets in that area.

"In other words, it's certainly possible, which is what we think, that the river was in the channel on the far side and the area where it is shallow is where they would have pulled up canoes and that sort of thing and we think we're probably on the very edge of the occupation. So, the river might not have washed that much away."

With the permission of Michigan Department of Environmental Quality, they have also been given access to explore under the dump (to the south and east.) They "accessed a backhoe" and discovered "material that is intact, undisturbed from the eighteenth century" in 2019.

"This was a dump for over 30 years," Nassaney said. "There is about four acres of it. It's a big area. A herculean challenge was figuring out how we were going to dewater the site. Now another huge challenge is what do you do with six feet of landfill over an area of let's say a half an acre? It's solvable if you had an unlimited budget. You just bring in backhoes and dump trucks and you could haul it all away I suppose, but you've got to pay to have it hauled away. They're not going to take that stuff free of charge."

Nassaney admits that the efficacy of doing that is debatable, although it's clear that he would like to better identify the actual location of the fort itself. He wrote that some in the "Save the Fort" group have long envisioned a reconstruction of the fort similar to that of Fort Michilimackinac.

"We haven't found any evidence of the actual palisades, but the area where we've excavated is very, very thick deposits of animal bone, and artifacts of all sorts," Nassaney said. "Broken knife blade, gun flints, rusty nails, annular nails and evidence of these houses. We're not exactly sure where the palisaded area was, but there are dense deposits of artifacts and what we call features, foundation walls and fireplaces and that sort of thing. So, we're still working to define the boundaries."

Even if they don't know the precise boundaries of the fort itself, Nassaney and his students have created an incredible roadmap to the neighborhood. And if that giant boulder isn't close to the walls of the old stockade, it still makes an impressive massive billboard for the historic structure that stood through the woods and down the hill behind it.

Visitors looking for more than a billboard should continue north on Bond Street past the Allouez cross and park near the canoe landing (or if necessary in the Riverfront South Park parking lot beyond it) and take a southerly stroll on the car path near the river until you pass an electric meter and see signs of archaeological field work.

COVID permitting, Nassaney planned to work the site in 2021 with 10 or 15 students as he does every July and August. He said there is public visitation "on a weekly basis, usually Friday" and an advertised open house that is usually scheduled for the first weekend in August. Their work at the 15-acre site has attracted over 10,000 visitors so far.

And what if the pandemic doesn't allow it?

"I don't want to give you the impression that this is all about digging," Nassaney said, "because it is about digging, but it's not all about digging. Now that we've recovered all of this material, there's probably 50 years of analysis time.

"We think if we never dug another shovelful, the students and others can learn from the ongoing analysis of the material. That's why we do this work. We're not digging to find more glass beads. There are a hundred thousand glass beads in the museum now. If we dig and we find another thousand, so what?"

31 FORT DETROIT

The imagination conjures a delightful image of old Detroit long before an epidemic of skyscrapers and asphalt took its life. It was a bustling little French town of traders, soldiers, missionaries and Native Americans with little shops, houses and churches lining streets with names like Ste. Anne, Ste. Honore and St. Jacques, in and around an old stockade.

When the imagination lets go, a grim twenty-first century reality sets in: Sometimes a city becomes so large that it seems to swallow up its distant past.

Detroit was born when French officer Antoine de la Mothe Cadillac erected Fort Pontchartrain du Détroit in 1701. It lived as a small settlement in and around the fort for much of the eighteenth century, a French and then British outpost that played an important role in both the history of the Old Northwest and the United States.

But the modern city of over four million radiates out of a mile-long phalanx of towering buildings from Riverfront Towers to the GM Renaissance Center along the Detroit River, leaving the site of an almost 200-foot square frontier fort lost amidst the mountains of glass and concrete. I found the most detailed description of the fort's location in an 1884 history of the city, a quest that requires more time than the average time traveler probably wants to devote to it.

But when you're standing on the sidewalk on East Jefferson Avenue between Shelby and Griswold streets and you know that you're within the walls of an ancient place that oozed American history, it's difficult not to feel a little awed.

Silas Farmer, our nineteenth-century tour guide, tells us that the front of the structure was located between Jefferson Avenue and Woodbridge Street in a spot that would likely place the fort's south wall in the four eastbound lanes of today's Jefferson. The fort occupied most of the block between

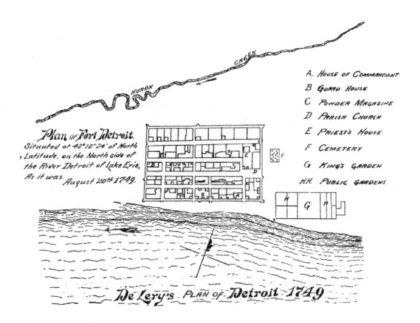

Griswold and Shelby streets, with the west side spilling over onto the other side of Shelby to take in part of the Crown Plaza Hotel. The Pontchartrain Hotel once stood here and the Market Exchange Hotel preceded the Pontchartrain. The back side of the fort lay on the south side of Larned Street.

The streets are the only open areas on the ground insides the palisades of the original fort, a big chunk of which is occupied by the 26-story 150 West Jefferson Building. The eight–story Standard Federal Savings and Loan Building adjoins the property to the east and takes up the rest of the fort's space. The building was being remodeled for use by the Church of Scientology on the day I was there, and a plaque on its corner wall on Griswold Street was partially hidden by a large sheet of plywood that had landed there for no discernible reason.

A chain link fence kept curiosity seekers like me from getting a look at both the plywood and the plaque, so I asked a middle-aged worker in the forbidden zone behind the fence if he could move the plywood so I could take a picture of the historical marker behind it. He not only moved it, but he invited me inside to take a closer look.

The marker announced this as the location of Sainte Anne's Catholic Church, which the French began building the day they landed here.

"There's a mistake on it," the grinning worker said, even before he had removed the plywood. "Look here, it says work on the church started on July 24, 1701, and it was completed only July 26, 1701. I don't think they built the church in two days."

This seems logical, but they weren't exactly building Notre Dame Cathedral. Given the church's small size, an exhaustive supply of building material – trees -- and the number of soldiers who could work on it, it's possible the dates on the marker are correct. The church stood just inside the east wall of the fort.

The worker introduced himself as Nick Serra and said his grandfather had helped build many buildings in downtown Detroit in the 1920s and 30s. He wasn't sure about this one but he seemed proud of the possibility of a connection. He said he had been working on the building for eight months and told me some of its history; it was constructed in 1927, two years before the Wall Street crash and the beginning of the Great Depression.

"It never closed its doors during the Depression, but it merged with another bank and moved out of here in the 70's," he said. He smiled. "That plaque used to be on that wall over there."

It occurred to me that Serra's interest in that crude log church extended beyond a possible typographical error on the historical marker. Both he and his grandfather had something in common with those long-dead Frenchmen who had once raised a house of God on or near this very spot. It's not every day you can feel such a kinship with strangers who had lived more than three centuries before, and something in his eyes told me that this isn't ancient history to him.

I thanked him for the information, took one more glance at the chain link fence, the dirt and the concrete and headed back to the beginning of the eighteenth century, when this place was surrounded by hundreds of miles of forests and countless tribes of Native Americans who called them home. None of that is reflected in the vicinity today, although the city of Detroit did erect both a large plaque in 2001 with the names of the French-Canadians who first settled here and a statue of Cadillac planting the French flag. It is located across Jefferson Street in a large riverfront events area called Hart Plaza.

On this Saturday the twenty-first century also encroached upon these memorials, the Ribs and Soul Festival having taken up temporary residence in the plaza. I launched my own voyage of discovery, looking for Cadillac and his traveling party amid the tents of clothing being hawked by weekend haberdashers and dress makers and the trailers of food vendors. Two tortuous trips through the plaza finally ended behind some vendor tents, where the statue and the plaque occupied a grassy area some vendors were using to pile up their excess products and garbage. I'm not sure the vendors would have treated a statue of Grandma that way, but at least the memorial isn't far from the accepted Cadillac landing spot near Jefferson and Woodward Avenue (Woodward ends at Larned Street today.) And the ribs did smell terrific.

Cadillac didn't land here by accident. He had been appointed commander of the French forts in the upper Great Lakes in 1694 and commanded Fort de Buade in St. Ignace on the Straits of Mackinac until 1696. He surmised that it wouldn't be as costly to operate the fur trade from a narrow point in the Detroit River that could control the flow of traffic between Lake Erie and Lake Huron, and went to France in 1699 to secure permission to build a fort here. Today, it seems like a natural move from a remote spot in the upper peninsula to the more centrally-located and populous region in Detroit. At the turn of the eighteenth century, it was a flip of a coin. Both were isolated spots surrounded by forests and their Native American custodians.

King Louis XIV gave Cadillac permission to build his fort and his party of more than one hundred departed Montreal on June 4, 1701. They emerged from their birch bark canoes not far Cadillac's statue on July 24 and almost immediately began building Sainte Anne's Catholic Church. Next, they finished the stockade with defensive bastions in each corner and began work on the buildings and streets inside of it.

Ste. Anne Street, about 22 feet wide, ran east to west along the southern wall. St. Joachim lay parallel to and north of Ste. Anne Street. St. Francois and St. Antoine were smaller and ran north-south in the enclosure. A very small street or alley was named Recontre. An early map shows that some of the buildings stood on ground now occupied by the westbound lanes of Jefferson Avenue. Cadillac's headquarters likely stood just inside the south wall in the eastbound lanes of Jefferson, just west of Griswold Street.

The new fort proved to be a magnet for Indian tribes interested in trading with the French. In July of 1702 – one year after its construction -- Cadillac sent his superiors in Quebec a report that six thousand Native Americans lived in the area. He wrote that an Ottawa village had been built near the foot of Belle Isle, a Miami village had been built along the river east of the fort and a Potawatomi village had been built near the mouth of now-gone Knaggs Creek, which ran to the Detroit River near Twenty-Fourth Street. Another source indicated that a Wolf (a division of the Sauk tribe) village had been built nearby in the "King's Commons (north of the fort)," and in June, 1703, thirty Huron families arrived from St. Ignace and established a village in the area that is now the foot of Third Avenue near the former site of Joe Louis Arena.

Cadillac wanted this to be an important settlement rather than just a frontier fortress and trading post and he brought his wife here from Quebec the following year. But French settlers were slow to come to the new outpost, because of both the distance from Quebec and the danger involved in making the trip.

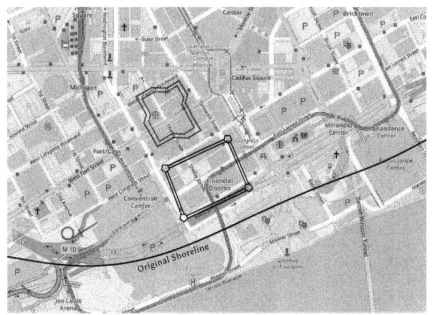

Cadillac had his own problems. He was ordered to return to Montréal and charged with illegal dealing in alcohol and furs in 1704; he returned to Detroit after being acquitted. He was away when the first major conflict at the fort occurred in March, 1706. The Ottawas attacked and killed several Miamis and the Miami tribesmen sought safety within the fort. The French soldiers killed about 30 Ottawa warriors when they attacked, and after the battle, the Miami attacked a nearby Ottawa village. During the course of this conflict, a French priest and a sergeant were caught outside the fort's walls and killed.

In March of 1708, Cadillac granted 68 lots to private individuals, which expanded the village limits to today's Washington Boulevard on the west and Larned Street on the north. A new street, St. Louis, was added to the south of Ste. Anne Street.

Cadillac departed again in 1710 because of accusations of corruption and this time he didn't come back. Jacques-Charles Renaud Dubuisson assumed command of the fort and many of Cadillac's Indian supporters subsequently left. The Fox tribe, recently relocated from what is now the state of Wisconsin, besieged the fort in May of 1712 with a mixed force of about 1,000 Foxes, Mascoutens and Sacs. Only 33 soldiers were stationed at the fort at that time and the Ottawa and the French-friendly Huron warriors were out on a raid in the Mississippi Valley.

This siege of Fort Pontchartrain du Détroit became the opening incident in the Fox Wars. The attackers fired blazing arrows into the settlement. Sainte Anne's Church and other buildings were torn down to reduce the risk of fire. The fastest boys from the local tribes took off to bring the warriors back; when they returned, many Foxes were killed.

The victory drove the Fox, Sauk and Mascouten tribes from the area. It didn't guarantee Detroit a prosperous future. The French built Fort Michilimackinac as their new fur trade headquarters in 1715, a repudiation of Cadillac's decision to leave the Straits of Mackinac 14 years before, and Detroit's influence shriveled.

France declared war on England in 1744 and that small French outpost on the Detroit River moved center stage and remained there. As the historic events of the next half century are recalled, this seems like a good place to purge our images of modern Detroit from the mind and remember that all of this mostly happened within what it today is at most about a ten-block area.

This is a lot of drama for such a small piece of real estate:

Chief Mackinac led a group of Ojibwa warriors from the north in an attack on Fort Pontchartrain in 1746, an attack thwarted by Pontiac and the Ottawas. This isn't the last we hear from Pontiac, who was on the other side in 1760 after the British gained control of the fort in negotiations that ended the French and Indian War.

In the spring of 1747, the Iroquois hatched a plot to murder everyone in the fort and drive out the French and they recruited local Hurons to join the plot. On a night following a church holiday, Indians asked permission to sleep inside the palisades and planned to kill those in the houses where they lodged. The massacre failed to materialize because an Indian woman tipped off the French to the plan.

The fort's commandant, Paul-Joseph Le Moyne de Longueuil, called the Huron chiefs together, told them what he knew and threatened severe punishment. The Hurons humbly asked forgiveness, pledged their allegiance and moved from Bois Blanc Island (near the southern mouth of the Detroit River across from modern Amherstburg, Ontario) to Sandwich (part of modern Windsor, Ontario). They settled around the mission house there, a short distance south of the fort at Detroit. The new Huron village was located in the area of what is now McKee Park, just west of today's Ambassador Bridge.

Major Robert Rogers assumed possession of the fort for the British in 1760 and Fort Detroit lost the Pontchartrain part of its name. At that point, it extended approximately 600 feet by 300 feet with boundaries at today's Larned Street, Griswold Street, Washington Boulevard, and Jefferson Avenue. The village population had swelled to about 500. Because the British didn't enjoy the same cozy relationship with the Indians as the French, Detroit would become the center of a new conflict.

The French had given the Indians more favorable trading terms than the British did. The British also limited the amount of ammunition sold to the tribes, which made it difficult for them to hunt. General Jeffrey Amherst, the architect of the British policy toward Native Americans, also cut back on gift-giving, a policy that the tribes had come to rely upon.

By 1761, Indian leaders wanted to drive out the British and restore French rule and Pontiac assumed leadership of the movement. He called a council of the Ottawa, Huron and Potawatomi tribes on a point of land near the Ecorse River on April 27, 1763, about 10 miles below Fort Detroit, to call for attacks on all of the English posts in the Great Lakes region and the Ohio Valley. He urged them to join him in launching a surprise attack on Fort Detroit. Today, the location of this conference is a 27-acre park with baseball and soccer fields in the suburb of Lincoln Park called Council Point Park.

The park is a half-mile west of the Detroit River, where the Ecorse splits in northern and southern branches forming the point. It has a large historic marker not far from a set of slides and playground equipment, an intrusion on the imagination that a modern visitor can overlook given the site's recent history: The property become a park in the late 1980s when the city of Lincoln Park purchased a series of small fields and woods from the Edward C. Levy Company, which hauls, processes and resells slag, an iron and steel production waste product. The city partnered with Michigan Department of Natural Resources to remove hazardous chemicals from the site, including heavy metals used in steel making.

There were no hazardous chemicals lurking in the ground beneath Pontiac's feet. It was a much simpler time. He could see the danger to him and his people.

"It is important for us, my brothers, that we exterminate from our lands this nation which seeks only to destroy us," he said, at the council. "You see as well as I that we can no longer supply our needs, as we have done from our brothers, the French. . . Therefore, my brothers, we must all swear their destruction and wait no longer. Nothing prevents us; they are few in numbers, and we can accomplish it."

Pontiac's words worked better than his battle plans. After forty warriors made a reconnaissance mission to the fort that was disguised as a friendly visit, he called another council on May 5 at the Pottawatomi village five miles west Fort Detroit where the village of Springwells is now located. He revealed what they had learned from their scouting mission and made final plans for the surprise attack.

It turns out that Pontiac was the one surprised. This time, he arrived at the fort with 60 warriors who had weapons hidden under their blankets. Once inside, Pontiac planned to give a signal and the Indians would kill the

130 British soldiers who lived there. But Major Henry Gladwin, the fort's commander, had been warned of the plan by an informer, and he had all of his troops armed and ready when Pontiac's group entered. The Ottawa chief quickly realized his plan had been foiled and he sullenly led his warriors out of the fort without attacking. Two days later, he directed his combined forces to lay siege to the structure, an effort soon joined by 900 warriors from other tribes.

Captain Donald Campbell's 1760 letter offers a fair snapshot of the structure under siege:

"The fort is very large and in good repair; there are two bastions toward the water and a large fast bastion toward the inland. The point of the bastion is a cavalier of wood, on which there are mounted the three pounders and three small mortars or cohorns. The palisades are in good repair. There is a scaffolding around the whole, which is only floored toward the land for want of plank; it is by way of a banquette. There are seventy or eighty houses in the fort, laid out in regular streets."

He described a settlement with narrow streets and shallow lots, with houses all made of wood and one-story. All of the streets in the village bore names that testify to the place's beginnings as a French missionary post. Their names -- Ste. Anne, St. Joseph, St. Louis, Ste. Honore, St. Joachim, St. James or St. Jacques, Sacrament, et. al – give today's reader visions of modern-day New Orleans, but only if he's looking at an eighteenth-century map. All have been paved over with asphalt and concrete.

Ste. Honore Street stood in nearly the same place as Shelby Street does today. Some 200 feet south of Ste. Anne Street nearly at the water's edge was a building used for holding Indian councils and lodging. With the exception of the church, Ste. Anne Street, which stood on or just north of modern Jefferson, was home to the traders. Immediately outside the pickets on the west end of Ste. Anne Street, were the barracks occupied by the soldiers, a small parade ground and a stone dwelling occupied by the commandant. The buildings and grounds constituted the "citadel" and were enclosed by another palisade still farther to the west.

The siege dragged on with no resolution in sight. Despite their superior numbers, Pontiac's forces were unable to take the fort and Gladwin refused to surrender. Finally, in June some British reinforcements under Captain James Dalyell arrived; the Indians had been unable to block water access to the fort.

Despite Gladwin's advice to the contrary, an overly ambitious Dalyell believed he could end the siege by attacking Pontiac's Ottawa camp about two miles northeast of the fort in and around what is now Elmwood Cemetery. Under cover of darkness on the morning of July 21, Captain Dalyell led 247 men to attack Pontiac's forces. His path is easily traced today on Jefferson Avenue, a busy six-lane street choked with cars and trucks because of numerous traffic lights, to a spot a short distance west of Mt. Elliott Avenue.

A plaque on the Players Club building identifies it as being close to the site of a small bridge that spanned Parent Creek, which Dalyell's soldiers crossed. Waiting Indians immediately surrounded and attacked them there. Pontiac had been tipped off about their planned attack, probably by one of the French settlers, and the Indians had an easy time of it, killing Dalyell and many of his troops. So much British blood flowed during the one-sided battle that Parent Creek became forever known as Bloody Run.

The creek is still there today – underground. An above-ground portion of it can still be found in Elmwood Cemetery, although it has been reduced to a small gully of water that doubtless looks nothing like the stream the British soldiers crossed on their way to eternity. The creek meanders around the cemetery and eventually goes under ground, not far from its entrance on Robert Bradby Drive on the eastern side of the cemetery.

Frenchman Antoine Cuillerier dit Beaubien's house stood on the far side of Pontiac's Ottawa camp on the other side of the creek. Shortly after the siege began, Pontiac took Captain Campbell and Lieutenant George McDougall prisoner after a peace council in Cuillerier's house, and Campbell was eventually executed. Pontiac considered Cuillerier the leader of the =French settlers who stayed in the area after the British took over, and he planned to have Cuillerier assume command of the fort after the British evacuated it.

That never happened. Despite the bloody defeat suffered by the reckless Captain Dalyell and his troops, Major Gladwin and his men remained safe inside the fort. As the siege dragged on and the season turned to autumn, Pontiac's support among the tribes eroded. It became clear that the French military support he expected wasn't coming and some of the tribes returned home. By November, the Ottawa chief finally realized he couldn't take Detroit and Pontiac and his forces withdrew and moved west. Pontiac's rebellion officially ended in 1765, but by then his Indian allies realized they had no choice but to trade with the British.

The next threat to Fort Detroit would come from the Americans, even though the main fronts in the Revolutionary War lay hundreds of miles to the east. Lieutenant governor Henry Hamilton, known by American frontiersmen as the "Hair-buyer general" because they believed he paid his Indian allies for scalps, assumed command of the fort in 1775. He lived in the two-story King's Palace, which stood in the gardens on the other side of modern Griswold Street from the church site. The gardens extended to the river.

George Rogers Clark took Hamilton prisoner in a surprise attack at Vincennes in February, 1779. Because of the rumored threat of a Clark attack on Detroit, British Captain Richard Lernoult ordered a new, stronger fort to be built. The structure, called Fort Lernoult and later also referred to as Fort Detroit, was constructed a few hundred yards to the north of the old fort that year.

A three-block walk north on Shelby Street from Jefferson Avenue will bring the modern visitor to the location of the newer, larger fortification, remembered by a historical marker on the side of the Detroit Bank and Trust Building (more recently a Comerica bank) at the southwest corner of Shelby and Fort streets. The new fort was loosely bounded by Lafayette Avenue on the north, Griswold on the east, West Congress on the south and Cass Avenue on the west. The United States Courthouse across Fort from the Detroit Trust building occupies a significant chunk of the land once occupied by the garrison.

The Americans never attacked the fort. It should have been surrendered with the end of the Revolutionary War in 1783, but the British hung onto it and continued to supply Indian tribes that attacked American settlers. After the Treaty of Greenville ended the Indian threat in the region, the British peacefully surrendered Fort Lernoult to American troops, led by Colonel John Francis Hamtramck, on July 11, 1796.

Fort Lernoult survived an 1805 fire that destroyed most of Detroit, including what remained of the original Fort Detroit; Fort Lernoult officially took the name of Fort Detroit at that time. That fort surrendered to the British without a shot in 1813 (during the War of 1812) and was renamed Fort Shelby after the Americans retook it that same year. American troops continued to use the structure until 1826, a year before the city tore it down. At that point, Detroit had approximately 2,000 residents, few with any recollection of Pontiac's siege or the city's French days.

Sadly, the modern visitor is left to wander the streets of a city with a rich history rivalling those of Boston or Philadelphia and French roots deeper than those of New Orleans, but one that has little to show for it in the twenty-first century.

The Charles C. Trowbridge House is the oldest documented building in the city of Detroit. It was built in 1826.

32. FORT SANDUSKY

The spot on the south shore of Sandusky Bay where the tragedy-marred eighteenth-century British stockade called Fort Sandusky once stood is one of those places where the past and the present collide, a spot where the sharp differences between the two are difficult to reconcile.

A historical marker places the fortification wiped out in 1763 by a band of Wyandots west of Cold Creek at the corner of Venice Road and Fremont Avenue, on the far west side of modern Sandusky, Ohio. It sits across the street from a restaurant-bar that proudly bills itself as "The Original Margaritaville," a local haunt that opened in 1981 and preceded Jimmy Buffett's Margaritaville chain by three years.

"Jimmy Buffett hates us," a bartender there said of the popular recording artist, "or at least his lawyers do."

It's intriguing to contemplate their "hate" against the emotions that led those Wyandots to kill 27 English intruders here over two centuries ago, if only to accentuate the differences between then and now at this seemingly benign location.

Buffett's "original" restaurant is in Key West, Florida -- you didn't really think it would be in Sandusky, did you? – but both the sign and menu for the true original feature a happy cartoon alligator lounging in a beach chair while sucking on a margarita through a straw. The business describes itself "as a longtime favorite of those looking for a fun, relaxed atmosphere."

The poor butchered British souls who occupied the fort got to this spot 250 years too early. Having this establishment near and/or sitting on the site of a fort that came to such a tragic end feels like a cruel joke on the soldiers who died here, a gruesome example of how in life, death and yes, even restaurant openings, timing is everything.

Lest anyone miss the irony of this, a replica of the fort was built in 1971 at the Cedar Point Amusement Park's Frontier Trail on the other side of Sandusky, about four miles away. The 15 soldiers and 12 traders who were massacred by a band of Pontiac's forces doubtless wouldn't have seen the amusement in this, even if the act of being remembered 250 years later is quite an honor for lost eighteenth century souls who probably couldn't fathom the presence of a modern city on the shores of Sandusky Bay let alone the concept of a modern amusement park.

Their Fort Sandusky wasn't the first in this area and it wouldn't be the last, though it arguably left the most compelling story of any of the garrisons in a region where the French and the British were in fierce compensation for a trade presence for many years.

The Wyandots under Chief Orontony or Nicholas established a camp on the north shore of Sandusky Bay in 1739, at the south end of a two-mile portage across a narrow peninsula between Lake Erie and the bay. This popular route became known as the "De Lery Portage" and was designed to avoid a hazardous 50-mile water route around Marblehead Peninsula. Fulton Street in modern Port Clinton traces the portage route today.

The English offered better trade goods at better prices than the French, and Nicholas invited British traders to his camp. By 1745 they had erected a fortified blockhouse and trading post called Fort Sandoski at the southern end of this portage.

Nicholas called together other tribes in 1747 and tried to put together an alliance to attack Fort Detroit and other French forts in the region and drive them out, but the plan never came to fruition. So when a group of French trappers unaware of his hostility arrived at Fort Sandoski and attempted to trade, Nicholas had them seized and tomahawked. Word reached Fort Detroit of Nicholas' intentions and the French sent an additional 150 troops to the fort, and in 1748 the French commandant decided to forcefully eject Nicholas and the English traders from the compound.

To avoid an impending disaster, Nicholas ordered the buildings at his village dismantled and the stockade and trading post burned down, then led 119 of his warriors and their families to a new home in Illinois.

The portage remained important, however, and the British rebuilt the fort on the same site in 1750. Having an English fort in the region again didn't sit well with the French, who in 1751 marched troops from Fort Detroit and regained the site from the fleeing English traders who deserted it.

A fat obelisk erected in 1912 by the Ohio Archaeological and Historical Society at the end of Fulton Street a short distance from the water marks the site of the fort, which the French apparently coveted only to keep it out of British hands. (To mark the portage, the society erected a similar stone marker at the other end of Fulton Street near the lakeshore.) Even after they had it back, the French apparently believed Fort Sandoski was too isolated from land routes to be of much value, and the fortification was found in ruins in August, 1754, a mere three years after they had taken it.

French officers apparently spied a better location for a fort to the southwest on the south shore of Sandusky Bay, where Sieur Gouin had been operating a trading post near the mouth of Pickerel Creek. They constructed a fortification near the trading post in 1754 and called it Fort Junandat (pronounced in French as "Wyandot.") It took its name from a nearby Wyandot village. Today this is part of the 3,200-acre Pickerel Creek Wildlife Area that bridges Townsend and Riley townships in Sandusky County. Most of that area has been restored to wetland with the remainder in woods, brush, and native grassland, and probably doesn't look much different than it did Fort Junandat's days. But the exact location where the fort/trading post stood likely has been reclaimed by Sandusky Bay, a victim of shoreline erosion and higher water levels. The remains of short-lived fort are likely buried in the sediments near the mouth of Pickerel Creek, off-shore from the wildlife area.

Trade took precedence over the military at Fort Junandat, which stood at the apex of Indian foot trails. A few French families located here and it may be the site of the first white baby born within the modern limits of the state of Ohio. But France's military setbacks in its ongoing war with Britain guaranteed that its importance to the region would be short-lived. The British captured Fort Duquesne (on the future site of Pittsburgh) after the French abandoned it in 1758, and when the British arrived at Fort Junundat they found that it had also been abandoned in advance of their arrival. They burned the empty fort and saw no reason to establish one of their own here.

That changed when the war ended in 1760. Major Robert Rogers stressed the importance of a having a fort in the Sandusky Bay region to serve as a communication link to Fort Pitt and other English forts to the east, and British commander Sir Jeffrey Amherst ordered one built. Lieutenant Elias Meyer scouted the area and wrote on September 1, 1761, that he had found a suitable location for blockhouse. It sat next to a spot where a cold-water creek entered the bay – today's Cold Creek. It also lay three miles from a village the Indians called Canoutout (at the site of the modern town of Castalia), where all of the traders loaded and unloaded their goods for Fort Detroit. Meyer quickly began work on a new fortification, 10 miles to east of old Fort Junandat.

Meyer and his soldiers completed the new fort by the end of November and christened it Fort Sandusky. Meyer remained in command at the post until the following July, when he received news of a severe illness in his family and requested a leave to go home. Ensign Christopher Pauli took charge of the post in his absence.

With the French and English no longer at war, this seemed like a relatively uneventful move for everyone but Pauli, who must have been thrilled to have command of his own 16-soldier post at the age of 24. And indeed, it might have been no more than a personal milestone if Pontiac hadn't been stirring up anger against the British and creating a confederacy of Indian tribes that he hoped would drive the English from the territory.

The following spring the Ottawa chief conceived a plan to launch a wave of surprise attacks on the chain of British forts in the West – Detroit, Pitt, Michilimackinac, Presque Isle, Sandusky, et. al. Fort Detroit never fell; by contrast, Pauli and his men were caught completely unaware by the Indians' surprise attack. At one point, Pontiac's forces controlled nine of the eleven British forts in the Ohio Valley.

The Fort Sandusky attack came on May 16, 1763. A large party of Indians showed up at the gate of fort and told the sentry that they wanted to council with Pauli. The Indians hadn't requested a council in a couple of weeks and the ensign assumed that they came with their usual request – more ammunition for hunting. Pauli was surprised when he got to the gate and found not just a handful of local Wyandot chiefs under Big Jaw but more than forty Indians, including a couple of chiefs he recognized as Ottawas.

Big Jaw greeted Pauli with a smile and a warm handshake and asked for a council, which the ensign agreed to within limits; the fort's council house was small and couldn't accommodate so many Indians. The others would have to wait outside. Big Jaw said he understood, and while Pauli led a party that included Big Jaw and a half-dozen chiefs into the council house, he noticed that maybe 20 members of the party had entered the gates and were milling about the fort.

Pauli and the chiefs smoked tobacco for several minutes in the council house when one of the chiefs near the door saw something outside, stiffened and gave a signal to the others. With that all of the chiefs dropped their pipes and those nearest Pauli seized him. The surprised ensign yelled for help and struggled furiously, but no one responded to his call. When he tried to yell again, one of the chiefs struck a glancing blow on his temple with a small war club, and while he tried to regain his senses the Indians tightly tied his wrists with strips of rawhide.

Even in a mental fog, he heard the sound of shrieks and grunts coming from outside the council house. When his captors dragged him out into the open, he saw the bodies of many of his soldiers, lying in pools blood, some with their throats cut and others with their skulls split and all with their scalps gone. The chiefs led him out of the fort toward the spot where Sergeant Delton had been tending his garden when the Indians arrived, and Pauli briefly hoped he had escaped. A few seconds later, he saw Delton lying in his garden face down, his throat split and his head scalped. On the way out, he also passed the blood-covered bodies of several traders.

Pauli spent the rest of the day in a painful daze, tied to stake near the shore while the Indians loaded the fort's provisions onto canoes. Night had fallen by the time they untied him and two Ottawas dragged him to a canoe. They told him that he would be taken to Detroit along with all of the scalps that had been taken. The commanding officer of Fort Sandusky would be presented to Pontiac and burned at the stake.

After the canoes paddled a goodly distance into the bay, Pauli could see flames rising from the shoreline where Fort Sandusky was burning. He inquired about the number of scalps taken and received an answer he didn't want to hear: 27. Besides him, there had been 15 soldiers and 12 traders in camp. Only Pauli had survived.

Pauli's tale hadn't reached its conclusion however, and nor had that of Fort Sandusky. Although his captors had planned to burn Pauli at the stake after they reached Pontiac's camp near Fort Detroit, an Indian woman there who had lost her husband decided to take him as her replacement mate. This stroke of good fortune bought time and eventually enabled him to escape to the safety of the fort. In the meantime, a detachment of men under Lieutenant Abraham Cuyler en route to Detroit was attacked by Indians and the survivors fled to Fort Sandusky for safety. They found the charred ruins of the fort instead, and hastened back to Fort Niagara and reported their discovery.

Two months later on July 26, Captain James Dalyell's force of 260 men on another relief mission to Fort Detroit arrived at the ruins of Fort Sandusky. Angered by the discovery of decomposing bodies amidst the burned remnants of the fort, Dalyell decided to stay a few days and punish the Indians responsible for the act. Dalyell's troops subsequently marched three miles to Big Jaw's village of Canoutout. The lodges were empty because the Indians had spied the British boats in the bay, but Dalyell ordered his soldiers to burn them down and set fire to the adjacent fields of standing corn. Dalyell's troops then continued their journey northward for Fort Detroit.

Dalyell's life ended there with 59 of his men when he persuaded the fort's commander to permit him to make a reckless night-time raid of Pontiac's camp at Bloody Run. Ensign Pauli participated in this battle and survived.

In the spring of 1764, the British were back at the fort's ruins. This time it was Colonel John Bradstreet with a force of over 1,180 men, who set out from Albany, New York, for Detroit with orders to punish the Indians wherever they appeared in arms. Bradstreet's troops camped near the ruins of Fort Sandusky, where the local Indians agreed with terms that had just been offered to other tribes at Presque Isle. Among those terms: if any Indian killed an Englishman he would be delivered at Fort Pitt for trial, and if one tribe violated the peace the others would unite in punishing them. Bradstreet spared the Wyandot villages from his attack, but many historians believe that Bradstreet had been duped, that the Indians weren't authorized to speak for other tribes and merely told the British colonel what he wanted to hear.

Either way, the local Indians escaped punishment and Bradstreet and his troops left for Detroit. In August, he sent Ensign Pauli back to Sandusky with a small detachment of troops with orders to rebuild the fort and meet with the Delawares and Shawnees who had promised to bring prisoners there for release. The tribes came but not with prisoners; they promptly captured Pauli and his men.

When word of this duplicity reached an embarrassed Bradstreet, he commanded a contingent that reached the ruins and demanded the return of Pauli and his men. The Indians refused, and held onto their prisoners until Colonel Bouquet sent word to them that he planned to march a huge army to the region and destroy all of the Indian villages if they weren't returned.

On that threat, Pauli and his men (and other prisoners) were finally released; Pauli would eventually rise to the rank of captain before dying while on duty in the West Indies in 1778. But Fort Sandusky, at least the one on west bank of Cold Creek, would never rise again. A final Fort Sandusky would be built on the west bank about 10 miles upstream of the Sandusky River from the bay in 1812, as a supply depot for the Americans. It was subsequently renamed Fort Stephenson. The British were the attackers in a battle fought there in August, 1813, which shows how much things had changed in the fifty years since the Indians had surprised and massacred Pauli's 15 troops and 12 British traders in 1763.

Other than that historical marker in the little island in the street across from the parking lot for The Original Margaritaville, there is no visible sign of the fort or of the gruesome things that happened here. In light of the violent history, I asked the bartender if there had ever been any ghostly events around here.

"Here, yes, but I don't know about over there, where the sign is," she said.

I explained that the fort may or may not have been exactly where the sign stood, that even a small fort could take up a lot of ground and some of the fort may have in fact been located right where we were talking. From her expression, it seemed clear that thought had never occurred to her.

"Some strange things do happen here sometimes," she said. "The lights go off and on. . . sometimes we turn off all the lights at night when we close and they're all on in the morning. A man was murdered or committed suicide in the parking lot years ago, and when that stuff happens, we joke about it and call it the 'Margaritaville ghost."

Ghosts.

33 CRAWFORD-BATTLE ISLAND

There's a small sign on U.S. 23 between Upper Sandusky and Carey with an arrow that directs the driver onto a road to the "Col Crawford Monument." There's been a sign there since my first drive on that mostly four-lane highway between Columbus and Findlay in the mid-1970s, and I have a clear recollection of the first time my curiosity proved stronger than my desire to get to my destination in good time.

The road led to an intersection with Ohio Route 199 that lies a quarter mile north of U.S. 23. A small brick church on the left with a Crawford United Methodist sign told me that the church and a handful of houses at this crossroads bear the soldier's name. On my right stood a small park with a pair of weary wooden shelter houses and a brick monument. My razor-sharp senses deduced this to be a tribute to Colonel William Crawford. The monument included three plaques, two of which listed all of the organizations (American Legion and Veterans of Foreign War posts, Daughters of the American Revolution, etc.) who had financed the monument. The middle plaque offered a brief bio of Crawford and a separate historical marker off to the side noted that Crawford was burned at the stake by the Indians on June 11, 1782, a half mile to the northeast "in revenge for the massacre of the Christian Moravian Indians by Williamson's earlier expedition."

A half-mile to the northeast?

The road that brought me there (county road 29) crossed Ohio 199 and continued northeast, so heading that way seemed like a no-brainer. With no reason to believe I would find anything at all, it pleased me to discover a small stone marker in the weeds on the side of the road, one which indicated that Crawford was burned at the stake near Tymochtee Creek not far from this site. A one-lane gravel road directly across from the marker split the farm fields in search of the creek maybe 1000 feet away. Maybe because I hadn't seen a soul – or a "No Trespassing" sign -- since leaving 23, I went for it. Sure enough, a pillar of gray Berea sandstone eight feet high that memorialized Crawford's death lay near the end of that lane, a memorial that had been erected in August, 1877, to mark the spot where Crawford endured two hours of gruesome torture before he died.

I climbed out of the car and took a close look at the monument, which vaguely noted that Crawford "was burned by the Indians in this valley," and then took a short walking tour of the area around it. It's hard to describe how I felt at that moment. In a noisy, hectic, in-your-face world, this isolated spot would have been a terrific location for a picnic or a nap. A soft breeze rustled the leaves in several large nearby trees, the beginning of woods that hid the creek a short walk away. For some reason, probably because I had recently read about the horrifying death Crawford suffered there, the silence seemed more unnerving than peaceful. After five or 10 minutes of trying to visualize a dying Crawford with his ears cut off and his body charred by fire, jabs by sizzling pokers and close-range blasts of gunpowder, I retreated to the car and used that little gravel lane to make it back to the twentieth century.

Not until the car reached 23 and my mind had caught up with it did it clear enough to form questions that I normally would have asked myself back there. Was that really the spot where Crawford was burned or, like so many monuments, was that just a convenient place to put it? I laughed at my own question. Convenient? That place?

My mind also returned to the sign that led me there. Which "monument" did the people who erected that sign want tourists to visit, the one in the park, where probably about 90 percent of the curiosity seekers stop, or the real one a half mile up the road? It occurred to me that state highway department officials who authorized that little sign on U.S. 23 probably didn't even know that sandstone marker was back there by the creek, and may not have cared if they did. The sign probably resulted from the lobbying of the organizations that paid for the monument. For highway department officials and even most of the people who managed to get a park and two shelter houses built in Crawford's honor that was probably good enough.

Fast forward to July, 2018, when I returned to the little park and retraced my route to the Crawford burn site. The stone marker on the side of road was gone, and the only gravel road to the creek that I saw bore a sign that pointed to the Crawford-Richey cemetery. The little road looked familiar. The end of it didn't. There was the Crawford monument, maybe 100 feet east of the cemetery, but, uh, where did that cemetery come from? That cemetery wasn't here the last time. Had someone moved the monument? They sure didn't move the cemetery. Could it be that my first visit didn't make the impression on me I thought it did? Maybe that cemetery was there and I just didn't remember it.

A closer look at the monument confirmed that at least the monument had changed: it was "erected by the Wyandot County Patriotic Citizens, August 27, 1994." Unless the old one had been defaced by Crawford haters --- and it hadn't been that long ago that a Crawford statue in Bucyrus, Ohio, had been beheaded – or the old one still sat somewhere not next to a cemetery, it didn't make a lot of sense.

My first indication that my memory was dead-on came when I read a paper that Reverend Parker S. Brown wrote for the *Western Pennsylvania Historical Magazine* in 1982 titled "The Search for the Colonel William Crawford Burn Site: An Investigative Report." Included is a map with his research that shows the location of the cemetery, the location of a long-gone brick house that old-timers remembered on the farm there and the location of the monument that I had apparently seen 40 years before. According to Parker's map, it was near the creek, but it was maybe a hundred yards southwest of the cemetery.

A few days later, Tom Hill, a former trustee for the Wyandot County Historical Society and the author of two books on local history, filled me in.

"The owners of the property where the old monument was just shut everything off," Hill said. "The guy who owns it is from around Findlay, Ohio, and I think their son was living there and he's was just real nasty about people walking back there. So the historical society decided to put up a new one so the public could get to it, and now they say that monument is actually closer to the burn site than the other one was."

There would be delicious irony in that, if true. But it has since become clear to me that a debate has been raging over the "exact" site of Crawford's execution for almost 200 years, the reason Brown wrote his 24-page analysis back in the 1980s.

People have always been fascinated with the story and early visitors to this area wanted to be taken to the site where Crawford was executed. For years, the Wyandots who lived in the area, some of whom had even been present on the day he died, were happy to show them where it happened, right down to the spot on the ground where no grass would grow.

Nineteenth century historians were also intrigued by the story, which merits retelling before we get back to the late twentieth century and the two granite monuments, one public and one not, that may or may not mark the place a 60-year old Crawford paid a high price for Colonel David Williamson's heinous actions at Gnadenhutten

After Williamson's troops of Pennsylvania militia murdered 96 peaceful Delaware Moravian Indians at Gnadenhutten on March 8, 1782, angry tribes in western Pennsylvania and the Ohio country began killing settlers and their families in retribution for it. To counter that, George Washington asked his longtime friend and fellow soldier William Crawford to come out of retirement and lead a combined force of Virginias and Pennsylvanians to quell the Indian uprising in a campaign against the Sandusky towns, the apparent source of many of the attacks.

A mounted force of just under 500 men assembled near the Ohio River at Mingo Bottom, the present site of Mingo Junction, Ohio, and departed for points west on May 24, 1782. Crawford was "chosen" to command the force over Williamson, even though Williamson was a popular choice among many of the militiamen.

Their route took them past the deserted ruins of Schoenbrunn, sister Christian village of Gnadenhutten. Crawford's men ignored his orders and

rummaged all over the place, trying to grab anything they could find of value. His scouts shot at and missed two Indians caught observing them there and Crawford knew then that he wouldn't take the Sandusky towns by surprise. In fact, the Delaware and Wyandot spies kept a close eye on the troops' progress, saw them reach the headwaters of the Sandusky River and begin following the left bank along a trail that led directly to their villages.

On June 4, the militia's route took it through a place where guide John Stover said the principal Wyandot village, Half King's Town, had been located. They found it deserted. Fearing an ambush ahead, this made the scouts and many of the men nervous, but the troops pressed on

CRAWFORD WAS PROBABLY EXECUTED NOT FAR FROM THE SITE OF THIS MARKER.

for three miles. Here they found several fine bubbling springs and Crawford decided to pause for lunch so he could have another council with his officers and consider the danger that might lie ahead. These springs, covered over now, were located in the heart of today's Upper Sandusky in front of the Elks Lodge at the intersection of Fourth and Wyandot streets.

With Major John Rose leading an advance detachment of two dozen men, the army continued three miles through shoulder-high prairie grasses to a large island of trees in the distance. Rose's men reached the other side of the grove and continued on an Indian path (the Scioto Trail) that led to Fort Detroit for a mile and half, when he spotted three Indian horsemen ahead. The Indians spotted the white men about the same time and fled; Rose's men pursued them for a few minutes, then turned back, wary of an ambush. Their intuition was correct. As soon they stopped, a huge force of Delawares and Wyandots poured out of a hidden ravine and charged after them. Fortunately for the Americans, they were just out of the range of fire and managed to make it the three miles back to the grove without losing any men.

Crawford's main force had just reached the grove of trees when it heard the sound of gunfire and realized what had happened. He ordered his men to spread out and defend the perimeter of the woodland. The Indians saw this and also spread out and attacked from all angles, bobbing up and down in the high prairie grass to fire and leave little target for their enemies. So began the battle of Sandusky. It is commemorated with the Battle Island monument on a road called the Tarhe Trail that used to be county road 47 (it's now 367) and dead ends in U.S. 23. It lies directly across 23 from a Harley Davidson dealership at the U.S. 30 exit.

"A lot of people come down and see where the monument is for the battle and think it was right there," Hill said. "The actual battle was actually spread out pretty good. I think it was out towards the field (to the northwest) a little more, because you can see part of a rise."

As the day wore on, it became apparent that the Indian force numbered between 600 and 1,000, a sign that the tribes had been preparing for this. That night, the Indians built more than 50 fires around the grove, leaving dark only the trail to the south that the army had used to get there and an expansive cranberry bog to the southwest of the grove.

Crawford's soldiers were exhausted as the battle resumed the following morning and continued all that day. By then it had become clear that the warriors had the grove surrounded, and the Americans would have to break out and retreat if they were to survive. Crawford came up with a plan for a full retreat to the south beginning at nine o'clock, which likely would have been more successful if one hard-headed captain named John Hardin hadn't been convinced that they would be retreating into an ambush. Unbeknownst to Crawford, he gathered his own men together and took them to the west, away from the main body of troops. When Crawford discovered this, he left his troops and set off in pursuit of Hardin in an attempt to bring them back in line; in the meantime, Hardin's men came under heavy fire, the sounds of which threw the entire retreat into confusion. Unaware of where the gun shots came from, men began to peel off into splinter groups and search for their own route of escape.

Realizing that the damage had been done and it was too late to stop Hardin, Crawford turned around and eventually caught up with the backside of his troops. But for some reason he deduced that his son, son-in-law and nephew were not with their unit and he returned to the grove to look for them. During the course of this search, he came across Dr. John Knight, who had lingered to treat dying troops, and joined up with him in an attempt to escape the knoll from the best route possible. With the Indians now in pursuit of the main body of soldiers, Crawford and Knight decided their best chance of survival lay to the north, opposite of the retreating army.

Meanwhile, the rear guard had fallen into a state of confusion. Upon encountering hostile fire, many of the men veered off into that cranberry marsh. Their horses soon became useless, and they continued on foot, slogging through waist-deep water and muck that at times reached their necks.

"If you're standing at the monument and you look a little north and left of that, you can see where the cranberry marsh was," Hill said. "When I was a kid, none of that was farmed because it was so wet. And over the years they put so much plowing into that and farmed it, but there's still spots where it stays wet all the time. So when you read the story and it says some of the men took off into the cranberry marsh and the direction they took off, you can kind of get a feeling of where that grove of trees was."

Crawford and Knight adopted a routine after they escaped from the battle site; they would go one mile east and then one mile south and continued to alternate those paths, hoping to eventually run into the main body of troops while avoiding the Indians. On June 6, they encountered four of their fleeing troops on foot led by Captain John Biggs who joined them. The next day, the group errored in choosing the wrong trail, one that led to the village of Wingenund, a Delaware chief who had been one of the leaders at the battle. Before the soldiers realized their mistake, a group of warriors captured the six Americans and took them to Wingenund's camp, which was located a half-mile northeast of the present Leesville, Ohio, and nine and a half miles east of the current city of Bucyrus.

This was the beginning of the end for Crawford. He knew Wingenund from his visits to Fort Pitt and the two had been friendly, but the Delaware chief said he couldn't help him now. He spoke of the Moravians who had been killed and said that even if Crawford hadn't been there that day, he had done nothing to see that Williamson was punished. He also reminded Crawford that he led this campaign to the Sandusky villages now. He said that because Williamson hadn't been captured, Crawford must pay for Williamson's crimes.

After three days there, Crawford, Knight and nine other prisoners were told they were being taken to Pipe's Town, the village of a Delaware chief called Captain Pipe (or Hopocan) on Tymochtee Creek. During a stop at New Half King's town, near the present village of Smithville, Ohio, Crawford saw Indian agent Simon Girty and asked him to try to get him released. Girty had known Crawford for a long time and said he would try, but he didn't think it would do any good. Some historians believe that he tried to buy Crawford's release but the Indians made it clear they had no intention of releasing him. After they reached Pipe 's Town, a short distance east of the monument and cemetery on county road 29 on farm property at the northeast corner of its intersection with county road 106, Girty supposedly tried again and Pipe let Girty know he had heard enough.

"We will free him only if you are willing to take his place for the burning," he said. A defeated Girty looked away.

Last that afternoon, Crawford and Knight were marched less than three-quarters of a mile to a bluff overlooking the Tymochtee Creek, where a fire burned in a clearing among white oak trees and several hundred people had gathered. A tree that had been stripped of its branches and cut off 15 feet from the ground stood in the center of it.

After some words from Captain Pipe, several warriors approached Crawford and stripped him of his clothes, with his wrists tied behind him with a length of rawhide. They led him to the post and the hooked the rawhide to a length of rope attached the pole. The rope left him with enough leeway to permit him to stray from the tree a few feet or circle the tree once a twice before having to shift directions. The fire burned six or seven yards from the post to which Crawford was tied.

Several chiefs spoke before Hopocan, who blamed Crawford for the deaths of the Christian Indians at Gnadenhutten and called for the execution to begin. With that a warrior broke from the assemblage, drew a knife from his belt, jerked Crawford's head down and quickly sliced off both of his ears. The spectators shrieked in joy as the blood rushed from both sides of his head; that in turn prompted numerous warriors bearing flintlock rifles loaded with only gunpowder to rush up to him and fire blasts at his body from close range, scorching his skin. Approximately 70 rounds were fired this way, leaving his body – including his genitals – scarred with dozens of painful wounds from the burning gunpowder.

Next, men, women and children approached the fire and each collected a slender hickory pole six feet in length that had one end burning. They began thrusting these at the officer, burning holes in his skin from his head to his feet, going for especially sensitive areas such as his nipples, genitals, rectum and armpits. He tried to stumble away and he couldn't escape, his reddened and blistered skin now blackened and curled in many places. Some squaws scooped up hot coals from the fire into carriers made of wide pieces of bark and heaved the coals on him. Once they reached the ground, they formed a floor of glowing embers and hot ash that scorched his bare feet with every step. As Dr. Knight watched all of this in horror, Girty told him that the same fate awaited him, not that day and place but at a Shawnee village two days later.

At one point, Crawford begged for Girty to shoot him through the heart, but the trader could do nothing but watch. After about two hours of this torture, Crawford finally fell at the base of the tree post and a frenzied warrior ran up and scalped him. That elicited a loud moan from Crawford, which pleased the crowd. With that, a Cherokee woman scooped some more hot coals and dumped them on his skull where his scalp had been. Again, he moaned and this time he struggled to his feet, an act of defiance that resulted in the resumption of the poking and prodding of his charred body with those sizzling pokers. Just before nightfall, he stopped stumbling and fell to the ground dead. After some words from Wingenund, two warriors stepped forward, grabbed his charred body by the ankles and threw it into the fire. The cheering Indians piled firewood on top of it until it was completely covered, thus ending the story of Colonel Williams Crawford and beginning an infatuation with his burning that has endured for over two centuries.

In an 1873 book about Crawford's Sandusky expedition, C.W. Butterfield did several interviews, consulted numerous sources and devoted several pages to both the execution and the burn site. Most of these sources put the burn site on the east bank of the creek on land then owned by Daniel Hoge; there are enough discrepancies in the various reports to cast some doubt on the exact location of it. At least one credible early witness – a former slave named Black Betty who had been sold with her to a mother to a Delaware warrior who had fought in the Battle of Sandusky – said the burn site was on the west bank of the creek, in a spot that would have been nearly opposite the new monument and the cemetery.

When the Pioneer Association of Wyandot County erected the Crawford monument, local historians likely used Butterfield's research to pin down the site. But local farmer Emil Schlup, whose father had been shown the site by friendly Wyandots, said around 1900 that the site for the monument was chosen because it was accessible, "a public place." This makes sense: an annual Pioneer's Picnic was held near the site until 1935, when interest in it waned.

But interest in the burn site itself never ceased. After doing extensive research on the Crawford expedition itself, Parker S. Brown wrote his 24-page account on the burn site in 1982. He concluded that the actual burn site was on the east side of the creek, in a field southwest of the old monument and the road which led to the old sandstone pillar. Like Butterfield and others before him, Brown intended this to be the last word on the subject; author Allan W. Eckert even accepted it as such in the end notes to the 1995 book *That Dark and Bloody River*. But it wasn't.

In 2007, Charles Ed Faber wrote an extensive piece in the *Bucyrus Telegraph-Forum* disputing Brown's conclusions, even though he wrote that he had tremendous respect for him as both a researcher and friend. He noted that Brown had dismissed two early and reliable sources who had placed the burn site on the west side of the creek, William Walker and Black Betty, and that "this location is clearly marked with an X in the *Wyandot County Atlas of 1879* and on an E.B. Finley's map enclosed in a letter to (Wyandot historian William E.) Connelley, and drawn from informants at the Pioneer Picnic.

Using Brown's own criteria, he places the burn site a quarter of a mile northeast, across the Tymochtee, and several hundred yards west of the Old Springville/Detroit Trail: now a cultivated field. . . private property, where alternately corn and soybeans are grown."

I found that county atlas on the Internet, and sure enough, there's the X, which may explain why the monument's erection on the eastern bank occurred, as Brown noted, "over the objections of such pioneers as George James."

After countering Brown's analysis, Faber concluded with a joke about those trying to find the exact location of the burn site. In doing so, he may not have anticipated the eventual consideration of new arbiter in this debate -- modern science.

"A couple of years ago, a geologist from Kent State came down and I showed him around," Hill said. "He had done all of these maps and aerial maps and all kinds of stuff. And he wanted to come down and do ground penetrating radar and find the actual sites, but I've never heard anything from him. He said he'd try to get a grant to do it, and you know what that's like.

"Crawford's bones are probably all destroyed, but you could still find charcoal and stuff like that. That's been an argument forever because nobody knows for sure. Nothing is final until you actually find it."

34 FALLEN TIMBERS-FORT MIAMIS

When I had last visited the Fallen Timbers battle site in the 1980s, the view of the rough terrain on the Maumee river-side plain where Anthony Wayne's momentous victory lodged firmly in my mind. I remember trying to imagine what it must have looked like with those tangled, storm-ravaged trees that gave the location its name, with Indian warriors crouched behind the trunks and branches and Wayne's army somehow driving them off the field.

As good as that experience seemed to me at the time, it was mostly a lie. It turns out that the ground before me wasn't the battlefield at all; that information had apparently come from legend or at least a map of a soldier who wasn't there on that fateful day. But hey, this is a risk we always take when viewing a spot where history is purported to have occurred. Think of how embarrassed the well-meaning folks who planned and built that beautiful monument in 1929 would be to know that the battlefield that paved the way for the Treaty of Greenville and opened up settlement in most of what became Ohio wasn't where they thought it was.

Anyone visiting the area today can go on a mile-and-a-half hike around the real site of the battle, which lies on the other side of four-lane U.S. 24, almost a mile from where the Fallen Timbers Monument and the supposed battlefield lay. If you take the Fallen Timbers Lane exit from U.S. 24, just west of Interstate 475 and south of Maumee, Ohio, you come to a stop sign with arrows point in opposite directions, one way to the monument and the other way to the battlefield. If you're inclined to think logically and don't know the story, that seems a little odd.

While pondering your choices, you may also notice an impressive one million square foot shopping mall called The Shops at Fallen Timbers off to your right, which is also part of the story. Historians say the mall site was a less significant part of the battlefield than the preserved 187-acre site but still a part of it nonetheless, a disturbing thought that is only made palatable when you discover that at one point the guy who sold the property to mall developers also had an option on the battlefield property that we can tour today.

For that reason, we all owe a debt of thanks to Dr. G. Michael Pratt, a Heidelberg College anthropology professor who has since become dean of regional campuses for Miami University. His research of firsthand accounts of the battle told him that the Fallen Timbers battlefield wasn't where legend – and a monument -- said it was. For several weeks in the summer of 1995, Pratt and a group of history-lovers with metal detectors scoured the field where he believed it to be and found more than 300 musket balls, rifle shot, uniform buttons, and even a smooth-bore bayonet.

The property, owned by the city of Toledo and leased to a farmer, had been under consideration for residential and commercial development. In 1999, with the help of state and federal legislators, the site earned National Historic Site status, and $5.5 million in local, state, and federal funds was raised to purchase the plot in 2001.

Toledo Metroparks raised more than half of the $1.1 million needed to build a bridge with a walkway over U.S. 24 from the monument to the battlefield in 2006, a creative solution that makes it almost seem as if it all had been designed this way. But it only seems that way until you cross the busy four-lane highway and realize that the battlefield isn't right in front you. A half-mile walk to the beginning of a mile-and-a-half battlefield walk wouldn't have bothered the soldiers, but it probably isn't a welcome surprise to most non-hikers. Fortunately, most of us will probably drive.

The case can be made that once everyone got over the initial shock of having the battle site wrong for 200 years it all worked out for the better. Now history buffs can walk through the woods and really imagine what it must have been like when small trees and weeds were growing through those fallen timbers and warriors crouched there. Toledo Metroparks also added a beautiful visitor center a short distance from the beginning and end of the battlefield loop. It was locked on a July Saturday morning when I visited; a sign on the window indicated that the facilities were in use for a private party when the building was empty. That's a small thing, but it struck me that when you had been advertising a battle site that really wasn't forever, a little truth telling even on something as simple as a closed visitor's center might be a good idea.

Not that anyone needs a visitor's center. When a battlefield lost for almost two centuries turns back an invasion of enemies bearing names such as P.F. Chang and J.C. Penney that should be good enough for any preservationist who has been on the losing end of one of these fights. The end result -- the Fallen Timbers Battlefield and Fort Miamis National Historic Site – is impressive collaboration. It adroitly managed to bring together three

THIS SHOWS THE PROXIMITY OF THE ORIGINAL MEMORIAL, BOTTOM CENTER, TO THE BATTLEFIELD, TOP RIGHT, AND THE SHOPPING MALL, LEFT.

elements with separate owners: the Ohio History Connection owns the monument site, Toledo Metroparks owns the battlefield, and the city of Maumee owns Fort Miamis, the British fortification five miles north where the Indians fled after the battle.

Those interested in a complete history of the battle should probably start their day at a location five miles south that isn't an official part of the project: riverside property opposite the massive Roche de Bout (also called Roche de Boeuf) outcropping of limestone in the Maumee River. Wayne's army of 2,000 troops reached that spot and camped on August 18, 1794, two nights before the battle. The rock, a sacred meeting site for Native Americans, reputedly was where Little Turtle, Tarhe the Crane and Blue Jacket met to plan their strategy against Wayne's Legion and also in earlier battles when the Americans were led by Josiah Harmar and Arthur St. Clair.

The rock is still there and noticeable under one of the concrete legs of an old interurban bridge. When the bridge was built in 1908, the move created a storm of controversy because builders destroyed one-third of the rock in the process. The crumbling bridge is abandoned and a frequent subject for photographers. Sadly, the rock doesn't look much like the landmark that drew the Indians there for war councils or Wayne's troops saw when they camped before the most important battle of their lives. That is clear from old drawings and postcards that show the rock formation before progress dropped a bridge on top of it.

After the soldiers set up camp, Major William Price returned with his battalion of scouts and reported that judging from the ground and the displaced foliage a large body of Indians had apparently laid an ambush for Wayne's legion.

All signs pointed toward the Indian confederacy having amassed a huge force for a battle, so Wayne ordered everyone to build a formidable breastwork called Fort Deposit on the morning of the 19th. This would hold all of the supplies that the men could not carry on their persons, a move that Lieutenant John Bowyer noted would mean "the men may be light for action."

A historical marker near the entrance of Farnsworth Metropark just south of Waterville and Roche de Bout notes that Wayne built Fort Deposit "near here" on August 19 and that he left Captain Zebulon Pike -- father of the well-known explorer for whom Pike's Peak is named -- and 200 soldiers to guard the equipment when the army left for the fateful battle the following day. (Famous Ottawa chief Pontiac had his village on Missionary Island directly across the river from the park from 1764 until his death in 1769.)

The rest of Wayne's army of 1,700 regulars and Kentucky militia continued its march north on the morning of the 20th, a few days after the Indian confederacy had expected it. The Indians had formed a line in the trees on the 18th, but the Americans failed to appear. They formed a line in the timber on August 19 and stayed from morning until nightfall and still saw no action. Many of the warriors had eaten only an evening meal for the past three days, adhering to a belief that being wounded in the bowels on an empty stomach offers a better chance of survival. The chiefs held a council and decided to allow the warriors to eat breakfast that morning, a concession that may have replenished warriors weakened by hunger when Wayne's attack finally came.

The Legion left Fort Deposit between seven and eight o'clock in the morning, blazing a route that Anthony Wayne Parkway mostly follows today. (Anthony Wayne Trail, through Waterville, joins up with it north of town.) Descriptions by General James Wilkinson of "deep, steep and short ravines, running at nearly right angles to the general course" of the bluffs and by Lieutenant John Clark of "the thickness of the woods" say that this was no parkway.

Native American forces, numbering about 1,500, waited in an area near the foot of the rapids of the Maumee River, drawn up in the crescent formation that had overwhelmed St. Clair's army almost three years before. The Shawnees under Blue Jacket were on the left wing, with the Miamis under Little Turtle, the Delawares under Buckongahelas, the Wyandots under Roundhead and the Ottawas under Turkey Foot. The confederacy also included Ojibwas, Potawatomis, Mingoes and a British company of Canadian militiamen under Captain Alexander McKillop.

The battle began when the mounted Kentucky militiamen riding in advance of the main force were ambushed by the waiting warriors, who drove the forward line back into the Legion's main body. Wilkinson's right wing formed a single line starting near the top of the bluff overlooking the river and running north toward today's Monclova Road. Lieutenant Colonel John Hamtramck led the left wing, which moved forward in two parallel lines.

In St. Clair's defeat, the confederacy's initial assault kept the soldiers on the run and in a panic; this time, the militia and the foot soldiers regrouped and stiffened, then combined to push the Indians through that tangle of dead trees that, judging by the recent growth, had apparently been felled by a tornado a few years before. Blue Jacket had taken a defensive position here, thinking that the "fallen timbers" would slow the advance of Wayne's Legion, if needed.

It was and it didn't. The Second and Fourth sub-legions, which made up the right flank, defended against the heavy fire from Shawnee, Mingo, Delaware and other nations while First and Third sub-legions absorbed a fierce attack from the Ottawas, Wyandots and Canadians and kept coming.

According to legend, Turkey Foot climbed onto a large rock as the Indians were in retreat and attempted to rally them to victory. But he was shot and killed within seconds of climbing on top of the boulder, a sign that only further convinced the retreating tribes of the futility of their resistance. Today, the rock occupies a place near the monument, affixed to a concrete base and lying above a weathered plaque that tells the story. What it doesn't say is that the rock once occupied a spot at the base of Presque Isle Hill not far from the river, which is where just about everyone but the participants thought most of the battle had been fought.

That's not to say that the Ottawa chief, whose Indian name was Me-sa-sa, might not have tried to rally his troops from a rock, but knowing where most of the battle was really fought calls that particular rock into question. It's hard not wonder whether this was simply a rock of convenience and even if the legend itself is true.

The fighting lasted only two hours. The Americans finally drove confederacy forces from the field and into a retreat toward Fort Miamis with a bayonet charge, which Wayne had ordered in order to flush the Indians out of their positions. The battle was over so fast that not all of Wayne's troops made it into battle; Pratt told the *Toledo Blade* that his surveys and research indicated that two companies of militia, elements of Wayne's forces that were not quick enough to engage the enemy, were on the shopping mall property when the battle ended.

Casualties were relatively light for a battle which had such lasting significance: Wayne's army had 33 killed and about 100 wounded. Legion soldiers reported they found 30 to 40 dead warriors on the battlefield. Alexander McKee of the British Indian Department reported that the confederacy lost just 19 warriors and six white men and that only 400 had participated; because he had strongly encouraged this fight, it is believed that he lied to save face.

After their victories over Harmar and St. Clair, the Indians had expected to easily defeat the Americans, so the relentless push by Wayne's troops stunned them. They received another shock when they reached Fort Miamis and discovered that their British allies had closed their gates and made it clear that they had no intention of helping them. With no choice but to continue their retreat, the Indians continued twenty miles north to the mouth of Swan Creek in what is now downtown Toledo.

This betrayal proved to be a devastating blow to the Indians. The confederacy had not suffered a tremendous number of casualties so the tribes might have pressed on with their campaign against the Americans, but the rebuff from their supposed allies delivered a demoralizing jolt psychologically.

Back at Fallen Timbers, Wayne prepared his troops for an attack by the Indians. When it became clear it wasn't coming, he marched his troops the five miles to Fort Miamis. The British fort had been built earlier that year at the foot of the Maumee River rapids to defend the southern land route to Detroit, control the river traffic, and distribute food, supplies and weapons to their Native Americans allies. They constructed the fort on heavily wooded land, and after clearing the area, the British dug a series of deep trenches outside the structure to deter attacking forces. The trenches were 25 feet deep and lined with sharpened logs. Today, the fort and the logs are gone, but the trenches remain at the riverfront end of a pretty park where Michigan Avenue dead ends into River Road northeast of downtown Maumee.

Because of the depth of those trenches and drawings of the British bastion that once stood there, a visitor can quickly gauge how difficult it would have been for Wayne's army to drive the British from the fort. Wayne wanted to assess the situation and ordered his troops to set up camp less than a mile from the fort, "in full view of the British Garrison." Wilkinson recalled that the Americans were content to enjoy the success they had already achieved that day, noting "we Beat our Drums, Blowed our trumpets & went to bed."

The Legion remained camped there all the next day, much to the consternation of the fort's commander, Major William Campbell. At one point, Campbell sent Captain Spears out bearing a white flag and a message for Wayne, essentially asking why his troops were so close to "a Post belonging to His Majesty, the King of Great Britain" and concluding with "I have no hesitation on my part to say, that I know of no War existing between Great Britain and America."

This launched a series of hostile exchanges between Campbell and Wayne. The American general had received information from a spy who had walked away from the fort that a company of Canadian militia armed with British muskets and bayonets had participated in the battle, evidence that Wayne considered an act of war. But even with this information and superior numbers – about 130 British soldiers manned the fort with 14 cannons -- he knew that the British post would be difficult to take. The British were at war with France and could not afford to get into another war with the Americans, one reason they turned the Indians away in the first place.

Under the circumstances, neither commanding officer wanted to be the one to initiate a battle. So the two of them used messengers to exchange insults that would have made entertaining fodder for a cable news channel debate or a Twitter fight 200 years later, but proved to be a slow, tedious process that accomplished little now. Wayne told Campbell that he was in commission of a post "far within the well-known and acknowledged borders of the United States, and erecting a fortification in the heart of the settlement of the Indian Tribes, now at war with the United States. This, Sir, appears to be an Act of the high aggression, and destruction to the peace and interest of the Union. . . " Campbell replied that "being placed here in Command of a British Post and acting in a Military Capacity. . . that I certainly will not abandon this Post at the Summons of Any power whatever, until I receive Orders to that purpose to from those who I have the honor to serve under. . . "

During the course of this 'discussion," the Kentucky militia were in the process of burning all of the gardens around the fort, including hundreds of acres of corn "in prime, roasting ear." In his final response to Wayne, Campbell warned him and his Army not to approach the fort with range of his cannons, "without expecting the Consequences."

In response to this message, Lieutenant William Clark (who later headed the famous western journey with Meriwether Lewis) later wrote that the soldiers "for spite Burnt all the Indian Huts throughout the vicinity of the Garrison and put the finishing stroke to the Destruction of the Cornfields, Gardens, Haystacks, etc." It's difficult to imagine that scene now in an area of Maumee covered with houses, but it must have been quite a sight at the time.

Because Major Campbell had no intention of surrendering and Wayne didn't have the firepower or provisions for a siege, the American general led his army back to Fort Deposit on August 23. While en route, the soldiers saw no Indians and wondered what had happened to them, a natural reaction after they had been witness to such a large, impressive force less than a week before. What Wayne's men didn't realize is that the confederacy had collapsed in the wake of the defeat and the abandonment of their British allies in their time of need. By this time, most of the warring tribes had gone home.

The British turned Fort Miamis over the Americans with the signing of the Treaty of Greenville in 1795. American troops abandoned it in 1798. Although it had fallen into disrepair, the British returned to it during the War of 1812 and used it to house supplies while their soldiers camped outside its walls during the siege of nearby Fort Meigs in April and May 1813.

After the Americans lost a battle that became known as Dudley's Defeat, captured Kentucky soldiers were taken to Fort Miamis and forced to run a gauntlet while British officers looked on. Shawnee chief Tecumseh's intervention and call to stop the bloodshed marked the final memorable moment in the bastion's relatively short history.

It would be almost 200 years before historians would formally bring all of the elements of the Battle of Fallen Timbers and Fort Miamis together into a national historic site affiliated with the National Park Service. They did it with facts rather than legend, not always easy with tales two centuries old. The Turkey Foot Rock is a clear example of that. While some historians debated whether it is the rock and others even questioned the existence of Turkey Foot himself, a retired Ohio State University librarian and researcher with a degree in geology named Jim Murphy examined the rock and the photos of the rock that had been taken over the years. He determined that at some point between 1931 and its last move to a spot near the Fallen Timbers monument in 1953, the rock was flipped over and is now lying upside down.

Murphy wrote a detailed article about this for the *Ohio Archaeologist* in 2007, outlining his research and presenting a pictorial history of the rock that seem pretty conclusive. But his letters to the Ohio History Connection, Toledo Metroparks and the Ottawa tribe didn't accomplish much.

The Indians seemed amused that the white man's attempt to use the rock for a touristy display should end up that way and an Ohio History Connection official indicated the organization didn't have the personnel or the funds to devote the time and research necessary for proving or disproving Murphy's theory. Murphy wrote that the only reaction he received from Toledo Metroparks to his contention that the rock had been turned upside down was a flip "I wouldn't be a bit surprised."

At this point. it's hard to believe that anyone could be.

35 FORT DEFIANCE

U.S. Route 24 can take a traveler from Toledo to Fort Wayne in about an hour and forty-five minutes. It approximates the route that Anthony Wayne took in 1794 after the Battle of Fallen Timbers, with concessions to modernization that have turned it into high-speed, four-lane freeway.

One of those concessions – rerouting around a city or town to bypass congestion -- occurs near Defiance, Ohio, where Wayne stopped for three weeks after the battle to strengthen Fort Defiance before going on to the Miami settlement at conjunction of the St. Mary's and St. Joseph rivers to build the fort that took his name.

A traveler today makes that trip without realizing why Defiance is here. At the Clinton Street exit that comes nearest to the heart of the city, a modern visitor finds a Wal-Mart, a Hampton Inn, a Quality Inn, Bob Evans and Frisch's Big Boy restaurants, a Lowe's home improvement center, a Walgreens drug store and Advance Auto Parts. In other words, Defiance could be Findlay or Lima or Fremont or any of a thousand other cities or towns.

It isn't, of course. What makes Defiance special can't be seen from a four-lane highway that misses its core by over a mile. To understand that, you have to take Clinton Avenue south past Defiance College, cross a bridge over the Maumee River and take a quick left on Fort Street. Two and a half blocks on the left, just past the Defiance Public Library, is Fort Defiance Park.

The park is an amazing monument to history, but what distinguishes Defiance from all of those other places is what lies on the other side of it, the junction of the Maumee and Auglaize rivers and the beautiful scene that unfolds before your eyes. No less a source than Lieutenant William Clark, who would eventually go on a famous western expedition with Meriwether

231

Lewis, couldn't refrain from gushing in his journal on August 9, 1794, about the fort site at the point. He wrote that it lies "directly in the angle of the two Rivers, which is very accute, & elegantly Situated commanding a handsome View up & down the Rivers, the Margins of which as far as the Eye can see are covered with the most luxurient groths of Corn, interspurced with Small Log Cabbins arround all of which you observe theire are well cultivated gardens, affording almost every Species of porticultural Vegitables in the greatest abundance."

The corn and vegetables have been lost to the steady drumbeat of modernization, yet the view down the Maumee from the point remains impressive over two centuries later. It is little wonder that various tribes of Indians settled here in abundance or that legendary Ottawa chief Pontiac is believed to have been born across the Maumee from the point in a place now called Pontiac Park.

Early French traders and missionaries who wandered among the Indian tribes living in this area between 1672 and 1712 named the river that meets the Maumee "rivière à la Grande Glaize" – the river of Great Clay – and this place became The Glaize or Grand Glaize, even after General Anthony Wayne built his fort at the point on the way to the history-altering battle at Fallen Timbers.

The area served as a hunting ground for the Ottawas and other tribes. But it flourished as a place of permanent residence when French and English traders established a trading post here, around which at least seven Indian villages inhabited primarily by Shawnees, Delawares, and Miamis were located. At its peak in 1792, the combined population of these towns has been estimated at several thousand.

The Indians often brought white captives here, and two white boys taken captive in separate incidents in the years prior to the Wayne's arrival eventually wrote of their experiences. The later remembrances of nine-year-old John Brickell and eleven-year-old Oliver Spencer give us a good picture of the area before the tribes abandoned it with the coming of the American army.

Indians captured Spencer between Cincinnati and Columbia (where he lived) in July, 1792, and took him to Grand Glaize. His captors left him with Coohcoocheeh, an old woman who had been a princess with the Wolf tribe of the Iroquois and greatly esteemed as a medicine woman. Her late husband, Cokundiawtha, had been a distinguished war chief with the Mohawks and removed here with his family from the Lake Ontario region after the Americans had defeated the British in the 1770s. They settled at a Shawnee village about a mile below the mouth of the Auglaize.

Cokundiawtha suffered a bayonet wound while fighting Harmar's forces under Colonel John Hardin and Major John Wyllys at Kekionga on October 22, 1790, died during the trip home and was buried there near the banks of the Maumee. His death prompted Coohcoocheeh to choose her own residence and she erected a bark cabin on the Maumee where Spencer was taken. A granite marker in Pontiac Park directly across the Maumee from the point identifies the spot of the "Bark Cabin Home of Coohcoocheeh & Captive Spencer 1792" and lists other events under it as "Indian Grand Council 1793 and Birthplace of Indian Chief Scout Capt Anthony Shane and of Chief Occonoxee 1757 Whose Son and Son's Wife Died Here."

Shortly after Coohcoocheeh moved here, she retrieved her husband's remains from his burial site and reburied them on the side of the hill not far from her cabin, so that "she might enjoy the happiness of conversing with him." Spencer wrote that he "was buried in a sitting posture facing the west, by his side had been placed his rifle, tomahawk, knife, blanket, moccasins, and everything necessary for a hunter and a warrior; and his friends had, besides, thrown many little articles as presents into his grave, at the head of which they placed a post about four feet high, painted red and having near its top, rudely carved, the image of a face; while below was marked the number of scalps of all colors, of hair of all lengths, which on some great occasions might be seen streaming in the wind, suspended from a high pole bending over his grave, where I once counted nineteen, torn from the heads of my unfortunate countrymen."

I recount Spencer's rather disturbing picture for those wishing to walk across the road from Pontiac Park and visit the grave of Cokundiawtha, which is marked by a granite marker on the side of the hill directly across from the driveway which leads to the site of Coohcoocheeh's cabin There are no scalps flying in the wind, but the thought of them might cause the visitor to look at a granite marker that says simply "Grave of Cokundiawtha Mohawk Chief 1790" with more than the usual amount of awe.

A half-mile to the east of Pontiac Park, two stone markers and a historical sign stand across from a house with a long lawn at 1010 East River Drive. The first word on one of the stone markers is Coohcoocheeh, which might seem problematic to accuracy seekers if they haven't visited already visited the cabin site and the site of Cokundiawtha's grave. This marker also claims this as the birthplace of Ottawa chief Shabonee in 1775 and the lodge of noted Shawnee chief Blue Jacket in 1792. It might have said, but didn't, that two of Coohcoocheeh's sons lived in Blue Jacket's Town, which from all available evidence was definitely located in this vicinity. An odd-shaped boulder is also marked as "Blue Jacket's chair" and a nearby sign notes that this is the location of Winchester Camp No. 1, referring to a War of 1812 army camp. There is no mention of Oliver Spencer.

Spencer has plenty of say about just about all of this, however. He noted that "The site of the cabin was truly pleasant. It stood a few rods from the northern bank of the Maumee with its side fronting the river, on an elevated spot. . ." and continued on for several paragraphs. He described Blue Jacket ("'"the most noble in appearance of any Indian I ever saw") and described his abode ("Around his lodge were hung rifles, war clubs, bows and arrows, and other implements of war; while the skins of deer, bear, panther and otter, the spoils of the chase, furnished pouches for tobacco, or mats for seats and beds. . . ") Anyone desirous of a detailed description can find a copy of his book, The Indian Captivity of O.M. Spencer," which was popular enough when it was published in 1835 to have been reprinted many times.

For our purposes, his descriptions of other parts of the area are more interesting. He describes the area at the point (the eventual site of Fort Defiance where the park is located) as an open space," extending from the Maumee a quarter of a mile up the Auglaize, about two hundred yards in width. . . Within this opening, a few hundred yards above the point, on the steep, high bank of the Auglaize, were five or six cabins and log-houses, inhabited principally by Indian traders. The most northerly, a large hewed log-house, divided below into three apartments, was occupied as a warehouse, store and dwelling by George Ironside, the most wealthy and influential of the traders on the point. . ." Ironside married one of Coohcoocheeh's daughters.

In order followed the houses of Pirault, a French baker; John Kinzie, a Scottish silversmith who exchanged silver broaches, ear-drops and other ornaments for skins and furs; and other French and English families. (Today, Kinzie is celebrated as one of the first settlers of Chicago.) Two American prisoners, a soldier named Henry Ball and his wife Polly Meadows, were captured at St. Clair's defeat and allowed to live here and work to pay their master's ransom by boating to the Maumee rapids. A small stockade stood about 50 yards from the bank fronting Ironside's log house with two log houses inside it, one belonging to James Girty (brother of Simon Girty) and the other to Alexander McKee and Matthew Elliott, British agents who lived at Detroit.

Spencer also described an Indian village standing a mile up the Auglaize on the east side, which today would put it in the vicinity of the north end of Powell View Drive. Historians say that camp belonged to Kekewepelethy, a Shawnee leader of the Mekoche sept known to whites as Captain Johnny. Blue Jacket reportedly lived there in 1794.

Spencer also wrote that "On the south side of the Maumee for some distance below the mouth and extending more than a mile up the Auglaize to an Indian village, the low rich bottom, about three-quarters of a mile in width, was one entire field covered with corn, which, being in tassel, presented a beautiful appearance."

Spencer lived with Coohcoocheeh from July 1792 to the end of February 1793, so it seems odd that he didn't mention the grand council that representatives from various tribes held at Grand Glaize in October, 1792, in his writings.

In the wake of the Indian confederacy's victory over Arthur St. Clair, the Council met a mile south of the point to decide whether to continue the war or sue for peace while they had the advantage. A plaque at the point calls it "the largest Indian council ever held on the American continent," which Defiance city historian Randy Buchman says is a key to pinpointing the location of it.

"We know where it wasn't held, and when you get the descriptions of the conference, it really focuses in onto what is now an industrial site," Buchman said. "We use the Auglaize River as our guide, and you go about a mile down from the confluence, you cross toward the east side from the Auglaize and you go in maybe 150 or 200 feet or so and that looks like the ideal spot.

"There is a company located there that used to be called Compo, they made mufflers. . . I can't tell you the name of the company now, but it's in that general vicinity, and realize how many Indians you had and how much was going on, it occupied a large area."

B and B Molded Products has that address now, although Compo Park occupies the northwestern corner of the property. There is a lot of flat, open space there, one Buchman and other local historians believe would have been necessary for such a large event. If it merely had been a council of local Indian tribes it would have been well-attended. Aside from the Shawnee towns of Blue Jacket and Captain Johnny, Buckongahelas, Big Cat and Tetepachsit had a Delaware town on the west side of the Auglaize, a little above (south) of Captain Johnny's and possibly near the end of Riverside Drive, and Little Turtle had a Miami town on the north bank of the Maumee about four miles above the Glaize.

Scattered among these important towns were small groups of other Indians, including Nanticokes, Cherokees, and Mingoes. But Indian tribes made the trek here for the Council from hundreds of miles away.

McKee represented British interests at the council and for a week in October, pro-war factions of the Shawnee and Miami tribes and Simon Girty debated moderate factions from Six Nations tribes represented by Cornplanter and Red Jacket. In the end, the council determined the Ohio River must remain the (northern) boundary of the United States and that the forts in the Ohio country must be destroyed.

Spencer was gone by the time Anthony Wayne arrived here with his Legion to build his fort on the way to victory at Fallen Timbers in 1794. But Brickell, who had been captured near Pittsburgh in February, 1791, was still a captive of a Delaware warrior named Whingwy Pooshies or Big Cat. (Big Cat had fought against St. Clair and returned with some of the spoils of victory, including a soldiers' coat, which Brickell wore.) Brickell returned to Grand Glaize from a two-month hunting expedition along Blanchard's Fork of the Auglaize River with two warriors and another boy the night before Wayne's Legion's arrived and found it deserted. They didn't know that the residents had fled when surveyor and probable spy Robert Newman deserted Wayne's army and alerted the residents of Grand Glaize that Wayne's army was on its way. Brickell's party thought residents had probably gone to Roche de Bout down the Maumee to receive their annual presents from the British Indian Department. They camped overnight in a cornfield on a nearby island and were awakened the next morning by an alarm whoop from an Indian who announced that the American army was closing in.

"We scattered like a flock of partridges and leaving our breakfast cooking on the fire," Brickell wrote. "The Kentucky riflemen saw our smoke, and came to it, and just missed me as I passed them in my flight through the corn. They took the whole of our two months' work, breakfast, jirk, skins and all."

On August 8, the Legion established a camp in the angle formed by the conjunction of the Auglaize and Maumee and the Kentucky troops set up camp on the opposite bank of the Maumee. The next day some privates and non-commissioner officers began cutting logs for use in the construction of a fort that Wayne had decided to build there months before.

Six days later, with the fort nearing completion, Wayne penned a boastful letter to Secretary of War Knox:

"We have gained possession of the grand emporium of the hostile Indians of the West, without loss of blood. The very extensive and highly cultivated fields and gardens, show the work of many hands. The margin of those beautiful rivers, the Miamis of the lake (or Maumee) and Auglaize, appear like one continued village for a number of miles both above and below this place; nor have I ever before beheld such fields of corn, in any part of America, from Canada to Florida."

The nearly square fort, standing in a commanding position at the rivers' junction, was equally impressive. As it neared completion Kentucky militia leader General Charles Scott examined the post, which had four blockhouses projecting outward from the corners from a line of pickets that connected them so artillery could be fired through small embrasures on three sides of the structure. After his inspection, he threw down his oft-quoted challenge: "I defy the English, Indians and all the devils in hell to take it."

Wayne must have liked the sound of it. He promptly dubbed the structure "Fort Defiance."

Even today, when you walk about the park that occupies the spot, you can see why this post would have been so difficult for an enemy to capture. Three-fourths of the structure was surrounded by water and attackers would have had to scale a steep shore just to get to the walls of the fort.

Today, the park is a beautiful spot. It has several markers with maps and diagrams telling the story of both Fort Defiance and the area that was Grand Glaize. In-ground markers note the site of the fort's gateway, officer's quarters, supply trench and blockhouses, making this a pleasant place for an imaginative soul to take a trip back in time.

Wayne's Legion left here on August 15 for a date with history at Fallen Timbers, and it returned here after the battle (and its standoff with the British forces at Fort Miamis). On the way here, the troops destroyed all of the crops and villages in their way; they hoped to shift the burden of war onto the Indians and make it difficult for them to survive the winter here. The Legion arrived on August 27 with a 15-round greeting from the fort's cannons, cannons Wayne had sent Captain Henry DeButts ahead to arrange. Wayne ordered work crews to strengthen the fort so that it could withstand an assault from the British, if one came.

Almost three weeks later on September 14, Wayne and his troops left for the Indians stronghold at Miamitown, where they would build the structure that became Fort Wayne.

Fort Defiance served no purpose after the signing of the Treaty of Greenville the following August and the military abandoned it in 1796. By the time William Henry Harrison wanted to put this vital location to use in the War of 1812, the old fort had fallen into ruins and he had a much larger Fort Winchester built just to the south of it.

After Wayne left, the old fort witnessed one more dramatic moment that one of the captive boys recorded for posterity. During negotiations for the Greenville treaty, the Indians agreed to a prisoner exchange and John Brickell wrote about what happened to him:

"On the breaking up of spring, we all went up to Fort Defiance, and on arriving on the shore opposite, we saluted the fort with a round of rifles, and they shot a cannon thirteen times. We then encamped on the spot. On the same day, Pooshies told me I must go over to the fort. The children hung round me crying, and asked me if I was going to leave them? I told them I did not know. When we got over to the fort and were seated with the officers, Whingwy Pooshies told me to stand up, which I did; he then rose and addressed me in about these words: 'My son, these are men the same color as yourself; there may be some of your kin here, or your kin may be a great way off from you; you have lived a long time with us; I call on you to say if I have not been a father to you? If I have not used you as a father would a son?' I said: 'You have used me as well as a father could use a son.' He said: 'I am glad you say so. You have lived long with me; you have hunted for me; but our treaty says you must be free. If you choose to go with the people of your color, I have no right to say a word; but if you choose to stay with me, your people have no right to speak. Now, reflect on it, and take your choice; and tell us as soon as you make up your mind.'

"I was silent a few moments, in which time it seemed as if I thought of almost everything. I thought of the children I had just left crying; I thought of the Indians I was attached to; and I thought of my people, whom I remembered; and this latter thought predominated, and I said: 'I will go with my kin.' The old man then said: 'I have raised you; I have learned you to hunt;

you are a good hunter; you have been better to me than my own sons; I am now getting old and cannot hunt; I thought you would be a support to my age; I leaned on you as on a staff. Now it is broken -- you are going to leave me, and I have no right to say a word -- but I am ruined.' He then sank back in tears in his seat. I heartily joined him in his tears -- parted with him, and have never seen nor heard of him since."

36 KEKIONGA-FORT WAYNE

In a short conversation with a prim, graying woman working the counter at Fort Wayne's "History Center," I casually mentioned the area's deep, rich history.

"If you take the time to pay attention to it, yes," she snapped. Her stern tone and expression were that of an impatient school teacher.

A boy would have opened his book and buried his nose in its pages to avoid eye contact. I tried to soften her with up a little commiseration, citing the indifference to history in my own hometown.

"I think that's everywhere," she said disgustedly, taking her frown back to her chair.

While it occurred to me that she was about as welcoming as a "Keep Off the Grass" sign, her irritation is at least understandable. She worked in a museum in a downtown Fort Wayne building that used to be City Hall, a sandstone Richardsonian-Romanesque structure that went up at the corner of Barr and Berry streets in 1893. All of the rooms that housed the city's courts, the mayor's office, the jail and the police department until 1971 hold interesting exhibits of Fort Wayne's past and present, and all but one were empty when I entered them. One large upstairs room temporarily held a model train exhibit and several guys from the local model railroad association were in there "discussing" it.

Two blocks away, at the northwest corner of Berry and Clay streets, a large rock holds a plaque that describes it as the site of the original Fort Wayne, the one General Anthony Wayne dedicated on October 22, 1794, two months following the Battle of Fallen Timbers. It's a big rock, but probably because of its cluttered location close to a red brick building, between a one-way sign and a tree on the narrow easement between the sidewalk and the street, it's easy to miss. The century-old Western Newspaper Union Building next to it houses a cinema dedicated to independent films and the Fort Wayne Dance Collective. That building, a realtor's office/house behind it, and parking lot behind both of them occupy the block that gave the city its name. Wayne may have picked the perfect place for a fort; he didn't pick the perfect place to remember one over 200 years later.

Across the parking lot and across Main Street in tiny Old Fort Park next to Fort Wayne Fire Department Station No. 1, the "Old Fort Wayne Well" sits under a large poplar tree. A concrete stand near the sidewalk 20 feet away explains that Wayne's original fort was "hastily built" so a second Fort Wayne replaced it on this site (of the well and the fire station) in 1798. The new one withstood the "Siege of Fort Wayne" during the War of 1812 and was replaced by a third fort on the same site in 1815. The third didn't have much shelf life; the army abandoned it in 1819 and the Indian Agency used it as school from 1820 to 1822. The land around the fort was offered in a public sale in 1830 and the last building connected to the forts was torn down in 1852. (A log structure at called "The Old Fort" at 1201 Spy Run Avenue is neither "old" nor a "fort." It was built in 1964.)

There's a lot of history in those two blocks and a lost soul stalking Anthony Wayne, William Henry Harrison, Little Turtle and Tecumseh probably isn't going to find what he's looking for here. But in fairness to local civic leaders, that's what usually happens when a relatively large city – Fort Wayne had a population of 253,691 in the 2010 census – grows up in a place whose history predates city planners and preservationists.

The area's importance preceded white settlers because of its location at the confluence of the St. Mary's and St. Joseph's rivers, which converge a block northeast of the original Fort Wayne to form the Maumee River. The principal Miami village of Kekionga stood directly across the Maumee from the site of Wayne's fort; it had been settled at least by 1712 and probably earlier as the Miamis moved east away from the hostile Fox. By locating here, the Miamis gained advantages in trade and protection because of the proximity to the French outpost of Detroit.

The northeast starting point of the seven-mile Maumee-Wabash portage also began in what today is West Swinney Park on the west side of town. The portage took early travelers to the Little River, which joins the Wabash, which in turn empties into the Ohio River, ultimately making it a vital link between the far away St. Lawrence and Mississippi river systems.

The French built a log fort called Fort Miami on the right bank of the St. Mary's River in 1722 at or near the site of a trading post built sometime between 1680 and 1706. A historic marker for this site was placed on a small strip of Guldlin Park near the southwest corner of the Van Buren Avenue Bridge in 1932. However, a map drawn by Father Joseph-Pierre de Bonnecamps in 1749 placed it between modern Jackson Street and the river between Superior and Greeley streets, in an area with a few houses and some unoccupied property east of the Norfolk and Southern railroad tracks. This is about 250 to 300 feet northwest of the site of the marker. Unless a new witness pops up and testifies to the good father's sloppiness, it seems likely the 1932 marker found its place more because of accessibility than historic accuracy.

With a garrison of 20 to 30 men not far from the portage, the post served an important military purpose and became a center of French activity among the Indians. In a normal year, 250 to 300 packages of furs were shipped from Fort Miami to Montreal by the way of Detroit.

In 1747, a British–aligned Wyandot chief named Sanosket led an uprising against the French. Believing that Detroit had been captured, the Miamis at Kekionga set fire to Fort Miami and captured the eight men who manned the stockade. French Captain Charles de Raymond had always believed the fort was in the wrong location and in 1750 he built a new Fort Miami on the left (eastern) bank of the St. Joseph River, a half-mile above the confluence with the St. Mary's at what today is the corner of St. Joseph Boulevard and Delaware Avenue. The buildings of the old abandoned fort were occupied by Cold Foot, a Miami chief and a good friend of the French. That became the center of an Indian settlement known as Cold Foot Village. During the winter of 1751-52, smallpox swept through the village and many of the inhabitants including Cold Foot and his son died.

When the North American front of the Seven Years War between France and England mostly ended in 1760, the French governor of Canada agreed to the surrender of several posts to the British, including Fort Detroit and Fort Miami. The Detroit post surrendered to Major Robert Rogers on November 29 and Lieutenant John Butler set out from Fort Detroit on December 7 with a detachment of twenty men to take over the fort on the St. Joseph River.

The British enjoyed three years of peace there until French-leaning Ottawa leader Pontiac showed up. He assembled a loose confederation of tribes unhappy with British rule and launched attacks on eight forts, including Fort Miami.

As difficult as it is to imagine now in a neighborhood of century-old houses, the story of this attack is the stuff of Indian legend. Ensign Robert Holmes, the commander in charge of the fort, had been sleeping with a young Miami woman named Ouiske-lotha Nebi – he shortened it to Whiskey -- for several months. His love for her had progressed to the point that he had started to wonder what would happen when he would have to leave here, whether he could take her with him and deal with the problems that would create or if she could even live in his world. He knew that he couldn't live in hers.

Even though Holmes didn't know of an attack on Fort Detroit that had already begun, he had been suspicious of Indian hostility in the region. He restricted his men to the fort and encouraged them to start making cartridges. When two Ottawa warriors and two Frenchmen arrived at Cold Foot's Village and told the village chief that Pontiac said the time had come for a surprise attack on Fort Miami, the chief told them of Holmes' suspicions, which he had learned from his conversations with the Miami woman. That troubled them and they tried to think of another way; then asked if the young woman could be counted on to help.

"If it is a matter of choice between her own people or him," he said, "Ouiske-lotha Nebi will stay with her own."

And so she did. On May 27, 1763, Ensign Holmes' beloved Whiskey pleaded with him to help her seriously ill sister. Even though he had ordered his soldiers to stay within the fort's walls for safety, he accompanied her toward a flimsy hut made of sticks about 300 yards away, and as they neared the structure, he didn't notice that she had drawn away from him. The first shot from the hiding warriors didn't kill him. The second severed his spinal column and he died on the spot. As Whiskey let out a strangled cry and ran away from her dead lover, a warrior rushed up and scalped him, and held the bloody trophy high. As a sergeant standing near the gate watched in horror, he was knocked unconscious and dragged away as the fort's gate slammed shut. A short time later, the leaderless nine-man garrison surrendered to the Miami. There would not be another garrison in the vicinity until the arrival of Anthony Wayne.

The Miami, Delaware and Shawnee tribes had villages here during this period, attracting a mixture of French and Indian traders and their families. General Josiah Harmar's soldiers counted seven distinct villages in the vicinity in 1790, the combination of which came to be known as the Miami Villages, the Miami Towns or Miamitown. The area served an important role for the British fur trade. By this point, an estimated 2,000 packs of furs were taken from the Miami region annually, far more than from Detroit north to Lake Huron.

Miamitown served as the home base for Indian raiding parties across the frontier, which explains why it landed in General Josiah Harmar's sights when Secretary of War Henry Knox ordered him to end the Indian threat in western Ohio in 1790. From his base of operations at Fort Washington, Harmar marched north with 320 regular soldiers and approximately 1,100 militiamen from Pennsylvania and Kentucky with the intent of destroying Miamitown, its occupants and its "villainous traders." He also planned to punish any Shawnee, Delaware and Miami Indians he found along the way.

In anticipation of a massive attack on Miamitown, the Indians abandoned and destroyed the villages themselves, took the traders' stores of ammunition and aided them in fleeing with what goods they could carry. When the

American arrived there, they burned everything that remained, including 20,000 bushels of corn. After destroying what remained of the Miami villages, Harmar inexplicably split his forces and ordered a detachment of 200 soldiers led by Colonel John Hardin to the northwest to destroy any Indian villages they found there. As soon as Indians scouts realized the direction Hardin's soldiers headed, chiefs Little Turtle and Blue Jacket set up an ambush where an Indian trail leading to the Elkhart River passed through heavy brush as it crossed the Eel River. Today, this spot can be found where U.S. 33 crosses the Eel River six miles northwest of the modern city of Fort Wayne.

Hardin had not deemed it necessary to send out a forward guard or flankers and his troops paid dearly for his carelessness. His men marched into the ambush and suddenly faced a deafening barrage of shots. The Americans panicked, turned and ran – it's possible that they never fired a shot – and left 70 dead bodies on the "battlefield." Harmar reported that only seven of the 30 regular troops on this mission survived.

Harmar critics looking for modern evidence of his stupidity will be disappointed in their visit here. There is not even a sign identifying this as the Eel River, let alone one that remembers the 70 Americans who died here. Where the Eel crosses U.S. 33, it's little more than a glorified ditch on the edge of some farm fields. There some brush on its banks, but nothing that would hide even an army of Leprechauns.

Further evidence of Harmar's ineptitude – or cowardice – may be seen in his reaction to the news. When the survivors reached the main body of Harmar's force, the general didn't order his troops into battle, but retreat. This infuriated many of his soldiers, who believed that he should at least return to the battle site and bury the dead.

After a march of about eight miles, he had his army set up camp for the night. He heard that some Indians had returned to Kekionga and reluctantly sent out another detachment, this time with about 360 men again under the command of Colonel Hardin and a force of 60 regulars under Major John P. Wyllys to wipe them out.

The detachment reached Kekionga in the early morning light of October 22. They split into four bodies and started moving toward different quarters of town, which thrilled an undermanned Indian force unsure that it could defeat a single force that large. With Blue Jacket and Little Turtle still leading their tribesmen, they routed the Americans again in a series of intense minor skirmishes that lasted over three hours. This time, 113 soldiers died and the survivors beat a hasty retreat back to Harmar's camp.

That battle is commemorated today with two markers in the grass at the base of a riverfront levy that is topped by the concrete Rivergreenway trail next to the Maumee River. It is across from a row of early twentieth-century houses on Edgewater Avenue, near Dearborn Street. The larger marker is on a boulder that bears a bronze plaque placed there by the Daughters of the

American Revolution in 1916 to commemorate the death of "Major John Wyllys and his brave soldiers who were killed near this spot in the Battle of Harmar's Ford, Oct. 22, 1790 with the Miami Indians under Chief Little Turtle." The other is smaller and newer and tells the story of "The Battle of Kekionga" in detail. Two blocks to the west across from the corner of Lafort Street and Edgewater Avenue another small marker marks this area as the site of Kekionga; if you didn't know, the description makes it clear that the marker doesn't do justice to a place as important as this:

"This area of the Three Rivers was a site of settlement of Native Americans for as much as 10,000 years. The collection of villages known as Kekionga, located in the present-day Lakeside neighborhood, was a center of the Miami nation in historic times. At the time of the Miami confederacy in the 1790s, Kekionga also was the gathering place for the Huron, the Ottawa, and the Shawnee.

"Tradition holds that Kekionga means 'the blackberry patch.' To the Miami people this also had the meaning of an ancient, sacred place. In the spring, the scattered families of the several clans came to Kekionga from their winter hunting grounds to conduct their business, prepare for war, and cultivate the fields.

"Kekionga was described in the 1790s as being a very large settlement called 'Miami Town' by eastern Americans who feared the place as the center of Indian resistance to the expanding United States frontier.

"Kekionga occupied the ground above the flood plain of the Maumee and the St. Joseph rivers and was surrounded by wide expanses of corn fields, as far as the eye can see," according to one observer. Anthony Wayne commented on the broad corn fields that extended all along the Maumee River. Others noted the herds of cattle and the many gardens growing pumpkins, melons, and squash. Dome-shaped houses, log homes, and bark-covered long houses, for business or religious purposes, covered the many acres of Kekionga.

"Kekionga remained a place of native settlement until the Miami were forcibly removed from Indiana in 1846."

While reading that, it's not difficult to understand why Harmar came this way and why the defeats that his troops suffered here were so devastating. When word of the loss at Kekionga reached Harmar, he marched his force of over 1,200 fresh troops, their weapons having never been fired, back to Fort Washington. He had lost 183 soldiers, including 75 regulars; much of the army's equipment and the packhorses carrying it had been left to the Indians. Only 27 of an Indian force of 150 had been killed; the courageous warriors had defeated an American army 10 times its size.

Northwest Territory governor Arthur St. Clair replaced Harmar and Secretary of War Henry Knox ordered him to order him to establish an American fort at Miamitown in 1791. St. Clair never got that far, suffering a devastating defeat in the so-called Battle of the Wabash in what later became Fort Recovery, Ohio, 54 miles away. It was left to Anthony Wayne to lead a third expedition in what became western Ohio, defeat the combined Indian forces at the Battle of Fallen Timbers, and after a stay or three weeks at Fort Defiance, cut a wagon road 48 miles through the wilderness to the Miami villages and build the garrison that became Fort Wayne.

Wayne's Legion reached the confluence of the St. Joseph and St. Mary's rivers late in the afternoon on September 17, 1794. At the old site of Kekionga, they found approximately 500 acres of cleared ground, the area giving the indication that it had once been "one of the largest settlements made by the Indians in this country." The area had "grown up with Thorn Crab and Plumb Trees," apparently having been abandoned since Harmar's destruction of it. Soldiers poking around in the brush on the old battlefield found an assortment of bones, "including skulls which had marks of the tomahawk and scalping knife."

The next day Wayne located the spot for his new fort. Cornet John Posey gushed that "Nature has never formed a more beautiful spot for the purpose, a high and commanding situation on the south side of the Miami and immediately at the confluence of the Rivers Saint Marie and Saint Joseph." Lieutenant William Clark showed more restraint, noting that the site is "tolerably elevated & has ready command of the mouth of the two rivers." The owners of the Fort Wayne Dance Collective have probably never described their location either way.

Construction of the new structure commenced on September 25 after several days of hard rain. Private Garret Burns gave the only contemporary description of the fort, writing that it "was built of the largest kind of oak logs" and noting that "the walls of the fort were double, the space being filled up with earth, afforded by a ditch being dug outside, which was 14 feet deep and as much wide."

Construction took about a month and Wayne put the time to good use, setting off on October 12 with Generals Charles Scott and Robert Todd and several staff members and aides to inspect the eight-mile portage to the headwaters of the Wabash River. They found tracks of wagons and carts still visible on what had been a good road, and when they reached the "landing place" the old camping grounds could still be seen.

Wayne announced that Lieutenant Colonel Hamtramck would be the commander of the new post on October 21 and said it would consist of approximately 300 soldiers from four infantry companies and one artillery battery. The garrison marched to the fort's gates and after a 15-gun salute, Hamtramck issued his first order, christening the structure Fort Wayne after the commander who had led them there. (Hamtramck had requested

LITTLE TURTLE'S BURIAL SITE WAS DISCOVERED TOWARD THE BACK OF THIS LOT DURING HOUSE CONSTRUCTION IN 1912. A SMALL PARK HONORS HIM THERE TODAY.

permission to name the new post earlier.) One week later, Wayne and the rest of his legion began the march back to Fort Greeneville.

As Wayne prepared for a peace conference to be held at Greeneville the following summer, the Indians asked that it be held at Kekionga, their old village. Wayne declined their request, realizing that it would be more difficult to bring supplies there and that he would be better protected at Greeneville in the event of trouble. When many of the tribes came to Greeneville in the spring, they came by way of Fort Wayne, overcrowding the post so badly that Hamtramck's garrison had to go on half-rations to feed the delegates.

Little Turtle debated long and hard over the concessions that Wayne demanded in and around Fort Wayne prior to the peace conference. The great Miami chief eventually lost most of his demands, but did secure one compromise from Wayne, a reduction of the land around the fort to be ceded to the United States. In his farewell address to the conference, Little Turtle also asked that the Captain William Wells be appointed as the resident interpreter at Fort Wayne. The U.S. government established an Indian agency at Fort Wayne by 1798 and Wells was chosen as the first agent. Both military and government officials believed he should be rewarded for his services during and after Wayne's campaign and knew him to be the most qualified person for the position. Wells knew all of the important Indians in the region and could fluently speak five Indian dialects.

Colonel Thomas Hunt took command of the post in May, 1798, and found that the fort had already started to decay. So he undertook the task of building a replacement about 300 feet to the north, in the area that is now

Old Fort Park. The new fort included six log barracks for the officers and men, a brick magazine, and smaller buildings around the parade ground within the palisade.

The frontier stayed relatively peaceful until 1807, when signs of the forthcoming Indian difficulties began to appear. With Ohio's move to statehood in 1803, this became the Indiana Territory, with former Wayne aide and future president William Henry Harrison as governor.

Governor Harrison came to Fort Wayne in September, 1809, to negotiate what proved to be his final treaty with the Indians in the territory. On the one side sat the governor with his servant, his secretary, four Indian interpreters, and the officers of the fort; on the other sat the painted warriors of the Miamis, the Potawatomis, the Delawares, and the Weas. On the third day of the council, 892 warriors were present. On the day of the treaty signing 1,390 were present, the largest number of Indians ever assembled to meet a representative of the United States.

A collection of government buildings and sutler establishments sprouted to the immediate west of the fort at the meeting place of two roads, Wayne's Trace to Fort Washington and the old Maumee-Wabash portage path. In time, these resembled a small village, which became the plat of the town when platted in 1824. A marker placed at the corner of Wayne Trace and New Haven Avenue by the D.A.R. in 1906 commemorates the old Indian trail Harmar and Wayne used between Fort Wayne and Cincinnati.

The fort played a critical role during the War of 1812. During the summer of 1811, it became the central point between the Prophet's Town on the Tippecanoe River and Malden, the British post across from Detroit where they distributed arms and ammunition to the Indians.

After the American forces under Harrison defeated the Indians at Prophet's Town in November, 1811, Tecumseh (who was not in the battle) visited Fort Wayne in December. The loss had severely damaged his plans, and he railed against Harrison, asked for and was denied ammunition and left, still believing he could achieve success with the help of the British.

On August 28, 1812, warriors from the Potawatomi and Miami tribes led by Chief Winamac gathered around Fort Wayne and began a siege. Chief Winamac's forces assaulted the fort from the east side and burned the homes of the surrounding village.

Kentucky Governor Charles Scott had just appointed Governor Harrison as Major General of the Kentucky Militia and authorized him to relieve Fort Wayne. Harrison quickly organized a militia force of 2,200 men and marched north from the Newport (Ky.) Barracks to the fort. While en route a scouting party reported that a force of 400 Native Americans and 140 British regulars under Tecumseh was also marching towards the fort, so Harrison now raced to beat Tecumseh.

Winamac attempted one last attack on Fort Wayne on September 11, suffered several casualties and broke off the attack. Harrison's troops moved to within 17 miles of Fort Wayne that night and expected a battle the next day. The Indians had prepared to give battle at a swamp five miles southeast of the fort, but finding Harrison's army too strong to attack, they withdrew and allowed Harrison's troops to march to the fort uncontested. Three days later, Harrison ordered two divisions from Fort Wayne to destroy any Native American village they found as punishment for the siege.

An American army under Harrison routed the British and Indian forces at the Battle of the Thames on October 5, 1813. Tecumseh died in the battle, and in effect, the Indian power was broken forever in the Old Northwest.

Although Fort Wayne had withstood the siege, the destruction of the village and its trade proved to be major setbacks. A new fort replaced the old one in 1815 and the military left it in 1819. Many of the families who left the area in 1812 to escape the Indian attacks never returned, causing visitor Thomas Teas to write that "the village before the late war was much larger than at present." Indiana became a state in 1816, but until 1818, all of northern Indiana was still considered Indian territory.

Two hundred years later, the Indians' fate is evident in a neighborhood of century-old houses in the Spy Run section of Fort Wayne. A tiny park is squeezed between two houses on the south side of Lawton Place, a long half-block west of the St. Joseph River and almost directly across from the site of the second Fort Miami. At the end of a narrow path lies a bronze plaque and a few story-telling markers that reveal this as the final resting place for legendary Miami chief Little Turtle, whose grave was unearthed during the building of a house in 1912, one hundred years after his death.

A ceremonial sword given to him by George Washington and other artifacts buried with him were given to the Allen County Fort Wayne Historical Society for display, construction plans were altered and he was reburied on the site, which also contains the graves of other Miamis.

Eleanor and Mary Catherine Smeltzly donated the land there for a memorial park to Little Turtle in 1959.

It would be interesting to know what the Miami chief would have thought of his need for such generosity.

V.

LAKES AND STRAITS

37 SAULT STE. MARIE

It's safe to say that few if any tourists have ever come to Sault Ste. Marie, Michigan, because it hosted the historic Pageant of Saint Lusson. For starters, they would have to know about the pageant to make a trip to this town on the Canadian border in Michigan's Upper Peninsula, and the most recent poll indicated that 98 percent of the American and Canadian public had never heard of it.

Well OK, there was no poll, but if there had been one 98 percent might even be a low number. The pageant is one of those events that might have led CNN's evening newscast at the time -- if cable news had existed in 1671 -- but it didn't have much staying power historically. The French used it to make an ostentatious display of claiming the Great Lakes country and beyond, and we all know how much of that it still rules. If Milwaukee or Minneapolis-St. Paul were part of New France today, Simon-François Daumont de Saint Lusson's pageant might still be celebrated as some sort of Midwestern Mardi Gras. Instead, his pageant has been swept into the dust bin of history.

That doesn't mean it wasn't suitable for prime time in 1671 or even worth commemorating three and a half centuries later. The French worried about the increasing influence of the English in an area where their explorers and missionaries had been poking around for a half-century. French explorer Etienne Brule didn't keep extensive journals documenting his travels, but he definitely visited the area at the eastern terminus of Lake Superior around the St. Mary River rapids in 1621 and may have been here during the winters of 1618-19. Jean Nicolet, another French explorer on a search for the Northwest Passage, passed through here in 1634 and some Jesuit missionaries visited here in 1641. Explorer/fur trader Pierre-Esprit Radisson stopped here in 1658 and wrote about it later:

"We found ye truth of what those men have told us, that if once we would come to that place we should make good cheer of ye white fish. Ye bear, castors (beaver), and oriniack (moose) showed themselves often, but to their cost; indeed, it was to us like a terrestrial paradise."

Father Louis Nicolas came to the Sault as resident priest in 1667 and in 1668 Father Jacques Marquette established a Jesuit mission here. With their long history in the area, it's not hard to see why the French would be uncomfortable if the English started casting their eyes in this direction. That is exactly what they feared when King Charles II of England granted Radisson and Médard Chouart des Groseilliers and their associates and successors a patent for trading in "The Bay called Hudson's Streights" in May, 1670, which marked the beginning of the Hudson's Bay Company.

Word of the defection of the famous pair and their trading activity spread rapidly and aroused the ire and anxiety of the French. Something obviously had to be done, so in the fall of 1670, Saint Lusson sent an invitation to tribes throughout the Great Lakes region to attend a ceremonial event in the Sault the following summer. Two thousand Native Americans representing 14 different tribes from as far as 400 miles away answered the call, arriving as early as May to camp along the shores of St. Mary's River and wait for the party.

On the French side, Saint Lusson represented King Louis XIV. Jesuit Fathers Claude-Jean Allouez, Gabriel Druillettes, Claude Dablon and Louis Andre also attended, as did explorers Nicholas Perrot and Louis Joliet and others (20 Frenchmen signed the record that day) who would probably be familiar to the seventeenth century French fur trade crowd.

The precise location of the ceremony is open to question, although eyewitness accounts indicate that Saint Lusson chose a spot at a height overlooking the village. In a place all could see, he planted a large wooden cross and raised the King's standard with all the pomp he and his fellow land grabbers could devise. Given that modern-day Portage Street is located a small climb from Water Street between Ashmun Street and Osborne Boulevard, that the foot of that area served as the landing place for the canoes of the French and the visiting tribes and that that part of Water Street eventually became the heart of the old Sault, the top of that "hill" on Portage seems like a reasonable guess as to a general location of the cross planting. Others have attempted to pin its location on two hills to the west, but one of those held an Ojibwa sacred burial ground (not the best place for a celebration) and dumping during the later construction of navigation locks we know today as the Soo Locks apparently created the other. With all due respect, the Portage location seems more likely.

Wherever it was, eyewitness accounts tell us that Saint Lusson held his sword in one hand and a clod of earth in the other (ah, symbolism) and tried to summon all of the oratory Martin Luther King might have mustered to move and impress the huge throng of Native Americans who had gathered there:

"In the name of the most high, mighty and redoubtable monarch, Louis the Fourteenth of that name, Most Christian King of France and Navarre, I take over this Sainte Marie du Sault, the

Lakes Huron and Superior, Manitoulin Island, and all the other countries, lakes and streams adjacent thereto, both those discovered and those which may be discovered hereafter, in all their length and breadth, bounded on the one side by the oceans of the north and west, and on the other by the South Sea, declaring to the nations therein that from this time henceforth they are subjects of His Majesty, bound to obey his laws and follow his customs; promising them on his part all succor and protection against their enemies; and declaring to all other princes and potentates, states and republics, to them and their peoples, that they must not seize or settle upon any part of the aforesaid countries, save only under the good pleasure of His Most Christian Majesty and of him who will govern in his behalf; and this on pain of incurring his resentment and the weight of his arms. Long live the King!"

That pretty well covers it, doesn't it? The French didn't know exactly what was out there but they wanted to make sure everyone knew that they owned all of it. The huge crowd of Indians must have been suitably impressed with all of the pomp and circumstance: the cross, the solemn sermon and powerful description of the king given by Father Allouez ("He is the chief of the greatest chiefs, and has no equal on earth!"), the French escutcheon attached to a cedar pole, the French soldiers who repeatedly shouted "Long, live the King!" and fired their muskets in celebration and the huge bonfire that closed the ceremony. Around that bonfire, the French sang the hymn "Te Deum," apparently to thank God on behalf of these poor souls now the subjects of so great and powerful a monarch.

This is probably a good place to note that Native Americans had been in this area for hundreds of years. Archaeologists say that the Ojibwas themselves had been residing in places around the rapids since about 800 A.D., or almost 900 years before the French stuck a cross and a flag on a hill and claimed it all as their own. The Ojibwa first arrived here in a westward migration, settled and eventually split into two branches of the tribe, a northern branch which migrated along the northern shore of Lake Superior toward Thunder Bay and beyond, and a southern branch which followed the southern shore and eventually founded an important tribal village at La Pointe (now Wisconsin),

The rapids of the St. Mary's River – "sault" is the French word for rapids or falls – stand a few miles east of the entrance to Lake Superior, which is 21 feet higher than the river on other side of the rapids that winds its way to Lake Huron. The natural bottleneck at this location coupled with the fabulous fishing the natives (the French called them Saulteurs) found there made this a natural place for tribes to congregate.

Sulpician priest Rene de Brehant de Galinee, who arrived here with Francois Dollier de Casson in May, 1670, wrote that the "river forms here a rapid so teeming with fish, called poisson blanc (white fish), or in Algonkin Aitikameg, that the Indians could easily catch enough to feed ten thousand men. Only Indians can carry it on, and no Frenchman has hitherto been able to succeed at it, nor any other Indians than those of this tribe, who are used to this kind of fishing from an early age. In short this fish is so cheap that they are given ten or twelve of them for four fingers of tobacco. Each weighs six or seven pounds, but it is so delicate that I know of no fish that approaches it. Sturgeon is caught in this river in abundance, and meat is so cheap here that for a pound of glass beads I had four minots of fat entrails of moose. It is here that one gets a beaver robe for a fathom of tobacco, or a quarter of a pound of powder, or for six knives, or a fathom of blue beads."

The Ojibwa called the area Bawating, which translates as "The Gathering Place," helping to explain why Marquette built a mission here. The original one, which stood near the modern intersection of Water Street and Bingham Avenue, burned two weeks after Saint Lusson's impressive pageant. A second mission was quickly constructed to replace the first and another fire nearly destroyed it in 1674. This blaze resulted from a squabble between the local tribe and visiting Sioux, ten of whom came here to negotiate peace with the Saulteurs, winners of a battle with them in the western part of the peninsula. A large band of Crees, enemies of the Sioux, heard of this and traveled here from north shores of Lake Superior, determined to prevent a truce if possible. Fathers Dablon and Druillettes took the Sioux into their home for safety and several Crees and Saulteurs followed them.

A Cree chief challenged the courage of one of the Sioux warriors and plunged a knife into his heart, beginning a bloody battle in which all of the Sioux and 30 of Saulteurs and Crees were killed. Somewhere in the chaos, the priests' house was set afire, and the mission itself barely missed being destroyed by the nearby flames.

Father Charles Albanel, the first white man to reach Hudson's Bay by the overland route, manned the mission from 1676 to 1696. The adventurous part of Albanel's life had ended, at least if you don't believe living in a northern wilderness village in the seventeenth century qualifies as adventurous. He reached Hudson's Bay in 1670 after a 2,400-mile journey from Quebec, and when he made the same trip four years later the British imprisoned him and sent him to England. He came here after returning from France and eventually died here in January, 1696. He is said to be buried in the vicinity of the Johnston house on East Water Street, a few modern blocks east of the old mission.

NATIVE AMERICANS FISHED IN THE SAULT RAPIDS FOR HUNDREDS OF YEARS. THIS PHOTO WAS TAKEN IN 1900.

Holy Name of Mary Catholic Church or St. Mary's somewhat tenuously traces its roots to that mission and is located on Portage Avenue, two and a half blocks southeast of the original mission site. The mission closed between 1696 and 1700; after the death of Father Albanel, there is no record of missionary priests at the Sault for more than a century. The first pastor of St. Mary's served beginning in 1834. The connection is understood, but whether that satisfies its claim as the third oldest parish in the United States is subject to debate.

The mission closed because the area lost its importance as a trading post, first to St. Ignace on the Straits of Mackinac and then to Fort Detroit, which Antoine de La Mothe Cadillac (who had been commander at St. Ignace) founded in 1701. He lured many Native Americans in the Mackinac and Sault area to Detroit to facilitate trade there. Historical references in the early eighteenth century make it clear the Sault was never abandoned, but the Ojibwa and French traders who lived and passed through decreased until they were few in number.

Because of its strategic location at the eastern end of the fur-rich Lake Superior region, it couldn't stay that way. In 1734, Louis Denys, Sieur de la Ronde, former commander of a French fort at Chequamegon, obtained rights for a trading post at the Sault. He brought ship materials and workmen in from Montreal and built a 25-ton ship at Point au Pins, a spot today occupied by a park at the far western end of the Canadian Sault. Five years later, he hired 12 Frenchmen in the Sault to build a forge and a smelter to process copper found in the western part of the Upper Peninsula.

With the threat of competition from the British growing, the King approved the governor of Canada's request to give French army officers Chevalier de Repentigny and Captain de Bonne permission to establish a seignory at Sault Sainte Marie where travelers from neighboring ports could find safe retreat. The permission came with a whopping 214,000 acres of land, a pretty stiff price for the fort that Repentigny built here in 1750. But the governor and his king probably knew what lay ahead; the rivalry between French and British traders would soon lead to war.

Repentigny built his garrison with 1,100 posts 15 feet tall and three buildings inside those walls. He completed it in 1751. Based on an old map in the U.S. Corps of Engineers office in the Sault and a mortar foundation discovered during excavation for a house in 1908, the site of the stockade would straddle today's Water Street about fifty feet east of Brady Street.

The construction came with a historical bonus: Repentigny induced a Frenchman named Jean Baptiste Cadotte to take a farm here with an Indian woman he had married at the Sault to help supply the post with corn. Cadotte was the grandson of Mathurin Cadot (the spelling of the name before it was Anglicized), a trader who had been present at the famous pageant. Their progeny would span multiple generations here; Cadottes still lived in the area at the dawn of the 21st century.

When Repentigny left the Sault in the spring of 1759 to aid the defense of Quebec against the British, he left Cadotte in charge. The French loss at the Plains of Abraham at Quebec City in September, 1759, proved to be a pivotal moment in the Seven Years War; it ended with the French cessation of its territory in North America to the British at the Treaty of Paris in 1763.

French citizens were given 18 months to decide whether to remain in the area as British subjects or move on. Repentigny left; Cadotte stayed and engaged in the fur trade business with his two sons, Jean Baptiste and Michel. He retired in 1796 and died here in 1804.

The arrival of the English changed the Sault. Alexander Henry, a young British trader who had come to Michilimackinac in 1761 at the age of 22, came here from the straits by canoe on May 19, 1762. He wrote in his journal that Cadotte's family were the only French then living here. He also reported finding "a village of fifty Chippeways (Ojibwa) warriors seated at this place, but the inhabitants reside here during the summer only, going westward in the winter to hunt. The village was anciently much more populous."

While Henry was there, a detachment of British soldiers under Lieutenant John Jamet arrived to take over the fort. It burned down on December 22, sparing only Cadotte's house, and the soldiers returned to Michilimackinac. Jamet remained in the Sault with Cadotte until late February to nurse injuries suffered in the fire. At that point, Cadotte, Henry, two Canadians and two Indians accompanied Jamet back to the Michilimackinac by snowshoe, a distance of 90 miles by the shorelines. His timing could have been better.

Jamet arrived in time to be killed in the famous massacre of troops at the fort by local Indian tribes in June.

Henry fared better. He survived the massacre because of a relationship with Ojibwa village chief Wawatam. After he spent a harrowing year in disguise to keep himself from being killed by other Indians, Henry escaped to Montreal. He eventually returned by way of Fort Detroit and ended up making a tidy profit as a result of a fur trading partnership with Cadotte in 1766. Henry enjoyed 15 more years of adventure and profits throughout the region and finally settled in Montreal as a general merchant in 1781. But he remained attached to the fur trade and made occasional trips to Michilimackinac after sustaining heavy losses following the conclusion of the American Revolution

Fur traders maintained a quiet presence in the Sault under the British. Recorded history picks back up with the arrival of the North West Company, a fur trading company launched in 1787 as a rival to the Hudson's Bay Company, and Irish-born trader John Johnston. He first passed through the area in 1791 en route to Lake Superior with five voyageurs and trade goods obtained at Mackinac Island.

The North West Company had its headquarters in Montreal and a heavy presence in the regions around Lake Superior. Grand Portage served as its assembling point in the north and all of its up-bound field supplies and down-bound peltries portaged around the rapids at the Sault. The portage, company offices and warehouses were all located on the south side of the river.

That land had been formally ceded to the United States in the Peace of Paris in 1783. Because of its isolation, the British didn't withdraw from the area until after the War of 1812. But when occupation by American troops seemed imminent in the late 1790s, the company moved over to British territory on the north side of the river.

Johnston understood; he considered himself an Englishman. He met Ojibwa chief Mamongazida at La Pointe during the winter of 1791; French commander Louis-Joseph de Montcalm died in Mamongazida's arms at the Plains of Abraham. A year later, Johnston married his granddaughter, Ozhaguscodaywayquay; fortunately for all of us, she also used the name Susan Johnston. If her father, Waubojeeg, didn't get to see Montcalm into the afterlife like his father, he still may have been the most famous Ojibwa chief of his time.

The Johnstons and their first child Lewis lived in the Sault by 1794. Despite the area's rich French history, Johnston is most visible reminder of its distant past today. The Johnston house on East Water Street is on the site of the original structure built in 1794 and destroyed by American forces in 1814 in retaliation for Johnston's aid to the British during the War of 1812. The part of the house that remains and can be toured by visitors was built in

1822; in 1910, a falling tree crushed a section rebuilt in 1815 immediately after the war.

While the surviving section of the house dates from that later period, its age and location on the river offers visitors an insightful look at what the area must have been like when Johnston traded furs for the North West Company in this remote, sparsely populated region.

The house faces the river and sits in a row of historic structures on East Water Street; Johnston laid out Water Street or Park Place behind his house and garden as the first street in the Sault in 1816. At the time, it extended but a few hundred feet west from the lot where his house stood, past the house of Mrs. Cadotte on the site of the old French fort. Next door is a house built in 1827 by Henry Rowe Schoolcraft and his wife, Jane, Johnston's daughter. Schoolcraft had become the first Indian agent appointed to the Sault five years before. Schoolcraft is remembered as an American geographer, geologist, and ethnologist who would eventually write a six-volume study of Native Americans. He also led an 1832 expedition to the source of the Mississippi River.

Sadly, the river and what remains of its rapids are about all that remains of Sault Ste. Marie's days as an early gathering place of Indian tribes and French and English traders. The village that sprouted in the middle of the nineteenth century was concentrated on Water Street. The section of it that once teemed with business and hotels in the late nineteenth century, a block below Portage Avenue and the start of today's business district, is mostly barren now.

Portage Avenue itself is a reminder of the old way of life here. Early pioneers were forced to carry their canoes – or portage -- around the rapids. When settlement of the Northwest Territory brought more trade and large boats, it became necessary to unload the boats, haul the cargoes around the rapids in wagons, and reload in other boats.

In 1797, the North West Company constructed a navigation lock 38 feet long on the Canadian side of the river for small boats to navigate around the rapids. That lock was destroyed in the War of 1812 and all freight again had to be portaged around the rapids.

Those portages passed into history with the coming of locks on the American side of the river. In 1853, Charles T. Harvey, accountant for the Fairbanks Scale Company which operated numerous mines in the Upper Peninsula, completed a system of two locks in tandem, each 350 long, within a two-year deadline set by the state of Michigan. The locks were turned over to the state in 1855, thus beginning an expansive series of locks that would make transportation between Lake Superior and the lower Great Lakes easy.

Today, tourists know Sault Ste. Marie – nicknamed the Soo – for the Soo Locks, which transport massive ships from one level to another. The area around the locks, once home to Indian tribes who fished the angry water in the river, is now awash in souvenir shops hawking everything from toy totem poles and Indian headdresses to moccasins and toy spears.

The modern American Soo is home to approximately 14,000 citizens, less than one-fourth the size of the much more industrial Canadian Soo, and only 17 percent of the population is Native American. Sad as that is, the Indians' loss of land and river here is at partially mitigated by their ownership of one of the most successful businesses in town:

Kewadin Casino, operated by the Sault Ste. Marie tribe of Chippewa (Ojibwa) Indians, regularly beats visitors with its table games and 800 slot machines. Long-dead Ojibwa warriors would doubtless see this as delicious irony.

38 POINT IROQUOIS

The Point Iroquois Lighthouse is one of those picturesque places on the south shore of Lake Superior that gets plenty of tourist action during the summer months, both from those who just happen by on West Lakeshore Drive and those who have been advised to go out of their way to stop there.

It is a pretty, 65-foot high, conical brick lighthouse with an accompanying two-story, Cape Cod-style keeper's house, and its location only a few hundred feet from the road makes it impossible for even the most inattentive driver to miss. Even for a driver in a hurry, and I have no idea why anyone would be in a hurry he re, stopping requires less time and effort than a freeway potty break.

All but the most devoted students of Native American history probably do that without giving the name of the spot a second thought. Truthfully, most of us don't give the names of anything -- roads, buildings, towns, lakes or rivers – even a fleeting moment of our time. So having the name of an Indian tribe on a point of land in a place where we all know there have been and still are lots of Native Americans seems natural. It is located a few miles west of Brimley, Michigan, home to two Indian casinos and the Bay Mills Indian Community reservation.

But the name isn't the norm here. The Iroquois' primary base of operations lay mostly in western New York, south of Lake Ontario, about 450 miles from this retired lighthouse, which was first illuminated in 1852 and decommissioned in 1962 in favor of beacon out in the water.

Again, it is the lighthouse that draws most tourists; these days, posing for pictures has become the primary purpose for many of these intriguing old structures. Visitors here also love to imagine what it must have been like in distant days when the then-isolated station housed the keeper, two assistants and their families and a little museum on the property paints a picture of that. But those who stop to climb the lighthouse stairs and gaze over two miles of water toward Gros Cap, the last tip of land on the Canadian side before the widening St. Mary's River becomes Whitefish Bay, may be surprised to find there's more to that name – Point Iroquois – than they expected.

The fierce, warlike Iroquois had their name attached to this place by the Ojibwa tribe that launched a surprise attack on a party of 100 of them camped here in 1662. The Ojibwas supposedly killed them all but one (or two, in another account) in a bloody, conclusive battle, leaving the sole survivor to return to his people and tell them of the crushing defeat. Some early accounts of it made the rout seem much larger, so even in those days, it was important to be wary of news sources.

In his description of the battle, French explorer Baron de Lahontan wrote that the Ojibwa tribe crushed an Iroquois force of one thousand warriors and well-known trader Great Lakes trader Alexander Henry later wrote that he was told 1,000 Iroquois had died in the massacre. Henry was married to the daughter of an Ojibwa chief who almost certainly knew the tribe's traditions forward and backward, so there's that to consider. But the editor of Henry's papers simply footnoted the figure and listed the number as 100, the accepted figure of historians who are doubtless aware that oral histories handed down through the generations are sometimes prone to exaggeration.

Either way, this qualifies as a huge historical moment, especially for the Ojibwas.

"The battle of Iroquois Point was not a minor skirmish, it was a turning point in Ojibway history," former Michigan governor Chase Osborn and his daughter Stellanova wrote in a book about Indian legends in 1944. "It was to them what Waterloo was to the nations who stopped the encroachments of Napoleon."

That hints at what the Iroquois were doing here, hundreds of miles from the primary base of operations. But this is a story that deserves all of its details, at least so far as we have them:

Beaver were disappearing from the lands that the Iroquois Confederacy (of five tribal nations and later six) controlled in the mid-1600s, in part because of the firearms they acquired by trading with the Dutch. They cast their longing eyes west, both to land where the Iroquoian-speaking Hurons lived in modern Quebec and Ontario and also to places where many of the tribes spoke the Algonquin language.

The Iroquois drove the Hurons north in the early days of the seventeenth century and came for them again on the St. Lawrence in the 1640s. They destroyed several important Huron villages in 1648 and also turned their wrath on residents of New France. They continued to push west and the Ojibwas and the Iroquois fought several battles in what is now southern Ontario over a time frame of more than a decade. The Iroquois' westward quest was bound to reach the Lake Superior region eventually and that finally happened in 1662.

A large Iroquois band approaching one thousand, determined to attack some fleeing Hurons and Algonquin refugees and their Winnebago allies, paddled through the Straits of Mackinac in their canoes and attacked them at Green Bay. The aggressors were turned back, and on their return lost a large number of warriors in a tremendous storm at the entrance to the bay.

At that point, their remaining force split in two, one heading south in Lake Michigan toward Illinois and the other heading back to the straits and up the St. Mary's River to the rapids. There they launched an attack on the resident Ojibwa and drove them from the village they called Bawating, today's Sault Ste. Marie. The victorious Iroquois took many prisoners, portaged around the rapids and headed up the river and camped at this spot at the entrance to Whitefish Bay to torture, kill and eat their prisoners, in their accustomed fashion.

In the meantime, Ojibwa chief Ningaubeon had collected and rallied his band of shell-shocked warriors at Gros Cap, across the bay. They crossed the water during the early morning hours and landed on the beach around dawn during a thick fog that provided the perfect cover for a surprise attack. The angry Ojibwa fell upon their gorged and sleeping enemies and the result wasn't a battle so much as a massacre. Iroquois blood soaked the beautiful beach where lighthouse visitors collect colorful rocks. Tribal traditions say that the lone survivor, minus his nose and ears, went back to his tribe with a message as insulting as it was graphic: next time send men and not women should you decide to attack the Ojibwa.

The victors decapitated the bodies of the victims and placed the skulls in a line on the shore that tradition says stretched nearly a mile in length – a tale that makes you wonder if those estimates of 1,000 victims isn't closer to the truth -- and they left the headless bodies unburied on the shore, prey to hungry birds and animals. A fur trader from Sault Ste. Marie observed human bones and skulls still visible on the beach at Point Iroquois in the late 1700s, over a century after the fact, which helps to explain how this place came to be known as the "Place of the Iroquois Bones" or the "Boneyard of the Iroquois."

The story provides us with a gruesome mental image, one that seems at odds with the picturesque lighthouse and the wooded park that lies mostly to the east of it. From the beach, a raised wooden walkway follows the beach and then rises up through the woods, exiting near the restrooms and parking lot. It is a beautiful walk through the white birch trees and towering pines. But once you know the story – maybe you don't even have to know the story – it's difficult to take a quiet, breezy walk through here without getting an eerie feeling.

Ghost hunter web sites on the Internet claim that the lighthouse is haunted (actually, if you look at those sites, you'd swear that most lighthouses are haunted). But even if you aren't inclined to believe in supernatural events, reports of visitors seeing shadowy figures in those woods and along the beach that are supposedly spirits of the restless dead from a horrific seventeenth century slaughter are downright creepy.

Whether this truly marked the end of Iroquois' ambitions in Lake Superior country is debatable. Apparently, descendants of the defeated eastern confederation at least came back this way on business, or maybe even as tourists.

In Stanley Newton's 1923 book *The Story of Sault Ste. Marie and Chippewa County*, he described what he called an occasional "echo of that epochal occasion on the streets of Sault Ste. Marie," when Indians from the east visit and were confronted by a local Indian.

"How do, Iroquois?"

"Huh, how do you know we're Iroquois?"

*'Oh, we know the Iroquois well. There are hundreds of them here."

"What, Iroquois here?"

"Yes, plenty. They came here to see us nearly three hundred years ago and they are here yet. They were looking for trouble, and we gave them such fine entertainment that they never went back."

39 ST. IGNACE

My discovery of a famous French explorer's grave in St. Ignace, Michigan, occurred before my twelfth birthday. It didn't make the news because someone, actually lots of someones, had found it first.

Being late to the game didn't matter to me. Father Jacques Marquette is one of those historical figures you learn about in elementary or middle school, a long-ago guy like René-Robert Cavelier, Sieur de La Salle and Henry Hudson who poked around North America long before Canada and the United States existed. And the St. Ignace I had first met as a toddler was a picturesque place on the southern tip of the Upper Peninsula of Michigan where you could buy some cheap souvenirs, grab a bite to eat and catch a ferry to Mackinac Island.

Marquette was buried here?

As I got older, the idea became more believable as the bigger picture of French exploration became clearer to me. French explorers had their fingerprints all over northern Michigan. La Salle and Louis Joliet also passed by this way, as did a considerable number of lesser explorers who have had their names attached to lakes, islands, inlets and towns in and around the waterways of the upper Great Lakes.

Marquette became part of St. Ignace, now a town of 2,400 on the north end of the Mackinac Bridge, because he established a mission here in 1671. Father Claude Dablon had built a birchbark mission on Mackinac Island and spent the winter of 1670-71 there, before helping Marquette move the mission across the straits where the horticultural prospects were better. Marquette and a party of Hurons landed their birch bark canoes on the beach across State Street from his burial site, probably on the beach that is part of a small park with a historical marker for Michilimackinac Cove. Presumably, he could have also landed in the asphalt parking lot adjacent to the Indian

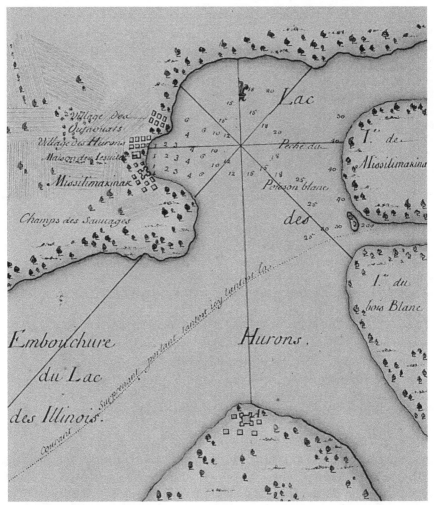

THIS **1717** MAP SHOWS ST. IGNACE MISSION AND HURON AND OTTAWA VILLAGES, UPPER LEFT, AND FORT MICHILIMACKINAC, CENTER, ABOVE.

Village souvenir shop that sits just to the south of that park – both of those are also part of the cove -- but it makes for a better visual picture to think that Marquette and other French explorers landed on that little unspoiled beach. He named his mission for St. Ignatius of Loyola (Ignace is French for Ignatius), the founder of the Jesuit religious order whose missionary priests were active across North America.

When Joliet came this way in his quest for the Mississippi River in 1673, Marquette joined his party. The group left St. Ignace in two canoes with five voyageurs of French-Indian ancestry on May 17. They crossed Lake Michigan, entered Green Bay and journeyed up the Fox River, nearly to its headwaters. The local Indians told them to portage their canoes a distance of slightly less than two miles through marsh and oak plains to the Wisconsin River. On June 17 they entered the Mississippi near present-day Prairie du Chien, Wisconsin.

While Hernando de Soto was the first European to "discover" the Mississippi when he located its mouth in 1541, Joliet and Marquette became the first non-Natives to locate the river's upper reaches, travel a big chunk of it (they went as far south as the mouth of the Arkansas River, 435 miles from the Gulf of Mexico before turning around) and map it.

They left the Mississippi at the mouth of the Illinois River, which the local natives said would provide a shorter route back. They reached Lake Michigan near the site of today's Chicago by way of the Chicago portage. Marquette and his party stopped at the mission of St. Francis Xavier, located in present-day Green Bay, Wisconsin, in September, while Joliet returned to Quebec to announce news of their discoveries.

Marquette returned to the Illinois Territory in late 1674 and became the first Europeans to winter in the area that became modern Chicago. He traveled westward in the spring of 1675 and celebrated Easter mass at the Grand Village of the Illinois near Starved Rock. He had hoped to found a mission in the Illinois county, but by then he suffered from exhaustion, dysentery and bouts of temporary blindness. Feeling that death might be near, he set out the next day for the St. Ignace mission where he hoped to be buried. He didn't make it, dying near the eventual site of Ludington, Michigan, at the age of 37. Two years later in 1677, Indians exhumed his body and carried him to St. Ignace to fulfill his dying wish.

The activity at the mission and on that little beach didn't end with Marquette's death. La Salle came this way on August 27, 1679, and stopped at St. Ignace while exploring the region on the Griffon with Louis Hennepin. The Griffon, believed to have been 30 to 40 feet long with a single mast and a weight of 45 tons, was the first ship to sail the Great Lakes and may have also been the Lakes' first shipwreck; it departed from the area near today's Green Bay, Wisconsin, bound for St. Ignace with a fortune in furs and was never seen or heard from again. The ship may have sunk in a violent Lake Michigan storm – or not. La Salle had separated from the crew for an expedition to the south, and he believed the crew may have scuttled the ship and stolen the furs.

Furs were a magnet. Louis de La Porte, Sieur de Louvigny built a fort at St. Ignace in 1681 primarily to protect a fur trading post. The post was called Fort Michilimackinac, Fort St. Ignace and Fort Frontenac in some early texts and finally took the name Fort de Buade after a French governor, Louis de Buade.

Antoine de la Mothe Cadillac became the commander of this post in 1695, and his description is worth sharing:

"It is very important that you should know, in case you are not already informed, that this village is one of the largest in all Canada. There is a fine fort of pickets, and 60 houses that form a street in a straight line. There is a garrison of well-disciplined, chosen soldiers, consisting of about 200 men, the best formed and most athletic to be found in this New World; besides many other persons who are residents here during two or three months in the year... The houses are arranged along the shore of this great Lake Huron, and fish and smoked meat constitute the principal food of the inhabitants.

"The villages of the savages, in which there are six or seven thousand souls, are about a pistol-shot distant from ours. All the lands are cleared for about three-leagues around their village, and perfectly well cultivated. They produce a sufficient quantity of Indian corn for the use of both the French and savage inhabitants."

Cadillac must not have been that impressed. The French closed Fort de Buade in 1697 and Cadillac founded Fort Detroit in 1701. He used every inducement he could to encourage the tribes to desert their northern villages, move close to the new fort and continue their trade relationship. The Jesuits at St. Ignace did all they could to prevent the Indians from moving, but they became more and more discouraged. They finally gave up in 1705, burned down their mission and returned to Quebec.

This alarmed the French governor and he eventually persuaded Father Joseph Marest to return to St. Ignace in 1714. Louvigny, a former commander, also returned with a few soldiers and re-established the fort; how long it lasted is unknown.

The mission continued to do its work until 1741, when it moved to the south side of the straits. The move made sense because of the increasing prominence of the trading post at Fort Michilimackinac and the migration of Indian tribes that had once populated the area. The mission's closing left St. Ignace nearly deserted,

The actual location of the fort in St. Ignace has never been discovered and it has become something of a mystery to amateur researchers. Some locals say the fort stood on a hill and some historians believe it occupied a spot close to the shore. Others say it sat on the site of the Museum of Ojibwa Culture which lies adjacent to the mission site where Father Marquette is buried. To date, none of these theories has been proven.

The Fort de Buade Museum at 334 North State Street is easier to find. It has been in the same place since 2007 when the City of St. Ignace purchased the site with funding from the Sault Ste. Marie Tribe of Chippewa Indians. The free museum houses a collection of some 3,500 area relics and is operated by the Michilimackinac Historical Society. While we can't be sure if the fort was located there. we do know that the building itself once held the first automobile repair shop in St. Ignace, having been opened in 1910.

The locations of Native American villages here during this period are no mystery. The Huron refugee village (the Hurons lived in the Georgian Bay area before they were driven out by the Iroquois) occupied space to the north of the St. Ignace Mission, on or near the site of the Museum of Ojibwa Culture. They lived here for about 30 years until they resettled in the vicinity of Fort Detroit at the invitation of Cadillac. An Ottawa village lay just to the north of the Huron camp. The two tribes had different languages, different customs and different residences; the Hurons lived in long log houses and the Ottawas resided in wigwams made of bark. Although the two tribes lived in close proximity, they didn't trust each other.

After the abandonment of the mission and the fort, some Indian tribes continued to live and congregate in this area. But the bulk of trading activity occurred in Sault Ste. Marie, 50 miles to the north; at Fort Michilimackinac on the south side of the straits and, after that was abandoned, near Fort Mackinac on Mackinac Island, across the water from St. Ignace.

When the Americans came to Mackinac Island during Northwest Territory days, the French who held land grants here began to come in greater numbers. By the 1830s, they petitioned for a church and built the first St. Ignatius Loyola Church on the corner of McCann Street. That church building, where the Museum of Ojibwa Culture is now located, was moved to site next to the old Father Marquette mission and burial site in 1954.

Even today, the Native American population of St. Ignace remains strong. In the 2010 census, Native Americans made up 27.8 percent of the city's population. A casino run by Sault Ste. Marie Tribe of Chippewa Indians sits just north of town, not far from the Castle Rock tourist site purportedly used as a lookout for Ottawa war chief Pontiac.

It is an area rich with history, and none is more important that than the little State Street plot with an arched concrete entrance that announces itself as Father Marquette Park. The explorer's remains were discovered in 1877, two hundred years after his burial, and a white stone monument was erected on his grave site and the site of his mission for St. Ignatius Loyola.

It can be a busy place in the summer. Carloads of tourists buzz up and down State Street, coming and going from ferry trips to Mackinac Island, where laws against motorized vehicles offer visitors a trip back in time.

But a real trip to the past can be taken in a quiet little park where a famous explorer once walked and a Catholic mission once stood – for free.

40 FORT MICHILIMACKINAC

As you descend Mackinac Bridge from the north, the image of Fort Michilimackinac appears on the right like a ghost that has lost its way. A replica of the old fort and trading post sits there on the exact spot that it stood over 300 years ago, guarding the Straits of Mackinac as it did for both the French and British and causing who knows how many first-time viewers to wonder "Am I really seeing this?"

It looks so natural sitting there, a beach to the north and woods to the south and east that there is almost a hallucinogenic quality about it, as if time had fractured and you really have a 300-year window through time.

The fort that the French built here on the northern tip of the lower peninsula of modern Michigan in 1715 to guard the straits, the deep five-mile wide expanse of water which connects Lake Michigan and Lake Huron, was reborn because of excavations started in the 1960s. The modern replica that includes subsequent expansions, the fort's walls and numerous buildings stands precisely where it did in the mid-1700s.

The surroundings contribute to the fascination of this place. The narrow strip of sand beach and the vast body of water north and west of the fort must look much the way they did before the British dismantled and burned the structure in 1783. The massive Mackinac Bridge that lies northeast of the fort is an obvious intrusion on this daydream, although those who made the one-hour trip to the Upper Peninsula on car ferries for over a half century before the bridge opened in 1957 were doubtless glad to make that sacrifice.

Even the partially wooded area immediately surrounding the fort suggests a time when Indian tribes were the only permanent inhabitants of the area. The village of Mackinaw City, a summer tourist mecca whose souvenir stores and fudge shops seem to outnumber its 800 residents, lies mostly to the east of the fort and of I-75. But the settlement appeared long after the fort had been abandoned. Edgar Conkling and Asbury Searles platted what would become the modern town in 1857. They reserved the northern part of their settlement for a park to accommodate a lighthouse and to preserve the area where the fort had stood. (The Old Mackinac Point Lighthouse, which lies just to the east of I-75, was built in 1889.) Even though the fort didn't rise again for more than another 100 years and their town didn't become the major metropolis they expected it to be, their vision is the reason we're able to visit the rebuilt structure on the same spot today.

When our kids were young, Mackinaw City was a frequent stop on fishing and camping trips. Sometimes this meant merely stopping off at The Fort restaurant, located across Louvigny Street from the reconstructed Fort Michilimackinac. From the second-floor restaurant, you could see the wooden palisades of the replica fort through the trees.

In later years, we toured the amazing structure several times. I have never forgotten the day when a tour guide talked about the British possession of the fort during Revolutionary War days. She said something about the King, then paused and asked the children in the audience if anyone knew the name of the King.

A boy who appeared to be five or six years old began waving his arm frantically until he was called upon.

"Elvis Presley!" he said enthusiastically.

His answer got a good laugh from the tour guide and his audience and gave me a story to tell. Although this is one building Elvis never left, this place has lots of good stories of its own.

For a long time, the action centered on the north side of the straits, where Father Jacques Marquette established his Jesuit mission in 1671 and Fort de Buade was built ten years later. After Sieur de Cadillac closed the mission and moved the French garrison to Fort Detroit in 1701, some French fur traders continued to operate in the area. Demand for furs continued to increase in the ensuing years and tensions with the Indian tribes in the area grew. As British traders of the Hudson Bay Company began to move in this direction from the north and east, the French again saw the military value of the straits.

The French sent soldiers here to try to convince local tribes of Ojibwa, Wyandot, Huron, Potawatomi and Ottawa to form an alliance with them against the Fox and Iroquois, trade partners with the British. They eventually decided to build a smaller version of the modern fort here in 1715. It held almost 40 houses inside its walls even before numerous expansions over the next 30 years turned it into the larger structure we know today.

Why so many residences in a place then about as remote as today's Arctic Circle? The isolated outpost turned into a bustling place in the summer months as Indians, voyageurs, clerks and merchants descended on the post for the annual trading season. The fort itself expanded to accommodate more

FORT MICHILIMACKINAC IS BACK IN THE SAME LOCATION AS THE ORIGINAL, BUT THE
VIEW TO THE NORTHEAST IS DIFFERENT: THE MACKINAC BRIDGE IS IN THE DISTANCE.

traders and by the 1760s a number of homes had been constructed in the area east of the stockade. Merchant John Askin wrote in 1778 that "there is near to one hundred houses in the subarbs (sic), and people are now building tolerable good ones."

While Fort Michilimackinac had a dual presence as both a military post and as a supply depot, the military primarily protected the dozens of traders who came through here on a daily basis. As trade competition between France and England heated up, the fort became a gathering place for all local tribes when they decided to declare their allegiance to the French in 1753, three years before the start of the French and Indian War.

French soldier "Jolicoeur" Charles Bonin visited the fort in 1754 and left an insightful look at the soldiers there:

"The fort. . . has thirty men in garrison who are changed every three years, if they wish. Their only renumeration is powder and lead bullets. This is enough because they cultivate maize or Indian corn, and go hunting and fishing, thus supplying their needs. Anyone who is contented there, and asks not to be transferred, is permitted to remain. I saw two men there who had stayed on, one for twenty years, and another, a Parisian, for thirty years. The latter was sixty years old. The soldiers of this garrison usually trade with the neighboring savages. It is known that some, when transferred from this post, have collected and taken with them, two, three or four bundles of pelts, which they have obtained by trade with the savages."

When the war ended, the victorious British took over the fort in 1761 and their occupation of it didn't make the local tribes at all happy. The British didn't know the Indians as well as the French, weren't as generous with gifts and supplies and weren't accommodating trading partners. Those conditions led to Pontiac's Rebellion, a series of attacks on British forts throughout the region. The grisly attack that occurred here is the most famous incident in the seventy years of the fort's existence.

On June 2, 1763, several hundred Ojibwas who camped near the fort gathered in the clearing outside the fort's south gate for a game of baggatiway, a sport similar to modern lacrosse. The Indians had done this before and the British soldiers often watched from inside the fort's walls. Ojibwa chiefs Minweweh and Madjeckewiss told the soldiers that this was a special game against the Sauks and said that it would be played in honor of the British king (no, not Elvis Presley), George III. As many as 30 or 40 warriors competed in the brutal game, and at one point the ball was thrown near the fort's open gate, where several Indian women lingered while wrapped tightly in bulky blankets that should have been a clue to their evil intentions. The women suddenly threw open their blankets and handed off knives and tomahawks to the athletes-turned-warriors, who began attacking the spectator-soldiers both inside and outside the fort.

Captain Charles Etherington had missed all of the signs of the impending attack and even encouraged his men to watch the game and he was captured with Lieutenant William Leslye and taken away. Lieutenant John Jamet, the fort's only other officer and likely the only armed soldier among the 35 troops, fought courageously with his sword but was hopelessly outnumbered. He fell wounded and the invaders cut off his head.

Young British trader Alexander Henry sat quietly in his cabin, writing letters he hoped to finish before some of the traders left for Montreal. He heard the whoops of the attacking Indians, sprang to his window and witnessed the warriors' savagery.

"Going instantly to my window I saw a crowd of Indians within the fort furiously cutting down every Englishman they found," Henry wrote later. "I saw several of my countrymen fall, and more than one struggling between the knees of an Indian who, holding him in this manner, scalped him while yet living."

Henry noticed that none of the French-Canadian traders living at the fort had been harmed, nor did they lift a finger to help their British hosts. He ran next door to the home of French-Canadian trader Charles Langlade for help. The trader answered in French "What do you want me to do about it?" and turned away, as did the other members of his family.

Fortunately for Henry, the family's Indian slave girl motioned for him to follow her to the attic, where he watched the scene unfold on the fort grounds below him from a hole in the attic wall.

Although Henry avoided capture that day, British soldiers rooted him from his hiding place a day later. He thought he faced immediate death; luckily, the killing spree had temporarily ended. He and other prisoners were paddled off toward an Ojibwa camp on Beaver Island, 30 miles west in Lake Michigan. Starved though he was, he turned down his captors' offer of chunks of bread cut with knives stained in blood the taunting Ojibwas moistened with their spit and smeared on the bread.

The Ojibwas likely would have killed Henry and the other captives had fog not forced their canoes to make a landing at the Ottawa village of L'Arbre Croche. The Ottawas were unhappy that they hadn't been asked to participate in the massacre and they took possession of the captives and paddled them back to Fort Michilimackinac, where they angrily confronted the Indians there and assumed control.

After a tribal council, the Ottawas gave Henry back to the Ojibwas, who again planned to kill him. This time, an Ojibwa village chief named Wawatam saved his life. Wawatam claimed the Great Spirit had told him in a dream that he would make an Englishman his brother and had identified Henry as that Englishman.

Henry's good fortune didn't help the other captives. While he sat within the safety of Wawatam's lodge, the Ojibwas killed seven of the captives who had been with him. The Ojibwas spared two officers who had been held prisoner in the fort because they hoped they would secure a large ransom. With the negotiation of their release in July the officers were taken to Montreal, leaving the fort in the hands of the Indians and a small group of French traders. The Indians didn't really want it. Like Pontiac, they merely wanted to stop British settlement, which they saw as a threat to their lifestyle. The Indians at Michilimackinac soon departed for their winter hunting grounds, hoping to escape retribution from the British for the massacre.

Twenty-seven Englishmen died in the attack and about a dozen were captured; the French suffered no casualties. Besides Michilimackinac, Pontiac and his allies took four other western forts – Miamis, Ouiatenon, St. Joseph and Presque Isle. It didn't matter. The war between the French and the English had already been ended by Treaty of Paris in February. Fourteen months after the Indians' savage attack at Fort Michilimackinac, a detachment of over 300 soldiers under the command of British Captain William Howard again took possession of the fort on August 26, 1764. Henry was among those who accompanied the troops. He had escaped death by living with his adoptive Indian family for over a year before finally making it back to the English side and had joined the expedition at Fort Detroit in hopes of recouping his losses in the area.

The old fort still had a little history left in it, though. Major Robert Rogers, well-known for his exploits as the leader of his guerilla warfare unit called Robert's Rangers that fought the French and Indians during the late 1750s,

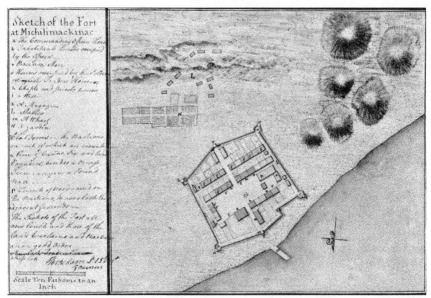

A SKETCH OF FORT MICHILIMACKINAC DONE BY PERKINS MAGRA IN 1766. THE COMMANDANT'S HOUSE (A) IS THE LARGE SHADED BOX, LOWER LEFT. THE CHURCH IS THE LONG RECTANGLE, CENTER RIGHT. GARDEN N) AND STABLES (L) ARE ABOVE.

received personal approval from King George III to mount an expedition to find the Northwest Passage. At the same time, the king named him governor of Michilimackinac and commanding officer of the fort.

Rogers arrived at the fort with his wife during the summer of 1766 and immediately launched the Northwest Passage expedition. Rogers also started planning a new British colony around the Great Lakes that would be ruled by a governor (wait a minute, that's him!) who had direct access to the King.

Thomas Gage, commander of the British forces in North America, didn't like Rogers and he certainly didn't like his plan. Gage was a bitter rival of predecessor General Jeffrey Amherst and Rogers was one Amherst's close friends. Gage used Rogers' quarrels with his subordinate officers to accuse him of treason, and Rogers' own soldiers arrested him on the Fort Michilimackinac parade ground on December 6, 1767. Gage's warrant claimed that Rogers planned to turn the fort over to the French if the British didn't approve his plan of governance.

Soldiers took Rogers in chains to Montreal for trial. Once there, he received support from Amherst's friends and a not guilty verdict, which had to be sent to the king for approval. But Rogers' star was ascending. The king accepted the verdict but tried to avoid embarrassing Gage by issuing a statement indicating that Rogers may be guilty.

Under the circumstances, Rogers couldn't go back to Fort Michilimackinac, where he had been held in jail by his own men. He had gone deeply in debt from spending his own money to equip and pay his Rangers and had never been reimbursed, so he went to England in 1769 to petition for debt relief. But George III had his hands full with the rebellious American colonists and no time for Rogers, who ended up in debtors' prison. He sued Gage for false imprisonment and won a settlement, but his best days were behind him.

The same could be said for the old fort. In 1770, Captain Beamsley Glazier wrote a scathing report to General Gage about the location of Fort Michilimackinac:

"As this Fort stands in so bad a place the landing is so difficult, large hills and deep gullies, which are within 40 yards of the west and south Bastions and spread themselves a Quarter of a mile in circumference, where 1500 Indians may (lie) under cover from any fire from the Fort excepting Shells, and the (reparations) this Fort will want in a little time; If I may be allowed to give my opinion it would be but little more (expensive) to build a Small Fort about ¾ of a mile from this, round the point to the Eastward where this is a good Cove for Landing and a high spot of ground very convenient; but the best place would be the island called Michilimackinac about 8 Miles North from this Fort where there is good landing and wood plenty, which in little time will be very difficult to be got here as we are not obliged to go 7 or 8 Mile for it and it is a great distance from the Shore there."

It took a while but the idea that the defense of Fort Michilimackinac could be a tactical nightmare eventually took hold. In 1781, the British began dismantling buildings and moving them seven miles to Mackinac Island, across the water in the summer and across the ice in the winter. This included Sainte Anne Church, a log building that was disassembled and moved to Mackinac Island, its new permanent home. (The log church was torn down in the 1870s and replaced by the current building, which was completed in 1874.) The houses outside the fort's walls also likely were either dismantled and moved or abandoned during this process.

The move took two years, but the British finished a new limestone fort on a hill, apparently also initially named Fort Michilimackinac, in 1783. That fort, Fort Mackinac, still stands on Mackinac Island today. Patrick Sinclair, lieutenant governor of Michilimackinac, ordered what remained of the old fort burned to the ground and before long no trace of it remained.

The fact that tourists, historians and curiosity seekers can view a replica of it on the spot today shows how much a relatively remote location can be a friend of history. Visitors can't poke around a replica of Fort Detroit or Cincinnati's Fort Washington because a big city grew up where those forts stood. In the 1960s, the site of Fort Michilimackinac was just a windswept park on the shoreline of the Straits of Mackinac, west of a tiny tourist town that all but shuts down in the winter.

Despite its remote location – or maybe because of it -- its rebirth took over 175 years. The Mackinac Island State Park Commission contracted with Michigan State University in 1959 to do a season of excavation at the fort site, a project that has continued every season since. Most of the western half of the fort was excavated and rebuilt during the 1960s. In the 1970s, archaeologists uncovered three row houses outside the fort walls during the building the "Colonial Michilimackinac" visitor center's under Mackinac Bridge.

Large scale excavations of the area surrounding the fort, which park officials call "the suburbs," have yet to occur. But visitors to the fort walk through that area, which lies between the visitor's center and the reconstructed fort.

Both the fort and the buildings inside it are remarkable reconstructions. If there's a down side to a visit, it's that a handful of tourists in shorts and baseball caps, pushing baby carriages and snapping photos with their cell phones, can't generate the kind of energy that surged through here when hundreds of traders, Indians, soldiers and merchants congregated at the height of trading season.

The fort is open to visitors from May 2 to October 7. The schedule alone offers supporting evidence to the annual metamorphosis this place underwent hundreds of years ago, from crowded, bustling place in the summer to a desolate, almost isolated outpost in the winter.

It wasn't open for business in those days either.

41 L'ARBRE CROCHE

The search for L'Arbre Croche, an important Ottawa village and Jesuit mission on the shore of Lake Michigan near of top of Michigan's lower peninsula, encounters the same problem of many other places whose location is tied to a perishable object.

L'Arbre Croche is French for "crooked tree," in this case a towering pine with a hooked top that stood on a bluff and served as an early landmark and navigation aid for voyageurs. The precise location of that long-departed tree is uncertain, as is the site of that tree in relation to the heart of that Ottawa village. The settlement was apparently large enough to put its stamp on the entire region that is today called Little Traverse because of its proximity north of a bay of the same name.

Some historians have placed that crooked tree near Middle Village, which not-so-coincidentally sits near the center of the region, while others believe it may have been located at Cross Village, 10 miles to the north. It's also likely that what early French and English explorers came to regard as L'Arbre Croche stretched all the way from Cross Village in the north to Harbor Springs in the south, a distance of about 20 miles. An 1819 census lists it as a region with ten towns with a combined population of 1,500.

There is no question where the name is most prominent today: Harbor Springs. With a population of 1,200, the city is not only the largest municipality within those boundaries, but it also has the L'Arbre Croche name on a private club and a real estate company and is the home base for the L'Arbre Croche community of Catholic churches.

There is no doubt that the final L'Arbre Croche mission was located there, which explains why the name attached itself to the budding settlement until

277

an influx of settlers in the middle of the nineteenth century began calling it Harbor Springs.

But where was L'Arbre Croche when the Jesuits built the mission in the latter half of the seventeenth century? Where was it when Ojibwas launched a surprise attack from a seemingly harmless game of lacrosse and killed all but a handful of Englishmen at Fort Michilimackinac in 1763? The attackers were taking four of the surviving English including well-known trader Alexander Henry to Beaver Island (probably to be killed and eaten) when they were intercepted by Ottawas, angry at not being consulted about the massacre of the English soldiers at the fort, and diverted to L'Arbre Croche. Exactly where was this L'Arbre Croche of Ottawa sub chief Okinochumake?

In 1917, H. Bedford-Jones' self-published a 26-page book called *L'Arbre Croche Mission. A Memorable Relation Briefly Setting Form the Historical Facts and Eschewing All Fable & Legend, as Erected by Untutored Minds Touching Upon the Justly Famed Mission of the Crooked Tree* to set the record straight.

Bedford-Jones had only 40 copies printed, so he must have had a particular audience in mind. His preface seems to indicate as much:

"This volume is not controversial. Its intent is to give concisely the actual story of a famous mission. A great deal of trash has been written about L'Arbre Croche by lazy or honestly ignorant dabblers; and this book is not copyrighted in hope that others may find profitable instruction therein."

Some "lazy or honestly ignorant dabbler" must have touched Bedford-Jones off. Lest we think that this is just some poor slob who decided to write a book for laughs, it should be noted that the Canadian-born Bedford-Jones was no slouch as a writer. When he self-published his book, he was only three years and six books into a career that would see him write over 100 novels and earn him the nickname "King of Pulps."

He apparently lived in Santa Barbara, California, when he wrote about L'Arbre Croche – he became a U.S. citizen in 1908 – and the little book's dedication to area historian Henry McConnell, whom he credits in the preface for compiling the material "contained herein" from original sources. Whether this was Bedford-Jones' mission, or McConnell's, it's clear one or both were determined to correct the record others had muddled and definitively put the mystery to rest.

"Henry locates L'Arbre Croche twenty miles west of the fort," Bedford-Jones wrote. "Puthoff's census of 1819 gives it as ten towns with a population of 1500. In the first gazetteer of Michigan it is placed ten miles southwest of Mackinaw. Farmer's map of 1846 places it at Harbor Springs. Andrews, in 1853, puts it twenty-five miles southwest of Mackinaw. Where was L'Arbre Croche? Puzzling as these varied locations have been to historians, it will be shown that all were correct."

This book is primarily concerned with the location of the early L'Arbre Croche and not that one that became Harbor Springs after the establishment of the state of Michigan in 1837. Bedford-Jones (or McConnell) seems pretty certain of his facts there.

He wrote that the Ottawas occupied a spot near Fort Michilimackinac in 1740, but were unhappy about the unproductive land there. The French wanted to keep them nearby for trade purposes and set up a meeting with the French governor in Quebec, Marquis de Beauharnois, who offered to help them clear land at several nearby locations. They settled at L'Arbre Croche the following summer and Beauharnois kept his word, sending French soldiers from Michilimackinac to aid the Indians in gradually clearing the entire shore-line down to Little Traverse Bay for tillage. Dotted with villages, the area took the generic term of L'Arbre Croche.

In Bedford-Jones' words "In 1742 came Joseph Ainse, a master carpenter. He built a church near the principal village and the crooked tree, where Cross Village now is. Here the abstract became the concrete name, and here was located "Le Registre de Nouveau Mackinac."

But Judge Thomas Linehan of Harbor Springs, writing in the *Michigan History Magazine* in April, 1918, shortly after Bedford-Jones' book, claims that the mission was established in the seventeenth century:

"In the latter part of the 17th century a mission was established by the Jesuit Fathers at L'Arbre Croche, the most densely populated of all the missions. The exact date of establishing the mission I am unable to determine; however, we have it of record that during the year 1695 the Franciscan missionaries traversed this region and visited the L'Arbre Croche Mission — this record is now at Mackinac."

Either way, the French apparently abandoned that mission sometime between 1764 and the 1780s, after the area fell under British rule. Father Gabriel Richard stopped at L'Arbre Croche on a tour of missions in 1799 and he found just one baptized Ottawa out of 1,300 – and the mission itself had been moved five miles to the south.

Linehan cites the memoirs of Father Samuel Charles Mazzuchelli, written between 1830 and 1834, who placed Old L'Arbre Croche at Middle Village and New L'Arbre Croche at Harbor Springs. He indicated that the mission consisted of four or five churches at this point.

The article doesn't mention Cross Village, which would probably have set Bedford-Jones and McConnell off if they had caught wind of Linehan's research. They were certain that this was not only the site of the crooked tree, but the principal L'Arbre Croche village during the period when both the French and English explored and settled the area.

Today, Cross Village is an airy, unincorporated community of 93 people (according to the 2010 census) in a ten square-mile township of the same name with fewer than 300. It took its name from a huge cross that the Jesuit missionaries erected on a bluff overlooking the lake there, possibly to take the place of the crooked tree. Father Gabriel Richard saw the cross there when he visited in 1799, more evidence for the theory that this was a special place within the Ottawa settlements up and down the Lake Michigan shoreline.

A replica of that huge white cross remains visible from the lake, although the village itself is probably more known for its location at the northern entrance to the 16-mile Tunnel of Trees, a scenic, forested drive on M-119 between Cross Village and Harbor Springs near the lakeshore, and Legs Inn, a one-of-a-kind, bar/restaurant created by Polish immigrant Stanley Smolak in the 1920s and still operated by the same family today. The inn's name was taken from the row of inverted cast iron stove legs Stanley used to create the decorative railing on the roof of the building, but the façade of stones, timber and driftwood create an odd blend of Old World European and Indian culture. Where else can you find totem poles, quality Polish food, deer heads and live music on the site of a historic Indian village and within a stylish log interior that makes it an unusual monument to a time when the lumber business thrived in this region?

Diners have the option of sampling a "Taste of Poland" or "Polska Kielbasa" in the rustic dining room or on the outdoor terrace, a short distance from the lake. Neither calls to the mind the hundreds of Ottawas who lived on this same spot, the council fires with other tribes held here throughout the eighteenth century or the day that 100 or so Ottawas surrounded a small band of Ojibwas with four white prisoners in 1763 and escorted them to shore, probably within sight of what would become Legs Inn's outdoor dining area and garden.

The Ottawas who lived here got around. They traveled hundreds of miles to help the French defeat Braddock at Fort Duquesne in 1755 and helped the French in their defense of Quebec at the Plains of Abraham in 1759. Some of them (but not all) fought with Pontiac around Fort Detroit in the 1760s and fought against Anthony Wayne at Fallen Timbers in 1794, before participating in the Treaty of Greenville.

The center of Ottawa activity here gradually moved southward toward Middle Village and eventually to Harbor Springs, which today is a pretty little resort community on Little Traverse Bay with busy harbor shielded by Harbor Point. The small Native American population of 4.8 percent (as measured by the 2010 census) is probably the result of the emigration of the Ottawas toward the northwest, one that eventually drew the life out of string of Native American settlements along 20 miles of shoreline.

If Harbor Springs has more modern ties to the L'Arbre Croche name, it's not the place to feel the presence of the Ottawa tribe that once lived here. You can feel it during a beautiful Tunnel of Trees drive through Middle Village, which wouldn't feel like a village at all were it not for St. Ignatius Mission Church (that replaced a much earlier structure destroyed by fire in 1893). Rows of white wooden crosses mark the graves of Native Americans who are buried there. Middle Village Park is not far away; it has a walkway through the woods that leads to the beach where dozens of Ottawas must have camped in ancient times.

But Cross Village is probably the go-to place for those looking to experience the ancient village of L'Arbre Croce. The little Catholic church here – Holy Cross Church -- was founded in 1847. It's not the one manned by those early French missionaries, but many of its early records are written in the Ottawa language.

Bedford-Jones wrote of how John Bernard Weikamp, a superior of the Franciscan order, became involved in serious trouble with Bishop Anthony O' Regan of Chicago and was given another chance at L'Arbre Croche by Bishop Frederic Baraga of the Sault Ste. Marie diocese. Weikamp came to Cross Village in 1855 and took charge of the missions. With four brothers and 12 sisters, he "was well able to discover and to graft the shards of the ancient tree," build new structures, operate a farm and "centralize" the region's other missions here.

After Weikamp died in 1889, his operation apparently went downhill quickly. The populations of Harbor Springs and Petoskey were growing and Cross Village seemed out of the way.

"The foundation did not long survive him," Bedford-Jones wrote. "It was controlled by a stock company and supported by the farm, but was finally abandoned in '96, the sisters retiring to Joliet, Illinois. Ten years later, what remained of the buildings was struck by lightning and destroyed.

"Thus perished the last stock of the famed crooked tree, probably nevermore to be revived. . ."

42 MACKINAC ISLAND

Mackinac Island is a terrific place to take a new bride, ride a bicycle, buy fresh fudge, pet a horse, peruse several blocks of souvenir/clothing/you-name-it retail shops, stay in a famous hotel, stay in some not-so-famous-but-should-be hotels, enjoy a wide expanse of gorgeous blue water in almost every direction and many other things that characterize one of America's great summer vacation destinations.

What probably isn't on the minds of most who ride the frequent ferries to the island from Mackinaw City or St. Ignace during warm summer months is the history that also awaits them there.

It would be interesting to know what percentage of day-tripping summer visitors make a stop at Fort Mackinac while they are on the no-motor-vehicles-allowed island. Anyone who has dodged the crowds, horse-drawn carriages and bikes on Main Street and visited the imposing fort on the limestone bluff on the eastern end of the business district knows it's not nearly as crowded up there as it is down on Main.

There are doubtless lots of reasons for this, but we can probably sum it up this way: many of us prefer to spend our time on an island resort sipping beer in a quaint little bar or restaurant or sampling sweets in a fudge shop than tramping around inside an old fort. The history lover in me would like to think the crowd down there is simply composed of visitors who have already toured the historic garrison, but I know better. It's obvious a huge number of the estimated 900,000 tourists who visit the island annually never make it up the hill to see what's behind those white-washed stone walls.

A bicycle ride around the island's perimeter covers eight miles, but the walk up the path to the fort takes the visitor even farther: it's a walk through the centuries. A little perspective is in order for anyone ascending the ramp leading up to the south sally port of the fort at the top of the bluff: none of those signs of modern and not-so-modern civilization behind them -- buildings, streets, ferries, bicycles and tourists -- were there when the British built the fort in 1780.

The British decided to close Fort Michilimackinac on the south side of the Straits of Mackinac and move here because it offered a better view of the area and would be much easier to defend against, ahem, American invaders. A visit to Fort Mackinac that follows one to the reconstructed Michilimackinac in what is now Mackinaw City makes this instantly obvious. If an army of canoes or skiffs bearing hostile Indians or soldiers had the elevated fort on Mackinac Island in its sight, lookouts could see the invaders approaching from great distances.

Native Americans saw value in this place long before the white man. Archaeologists have discovered fishhooks, pottery, and other artifacts that establish a Native American presence on the island around 900 A.D. or at least 700 years before European exploration. The island's earliest inhabitants considered it a sacred place.

The Anishinaabe tribe believed it to be home to the Gitchie Manitou, the "Great Spirit." Tribal legend says that Mackinac Island was created by one of their gods, Michabou (the Great Hare), and that he invented fish nets here after having attentively considered a spider while it constructed its web for catching flies. Legend claims that it was the first land to appear after the end of the Great Flood. It was the burial place of tribal chiefs.

The Ojibwas gave it the name it has today. They likened the shape of the island to that of a turtle so they named it "Mitchimakinak," Ojibwa for "Big Turtle". The Ottawas had a settlement on the island before European exploration began and a nineteenth century Ottawa historian tells of a small local band of tribesman who would have been annihilated by an Iroquois force had two of the local tribesmen not hidden in what now is called Skull Cave.

In 1651-52, the small tribe of Tionontate Hurons who had lived in southern Ontario near Georgian Bay reached Mackinac Island in flight from the Iroquois and believed the island offered them safety. They held it for about two years and are credited with clearing some of the wooded parts for farming before they got anxious with the approach of the Iroquois and retreated to the islands at the mouth of Green Bay.

During the winter of 1670-71, Father Claude Dablon came Mackinac Island from Sault Ste. Marie and established a birchbark mission there. His reports at the time make it clear that he didn't land here by accident:

"Missilimackinac is an island famous in these regions, of more than a league in diameter, and elevated in some places by such high cliffs as to be seen more than twelve leagues off. It is situated just in the strait forming the communication between Lakes Huron and Illinois (Michigan). It is the key. . . and the gate for all of the tribes from the south as the Sault is for those of

FORT MACKINAC PEERS OVER MACKINAC ISLAND IN THIS 1899 PHOTO.

the north, there being in this section of the country only those two passages by water. . . This presents a peculiarly favorable opportunity, both for instructing those who pass here and also for obtaining easy access and conveyance to their places of abode."

What it didn't present was a location good for horticulture, and after contemplating the rocky ground during the winter months, Dablon helped Farther Jacques Marquette move the mission to the northern shore of the straits where he established the Mission of St. Ignace.

Some of the local tribes followed the Jesuits and congregated there, and the number of Native Americans who remained on the island is open to conjecture. After the massacre of the English at Fort Michilimackinac on the straits' southern shore in 1763, English trader Alexander Henry was spared by Ojibwa sub chief Wawatam, who claimed a special kinship to Henry and spirited him away to his own lodge. Several days later, local Indians again threatened Henry and Wawatam came to his rescue and hid him overnight in Skull Cave, located four-tenths of a mile north of today's Fort Mackinac.

Henry later wrote about this experience, which has become one of those historical moments that even many island visitors who aren't interested in touring an old fort love to revisit:

"On going into the cave, of which the entrance was nearly ten feet wide, I found the further end to be rounded in its shape, like that of an oven, but with a further aperture, too small, however, to be explored. After thus looking around me, I broke small branches from the trees and spread them for a bed, then wrapped myself in my blanket and slept till day-break. On awaking, I felt myself incommoded by some object upon which I lay, and, removing it, found it to be a bone. This I supposed to be that of a deer, or some other animal, and what might very naturally be looked for in the place in which I was; but when daylight visited my chamber I discovered, with some feelings of horror, that I was lying on nothing less than a heap of human bones and skulls, which covered the floor!"

Henry later recalled hearing female members of Wawatam's clan signing a song of lament as their canoes approached the island, music designed to pay respect to family members buried there. While there's no way to know today whether Henry had slept with some of those deceased relatives, Wawatam obviously knew the cave well enough to see it as a good hiding place. Today, a historical marker directs visitors to the spot and a wooden fence has been erected to keep visitors out of the cave. Even though the bones are long gone, park officials know that wouldn't dissuade curious tourists from trying to "find" a unique souvenir with a shovel, pick or any other tool they just happened to have in their daughter's baby carriage.

In light of those Ojibwa burials, it should come as no surprise that before Lieutenant Governor Patrick Sinclair arrived on the island in 1779 to relocate the British fort there from the straits' south shore, he first had to secure title to the island from Ojibwa chief Kitchienago, who occupied it with his band.

Sinclair's soldiers didn't have much time to go skull hunting. In the early months of 1780, they hauled the timbers of Ste. Anne's Church at Fort Michilimackinac over the ice to the island six miles away and rebuilt it on the shoreline near the foot of today's Astor Street. The church moved to its current location on the east side of the island harbor in the mid-1820s and the old building was torn down and replaced in 1874.

In the summer, the soldiers moved smaller items by boat and when the ice again formed on the straits during the winter of 1780-81, the troops started hauling the barracks and other buildings made of cedar timbers from the old fort to the island. They transported doors, windows, bricks and provisions in boats during the fall of 1780 and in the spring and summer of 1781. The new fort clung to its old name, Fort Michilimackinac.

There's at least one building on the island today that may have been moved across the straits on the ice, the one-story McGulpin House on Fort Street near Market Street across from the fort. It is a log house of piece-sur-piece construction with a steeply-pitched gable roof in the French Colonial style and is believed to have been built around 1781. It was moved again to its present location from a spot behind Ste. Anne's Church in the 1980s. It has been restored to its appearance in the 1820s with clapboard siding. The Biddle House on Market Street is also a log house of piece-sur-piece construction that dates to the eighteenth century, although its history before 1797 is unknown. A pair of one-story and a half log houses on the opposite sides of French Street might also date the 1700s, as does the building which houses the Mustang Lounge on Astor Street. It is believed to have been a row house or a fur trader's warehouse in its early life. It has been extensively remodeled with its original log timbers, the last time in 2008, and dubs itself "Michigan's Most Historic Tavern."

The first troops moved to the new fort on May, 24, 1781, although all weren't stationed there until later that summer. The Officers' Stone Quarters, with walls up to three feet thick, became an integral part of the south fort wall when construction began in 1780.

After all that backbreaking labor, it seems almost cruel that the peace treaty the Americans and British signed in Paris on September 3, 1783, placed the new outpost within the boundaries of the United States. That would seem to be a plausible explanation for why the English refused to withdraw their troops for another 12 years, but it's not the real reason: the British didn't relinquish their hold on Fort Mackinac, Fort Detroit, Fort Ontario (at Oswego), Fort Niagara, and Fort Miamis because of their importance in the fur trade and their critical alliances with Indian tribes.

Finally, the Jay Treaty between the United States and Great Britain ratified by the U.S. Senate in June, 1795, resolved lingering issues from the Treaty of Paris, including the withdrawal of British Army units from forts in the Northwest Territory. Two companies of American troops under the command of Major Henry Burbeck, with Captain Abner Prior and Lieutenants Ebenezer Massay and John Michael, arrived and took possession of the post in October, 1796.

Early reports of the number of buildings in the town beneath the fort between 1796 and 1802 are all over the place, ranging from about 50 to 89. Residents occupied only about half the houses in the winter, but the population exploded during the summer months and some of the visitors had to take up residence in tents.

The British laid out the little village behind stockade walls. Market Street became the town's main street. Astor Street, Windsor Street and French Lane connected Market with Huron (Main) Street and the lakeshore Fort Street separated the east end of town from the government grounds below the fort. The village remained sparsely settled until the mid-nineteenth century. Following the Treaty of Paris in 1783, the townspeople began to move outside of the town walls, building homes on the east side of Haldimand Bay and settling on small farms in the interior. The stockade walls were gone by the 1810s.

American forces worked to repair and improve the defenses of the fort, which the British had allowed to deteriorate in their years as military squatters. Between 1797 and 1800, the Americans built new stone walls where wooden walls had rotted, built stone and hewn timber blockhouses on the old bastions, and finished the Officers' Stone Quarters that the British had failed to complete. Today's fort appears much as it did in 1800 after the Americans had finished their rehabilitation of the original. Fort Mackinac ranked as the sixth largest army post in the U.S. in 1803 with more than 120 soldiers.

The British weren't through with the island, however. A small garrison of about 60 men manned the fort in what was then called Michigan Territory when the War of 1812 erupted. On July 17, 1812, a combined force of approximately 600 British soldiers, Indian warriors, French Canadians and Metis voyageurs in seventy war canoes and ten bateaux under the command of British Captain Charles Roberts sailed from Fort St. Joseph about 40 miles away and landed on the north side of the island. Today, a replica of a British cannon marks the site, and a nearby nature center, concession stand and picnic tables make this a popular place for bicycle riders to rest.

The British came on a more serious mission. They aimed two cannons at the fort, and American Lieutenant Porter Hanks realized that his forces were greatly outnumbered and surrendered without a fight. Hanks' sad tale doesn't end there. The British paroled the Americans provided they agreed not to take up arms against them again, and Hanks made his way to the American military post at Detroit. The officers there charged him with cowardice in the surrender of his fort, but the British attacked Fort Detroit before his trial could begin. A British cannonball crashed through the room where Hanks stood, cutting him in half and also killing the officer next to him.

In the two years that the British flag flew above Fort Mackinac, they built Fort George, a stockade and blockhouse on the highest point of the island that can still be viewed today. It is the primary reason the Americans first attempt to retake the island in July, 1814, failed; the new blockhouse stood too high for the Americans naval guns to reach. They withdrew in a dense fog after about a week, then returned in a landing on the north shore near the site of the British invasion.

The British were waiting on Michael Dousman's farm in the center of the island when the Battle of Mackinac Island took place on August 4, 1814. The Americans attacked and 13 American soldiers including Major Andrew Holmes were killed and 51 were wounded before the Americans retreated again. The Americans finally regained the island in July, 1815, with the signing of the Treaty of Ghent at the end of the war. They renamed the new British fortification Fort Holmes for their fallen commander.

While that ended the fort's military significance, the island enjoyed new life as an important fur trading outpost. John Jacob Astor's American Fur Company merged with the Montreal Michilimackinac Company in 1811 and Astor capitalized on anti-British sentiments to challenge the British commercial dominance in North American fur trade. After the war, Astor reestablished Mackinac Island as the American Fur Company's center for interior operations, bringing in a large number of clerks from Montreal and various U.S. locations to the island.

Traders fanned out over the Great Lakes during the winter months and traded for furs from Indian trappers, then returned to the island with their pelts in the summer. There, American Fur Company clerks counted, graded, sorted and packed their pelts and shipped them back to New York City, the new eastern destination. In return, trade goods were shipped to Mackinac Island for the next winter's trading.

The company grew to monopolize the fur trade in the United States by 1830. But a decline in fur's popularity prompted Astor to sell the American Fur Company in 1834 to a group of investors led by Ramsey Crooks and Robert Stuart, who managed the factory. The Stuart House on Market Street, which dates from the 1817, is operated as a museum by the city; the fur company's warehouse next door, circa 1810, is used for city offices and a community hall. Crooks moved the company's primary western outpost to LaPointe, Wisconsin, and Astor invested his money in New York real estate on Manhattan, a move that paid off handsomely.

John Jacob Astor was the richest man in America with an estate of over $20 million -- over $100 billion in today's dollars -- when he died in 1848, a year after the American Fur Company went out of business.

A house on Cadotte Avenue is named for Astor's son, William Backhouse Astor, who succeeded him as CEO of the family firm and oversaw its business interests. Oral history on the island suggests that he lived in this structure when he visited the island, but it is uncertain how often that happened, if at all. (The house was originally built as a log house in 1816.) When his father died, William Backhouse Astor succeeded him as the richest man in America. If he felt strong ties to the island that once occupied such an important position in the family empire, he didn't show it by spreading his wealth.

When the elegant Grand Hotel was built on the island in 1887, two-thirds of the money for it came from East Coast business interests.

The Astors?

Nope. The Vanderbilts and the Michigan Central Railroad they owned put up the New York share of the money to build the plush hotel that remains world famous today.

VI.

FRENCH INDIANA-ILLINOIS

43 STARVED ROCK

It's hard to know how many visitors to Starved Rock State Park have heard the story of how the 125-foot high, tree-covered sandstone monolith at the heart of it all got its name. It's even harder to know how many of them believe the legend when they hear it.

It almost goes without saying that a landmark called Starved Rock would have a terrific back story. Places with much less evocative names come with dramatic tales that sound like they sprang from the keyboard of a Hollywood screenwriter, so it's not surprising that this massive butte next to the Illinois River inspired a legend that would make a terrific movie. Although there are several variations of the story, the most popular one goes like this:

A member of one of the Illinois subtribes murdered famous intra-tribal leader Pontiac in Cahokia on April 20, 1769. Potawatomi, Ottawa and Meskwaki warriors, angered by the senseless killing, engaged in a war of retribution against members of the Illinois confederation. That grouping consists of 12 or 13 different tribes, including the Peoria, Michigamea, Kaskaskia and Cahokia.

The Illini were driven across modern Illinois and finally took refuge on top of Starved Rock – presumably, it was simply called "The Rock" at that point – where they were safe from their enemies. Unfortunately, it offered no source of food or water. Because of this, their attackers kept the Illini under siege until they all died of thirst and starvation, the reason there are no surviving Illini people today.

There are lots of problems with this "legend," starting with the fact that members of the Peoria and Kaskaskia subtribes of the Illiniwek are still among the living. If this legend works for some of us, it's probably because we wouldn't know a modern member of the Illini tribe if we saw one. (Here's a hint: It's probably not the guy wearing an orange Fighting Illini t-shirt in front of you in line at Chipotle.) Anyone who climbs the wooden stairs to the top of Starved Rock and walks the perimeter would also have to wonder if all of the members of the Illinois tribe could have even fit up there before they starved to death.

To be fair, Starved Rock has been as a magnet for other legends as well. There is a story of doomed Native American lovers from warring tribes who leap to their deaths rather than face living without their true love. (Visitors can follow a path to "Lovers Leap" elsewhere in the park.) Some suggest that Starved Rock and the nearby canyons are haunted. There is even the seemingly mandatory "buried gold" legend, one suggesting that French army officer Henri de Tonti returned here many years after his supposed death -- he died near Mobile, Alabama in 1704 -- and buried an undiscovered cache of gold nearby. Far be it from me to say that Tonti didn't bury some gold near the rock, but it strikes me that the enormous number of these buried treasure stories are mostly bad for the credibility of legends and good for the metal detector business.

I'll concede that it would probably be more fun simply to accept some of the legends – "Wow, you mean all of the members of the Illini tribe died of starvation right here? – than look at the real history of the place. But that history is actually pretty fascinating without wild tales involving the extermination of a historic tribe.

Archaeologists say that human habitation around Starved Rock goes as far back as 8000 B.C. There are five sites including Starved Rock in the 2,630-acre park on the National Register of Historic Places and several other sites of archaeological significance. Three village and mound sites lie within park boundaries.

When Father Jacques Marquette and Louis Joliet passed by here on the return home from their famous "discovery" of the Mississippi River in 1673 they called it Le Roche. They were welcomed by the Kaskaskias, whose Grand Village of the Kaskaskias stood just across the Illinois River and slightly upstream from the rock. The Kaskaskias lived in wigwams made of light-weight material that could easily be dismantled when they traveled to hunt bison twice a year. When Rene-Robert Cavelier, Sieur de La Salle paddled by here in December, 1679, the Kaskaskia were away on their winter hunt, but he estimated that the village had 400 or 500 cabins, each big enough to house five or six families. The village extended along the north bank of the Illinois for about a league (about three miles), with a width of about a quarter of a league (three-quarters of a mile.) Marquette returned two years later and established the Mission of the Immaculate Conception here and fellow Jesuit priest Claude-Jean Allouez came here to work among the Illinois in 1677 after receiving word of Marquette's death.

La Salle and his lieutenant, Tonti, continued about 65 miles down the

STARVED ROCK AS IT APPEARED ON A 1922 POSTCARD

Illinois River and on January 4 or 5, 1680, discovered an Illini village of about 80 cabins at the southern end of Peoria Lake. All of the warriors had gone away on their winter hunt and those who remained initially worried that the French were part of an Iroquois war party. La Salle assured them of his friendship and built Fort Crevecoeur near the village.

Tonti was still there that spring when he received word of the Iroquois' intent to attack the Illini. He went to Starved Rock to help prepare the Illini to defend themselves. The women and children had already fled down the river when the Iroquois arrived and only about 500 Illini remained in the village that once consisted of 7,000 or 8,000. Tonti tried to negotiate peace between the tribes, but after being stabbed and severely injured he realized that the Iroquois had no interest in peace. The Illini who had stayed behind moved downriver, Tonti moved north to Green Bay and the angry Iroquois burned the village, desecrated the Kaskaskias' cemetery and destroyed their fields of corn.

La Salle had noted the natural fortification provided by Starved Rock when he passed here earlier and in December, 1682, he and Tonti returned to construct Fort St. Louis atop the rock. They envisioned it as part of a chain of French forts between Montreal and New Orleans that would discourage the British westward expansion, one that would also provide protection for their Illinois allies from the aggressive Iroquois. But they found the village deserted when they arrived, the Kaskaskias having fled across the Mississippi in fear of an Iroquois attack. The fort La Salle built had oak palisades, a parapet and bastions, with a storehouse, chapel and several cabins for trade inside its walls. Tonti served as commander of the structure, which functioned as the headquarters for the French and Indian trade and also as the diplomatic center for the region.

A model of the fort in the park's visitor center makes it easier for a modern sightseer to imagine what it must have been like to live on top of a butte. Visitors ascending the wooden stairs that frame the rock will get a better feel for the climb the French faced if they check out the woods and the steep rock beside them. On a hot, humid August day it occurred to me how miserable it would be living under siege in this place with the only water at the bottom. But it also occurred to a mom with a toddler I passed near the bottom that the rock isn't "baby carriage friendly," so it's all a matter of perspective.

Either way, La Salle had big things in mind for it. In the fall of 1683, he and the Miamis invited the Kaskaskia, Peoria, Moingwena, Tamaroa and Cahokia subtribes of Illinois to come here and join the Miami, Mascouten and Shawnee tribes to form a confederacy against the invaders.

Jean-Baptiste-Louis Franquelin's 1684 map shows what a bustling place the area around Starved Rock and Fort St. Louis became; 1,200 Illini warriors living on the north shore of the river across from the fort, 500 Wea warriors just west of the Illini, 200 Shawnee warriors living south of the fort, 1,300 Miami warriors located just up the Vermilion River (which empties into the Illinois a mile and a half to the west), 150 Piankashaw (a Miami subtribe) warriors just up the Illinois, and several others. La Salle's confederacy had mustered 3,800 warriors around his fort; when their families are counted, the number of Native Americans here probably exceeded 20,000.

La Salle returned to Canada in August of 1683, and with Chevalier de Baugis in command and many of the warriors away, an Iroquois war party attacked Fort St. Louis in 1684. The defenders withstood a six-day siege, but the Iroquois didn't go away. They continued to pillage French canoes and skirmish with the scattering Illini, and the French finally came to the conclusion that it was too difficult to secure water and firewood on Starved Rock while under attack. The French abandoned it in 1702 and moved to a more convenient location at Peoria Lake that would also be called Fort St. Louis.

The ruins of the fort atop Starved Rock burned sometime in the eighteenth century. Nothing remains of the fort today, although a wooden walkway that takes sightseers around the perimeter of the butte hints at what it must have been like to have been stationed up there. On a clear day, you can see for miles in every direction. The Illinois River flows just to the north of it, and to the east, in the vicinity of the site of the Kaskaskias' Grand Village, the Starved Rock Lock and Dam was constructed between 1926 and 1933. Even with the dam as a modern intrusion to a historian's fantasy, the view of the woods to the south, Plum Island to the west and the prairie to the north is spectacular. The wooded "interior" view should is also worth noting: it takes us past three species of confers (eastern white pine, northern white cedar and eastern red cedar) that aren't common in most parts of the modern state of Illinois.

It seems odd that Starved Rock is as much of a voyage of discovery for many of us as it was for Marquette, La Salle and Joliet, but out of sight out of mind: we don't usually travel by river these days and it's not visible from a speeding car on a freeway several miles away. Most of us don't see the physical aspects of the earth the same way as our ancestors did, if we see them at all.

"Who knew we had a place like this so close to Chicago?" one Internet reviewer wrote.

"Had never even heard of Starved Rock until about a month ago," wrote another, this one from Wisconsin. "But I think I saw a photo on Facebook and we decided to go. . ."

This place obviously meant a lot more to the local tribes than it does to us, and the Native American presence on and around Starved Rock continued long after the French abandoned Fort St. Louis. By 1712, part of the Peoria tribe established a settlement at Starved Rock under the leadership of a powerful chief named Chachagouache. But they were at war with the Kickapoo, Mascouten or Fox tribes almost constantly and by 1719, when the Foxes attacked, the Illini there consisted only of about 800 or 900 people. Those Illini had been forced to make their village on an island at the foot of Starved Rock in order to best defend themselves, the island where the Plum Island Eagle Sanctuary is today. The Illini had a second village at the southern tip of Peoria Lake, which also came under attack, and in 1722, they joined those at Starved Rock for protection. Later that year, the Foxes surrounded the Illini village and forced the surrender of 80 women and children, and the Illini immediately left Starved Rock and settled with other members of the Illiniwek at Cahokia, Kaskaskia and Michigamea.

Some Peorias eventually returned to Starved Rock and were living there in July, 1730, when a party of 350 Fox warriors and 1,000 in all came here for an attack and found themselves surrounded by Illini warriors from other villages who had heard of their approach. The Foxes retreated and established a "fort" about 63 miles south of Starved Rock, where a combined force of Illini, Weas, Piankashaws and French troops all but annihilated them.

But the Illini's numbers were also shrinking and so was the importance of Starved Rock. Little bands of Illini kept leaving the main villages, many going west of the Mississippi River, and it became difficult for the tribe to defend itself. A Sioux war against the Illini in 1740 took its toll and the Potawatomis, Mascoutens, Menominees and Ojibwas sent war parties against the Illinois in 1751. At that point, only four cabins of Illini still lived at Starved Rock.

By the time Pontiac had been stabbed by a Peoria in Cahokia in 1769 and the northern tribes sought to punish the Illiniwek – remember the legend? --

500 to 600 fleeing Illini sought protection at Fort de Chartres, and not Starved Rock. By then, the weakened Illini had abandoned their Illinois River sites and no other tribes had moved in to take their place.

Daniel Hitt purchased the land that became Starved Rock State Park from the federal government for $85 in 1835 as compensation for his service in the army, and Ferdinand Walther bought it from him in 1890 with the eye on creating a resort there. Walther built a hotel near the base of Starved Rock and also added a dance hall and concession stand. The site was accessible only by railroad and Walther couldn't make a go of it financially; he sold the land to the Illinois State Park Commission in 1911 and it became a state park a year later. The rock became a national monument in 1960, although its rich history suggests that it had been one long before it received an official designation.

One of several high school students who followed me up the steps begged to differ as he came within sight of the top. He drew in a couple of hard breaths and exhaled the words with the last one. "This would be better if there weren't so many stairs."

Or worse with no stairs at all

44 PEORIA

Driving north on Northeast Adams Street out of downtown Peoria, Illinois, thoughts don't naturally turn to history. Mixed among the old warehouses and empty lots are an electric supply company, a pump company, a bearing distributor, a sheet metal company, a heating and cooling company, a mortuary services business, a pest control company and a handful of houses, most of which were probably built in the 1950s. For most of the mile-and-a-half drive, first the Illinois River and then Peoria Lake is over there somewhere, no more than 200 yards to the east but hidden by the buildings and loading docks that front on Adams.

In an empty lot at southwest corner of Mary Street, a granite marker with a bronze plaque announces the site of Camp Peoria, where some volunteer regiments of Union soldiers were encamped for several months during the Civil War in 1862. What it doesn't say is every bit as interesting: A large village of the Peoria sub-tribe of the Illinois was located in this vicinity in the seventeenth and eighteenth centuries, the reason the French built the first enduring fort of what is now Peoria in 1691 one block to the north, near the corner of Cornhill and Adams streets.

Isn't that history as important as that of a temporary Civil War camp?

To be fair, the "George A. Wilson Circle No. 49 Ladies of the Grand Army of the Republic" erected the Camp Peoria marker in 1911, and they probably didn't know or care about the other history in the vicinity. And there is nothing in the area (outside of that marker) to suggest that anything of note happened here. This isn't exactly Boston's Freedom Trail.

A park across Mary Street from the marker is intersected by a railroad track and occupies the block that stretches to Cornhill Street. A bar or private club with lighted beer signs and no visible name is located on the other corner at Cornhill; the O'Brien Steel Company lies directly across Adams from both the park and the bar.

While I studied the park and tried to imagine it without the encroachments from the twenty-first century, a silver-haired man with a face lined like a road map ambled past on the street in front of me. He nodded and smiled as I snapped a few photos of the park with my cellphone and I felt obligated to explain what I found so interesting in a rather drab little park.

He told me that he lived nearby and confessed that he didn't know much about history. I thought about the Peorias whose village once spread out over the area where we stood and asked him something when I already knew the answer.

"This is going to sound like a weird question," I said. "But do you know any Indians?"

He looked puzzled. "Indians?"

"You know. . . Native Americans."

He shook his head. "Can't say as I do."

"Just curious," I said.

I left it there. He didn't steal his neighborhood from the Illinois tribes. He just lives here.

The Illinois lived here first, or at least before the white man. If you discount Rene-Robert Cavelier, Sieur de La Salle's construction of a small, fleeting compound he called Fort Crevecoeur in January, 1680, on the east side of the Peoria River where the modern suburb of Creve Coeur is located (more on that later), this is apparently where the story of Peoria begins.

Henri de Tonti, the trusted lieutenant of La Salle before the French explorer died in 1687, arrived here during the winter of 1691-92 and began constructing a fort to replace the one at Starved Rock. History doesn't remember Tonti with the same enthusiasm that it does La Salle, but the Native Americans who dealt with Tonti did; he was called "Iron Hand" by the natives because a grenade had blown away most of his right hand during a battle at Libisso, Sicily, and an iron hand or hook, usually covered by a glove, had replaced it.

Like the one at Starved Rock, Tonti's new structure would be called Fort St. Louis, after French King Louis XIV. Two large buildings, one for lodging and one a warehouse, and two small buildings to house soldiers sat inside a wall of 1,800 pickets. The design would allow friendly Indians to come inside for protection against the hostile Iroquois.

Father Jacques Gravier had started a Jesuit mission at Starved Rock in 1689 or 1690 and he likely came here with Tonti or shortly afterwards. He worked here among the Indians until 1706, when a prominent member of the Peoria tribe who hated the French attacked him. Gravier was struck by five arrows and eventually had to be taken to a Kaskaskia village and then to Mobile for further treatment, thus ending his missionary work with the tribe.

Tonti and his cousin and trading partner, Francois Dauphin de La Forest, continued their operations here until at least 1703, but they also seem to have left because of the bad feelings among the Peorias. A few years later the Peorias were eager to have the old mission reopened, so Rev. Jean Marie de Ville came here in 1711 and stayed for several years.

Shifting French trade policies made this a period of uncertainty. The fort closed in 1713 and opened again two years later with a sergeant and a band of eight soldiers. Finally, when the French abolished the permit system at the fort and the Company of the West absorbed all of the trading, the garrison was called back to Montreal. The French military finally abandoned the fort in 1720, and when Father Charlevoix passed through in 1721, he reported several hundred Indians and four Frenchmen at the site. But De Lisle stopped the following year and found no one in the area, the Peoria tribe having joined the other Illinois tribesmen at Starved Rock.

The Peorias returned in 1733 and by 1750 the tribe's village numbered 1,200, Father Sébastien Louis Meurin had a Jesuit mission and the French again manned a small garrison. The old fort had probably been rebuilt numerous times and remained operational when the British took control of the area in 1765. It had acquired the name of Fort Pimiteoui (the name the Illini attached to the Peoria Lake) and had "stockades of green timber, enclosing a square with log structures within."

A handful of French settlers built houses and farmed here and at one point, this "Old Peoria" village had a horse mill and a blacksmith. For most of the next 30 years its population ranged from six to 15 residents, not counting the local tribes. One of them was a free black trader named Jean-Baptiste-Point DuSable, who bought a house and a three-acre farm in 1773 and later became (according to some) the first resident of Chicago. But Indian attacks during the American Revolution resulted in the settlement's abandonment. A man named Patrick Kennedy visited the area in 1773 and found the fort's stockade destroyed by fire and the houses in the village still standing.

Trader Jean Baptiste Maillet lived in one of those houses and sometime before 1778 he moved a mile and a half south and built a stockade house near the foot of modern Harrison Street in downtown Peoria. When other village residents began to follow him, it marked the beginnings of a new settlement the French called Au Pied du Lac, meaning "at the foot of the lake." By 1796, all of the former residents of "Old Peoria" were gone, although parts of the fort's blockhouses apparently remained standing. Thirty years later, the property owner there found fragments of burned pickets and heaped earth at the foot of Mary Street he thought were the remains of the fort. Presumably, this was across modern Adams Street from the "Camp Peoria" marker, in the area occupied by the parking lots and buildings of

O'Brien Steel. A boat launch and parking lot lie behind the steel company's property on the shore of Peoria Lake today.

Maillet's settlement or "New Peoria" grew considerably larger than the old village on Peoria Lake. His "house" became part of a fort, with two blockhouses. Maillet lived in one blockhouse and the other held a store. Earthworks and palisades surrounded it, and a gateway on the south side of it opened to the burgeoning town. Today, this property is occupied by the Ameren power company, which has a fenced lot on the Illinois River at the foot of Harrison Street.

George Rogers Clark sent three soldiers and two Frenchmen to the little village in 1778 to tell its residents that British authority had ended and they had become citizens of the United States. One of the soldiers, Nicholas Smith, described it as a large town with narrow, unpaved streets and houses made of wood. There was a church with a wooden cross on its roof and gilt lettering on the door and a windmill nearby for grinding grain. The town's six stores were filled with goods for the Indian market. He said the inhabitants included French settlers, Indians and people of mixed heritage, and none of them could speak or understand English.

During the winter of 1788, several Indians came to the village to trade and lodged in the empty fort, which Maillet no longer occupied. They all got drunk and burned the fort down, abruptly ending that chapter in the village's brief existence. Detroit trader Hugh Heward visited there in May 1790, and found "seven French settled among the Indians." One of those was Maillet, whom he called "Capt. Mye."

According to a nineteenth century U.S. survey, this village occupied the land from the river to Washington Street on the west and Oak Street on the northeast. That this small area extends no more than three modern city blocks in any direction offers perspective in just how tiny the settlement was compared to the modern city of Peoria.

No matter. Like the original settlement out there at Adams and Cornhill streets, this Peoria also wouldn't last. The end came with the War of 1812, which reached here when mounted militia under Colonel William Russell from Kentucky attacked a Potawatomi village at the head of Peoria Lake and killed 25 to 30 people without waiting to see whether the tribe was friendly. When expected reinforcements failed to arrive, the troops departed; several days later, another militia company under Colonel Thomas Craig finally showed up and found New Peoria half empty, probably because the settlers feared retaliation for Russell's attack. The militia decided to loot the vacant houses -- they came here to protect the settlers, right? -- including the warehouse of traders Thomas Forsyth and John Kinzie.

Forsyth returned and demanded that the goods be returned, a request only partially met. Shots were fired at Craig's boats during the night and Craig rounded up the remaining inhabitants of the village for their "protection."

Forty-one men, women and children were taken to Savage's Ferry near Alton and held for four days before Illinois territorial governor Ninian Edwards ordered their release. In the meantime, Craig had, in his words, "burnt down about half of the town." It wasn't resettled. Five more years would pass before seven settlers came here in 1819 looking for a favorable place to live and the beginnings of the modern city of Peoria sprouted. But those who lived in both of the deserted Peoria settlements didn't forget: The claims of the French who had occupied the property were mired in the courts for more than a half-century.

The previous owners – the Peoria tribe of the Illinois – weren't party to any of those claims, of course. In the 2010 census, only .3 percent of the population of the city of 115,000 residents identified as Native American. They comprised 100 percent of the population when the French arrived.

The other side of the Peoria River has its own history. The American Fur Company established a trading post on the east side of the Peoria River in 1818 called Opa Post. Today, that trading post would be in the village of Creve Coeur, which took the name of the fort that La Salle built and briefly occupied in that area in 1680.

La Salle and Tonti began construction of the fort on January 15, 1680, and the Recollets -- Gabriel de la Ribourde, Zenobius Membre and Louis Hennepin – celebrated a mass there. They finished building the fort in early March, naming it Crevecoeur, French for "broken heart." Historians believe this referred either to the loss of the Griffon, the sailing vessel La Salle had built to help find the Northwest Passage several months before, or the hardships the French had encountered on this mission. I would suggest that they keep trying.

On March 1, La Salle set off up the Illinois River for supplies, leaving Tonti in charge of the fort. When he reached Starved Rock, he concluded that it would be a better location for a fort and sent word back to Tonti. Tonti left Fort Crèvecoeur on April 15, 1680, with Father Ribourde and two other men for Starved Rock. The next day, the remaining seven men at Crevecoeur led by Martin Chartier pillaged the fort of all provisions and ammunition, destroyed it and headed back to Canada.

Today, the village of Creve Coeur is home to Fort Crevecoeur State Park, which has a modern rendition of the fort and a historical marker commemorating Fort Crevecoeur. The marker stands at the end of 100-foot, brush-lined path off a cul-de-sac at the end of Park Road, a pretty street in a residential area off Illinois Route 29.

It is a dramatic setting for a stone marker, but whether that is the fort's actual location has been debated for centuries.

La Salle's description of it in his journal seems precise:

"On January 15, toward evening a great thaw, which opportunely occurred, rendered the river free from ice from Pimiteoui as far as [the place chosen for the fort]. It was a little hillock about 540 feet from the bank of the river; up to the foot of the hillock the river expanded every time that there fell a heavy rain. Two wide and deep ravines shut in two other sides and one-half of the fourth, which I caused to be closed completely by a ditch joining the two ravines."

In 1902, the Daughters of the American Revolution conducted a five-year study and determined this as the site of the fort. But because others still insisted it wasn't, the Illinois Historical Society named a committee to study the information and conduct its own search. The panel finally decided in 1921 that it was impossible to determine the exact site. It agreed to accept the conclusion of the DAR, which promptly erected a stone monument on the spot starting with the inscription "In 1680 upon this spot stood Fort Crevecoeur. . ."

Unfortunately, as we have seen in other places, simply making a claim on a marker doesn't make it true. In 1919, Dan Sheen of Peoria wrote a detailed analysis of five locations that had been proposed as the site of La Salle's fort, including one in East Peoria "about on a line with Fayette Street in Peoria." That would place it just north of modern I-74, in a location that today holds a Bass Pro Shop.

In 1978, Richard Phillips submitted a National Register of Historic Places nomination for the Upper Hill site, also on Sheen's list, to the Illinois Historic Sites Advisory Council as the site of both Fort Crevecoeur and Fort St. Louis. The council "was not convinced." For those interested in drawing their own conclusions, Phillips, a former photographer and newspaper publisher with the *Peoria Journal*, donated 30 boxes of material on the fort to the Illinois History and Lincoln collections of the University of Illinois Library. The line to view them is undoubtedly enormous.

After investigations of the Upper Hill site failed to prove French occupation there, field investigators from Illinois State University examined seven other sites – note that the number is growing -- with similar results. They determined that because the areas had all been so badly disturbed there is a good chance the actual site will never be found.

Lest anyone wonder, the name of the village of Creve Coeur came after the DAR decided to put its historic monument there. The unincorporated community of Wesley City voted to incorporate as the village of Crevecoeur on May 5, 1921. It changed its name to Creve Coeur in 1960 because Mayor Carroll Patten believed "Crevecoeur" was a misspelling.

Fortunately, he didn't offer an opinion on the fort's location.

45 KASKASKIA

When I asked a history-minded friend what he knew of Kaskaskia, he scrunched his face into a pained expression, one that said he would have to dig around his mental attic looking for something he put there 40 years ago.

"Kaskaskia?" His repeat of the word gave way to a tortured five-second pause. "Uh. . . isn't that the place George Rogers Clark captured during the American Revolution?"

It didn't surprise me that he got that right, or that he next correctly guessed that it is located in the state of Illinois. But the bonus question – what else can you tell me about it? – stumped him.

"Nothing," he said.

I tried this out on several others and the conversation played out pretty much the same way, at least among those who knew of Kaskaskia at all. They generally surmised that it must have been an important place in its day or we wouldn't remember that Clark captured it, but no one seemed to know exactly where it is or what happened to it afterwards.

But when you set out on a personal mission of discovery, the mystery of Kaskaskia, if you want to call it that, starts to make sense. Locating it on a map is one thing; it's there in southern Illinois a short distance from the Mississippi River. And then you look closer and realize that it's on the wrong side of the Mississippi. The Mississippi and Illinois are over there, and Kaskaskia is over here, on the Missouri side, but still in Illinois. You can't get there by car from the Illinois side without taking a roundabout path on Illinois Route 51 across the bridge in Chester, Illinois. Then you circle around and slip in the backdoor from tiny St. Mary, Missouri, using the Old Channel Road Bridge. The Mississippi changed course and Kaskaskia is now on an island – that's the old channel of the river that you cross (Old Channel Road, get it?) to reach it -- and it's the only way to get there. By car, Kaskaskia is 17 lonely miles from the bridge at Chester. It feels like 40.

But this is only the beginning of the story. The Kaskaskia that the road takes us to is not the Kaskaskia that Clark captured back in 1778, the one that eventually became the capital of the Illinois Territory and the state's first capital. This Kaskaskia, referred to by some as New Kaskaskia, is about three miles south of the old one, which was swallowed by the river as the Mississippi changed course.

That happened over a period of years in the late nineteenth and early twentieth century, but the beginning of the end came in April, 1881, when the Mississippi shifted eastward during flooding and took over the lower 10 miles of the Kaskaskia River. By that time, some old Kaskaskia residents had already started to move south to a safer place as the river began to eat away at the banks of the ancient town. The new location, never as prosperous as the old, had 177 residents in 1900. Today, it has only 12, in part because it is located in an island no-man's land, and also because the area is subject to some serious flooding. Residents rebuilt a handful of the old structures with the bricks from the buildings as they fell into a state of collapse, so at least parts of the old town survive in this new location. Today, it consists of four scattered brick buildings that are framed by a couple of occupied houses and a lot of empty space. Truthfully, it doesn't even make for a good ghost town.

The original Kaskaskia stood on the west bank of the Kaskaskia River. A narrow neck of land separated the Mississippi and the Kaskaskia just north of town, By the 1860s, the Mississippi was rapidly eroding the banks that led to the smaller river, and in the 1870s the federal Mississippi River Commission erected substantial barriers to try to stop it. But the harsh winter of 1880-81 delivered heavy snow in the northern part of the Mississippi watershed and ice covered the river as far south at Cairo, Illinois. An early thaw in February caused the Mississippi to rise eight feet in one day, and the ice and water roared wildly downriver, tore away at banks and man-made obstructions and finally flowed into the Kaskaskia River just above the town.

When the water receded, the Mississippi returned to its old channel, but the damage had been done. During times of high water over the next few years the Mississippi joined with the Kaskaskia and each time it further cut into its banks. By the mid-1880s, the Mississippi continually flowed into the Kaskaskia River, dooming the historic town that lay beside it. Limestone bluffs resistant to erosion lined the east bank of the Kaskaskia and the town stood on the west side where the soil consisted of easily eroded alluvial deposits. The smaller Kaskaskia river channel couldn't accommodate the Mississippi, so the influx of new water began to carve out its new riverbed on the western side.

The Mississippi claimed some outlying buildings in the first few years of its consolidation with the Kaskaskia, and as the bank widened, building after building after building collapsed into the river during the course of the next twenty-five years, destroying the town completely.

THE WIDENING CHANNEL OF THE MISSISSIPPI RIVER CLAIMS ONE OF KASKASKIA'S BUILDINGS.

Dramatic photos of historic buildings in a partial state of collapse into the river can be found in books, libraries and on the Internet that illustrate this traumatic time for local residents and define the tragedy from a historical standpoint. One from the Abraham Lincoln Presidential Library and Museum library from 1900 shows the Territorial and State House perched on the edge of the bank with part of the building gone. The building hosted the Illinois territorial legislature from 1809 to 1818 and the Illinois state legislature in 1818 and 1819.

By the time the Mississippi River took dead aim on Kaskaskia, the old French village had already fallen into a steep decline. When the state capital moved to Vandalia, Illinois in 1819, in part because of repeated flooding in Kaskaskia, many residents resettled there. The population of the town supposedly peaked at over 7,000, but some historians say it never came close to this figure. In the quest for statehood in 1818, backers estimated the population estimate for the entire territory at 36,000, a generous guess designed to get it nearer the 40,000 Congress had set as a requirement. Kaskaskia's population and influence steadily declined after that.

Still, it had been a good run. The Kaskaskia tribe first occupied the area in 1703, moving here from just south of modern St. Louis probably in fear of an attack by the invading Iroquois. They settled on the southern bank of the Kaskaskia River about six miles above its confluence with the Mississippi; the Kaskaskia offered safer anchorage than the swift-flowing Mississippi. At that point the rivers ran parallel to each other here, two to three miles apart.

Jesuit missionaries and a few French traders who had married Kaskaskia women accompanied the Indians, and all took advantage of the abundance of good, tillable farmland. The Jesuits built a mission church in the year of their arrival. In 1719, the Indians moved several miles up the Kaskaskia River and established their own village, leaving a growing group of French in the original settlement. It is not clear what caused this, but the French and Indians remained close, despite living in separate villages, The Jesuits built a new church and parochial residence in Indian Kaskaskia, while keeping their headquarters in the French village.

By 1723, 196 people lived in Kaskaskia, excluding Indians, slaves, troops, transient traders and voyageurs. A census taken in 1732 showed that the village had grown to 352, which amounted to more than half of the people living in the Illinois country, excluding Indians who lived in tribal villages and transients.

A threat from the Chickasaws in 1737 convinced the French that Kaskaskia needed a fort to defend it, and they eyed the bluff across the Kaskaskia River. The local commander ordered stone quarried for the fort but stopped construction when confronted with the high cost.

Because the old log church built in 1703 had deteriorated, the French decided to use the stone that had been quarried for the fort for a new stone church. Building of the Church of the Immaculate Conception began in 1737 and finished in 1740. Its "1737" cornerstone has survived and is part of the Kaskaskia Bell State Memorial in New Kaskaskia today. The 140-pound church bell, known as "The Liberty Bell of the West," was a gift from King Louis XV of France to the Catholic Church of New France. It was cast in 1741 in La Rochelle, France, and also survives as part of that memorial in New Kaskaskia. The French settlers finally completed Fort Kaskaskia on the bluff on the east side of the river around 1759, although it was technically not a "fort" but an earthen redoubt.

Throughout this era, Kaskaskia remained the largest French village in Illinois and a relatively small place. A new census conducted in 1752 found 350 French, 246 black slaves and 75 Indian slaves living here. Historians say there also may have been as many as 200 soldiers and transients living there at the time.

How could such a slave-dependent community thrive in what became the modern state of Illinois? Maybe because at the time it was part of the French province of Louisiana. But it does make you wonder if the "curse" some believe ultimately brought Kaskaskia down isn't traceable to its early enthusiastic embrace of slavery. (And then again, maybe it was just the natural erosion caused by the Mississippi.)

The end of the French and Indian war brought British occupation to the region in 1765; British soldiers stopped at Kaskaskia briefly on their way to Fort de Chartres. The arrival of the British caused some of Kaskaskia's

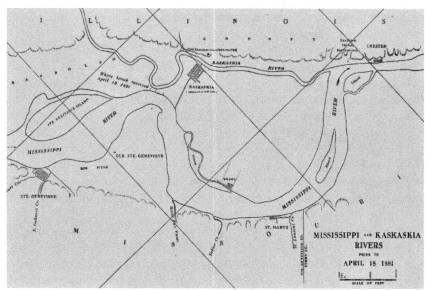

MAP OF THE MISSISSIPPI AND KASKASKIA RIVERS PRIOR TO APRIL 18, 1881

French to move to the western (Spanish) side of the Mississippi to New Madrid, Ste. Genevieve and other settlements.

With the Mississippi encroaching on Fort de Chartres' banks, the British abandoned the fort in 1771 and moved their troops to Kaskaskia. They moved into an old stone house the Jesuits had abandoned several years before, surrounded it with a picket fence, constructed two wooden bastions to house two small cannons and named it Fort Gage. Captain Hugh Lord left this "fort" in 1776 to join the British troops in the east, leaving Philippe-Francois de Rastel de Rocheblave in charge – with no soldiers under him.

Two thoughts immediately leap to mind here: Rocheblave is French, not English, so why was he put in charge? And if he didn't have any solders under him, exactly who or what was he in charge of?

In fact, Rocheblave had been a French officer, went to the Spanish side of the Mississippi when the British took over, and eventually came back and befriended Captain Lord. When Lord left Rocheblave was supposed to be little more than a caretaker for the British government; it's doubtful the British would have entrusted a former French officer with more, regardless of what Lord said. But Rocheblave took his new job seriously, and with the outbreak of the American Revolution, he repeatedly cautioned his superiors about the vulnerability of the region to attack.

They didn't listen to him, of course, which is where George Rogers Clark comes in. Clark had appointed himself head of the Kentucky militia and in 1778 Virginia governor Patrick Henry authorized him to lead an expedition against the British in the Illinois country. This was, believe it or not, territory claimed by Virginia, a claim that was good for Kaskaskia but probably didn't do much for local slaves.

Clark and his 175 men moved down the Ohio River and camped a short distance from the abandoned French post at Fort Massac, then made a 120-mile cross country march north to Kaskaskia. Clark's troops imprisoned Rocheblave and his wife in their quarters and took the territory's largest town without resistance. As alarmed as the French settlers must have been by the appearance of Clark and his Virginia troops, they enthusiastically declared their loyalty to the Americans. They had never cared much for the rival British, and simple pragmatism -- and Father Pierre Gibault -- told them that American rule might be better. Gibault and Dr. John Baptiste Laffont accompanied Clark and his troops to Vincennes, where they also urged acceptance of American control.

It may be difficult to believe that the Kaskaskia is remembered in American history for being taken by George Rogers Clark without any resistance. But Kaskaskia and Vincennes were important cities in the west at the time, and Clark's success in taking both proved unsettling for the British at Fort Detroit.

Clark pulled his remaining troops out of Illinois in 1781, which initially made the Kaskaskia French happy. After a period of time, the relationship had become strained. But this started a period where the area functioned without governance. While Cahokia seemed to function adequately under this arrangement, Kaskaskia became the wild Northwest.

In 1785 the area experienced the worst flood in the residents' memories and water inundated every building in Kaskaskia. Again, some of the area's French citizens moved to the Spanish side of the Mississippi. The exodus initially cut into the town's population, but settlers started streaming into the region from 1790 to 1800 and Kaskaskia received a surprising jolt of prosperity. Many settlers destined for Illinois and Missouri came here first and many settled here, including some of those who would become prominent in the early years of Illinois statehood.

This became a go-to place for westbound travelers including the most famous of them all, Meriwether Lewis and William Clark. They arrived here on November 29, 1803, in preparation for their western expedition and consulted with three of Kaskaskia's leading citizens -- Pierre Menard, William Morrison and John Edgar. They recruited 25 men for the Corps of Discovery, many from the two army companies stationed at Fort Kaskaskia, and left on December 3.

At this point, it would have been difficult to imagine Kaskaskia turning into a transient, second-rate ghost town. The first land office in Illinois was located here, and the Colonel Sweet Hotel, a well-known, story-and-a-half building which stood on Chartres Street near Pierre Menard's ferry, is believed to have been built a few years before. Marquis de Lafayette was honored with a large dinner there when he visited Kaskaskia in 1825.

But when the capital moved to Vandalia, many residents went with it. The Lafayette dinner was the last hurrah for the sleepy town. The Kaskaskia Indians who used to come to Kaskaskia to trade had declined in number, and many of those still living in Indian Kaskaskia crossed the Mississippi and settled near the Peorias in Missouri that same year. In 1832, the few remaining Kaskaskias and Peorias signed a treaty relinquishing their last holdings in Illinois and Indian Kaskaskia was dead.

Kaskaskia itself endured a steady decline over the course the century. A main support beam of the Church of the Immaculate Conception broke and the building partially collapsed in 1838; a brick church was erected to replace it. After the Mississippi threatened the church with destruction in 1892, the local citizenry tore it down the following year and moved the materials to the new settlement. They built a new church that still stands out of the old brick.

Kaskaskia's three cemeteries had also come under siege by that point and the state acted to move the graves across the river to Garrison Hill, near the old earthworks of Fort Kaskaskia. Approximately 5,000 graves and many gravestones were moved, despite the prostrations of some who thought the dead should be left undisturbed and claimed by the Mississippi. Today, visitors to Garrison Hill Cemetery can see the graves of many Kaskaskia pioneers and during winter months when the trees are barren they can peer over (and into) the Mississippi where the town once stood. In the solitude of an old cemetery, viewing a swift flowing river that occupied the space where they lived can be a, uh, moving experience. An overlook a short distance north of cemetery offers a stunning year-round view.

The two-story Pierre Menard house is built into gently sloping land at the bottom of the bluff occupied by the cemetery. It's a spectacular example of French Creole-style architecture with a steep double-hipped roof and a porch that wraps around the building's front façade and gable ends. Menard had been one of the leading citizens of Kaskaskia and his house may have been the grandest home in the area at the time.

Born near Montreal in 1766, he went to Vincennes about 1786, before moving to Kaskaskia and opening a store in 1790. The three large central rooms in his house were built about 1802 and it expanded with his wealth.

It is with us today as a state historic site, open for guided tours from May until October, because it stood on the east side of the old Kaskaskia, which the curse and the mighty Mississippi didn't touch.

Its contemporaries on the west side of the river are all long gone.

46 CAHOKIA

When I was on the major league baseball beat in the 1980s and 1990s, a 24-hour bar called Pop's in Sauget, Illinois, was an occasional late-night stop for Cincinnati beat writers after St. Louis Cardinals' night games. I knew all of the important historical landmarks on the Missouri side of the river, including the surprising plaque on a building at the corner of Broadway and Walnut streets in St. Louis that claimed to be the burial site of Pontiac. But it pains me to think that a history-obsessed guy like me had no idea that that bar across the bridge in Illinois sat only two and a half miles from the well-known French (and later British) settlement of Cahokia, a place captured by George Rogers Clark's troops during his campaign against Britain's western forts in 1778.

A closer reading of that plaque might have helped; Pontiac was killed in Cahokia and his body was supposedly brought to St. Louis and buried. Still, a history lover's ignorance of Cahokia's close proximity probably qualifies as more anecdotal evidence that frontier history seldom receives the attention it deserves.

In retrospect, Cahokia's location on the Mississippi River seems like a no-brainer. Just about every fort in the seventeenth and eighteenth centuries was perched near a river somewhere, and given Cahokia's importance, the Mississippi is the obvious choice. But for some reason it never occurred to me that it might be a St. Louis suburb, particularly when my baseball-writer cronies and I were looking for a place we might still be able to buy a beer after we had worked a late-night game.

Jesuit Father Hugues Pinet had no visions of baseball or twentieth century bars in 1670 when he established a mission destined to be the first permanent settlement in Illinois, and didn't even know that a great city would be located nearby.

A short drive south on Illinois Route 3/South Mississippi Avenue from Pop's will take the visitor within a couple of hundred feet of the Church of the Holy Family, which lies just off Illinois 3 on East First Street. Construction began on the old church that survives there in 1786 although it was formally consecrated in 1799. It is a mostly unaltered example of a distinctive French colonial construction style known as poteaux-sur-solle (posts on a sill), where the logs are placed vertically rather than horizontally as in most log structures. The building's posts are grounded in a foundation sill to retard wood rot.

A bronze plaque detailing the history of Cahokia in a park across the street from the church indicates that "a mission party -- guided here by famous explorer Henri de Tonti -- selected a site for the Mission of the Holy Family that was adjacent to a village of Tamaroa and Cahokia Indians" in 1698. Pinet left in 1685, which apparently disqualified him for a spot on the plaque.

The French village of Cahokia grew up around the mission, although there is little around the old structure to give a modern visitor a sense that this used to be a center of French influence in the upper Mississippi River valley. The little church is flanked by the modern, brick Holy Family Catholic Church that eventually succeeded it and the Holy Family Parish Hall. The Nicholas Jarrot mansion, a two-story brick house built by a former French fur trader, lawyer and judge in 1810, lies on an acre of ground a short distance to the east of the modern church. It looks its age, but it is a Federal style house that might have been built by an Englishman from Virginia.

To find another structure that looks like it could have been built by French missionaries, you have to backtrack across Illinois 3 and go three blocks to the Cahokia Courthouse, constructed as a house in 1737 in the same unusual architectural style as the church. It sits in a residential area at First and Elm, in the midst of a small park that abuts a modern village hall/police station made of brick.

Unlike the church, much of the wood in the old courthouse has been replaced because of three reconstructions. It was deconstructed and moved to the St. Louis World's Fair in 1904, deconstructed and moved to Chicago's Jackson Park for display in 1906 and then deconstructed and moved back to its original location in the 1920s by local residents upset that the oldest building in Cahokia no longer lived in Cahokia. Unfortunately, all of these teardowns and rebuilds took their toll – imagine a family of boys continually playing with a set of Lincoln Logs made of 150-year-old wood – and some of the old wood had to be replaced each time the structure was reconstructed.

The small park that surrounds it makes for a pretty setting, although the mood is easily lost because many of the houses in the area appear to have been built in the 1960s, 70s and 80s. Amidst several blocks of houses, most of the streets are narrow and there are no sidewalks, which gives the area a rural feel that is unexpected so close to downtown St. Louis. The river lies over a quarter of a mile to the west, where the Consolidated Grain and Barge Company occupies a large chunk of the low-lying riverfront property.

Frequent flooding of the Mississippi is one reason that Cahokia never grew large while under French control. The establishment of Kaskaskia and Fort de Chartres (and nearby Nouvelle Chartres and Prairie du Rocher) also affected its growth. French-speaking immigrants, mostly from Canada, settled in all of these villages on the east side of the Mississippi because the alluvial soil was especially fertile.

Shortly after missionaries arrived, several French traders moved here and by 1715 Cahokia became one of the chief trading posts south of Canada. In 1733, troubles with Indians eventually resulted in the building of the first French fort, garrisoned by 20 men. Henceforth, it became an important location in the land acquisition game played between the England and France through much of the eighteenth century.

Despite all of the activity, Cahokia didn't have a large number of permanent residents for many years. When Diron d'Artaguiette made the first official estimate of its population in his census of the Illinois Country in 1723, he credited the village with 12 residents -- seven habitants, one white laborer, one married woman and three children. (By contrast, Kaskaskia had 196 inhabitants and the new village of Nouvelle Chartres had 126.) Although this didn't include those attached to the mission, traders who came and went in their business with local Indians or merchants who visited from Canada on a seasonable basis, it makes it clear that Cahokia didn't immediately become a burgeoning metropolis.

The village finally began to grow in 1731, when the mission bought a parcel of land 30 acres wide by 10 acres deep from the Indians in order to give "tracts of land gratuitously to all." The next census in 1752 reported a total of 136 permanent residents, which again didn't include those at the mission or the soldiers.

The early maps show First Street running just south of Dead Creek, then an active channel of the Mississippi River and today a barely noticeable ditch in most spots. In those days, Cahokia was screened from the river's main channel by what used to be Cahokia Island. The rest of the town mostly huddled in the blocks two streets behind First. Today, First ventures just two blocks west of Illinois 3 before it turns south at Elm. It extended a few blocks farther to the west until the lateral movement of the Mississippi (to a point 600 feet west of the Cahokia Courthouse) in the 1860s destroyed the western portion of the French colonial village and the remains of an Indian village and burying ground.

The days of French control of the region were about over. When the French lost the French and Indian War, France ceded large parts of today's state of Illinois to the British in 1763, including Cahokia. Some contemporary accounts indicate that by the time of the transfer, the population of Cahokia had tripled since the 1752 census; after the treaty, many of the French-speaking residents in the area refused to live under British rule. They moved west of the Mississippi River to territory that the French had ceded to Spain in 1762.

Cahokia had only been under British rule for about six years when vanquished war chief Pontiac came to the area in April, 1769. He stopped in St. Louis for a few days to visit its commander, Captain Louis St. Ange de Bellerive, and then crossed the river to Cahokia. At the time, it consisted of about 45 houses stretched out along the river for three-quarters of a mile.

Pontiac entered the store of Philadelphia merchants Baynton, Wharton, and Morgan in Cahokia with the nephew of Peoria chief Black Dog. As they left the store, which author Bonnie L. Gums located across the street from the courthouse, Pontiac was clubbed from behind and then stabbed to death by Black Dog's nephew as he lay in the street. The courthouse backs up to First. The buildings on a 1766 map, the closeness of Dead Creek across First and the public square immediately east of the courthouse make it seem likely that Pontiac died in First Street, probably between Elm and Main. If that's true, it would have been the perfect place to solve a modern murder: the Cahokia police department also backs up to First at the corner of Main and a parking lot full of police cars borders the street.

In this case, we can't be sure precisely what happened or the motive of the killer. Months earlier, Pontiac got into an altercation with Black Dog and killed him; reasons for that fight also aren't clear. But some historians believe that the murder may have been in retaliation for Black Dog's death.

And then again, this was Pontiac, and it's not like others didn't have reasons for wanting him dead. Some Indians had grown angry over Pontiac's increasingly amicable relationship with the British; rumors flew that Pontiac had sold out his old allies and taken money and gifts from his old enemies. So maybe this had nothing to do with Black Dog at all.

Pontiac was dead either way and most believe his body was taken to St. Louis at St. Ange's request and buried. Again, there are questions. Some think he may have been given a proper Indian burial in Cahokia to satisfy a request from Lieutenant Colonel John Wilkins, the new commander Fort de Chartres. Wilkins worried that the Indians would believe a story spread by the French about the British sending an Indian to kill Pontiac. An 1866, story in the *St. Louis Evening News* indicated that Pontiac's grave "is in the outskirts of (Cahokia), over which a tombstone was erected by Colonel Clarke in 1778."

Nonetheless, the prevailing theory is that Pontiac's body was taken to St. Louis, where his final resting place is no clearer. Some say he was buried in St. Louis' only cemetery, a Catholic graveyard next to the Cathedral, which faced Second Street between Walnut and Market. The Missouri Historical Society determined that the exact spot of his burial lay 20 feet east of

Broadway and 50 feet south of Market, two blocks west of the graveyard. The Daughters of the American Revolution placed a tablet in the corridor of the Southern Hotel, which was razed in 1934. The hotel stood at the corner of Fourth and Walnut and stretched between Fourth and Fifth. That puts the DAR's tablet close to the MHS site. Today, a newer marker is on the side of the Stadium East parking garage at the corner of Broadway and Walnut. I'm not sure where the marker was when I first saw it, but it wasn't on the parking garage.

Depending upon your perspective, Pontiac's murder ranks as either the highlight or lowlight of Cahokia's time under British rule. The old French fort had fallen into decay and the British converted an unfinished stone presbytery that had been part of the mission into a fort. The American Revolution broke out shortly after that and in 1778 George Rogers Clark conceived his plan for taking the country back from the British, including forts at Vincennes, Kaskaskia and Cahokia.

Clark captured Kaskaskia with a force of about 175 men on July 4 without firing a shot. The next day, he dispatched Captain Joseph Bowman and a company of about 30 Americans to take Cahokia, which they did again without using their weapons. (The British fort became Fort Bowman, and the foundation of that old presbytery supposedly served as the foundation for the new Church of the Holy Family when construction began in 1786.) The garrison at Vincennes along the Wabash River, which the British called Fort Sackville, surrendered to Clark in August. The garrison was retaken by a small British force in December, but three months later, Clark took it back and also captured British lieutenant governor Henry Hamilton, who had planned to retake all of the western forts.

Clark knew that the people of the Illinois Country had been living under military rule. He spent five weeks in Cahokia in August to secure the area militarily and set up a local civil court and government to give the locals a taste of what it meant to be an American. Then he turned his attention to the Indians.

"In a short time, the Indians of various tribes inhabiting this Region at Illinois in great numbers came to Kohokia in order to make peace with us," Clark wrote. "Those treaties which commenced the last of August . . . continued between three and four weeks."

Some of the tribes came from as far as 500 miles away for these conferences. One party from the north came on the pretense of making peace when in fact they hoped to kidnap Clark and take him prisoner, but he uncovered their plan and foiled their attempt.

In April, 1780, a combined force of Indians and British soldiers from Fort Michilimackinac attacked St. Louis and Cahokia and the attack was repulsed. Two weeks later, a combined force of 350 Americans and Illinois French pursued the enemy but never came in contact with it. Throughout the summer, joint patrols of St. Louis and Cahokia militia watched the waterways to the north for signs of an impending attack that never came.

Life here during this period was less than idyllic. The civil court founded by Clark and Bowman continued to operate. But problems created by depreciated currency, the unpaid debts of Virginia, wild land speculation, and differences between military and civil officials and French and American parties made conditions difficult. The population of Cahokia remained decidedly French, regardless who controlled the land.

The creation of the Northwest Territory with the Ordinance of 1787 promised better times and didn't immediately deliver: Governor Arthur St. Clair didn't make it here for two years. When St. Clair County was established in 1790, Kaskaskia became the seat of government and Cahokia retained its independence and its own courts. After a judge came to Kaskaskia four years later and interfered with Cahokia's autonomy, St. Clair created Randolph County out of part of St. Clair in 1795 and Cahokia became the seat of St. Clair County. At the time, St. Clair County comprised today's 80 northernmost counties of Illinois. For many years, the Cahokia Courthouse served as the legal and governmental center of a sizeable area extending to the Canada–U.S. border. An influx of Americans effected the removal of county government from Cahokia to Belleville in 1814, effectively ending the village's importance as a government or commercial center.

Today, the name is mostly associated with the Cahokia Mounds, a large prehistoric Mississippi culture city designated as a UNESCO World Heritage site in 1982. It is located several miles to the northeast.

Cahokia's population, as a mostly-residential St. Louis suburb, was listed as 15,241 in the 2010 census. Its relative importance isn't one-tenth of what is was in the 1750s when an official census listed the number of permanent residents as 136.

47 FORT DE CHARTRES

A tourist who chances to be driving on Illinois Route 155 a couple of miles west of Prairie du Rocher, Illinois – and to be clear no one just happens to be driving on the two-lane road that splits miles and miles of farm fields – might be surprised to see a brown sign with an arrow pointing to the Fort de Chartres historic site.

This is one of those places where you either live or go out of your way to see as a historically minded visitor. Most of the latter do that for its annual June "rendezvous," its October "French and Indian War Encampment" or one of its smaller special events. The only other people who intentionally came here were the French soldiers who built the first of four forts here in 1720 and French settlers who clustered nearby and created the lost village of Nouvelle Chartres.

That first fort stood out there in those farm fields somewhere, a half-mile south of the current structure built on the site of the fourth and final fort.

It is worth noting that neither of these sites are particularly close to the Mississippi River.

"The river is about a mile away now and it was less than a quarter of a mile when the fort was first built." Tim Helms said. "Then all of a sudden the river changed its course and it never came back."

It was the middle of October and Helms was holding down the empty fort. A full-time "seasonal" worker who said he worked at St. Louis country music station WIL for 20 years and "failed at my retirement," Helms had been using a paint brush to keep what is called "an imaginative reconstruction" of portions of this fourth Fort de Chartres from, uh, looking like it is 250 years old.

FORT DE CHARTRES AS IT HAS BEEN RECONSTRUCTED TODAY

It's an impressive structure, although the setting would seem even more realistic if modern visitors couldn't see a massive levee sitting 200 feet west of it and no sign of a river behind it. But some things never change.

"In '93, the water was all the way up to the top of the levee," Helms said. "The only thing exposed was just the tip of the levee. It was under water for like two months. We lost 150 trees in the 800 or 900 acres we have over there. It was terrible, a terrible year."

"Terrible" years were common around here in the early days, which is why it is a wonder that any fort is sitting here. A little imaginary deconstruction of the modern fort is in order, if only to make the visitor see what this place would look like without a faux fort inducing us to come inside and take a gander at it. Without the fort and the accompanying park and parking lots, we would be looking at rich, agricultural bottomland no different than thousands of other places of the modern Midwest.

This isn't unusual in our modern quest to find the Old Northwest – important historical sites sometimes seem to turn up in the most unlikely places – but there's no reason for a twenty-first century soul to think that this remote place once served as the military, administrative and diplomatic capital of French Illinois. Or that the commandant here presided over a large region that stretched to modern Terre Haute, Indiana, (the southern border of Quebec) to the Arkansas River. The Company of the West, which held proprietary rights to French Louisiana from the French crown, sent troops north from New Orleans under Pierre Duque de Boisbriand to choose a location for a fort. The reason he chose this spot made sense at the time: It lay between two widely-separated French villages, Cahokia to the north, Kaskaskia to the south, should soldiers ever need to quickly intervene in either place. Again, the choice appears random to the modern visitor because neither town holds any special significance today.

Boisbriand, a French Canadian commissioned first king's lieutenant for the province of Louisiana, went first to Kaskaskia and established a temporary headquarters in December, 1718. After 18 months, he found what he considered a convenient site for the new post 18 miles northwest of Kaskaskia, and he led a large group of laborers and mechanics here to clear a place in the forest and begin building. The palisaded structure measured approximately 190 feet on each side and included three buildings that housed up to one hundred men. They completed it in 1720.

Although the fort stood about a quarter-mile from the Mississippi, its wood construction, frequent flooding and poor maintenance all but assured that it wouldn't last. It had to be replaced in 1725 with a second wooden structure, this one slightly smaller than the first but with four corner bastions. Though it seems to have been built better and farther from the river, it was in the vicinity of the first and still subject to flooding. Consequently, a third wooden fort was apparently built to replace it in 1732. This structure also deteriorated, and by 1742 French officials discussed the possibility of replacing it. Five years later, with the fort now in miserable condition, they decided that simply moving the garrison to Kaskaskia would be a better option.

The decision affected more than just the military however. Shortly after the completion of the initial Fort de Chartres, French and Canadians settlers started to move near the structure for their safety. The cluster of settlers created the village of Nouvelle Chartres on the bottom land between the fort and the river. The company built its warehouses here and enterprising Jesuits constructed the church of St. Anne du Fort de Chartres. The village grew slowly but steady; Commander Jean-Jacques Macarty's 1752 census shows that the village included 198 French, 89 black slaves and 36 Indian slaves, making it the third most populous village in the Illinois country behind Cahokia and Kaskaskia.

That may have had an impact on the 1751 decision to move the garrison back to Fort de Chartres and build another fort near the sites of the other three. This time, the French showed that they had finally learned from their previous mistakes. In 1753, they started building this new fort out of stone, about half-mile west of the previous ones. It is this fort that has been reconstructed with the help of archaeology and imagination for modern visitors.

Fort de Chartres' walls were made of locally quarried limestone, were over two feet thick and at least 15 feet high. They were capable of supporting 20 cannons, none of which were ever fired in combat. The fort's perimeter covered 2,000 feet and enclosed four acres, enough to house 300 soldiers.

Construction crept along. The stones had to be transported several miles from north of Prairie du Rocher, a town four miles east that had also been settled because of its proximity to the fort. Experienced labor was hard to find in the middle of nowhere. Costs soared.

At one point, the French crown threatened to end construction and it might have if the new governor of New Orleans hadn't offered assurance that the fort was almost finished. It wasn't and when the fort was finally completed in 1760, the French were in the midst of a losing effort to Britain in the French and Indian (Seven Years) War.

The story takes an unexpected turn here. In 1762, the New Orleans firm of Maxent, Laclede & Company obtained an exclusive license from the governor to trade with all Indian nations on the west side of the Mississippi up to the present site of Minneapolis-St. Paul for a period of six years. The focal point of this would be the fur rich Missouri River Valley, and the company would develop a trading town that would support the venture and provide a solid base. As the senior partner in the firm, Gilbert Antoine de St. Maxent took charge of ordering and preparing the goods that would be shipped there, and he gave Pierre Laclede the job of finding a suitable location and setting up the new town.

Laclede, his 13-year-old stepson Auguste Chouteau and five river bateaux (flat boats of shallow drafts capable of carrying up to forty tons) and their crews arrived at Fort de Chartres with several store-boats heavily stocked with trade goods on November 3, 1763. The trade goods would have to be stored while he searched for the best town site and he also stored 300 pounds of the king's gunpowder in the fort's powder magazine, the only structure in the complex still standing today. Commandant Neyon de Villiers found a house for him in Nouvelle Chartres that Laclede used as his base of operations. The house stood a short walk from the fort, near the church of Ste. Anne and on the King's Road that connected Kaskaskia and Cahokia. That made it an excellent location for Laclede to conduct his business for as long as he was in Nouvelle Chartres. University of Illinois archaeologist Dr. Robert Mazrim located the house site during excavations in 2006, and a sign now marks the site of Ste. Anne on the west side of Route 155 about a quarter of a mile southeast of the modern fort.

The spot Laclede ultimately chose for his town and trading post became the modern city of St. Louis. In some ways, this may be the most amazing part of the Fort de Chartres story. Laclede, memorialized today by the Laclede's Landing riverfront entertainment district in St. Louis, recruited most of the early settlers for his new town from Nouvelle Chartres.

The first small wave of settlers who moved to St. Louis in 1764 grew into a torrent. When Villiers pulled his troops from Fort de Chartres and took them to New Orleans as part of French abdication of the territory on June 15, 1764, it became easier for settlers to follow their friends to St. Louis. No one could be sure when or even if British troops would arrive and afford local residents with a modicum of protection against hostile western tribes. As the town's population withered, St. Anne du Fort de Chartres in Nouvelle Chartres closed and parishioners had to attend services in Prairie du Roche, four miles away. By 1766, a thriving place that had been the third largest town in the Illinois country had been reduced to three or four poor families. Amazingly, French authorities in Louisiana didn't learn until late 1764 that among the "secret" terms of the peace treaty, France had ceded Louisiana to Spain.

J. Frederick Fausz's 2011 book on the founding of St. Louis noted that "At least four waves of charter colonists populated St. Louis between February 1764 and March 1766 and Nouvelle Chartres was clearly the indispensable mother settlement of Laclede's infant town." Of 21 men whom Chouteau listed as members of the work crew who constructed the first buildings of St. Louis, Fausz noted that 20 of them lived in or near Nouvelle Chartres. After that, Nouvelle Chartres was nearly deserted, a fate that awaited the nearby fort.

Before Villiers pulled his troops out of Fort de Chartres in June, 1764, he had to deal with unexpected drama on April 12 created by the unexpected arrival of Pontiac. The Ottawa chief's siege of Fort Detroit had ended in failure, both because of the defection of some of his allies and the peace treaty that eliminated his chances of receiving military support from the French.

He knew the British troops were on their way from New Orleans to assume command of Fort de Chartres – neither he nor Villiers were aware that they had been turned back by a party of Indians 240 miles north of New Orleans – and he showed up and spent two days lobbying the Illinois to resist the British when they arrived. He also requested a council with Villiers -- held in his quarters on April 17 -- where he falsely represented the status of his army at Detroit and pled with him to continue the war against the British.

Villiers explained that the king had ordered both the French and the Indians to maintain peace with the British. Pontiac insisted that he "hated" the British and that the peace wouldn't last. As Pontiac argued, the French commander grew impatient and finally told Pontiac to reflect on their conversation and return tomorrow when they would talk again. The unhappy chief never returned.

During the first week of October, 1765, Captain Thomas Stirling and 100 Highlanders of the 42nd British regiment from Fort Pitt arrived to assume control of Fort de Chartres. Captain Louis St. Ange de Bellerive formally surrendered the post on October 10. The French flag was taken down and replaced by the red cross of St. George, and St. Ange and a company of 30 men departed by boat for St. Louis, as so many Nouvelle Chartres residents had already done.

Stirling's command of Fort de Chartres didn't last long; he was replaced by Major Robert Farmer and a detachment of the 34th British foot from Mobile in early December. They renamed the place Fort Cavendish after the regiment's colonel, although the name didn't stick. Another unit replaced them the following the year.

The fort obviously needed more than a name change. The British also struggled with the frequent flooding and soil erosion problems that their French predecessors had encountered. In the spring of 1772, while Fort de Chartres was under the command of Captain Hugh Lord of the 18th British regiment, the Mississippi flooded the adjacent bottom and the south wall and one bastion collapsed into the river. Captain Lord and the garrison bid a hasty departure from the fort and took up quarters at Kaskaskia. They never returned. Kaskaskia remained the local seat of British authority until the Virginia militia under Colonel George Rogers Clark took control of it for the United States in July, 1778.

The deserted fort fell into gradual ruin after that. In 1804, Major Amos Stoddard visited the site and reported that "the area of this fort is now covered with trees from 7 to 12 inches in diameter." Twenty-five years later, writer James Hall visited and found the ruins "covered with a vigorous growth of forest trees and a dense undergrowth of bushes and vines. . . and the vines creeping over the tottering walls. . . between the water's edge and the river bank. It was curious to see in the gloom of a wild forest these remnants of the architecture of a past ago."

Eventually, settlers took over the property, cleared it of trees and built a cabin within it, the process of demolition hastened by scavengers who came there looking for building material."

The state of Illinois purchased the nearly 20 acres of land occupied by the ruins of the old fort in 1913, established it as a state park and started restoration of the powder magazine in 1917. Partial reconstruction of other parts of the fort occurred over decades, resulting in the structure that exists today.

The British soldiers who abandoned the crumbling fort in 1772 would probably be shocked to discover it there today, even as an "imaginative reconstruction." They might even be shocked that Prairie du Rocher still exists, especially after the disappearing act performed by Nouvelle Chartres.

Prairie du Rocher also lost some residents to the new settlement of St. Louis. Its population had been on the decline even prior to that, in part because the farming community didn't practice fertilization and the rich soil became exhausted and couldn't produce enough food to feed residents. Fleeing Prairie du Rocher residents founded the town of Ste. Genevieve on the western shore of the Mississippi in 1750. Some Prairie residents also moved there with the coming of the British in 1765.

George Rogers Clark's capture of the town during the American Revolution caused even more residents to flee, although some of the subsequent settlers were members of Clark's campaign.

The French influence remains in the ancient town however. Twelve houses in the modern village of 600 survive from the eighteenth century, the oldest of which (the Melliere House) dates from 1735.

La Guiannée, a caroling custom that dates back to French medieval times, has been celebrated every New Year's Eve since the settling of the town in 1722. That's not bad for a small town settled only because of a fort that has been gone for almost two and a half centuries.

The levee is probably one reason it has survived. It turns north at Prairie du Rocher Creek southeast of both the village and the fort and runs on both sides of it, providing protection to the village in the shadow of the limestone bluff behind it. Because of the levee, the distant Mississippi River behind the fort doesn't appear nearly as threatening as it must have to those early French and English soldiers.

But don't tell Helms that.

"Last year (2019), it was about two-and-a-half, three feet from coming over," he said. "We had a boil down there and the Army corps came and fixed that. I was the only one down here last year and they told me if I heard the siren, you've got two minutes to get out of here or you're under 53 feet of water. I said "Two minutes?"

"So, I studied the flood. They'd always ask me that if it broke, where would you go? I said 'Straight to the levee. Straight up there.' Because if it broke the water's rushing in, it's going to level off and subside eventually. There's a lot of ground for the river to fly out to. You've got five miles to the bluff, so by the time it gets to the bluff, it would probably get to your knee."

He laughed.

"People said 'But what about that boat? Go over there and get that boat.' I said 'What do I do, carry it around with me all day?' They had like nine padlocks on it and a sign that said 'See Jerry for the key.' Who the hell's Jerry?' I just made the best of a bad situation. I could actually see the levee breathing, coming in and out. We were getting seepage. It started coming up out of the foundation. It was just brutal. I was ankle deep in water when I left."

When that happened to the British, they moved to Kaskaskia.

48 VINCENNES

Before interstate highways dominated the American transportation system, a family of tourists might have happened by Vincennes, Indiana, on U.S. routes 41 or 50 and have been surprised by what they found there. A beautiful circular white granite structure surrounded by 16 fluted Greek Doric columns sits near the banks of the Wabash River, one that looks like the architect may have planned it for Washington D.C. only to have it end up here by mistake.

It is no mistake. It seems out of a place in this relatively remote town in southwestern Indiana only until you realize who it memorializes and why it is here. The structure honors George Rogers Clark, who led his men on a heroic mid-winter march from Kaskaskia in February, 1779, to a victory over the British at Fort Sackville that is remembered as one of the most heroic feats of the American Revolution. The victory solidified American land claims in the Ohio Valley and helped lead to the United States acquisition of much of the land in the 1783 Treaty of Paris that became the Northwest Territory.

In 1936, the memorial was dedicated by President Franklin Delano Roosevelt on what was believed to have been the site of the British fort. As hard as it is to believe that the boundaries of the old fort could have been forgotten in a history-obsessed city as small as Vincennes (18,000 in 2010), this seems to have happened when the town's population "boomed" in the nineteenth century. (Number crunchers take note: The town's most dramatic growth occurred from 1850 to 1860 when it nearly doubled to 3,900, but even by 1900, there were only 10,000 residents in this riverfront town.)

Nevertheless, someone had to find it and the job fell to the Daughters of the American Revolution, as it often did in those days. The D.A.R. did some

323

research and placed a stone marker on what they believed to be the location of the fort in 1905.

President Calvin Coolidge authorized the erection of the memorial to Clark in 1928 and it was finished in 1933. It has a 12 ½-foot bronze statue of Clark in the interior, and the walls surrounding him are adorned with colorful murals. The memorial and the 24-acre site that surrounds it became the George Rogers Clark National Historic Park in 1966.

Again, it looks like it landed on the wrong river, like it belongs on the Potomac instead of on the Wabash.

"I know, it has that feel," GRCNHP head ranger Joe Herron said. "It's of that time. It's just a short period in our history where we would commemorate with large round monuments like this, Roman style. It's become more Americanized over time. It's a very different way that we memorialize today than during this particular time period."

But what about the location?

Evidence of the fort was found in the 1930s when the memorial was under construction and Indiana University conducted archaeological investigations from 1969 to 1971 north of the memorial. Researchers discovered some eighteenth-century artifacts as well as portions of stockade walls. Unfortunately, it was impossible to identify their origin because three different forts were located on or near this site -- the 1732 French stockade, Fort Sackville, and the third Fort Knox, built in 1812

CLARK MEMORIAL

"They have a pretty good idea with Sackville, but again in the 30s they couldn't really identify what they had found," Herron said. "The problem is from 1779 you have 150 years until they were actually building the building, so you had developments, you had factories, you had a pig farm right up here, a glass factory and then coal gasification on this end and then homes by the turn of the century that were on this spot. First Street ran right down the middle of it. It's all been built up over and over, so any good archaeology is way down because they were trying to build on the river."

Today's Vincennes has two heroes instead of one. William Henry Harrison, the nation's ninth president and a hero in the War of 1812, built a mansion here while he served as the governor of the Indiana Territory (and Vincennes served as its capital) from 1801 to 1812. Tours of the house, called Grouseland because of an abundance of grouse on the property, are second only to the Clark memorial as a local tourist attraction.

In 1810, with the tension growing on the Indiana frontier, famous Shawnee chief Tecumseh accepted Harrison's invitation to come here and speak with him, which they did in the grove on southwestern side of Grouseland. The talk was a disaster – more on that later – but it is another chapter in the story of a historic town that today receives relatively little attention from the outside world.

In that respect it is not unlike other trading posts, villages and towns in the Old Northwest that have seen their importance dramatically diminish over time. But the decline seems particularly acute in the case of Vincennes, a place believed to have been inhabited by prehistoric Indians, founded by French traders in 1732 (and maybe earlier) and to have played a key role in the early history of the United States.

This site's story likely begins with the Buffalo Trace, the path inadvertently cleared by tens of thousands of bison eons ago that crosses the Wabash River at this spot. This may have brought the Moundbuilders here -- there are numerous mounds in the area -- and probably had a hand (or feet) in causing the Piankeshaw tribe to establish a village here long before the first white men arrived.

La Salle came by here in 1669, called the river the Ouabache and may have stopped at the Piankeshaw village, although that is pure speculation. More speculation centers around the site of the first trading post on the Wabash, which was established by Charles Juchereau de St. Denis, the lieutenant general of Montreal, in 1702 to trade the Indians for buffalo hides. Again, because the Buffalo Trace crossed here, it makes this a good guess for the location of his trading post, but again this is speculation. Wherever it was located, Juchereau's traders had already collected 12,000 buffalo hides when he died in the autumn of 1702 and Poste Juchereau was abandoned.

Thirty years later, the French came back to stay. François-Marie Bissot, Sieur de Vincennes was commissioned to build a trading post on the Wabash to discourage the Indians in the area from trading with the British and he chose the site that was at first called simply the Post. He picked it because of its location near the Buffalo Trace and the fact that it also wasn't far from the White River, and he built a fort and trading post there.

Vincennes encouraged Canadian settlers to locate here and moved here with his own family. But settlers were slow to move here because of the remote location. At the time, the French considered this part of the province of Louisiana and he struggled to get trade supplies from there. Problematic as that was, it wouldn't be a long-term issue for him. Vincennes was captured during the French war with the Chickasaw nation and burned at the stake near the modern Fulton, Mississippi, in 1736. His death resulted in the Post being renamed Post Vincennes in his honor, one trade he probably wouldn't have made.

After Vincennes death, Louis Groston de Saint-Ange de Bellerive commanded Post Vincennes until the British assumed control of the territory at the conclusion of the French and Indian War in February, 1763. The end of French rule didn't change much. Vincennes remained a French settlement.

The first houses were durable structures made of timbers set upon end, thatched with straw and plastered with adobe. Many of them are known to have stood for more than 100 years and some were considered in a good state of preservation when local residents tore them down to build more modern buildings. The village's first church, St. Francis Xavier, was built in this style and held services for about 80 years and then used as a pastoral residence. None of those early structures survive, although that little church was the first of three on the site. The current one, St. Francis Xavier Cathedral, was built in 1834; it is located opposite the park and is flanked by the graves of several early settlers.

When the British gained control of the territory in 1763, St Ange left for Fort de Chartres. That marked end of civil government for the town until Lieutenant Governor Edward Abbott arrived from Detroit and formally took possession of the place for the British on May 19, 1777. Alarmed that so many Indians freely roamed about the town, Abbott built a new stockade around the headquarters building on the site of the old French fort. He named it Fort Sackville in honor of Lord George Germain, long known as Lord George Sackville, who had been named Secretary of State for the Colonies in 1775. Some historians blame Germain for the strategic and political mistakes in the American Revolution that cost Britain its colonies.

This is the point where George Rogers Clark enters the story. Clark lived in Kentucky, where Indians allied with the British crown regularly harassed settlers. Because Virginia claimed that territory, Clark went to Virginia Governor Patrick Henry seeking his support to raise and lead an army to capture the British forts at Kaskaskia, Vincennes and Detroit. Henry balked at first, but finally gave Rogers his approval to recruit 350 men for his campaign.

Clark recruited the men and assembled them near modern Louisville; many departed after being told the details of the mission. Undeterred, Clark floated down river with the 150 men who remained and captured Kaskaskia on July 4, 1778.

The cordial welcomes his troops received from the French residents led him to believe that those at Vincennes might be just as ready to accept American control. Father Pierre Gibault offered to go to Vincennes with a companion to scout it out for Clark – a statue of Gibault stands in front of the church today -- and when he got there, he discovered that the British commander had gone to Detroit with his troops. The French there were happy to take an oath of allegiance to America, and they took possession of

Fort Sackville. When Clark received word of this, he sent Captain Leonard Helm and one of his men to assume control of the fort.

If that had been the end of it, there would be no white granite memorial to Clark in Vincennes and this chapter might be about Helmsburg. But British Colonel Henry Hamilton, lieutenant governor Detroit at the time, flew into a rage over the news from Vincennes and assembled a force of 500 regulars, militia and Indians and headed there. Helm didn't learn of the British army's approach until it was about three miles away, time enough only to allow a handful of friendly Vincennes residents to return to their homes. That left him and his one American soldier to defend it. Although Helm tricked Hamilton into believing he had a much larger force and used that to negotiate more generous terms of his surrender, the British still regained control of Fort Sackville.

Hamilton captured Francis Vigo, a St. Louis fur trader who had been sent to Post Vincennes by Clark to check on conditions there, but eventually released him on the condition that he wouldn't harm British interests on his way back to St. Louis. Vigo didn't, but immediately returned to Kaskaskia from St. Louis and told Clark about the British takeover. (Vigo eventually moved his fur trade business to Vincennes, founded Vincennes University and is honored with a statue on the river side of the Clark memorial.) By then, a few months had passed before Clark learned that Hamilton had retaken the fort.

Clark found himself in a tough spot. Most of his men's terms of enlistment would soon expire. If he waited until spring to attack he would have fewer soldiers and Hamilton's troops would have received reinforcements. A winter campaign would be less than ideal – OK, it would be miserable -- but he felt he had no choice.

He sent 46 of his men on boats carrying provisions and ammunition and set off on a march of almost 200 miles with 170 men on February 5, 1779. The rain began to fall shortly after they departed and they had gone only a few miles before they came upon land flooded with icy water. They plunged in and marched in water for much of the journey. When they came to a spot that wasn't flooded, they often chose that spot to camp for the night. Sometimes they had no choice but to sleep standing in water.

They finally arrived on the heights to the rear of Fort Sackville on February 23 and had their first chance to dry their clothing. Clark secretly sent news of their arrival to the French citizens, who hated Hamilton and sent food to the hungry men. That night the American troops fired on the fort and completely surprised British; the attack continued until 9 the next morning when Clark demanded their surrender. Hamilton had been dismayed at the fort's condition since his arrival. He felt that it would be difficult to defend so he gave in to Clark's demands.

"(Fort Sackville) was about where the memorial is, but more forward," Herron said. "So, some of that parade ground in front of it makes up the interior of the fort. You almost have to go down to about the third bench to reach the front wall, which would have faced kind of northeast, so that bridge approach that has all the stone writing on it, that would be about where the surrender took place."

Clark sent Hamilton and his men to Williamsburg, Virginia, to be jailed, and renamed the stockade Fort Patrick Henry. Clark returned to Kentucky with hopes of raising more troops for an assault on Fort Detroit; his inability to do so ended his campaign. The Virginia troops he had raised withdrew from Vincennes in the spring of 1780 and left the fort in the control of local militia. The Americans abandoned it at the conclusion of the American Revolution.

Major John Hamtramck and his soldiers camped on the ruins of Fort Patrick Henry during the campaign against the Wabash tribes in the fall of 1787 and found it in shambles. A new fortification called Fort Knox was eventually built north of the old fort site and occupied until 1803, when Governor Harrison requested that a new fort be built. That structure, built three miles north of town on the Wabash at a landing called Petit Rocher, also was called Fort Knox and is known as Fort Knox II by historians. Today the site is state and national historical site and is known principally as a place where Harrison mustered troops in 1811 prior to his march to Prophetstown and the Battle of Tippecanoe.

In 1812, the military determined that it couldn't provide Vincennes with protection from that distance and dismantled the structure and reassembled it in the vicinity of the original Fort Knox. When the solders there (Fort Knox III) moved to Fort Harrison in 1816, the town's final military garrison was abandoned. Within weeks, local residents had stripped it of all usable material.

As the story unfolds, it becomes easier to sympathize with early Vincennes residents unsure about the exact locations of the forts. History-minded souls who might normally have committed every detail to memory may have had their thoughts muddled by the continual churn of construction, destruction and movement of these old fortifications. When they started digging more than 150 years later, even archaeologists who often can fix flaws in memory conceded they couldn't be sure whether they were finding Post Vincennes, Fort Sackville or one of the two Forts Knox.

Thankfully, we don't have to wager too many guesses concerning the Harrison side of Vincennes' history; Grouseland is sitting there on Scott Street, about 10 blocks northeast of the Clark memorial and probably one or more of the forts, and open daily (except Sunday) from 12 to 5 p.m.

Harrison had served as secretary of the Northwest Territory for two years and as the territory's representative to the United States Congress when

President John Adams named him governor of the new Indiana Territory in 1800. The territory was created because of Ohio's impending statehood and Vincennes became the territorial capital. It consisted of all the original Northwest Territory except for Ohio and eastern Michigan, which was still called by the old name until the admission of Ohio to the Union in 1803.

Harrison served as governor until 1812, when he resigned to resume his military career because of the War of 1812. He had the two-story brick plantation-style house built about 100 yards from the river between 1802 and 1804 on 300 acres of property he purchased adjacent to the town. It resembled the aristocratic homes where Harrison spent his childhood in Virginia.

The house, possibly the first brick structure in what became modern-day Indiana, is believed to have cost Harrison $20,000 to have built and stood in marked contrast to the other mostly log structures in the territory. At the time, Vincennes had a population of only 700 French and

GROUSELAND'S SOUTHWEST PORTICO

American residents. During Harrison's time in Vincennes, his wife Anna gave birth to three of their children and the couple frequently entertained and lodged visiting legislators and other dignitaries in the 17-room house.

Harrison's position also permitted him to negotiate treaties with Indian tribes in the region. Besides Tecumseh, he is known to have met Little Turtle and Buckongahelas here. Five of the 11 treaties Harrison negotiated were consummated here including the Treaty of Grouseland, signed in the mansion's main floor parlor in 1805. It secured land in southern Indiana, northeast Indiana, and northwestern Ohio controlled in principle by the Miamis. That treaty and others led to that dramatic confrontation between Tecumseh and Harrison at Grouseland in 1810.

Harrison invited Tecumseh to the house for what he hoped would be peaceful conference. Harrison promised Tecumseh that he would be treated courteously and asked him to come unarmed. On August 10, Tecumseh came down the Wabash with a party of 80 of his followers, who were stopped briefly for inspection by Captain George Floyd at Fort Knox. They continued downstream and camped along the riverbank, two miles from the fort and one mile from Grouseland.

When Tecumseh's delegation showed up at Grouseland on August 15, he left all but 11 of his men at the fringe of the woodland about 700 feet away. He approached the house with the others, stopping about 40 yards from it in a grove of trees. Harrison had military personnel stationed at various spots in the house and on the grounds.

Harrison had set up benches and chairs set up under the column portico on the southwest side. Tecumseh announced that he didn't care to talk with a roof above him and said he wanted to have the conference where he stood. Harrison consented and ordered the chairs and tables brought into the grove. This put the location of the conference in the vicinity of today's Scott Street.

Tecumseh's followers chose to sit in the grass about twenty feet behind their leader, who spoke first. He gave an impassioned speech in the Shawnee tongue; Harrison had arranged for the chief's nephew to serve as interpreter. Tecumseh went into stark detail about the ways the whites had mistreated the Indians and included details of several instances where Harrison had negotiated treaties for land secession from tribes that didn't own it. He demanded that the land be returned to the Indians and said that if it wasn't, Harrison would have a hand in the killing of those chiefs who had unlawfully made those concessions.

When Tecumseh finished, he took his place with his followers on the ground. Harrison stood up and began to speak. He called the Shawnee chief's land complaints ridiculous, explaining the land the Miamis had given up belonged to them, as had been the case with previous negotiations. He paused to give the interpreter a chance to catch up, but Tecumseh had understood what he said. He leaped to his feet and screamed "You are a liar!" in Shawnee and said that nothing that Harrison said could be trusted. "You lie and you cheat!"

General John Gibson, seated not far from Harrison and fearing the worst, ordered a lieutenant seated near him to bring up the guard. Five of Tecumseh's lieutenants saw this, jumped to their feet and formed a circle around their leader, tomahawks in hand. Harrison drew his sword. Tecumseh uttered shrill cry to his waiting warriors and they rushed up from the rear; Harrison's guard moved behind him, rifles in hand. Some scared spectators who had gathered to watch the ceremony sprinted away to safety, while others pulled their own weapons or grabbed a nearby chunk of firewood for possible use in the fighting.

Harrison asked the interpreter exactly what Tecumseh had said and Harrison's face grew redder with each word he uttered. When he finished, the visibly angry Harrison announced that the conference had ended and said he would have no further communication with his visitors. He told Tecumseh that he and his people could go safely, but they must leave immediately, which they did.

So ended one of the most dramatic moments in the history of Vincennes and one that isn't hard to envision on the southwest side of the mansion, even with a street and a parking lot for Grouseland occupying the space where it happened.

Again, we have the D.A.R. to thank for giving us the opportunity to indulge our historical fantasies. In 1909, some self-serving idiots who worked for the Vincennes Water Company purchased the property where Grouseland stood with the intention of tearing the house down so the site could be used for other purposes.

To be sure, the home had lived a long and checkered life. After the Harrisons moved out in 1812, Judge Benjamin Pike lived in it until 1821, and Harrison's son, John Cleves Symmes Harrison, and his wife Clarissa (daughter of explorer Zebulon Pike) and family lived there for about 10 years after that. It stayed in the Harrison family until about 1850, but then served a variety of purposes, including a hotel, a library and even a grain warehouse.

Fortunately, the Francis Vigo Chapter of the D.A.R. raised the money to put a down payment on the property and save it from demolition, and in 1911, it opened as a historical museum.

Today, history is what the small city on the Wabash River in southern Indiana with no industry to speak of has to sell to the public. The house that was home to a future president and hosted countless dignitaries and Indian chiefs has Vincennes University behind it and a row of historic buildings, including the Indiana Territorial Capitol building, in a park to its immediate southeast.

Vincennes is known for its illustrious history, which is the only reason a lot of people stop here. No one talks about its terrific water company.

49 FORT MASSAC

You don't have to be a real estate professional to realize that the Fort Massac site once stood in the way of progress. It sits on a bluff about 50 feet above the Ohio River and probably no more than 200 feet from the old, abandoned Laidlaw Corporation wire hanger plant. Concrete and recycling companies peer over the plant's roof from the lots on the other side, the eastern doorstep of the town of Metropolis, Illinois. There, but for the grace of God, go it.

Riverfront property has always been in demand, even in the middle of the eighteenth century when the French first decided to build a fort here. At that point, there was no thought of a Metropolis, either a sprawling imaginary city that would require the heroic services of Superman or a small one of 8,000 that would pair with Paducah, Kentucky, a short distance up river on the opposite shore.

What attracted both the French and nearby Indian tribes in those days was the mouth of the Tennessee River. It empties into the Ohio at Paducah, about five miles from the rocky heights where the French finally built their fort in 1757. The site overlooks a broad sweep of the Ohio and is about 45 miles by water to the river's confluence with the Mississippi.

Thick herds of buffalo roamed southern Illinois early in the eighteenth century, one reason early historians believed that Charles Juchereau de Saint Denis built a trading post and tannery here in the autumn of 1702. While that's possible, most modern historians believe Juchereau actually built his post near Mound City, Illinois, about 40 miles downriver and about six miles from the Ohio River's confluence with the Mississippi.

Some reference books avoid the issue by saying that Juchereau may have built several smaller trading posts including one at or near the eventual Fort Massac site, either a diplomatic or cowardly way to take this away from the area without having to deny it completely. But suffice it to say that more prominent historical figures than Juchereau would eventually find their way here.

After the French and Indian War broke out with the British in 1754, the French decided to build a defensive chain of forts that stretched west from Fort Duquesne (Pittsburgh) and they constructed a fort here near the riverbank in 1757. They initially called it Fort De' L' Ascension, and after they strengthened it in 1759 they renamed it Fort Massiac in honor of a French minister. George Rogers Clark came here and took control of the fort site from the British in 1778, and the name would eventually be shortened to Massac when the Americans rebuilt the fort on the orders of George Washington in 1794

History kept returning here like a persistent salesman. Meriwether Lewis and William Clark came this way looking for volunteers for their famous journey west and this became a point of intrigue during vice-president Aaron Burr's conspiracy to head his own empire. So it should have been apparent that after the evacuation of the fort in 1814 and the eventual stripping of its remaining wood and bricks by nearby settlers, it deserved commemoration of some sort.

It took nearly a century for someone to act on that. Had it taken much longer, the folks who come here hoping to teach their kids a little frontier history on their weekend camping trip might have had to pitch their tents on the parking lot of an empty warehouse or settle for a tour of a widget factory. As it is, they can check out the outline of the original fort marked by posts in the grass and tour see a modern replica of it a short distance to the north, unless it's still closed due to structural problems. Both are part of a 1,450-acre state park that serves campers, boaters, picnickers, and dare we say it, riverfront industrialists, as well as history enthusiasts.

Julia Green Scott is the person most responsible for putting the project in motion, as progress inched eastward and the Ohio River threatened the Fort Massac site from the south. The widowed Scott lived in Bloomington, Illinois, was descended from the family of George Washington on both sides and was the vice president general for the National Society of the Daughters of the American Revolution at the time. She recognized the importance of saving the site before it was too late – evidence of the fort's ramparts was still discernible in the ground -- and helped throw the weight of the D.A.R. behind her effort. Scott made a presentation to the State Historical Society of Illinois on January 28, 1903, on behalf of the six-woman D.A.R. committee charged with getting it done. And on May 7 the legislature appropriated $10,000 for the purchase of the 20 acres needed for the park and the development of it. Reed Green, an attorney in Cairo, Illinois, sold the property for $3,500 and the other $6,500 was used for grading, construction of roads and walks, removal of dead timber and the construction of a keeper's lodge. It was dedicated five years later as Illinois first state park. In 1908, the trustees of Fort Massac State Park placed bronze plaques on the concrete entrance columns to the state park that explain the site's history. The plaque diplomatically notes that Juchereau built his trading post "at some unknown place between this site and the mouth of the Ohio River."

While no major battles were fought here, its cavalcade of historical figures should be enough to draw our attention.

According to legend, the Spanish explorer Hernando de Soto and his soldiers constructed a primitive fortification here to defend themselves from native attack as early at 1540. In the absence of proof this seems even less plausible than the Juchereau story, but hey, see if you can prove that they didn't. There is no denying that the French considered building a stone fort on this site in the 1740s or that the French erected Fort De L' Ascension here under the authority of Captain Charles Philippe Aubry in 1757 in the midst of their conflict with Britain.

Fort Duquesne's fall in November, 1758, proved to be a real blow to the French; the post probably held out longer than it would have were it not for the provisions supplied to it from the Illinois country. Fort De L' Ascension remained important as a communication link to Post Vincennes and to the lower Ohio and Louisiana authorities stressed its importance in safeguarding the Mississippi convoy route.

As the fall of Quebec and Montreal became more and more likely, the French weighed how to defend Louisiana and save that region for France in the event of a negotiated peace. One proposal involved transplanting French settlers in Canada to Louisiana and the lower Ohio region, with a second group of habitants settling near the mouth of the Ohio, where a city would be built and fortified as the new capital. If it had happened, it might have made Fort Massac another Quebec, probably an unwelcome prospect for today's Metropolis residents who enjoy their small-town life.

But alas, nothing came of this. Quebec and Montreal fell in 1759, and in negotiations for the Treaty of 1763, the French were forced to give up Canada as well as the Ohio Valley and the east bank of the Mississippi. In July, 1764, Fort Massac, Post Vincennes and other western posts were evacuated. The British initially planned to garrison Fort Massac with 60 men, but before they could occupy it, the Chickasaws burned it to the ground. The British considered rebuilding it, but that's all they did. The fort didn't rise again until after the Americans were in control of the site in 1794.

George Rogers Clark came here with a command of 160 men and camped at the mouth of Massac Creek, a few hundred yards east of the fort site, on their march to capture Kaskaskia in 1778. It is possible that Clark raised the first American flag over Illinois here at that time – there is a statue of Clark here -- although that was the last time for 16 years that anyone thought much about it.

This time, conflict with the Indians, who had been wreaking havoc with settlers in the Old Northwest, put the site back in the minds of the military. General Anthony Wayne was in the midst of his Indian campaign in the Ohio country early in 1794 when he received orders from George Washington to refortify the site of Fort Massac. Wayne chose Major Thomas Doyle of the first sub-legion as the leader of the expedition, and those troops, along with two subcontractor boats, left Cincinnati on May 24. They arrived at the fort site eight days later and Doyle had his men throw up temporary breastworks about one corner of the old French works, thus making "a good posture of defense." He completed the new fort October 20, exactly two months after Wayne led his troops to the decisive victory over combined Indian forces at Fallen Timbers.

The fort stood on a bank approximately 75 feet above low water level. But it stood so near the river bank that by the time French agent Victor Collot visited in 1796, he wrote that the two bastions facing the river were already in danger of being undermined by the caving of the river banks and that part of the ditch and palisade had already fallen into the river. Anyone visiting the site today would have no difficulty believing that. It is that close.

Nearby attacks of hostile tribes placed the post in jeopardy until December, 1795, when strong reinforcements reached Fort Massac and command of the post passed to Captain Zebulon Pike. This was the father of Zebulon Montgomery Pike, the explorer, who was also a junior officer at Fort Massac.

During this period, Fort Massac became a major port of entry for settlers entering the Illinois country by way of the Ohio River. In 1799, it was placed under direct control of Alexander Hamilton, newly commissioned as a major general in the new army being raised by the government in preparation for war against the French. Plans to garrison 1,000 men at the fort in response to a French threat were scuttled in favor of the new "Cantonment Wilkinsonville" post erected early in 1801 at a site 12 miles downriver. That caused Fort Massac to be temporarily abandoned as a military installation; matters with the French improved within a few months and the soldiers returned to Massac under the command of Captain Daniel Bissell.

Meriwether Lewis and William Clark stopped here on November 11, 1803, looking for soldiers to accompany them on their journey west. They expected to rendezvous with eight soldiers who had volunteered for the trip at South West Point, Tennessee, and were disappointed to discover the eight had not arrived. Lewis didn't wait. He hired a local woodsman named George Drouillard to find the soldiers and report with them near St. Louis, and the troupe left for Kaskaskia on November 13. Only two volunteers from the post met Captain Lewis's standards and joined the expedition.

Fort Massac had another brush with history in 1805 when former vice-president Aaron Burr and then-governor of the Louisiana Territory James Wilkinson, old pals from Revolutionary War days, conferred there for unknown reasons. At the time, Burr was suspected of trying to set up a new country west of the Alleghenies and Wilkinson is known to have been a paid spy for the Spanish Empire while serving as a commanding officer in the U.S. army. Little is known about their discussions at Fort Massac, but some believe Burr tried to enlist Wilkinson in his scheme. Burr knew Wilkinson, so he knew Wilkinson would do what's best for Wilkinson, a desirable trait when you're recruiting a potential traitor.

As it turned out, Wilkinson seems to have hatched a plan to move troops to a post on the Mississippi to stop Burr, a plan never carried out. Nevertheless, some historians see the double-dealing Wilkinson as a hero for trying to thwart Burr's plans. It's a curious use of the word "hero."

Whatever Wilkinson did or didn't do doesn't seem to have fazed the former vice-president. On December 26, 1806, Burr's party assembled at the mouth of the Cumberland River, about 30 miles upriver, and he sent a representative to Fort Massac to ask Captain Bissell whether he would attempt to prevent the expedition from passing by the fort. Bissell's response is open to conjecture, but Burr's boats subsequently passed between midnight and 1 a.m. on the morning of December 30 and apparently landed two miles west of the fort. Bissell later came under harsh criticism for his inaction; one of his aides testified that Bissell told him that he had been on the boats and had seen "no appearance of arms or ammunition." Some historians say he didn't see any because he didn't search them. Others say he couldn't have stopped the boats from passing if he had wanted to; the fort didn't have many soldiers and didn't have any cannons that might have challenged Burr and his conspirators. As it is, the last big moment in the fort's history passed, between midnight and 1 a.m., in dark silence.

The fort served primarily as a training center for troops after that. It might have played a key role in the War of 1812, but the action shifted well away from here. With the war over in April, 1814, the troops stationed at Fort Massac were removed to St. Louis and the fort evacuated. A visitor to the site in 1817 described the old post as having been "dismantled" and in 1833 apparently only stones remained.

Under the circumstances, it's impressive that Scott and her group were able to stand before the march of progress 80 years later. Now that their tiny park has been all but swallowed up by a huge state park that serves so many other purposes, it's easy to forget the genesis of it. But anyone whose personal quest to visit and discover a historical riverfront location ended at a steel factory or a power plant can appreciate how easily the Fort Massac site could have ended up that way.

A visitor can walk within the confines of a French fort built in the days of the French and Indian War, imagine Meriwether Lewis stomping around here in anger over the tardiness of eight supposed Corps of Discovery volunteers and stand near the shore and almost see Burr's expedition slipping silently past the fort that might have stopped it.

This is a lot better than another closed wire hanger factory.

50 FOX FORT

One hundred years ago, historically-minded tourists interested in visiting the tribal fort where the Fox tribe made its last stand in 1730 might have gone to a spot in Kendall County, Illinois, just west of Chicago. A huge carved boulder not far from the Fox River bore an inscription that claimed the battle happened there, based on information researched by historian John Francis Steward in 1902.

If it's carved on a giant boulder, it must be true, right?

Well, no. In the 1930s, amateur historian and archaeologist William Brigham, superintendent of schools for McLean County, Illinois, determined after much study and digging that the site of the Fox fort actually had been located there, just southeast of the village of Arrowsmith and 90 miles south of Steward's site. Brigham convinced the McLean County Historical Society to place a marker near the site in 1937, and although it was a smaller rock than the one in Kendall County – heck, Pluto might be smaller than that rock -- it was no less definitive:

"ETNATAEK: Here French and Indian Allies Defeated Fox Tribe 1730".

According to Brigham, Etnataek was the Algonquin word for "where the fight, battle or clubbing took place." His (or the Algonquins') one-word description of that "battle" never caught on with historians, t-shirt markers or anybody else. But the rock is still there by the side of the road, near the Smith farm where most now think a combined force of 1,400 French soldiers and allied Indians besieged and eventually nearly wiped out the fleeing Fox. By the way, Steward's rock is still on Maramech Hill too, or at least it was in 2016, when a former Kendall County resident returned home, asked the owner of the property for permission to visit it, photographed himself in front of it and posted it on the Internet. The rock sits alone and uncelebrated, its letters fading, partially hidden in red pine forest.

If other researchers had been so inclined, there might have been inscribed rocks all over the state of Illinois. In 1980 historian Joseph L. Peyser published a list of twelve locations that had been proposed as the fort site by historians and researchers over the years, including the two already described. Peyser published the list after locating an ancient map in the Archives Nationales in France that he thought proved that the site southeast of tiny Arrowsmith (2017 population, 283) in eastern McLean County was the site of the Fox fort.

An eyewitness account of the 23-day siege by interpreter and scout Jean-Baptiste Reaume (there had been two previously) discovered in Paris in 1989 and excavations by archaeologists since then have provided further evidence that this is in fact where the siege took place, regardless of what a giant boulder in Kendall County had been saying about it for years.

The rock in McLean County is decidedly smaller than the one in Kendall County, which was apparently placed there by Steward, but fortunately this isn't a case where the largest rock wins. The archaeology matters, and the numerous excavations of the Arrowsmith site by Lenville J. Stelle, a professor from Parkland College in Champaign, Illinois, confirmed that a large battle took place there and that the French and the Fox were both there at some point. It's not like the French etched the date and occasion of the battle on their musket balls before firing them, so to date, there has been no definitive proof that this was the fort site. But everyone including even a lot of civic-minded Kendall County citizens have pretty much accepted this as the location of the siege.

It's remarkable that researchers were eventually able to figure it out from the scant and conflicting evidence about it. At the time of the siege, this region was mostly unknown to mapmakers and natural features couldn't pinpoint the spot.

The location wasn't even familiar to the principals in the battle. Historically, the Fox or Meskwaki tribe had resided along the Saint Lawrence River in Ontario and at one time in the late seventeenth century may have counted as many as 10,000 in the tribe. Years of war with the Hurons and the French colonial agents who supplied them arms caused Fox to migrate first today's eastern Michigan and later to southern Wisconsin.

The Fox were known as intense fighters who showed little or no mercy to their enemies, who seemed to be just about everybody else. It's not surprising then that they were fiercely resistant to the French and their Native American allies, or that their near-constant battles came to be known as the Fox Wars.

The Fox' persistent warring had reduced their numbers to about 3,500 by the start of the First Fox War in 1712, and by the end of the Second Fox War in 1728, their numbers had fallen to about 1,500. Although the French were gradually winning, they had grown weary of the tribe's hostile ways. The Fox harassment so annoyed the French king that he ordered the total extermination of the tribe.

The tribe suffered several major defeats and by 1730 the 900 or so Fox who remained (600 warriors and 300 women and children) felt they could no longer stay in southern Wisconsin. They were on the run across Illinois in hopes of reaching the allied Iroquois in the east when the French allied tribes of Potawatomi, Kickapoo, Mascouten, and Illini blocked their trek.

The fleeing Fox decided it would be best if they stopped and built a fort in the middle of a grove of small trees along the banks of the Sangamon River, believing that they had ample supplies of gunpowder and food to cause their enemies to lose interest in maintaining a long siege. The Fox built the walls of their fort of piled up dirt with a wooden palisade on top. They left open the river side and built the walls on three sides, 150 feet wide and 350 feet long. The houses inside resembled bullet-proof bunkers, dug to a depth of two or three feet.

While the Fox built their fort for what they thought would be a short stay, their Native American enemies sent word of their location to the French commanders at Fort de Chartres and Fort St. Joseph. French captain

Nicolas-Antoine Coulon de Villiers received word at Fort St. Joseph on August 6 and left with 50 French soldiers and 300 Sacs, Potawatomis and Miamis four days later. He also sent word to Fort Miami and Fort Detroit before he departed. Meanwhile, Lieutenant Robert Groston de St. Ange left Fort de Chartres with 100 French soldiers and traders and 100 Native American allies and picked up another 300 Illini on the way.

St. Ange arrived first on the morning of August 17 and his army joined forces with the Indian allies already there. Villiers arrived around noon the same day and the combined forces surrounded the Fox, attempted to cut off their water supply and put the fort under siege. Without artillery, it was difficult to do much damage, and the Fox had had the foresight to dig a series of tunnels to the river that enabled them to maintain their water supply. At that point, the Fox believed they could outlast the French and beat the siege.

The stifling August heat began to exact a toll on them however. A steady fire from their enemies kept many of the Fox women, children and elderly holed up in those windowless bunkers, where the heat must have seemed like a high price to pay for their safety.

Finally, the Fox tried to use the closely related Sacs as intermediaries who could help them negotiate terms of their surrender. But on September 1, Nicolas-Joseph de Noyelles arrived from Fort Miami with about 10 French soldiers and 200 Huron, Potawatomi, and Miami warriors and word from Governor Charles de la Boische, Marquis de Beauharnois of Detroit that there would be no negotiated peace. If the French could exterminate the Fox and rid themselves of the tribe forever, that's what they intended to do.

When a huge storm with heavy rain, hail and high wind rolled in on the evening of September 8, the desperate Fox seized their chance for escape. With clouds blocking the stars and moon and the night plunged in total darkness, they began a chaotic escape from the fort. Their children's cries alerted the enemies of their exodus and many of the Fox became confused in the total darkness and became separated from the rest of the tribe. French commanders wanted to pursue them, but their Native American allies refused to go after them in the severe storm and total darkness. The next morning, a combined force of 1400 French and Indians set out after them and caught the exhausted Fox on prairieland about 12 miles southwest of the fort. The Fox warriors hastily formed a skirmish line, hoping to give their women and children a chance to escape; their pursuers charged rapidly and began cutting down the Fox, some of whom sang their death song. Approximately 50 warriors escaped, but the bodies of 200 warriors and 300 women and children lay dead on the battlefield. Most of the surviving women, children and elderly were taken prisoner and later sold as slaves. Some of the escapees were hunted down, taken back to the enemy camp, tortured and burned to death.

In the months after the battle, Governor Beauharnois estimated that only about 450 Fox remained alive and said that most of those were held captive by French-allied Indians. He noted that some Fox hunting camps were still occupied in Wisconsin, and said they numbered no more than 30 lodges. Despite the high cost of the campaign (about 22,000 livres), he told his superiors that "peace and tranquility. . . now reign in the upper Countries." Others boasted that the fur trade would explode without the Fox to disrupt it and even that the farmers in the vicinity of Fort Detroit could now cultivate their crops in complete safety.

After reading those accounts, one might suppose that this moment in time would be forever remembered with an impressive memorial and that the Fox would quietly fade into history. Neither happened. The relative handful of surviving Fox eventually joined with the Sacs, and a century later, their descendants constituted a considerable portion of Black Hawk's followers in his war against European-American settlers in Illinois and present-day Wisconsin in 1832.

The exact location of the fort was all but forgotten, in part because the French failed to record a precise location of it at the time. Early descriptions of the battle indicated that it occurred on an open prairie between the Wabash and Illinois Rivers, approximately 145 miles south of Lake Michigan and east-southeast of Starved Rock on the Illinois River.

Part of the confusion stemmed from the fact that the French commanders reported to different governors - St. Ange to Louisiana and Villiers to Quebec – who apparently received different info which resulted in different maps. Steward used a 1730 map drawn in Quebec for his conclusion that the battle was on Maramech Hill in Kendall County, even though that placed it mostly at odds with eyewitness accounts. A map drawn in New Orleans in 1731 that was discovered in Paris more closely fit the participants' descriptions, which strengthened the case for McLean County.

The Arrowsmith site had been settled in 1841 by Jacob Smith, who found musket balls and other relics when he began plowing the land. In May of 1897, Captain John Burnham and members of the McLean County Historical Society excavated several pits on the land and found lead musket balls, iron, and bone fragments. The site was excavated again in 1932 and 1934, and over time arrowheads, French knife blades, gun parts and even a French brass button turned up.

While that may not be considered as definitive "proof," this tranquil farm along the winding Sangamon River in central Illinois seems like as good a place as any to pause and reflect on the French's determination to commit an act of genocide against the Fox tribe.

The French's failure to complete the job doesn't make the act any less horrific.

51 FORT OUIATENON

Until 1967, visiting Fort Ouiatenon couldn't have been easier. Signs directed visitors to a county park with a replica blockhouse that some visitors thought might be real, a spot with a plaque placed there by the Daughters of the American Revolution that identified this as the site of the fort/trading post built by the French in 1717.

There was just one problem: The real site of Fort Ouiatenon actually lay a mile to the west, disguised as a corn field.

If you've been reading this book from the beginning, you're probably already muttering something like "Not again." It seems remarkable to a twenty-first century visitor that early historians could misplace something as big as a fort or a battlefield, particularly a place that once had a community of 3,000 people and produced a stack of historic credentials.

Crazy as this seems, it probably happened here because the site has been farmland since the late eighteenth century. The city of Lafayette, Indiana, was founded on the opposite shore three miles up the Wabash River in 1824, and even when Purdue University was born on the same side of the river as Ouiatenon in West Lafayette in 1869, the town didn't grow in this direction. By the time anyone got around to worrying about exactly where Fort Ouiatenon had been, all visible traces of the old trading post had been gone for over a century, which cuts down on the number of living witnesses to its location.

The founding of the Tippecanoe County Historical Association by Dr. Richard B. Wetherill and some of his associates in 1925 finally put the old French fort on someone's radar, even if their radar needed recalibrating. Three years later, Wetherill purchased the land at 3129 South River Road where the D.A.R. had placed that small commemorative marker locating the fort in 1909, and in 1930, he built a 452 square foot replica of a blockhouse of a fort on the property. With no actual drawing to go on the "replica" was patterned after the more typical British fortifications than French, but at this point, that seems like a minor glitch. That marked the beginnings of the Fort Ouiatenon Historical Park that we know today, a pretty place for picnics, nature hikes, a museum (in the blockhouse) and the annual Feast of the Hunters' Moon, a historical reenactment of the annual fall gatherings of the French and Native Americans held at Fort Ouiatenon in the eighteenth century.

By all accounts, it is a wonderful event, one that has been held here on the banks of the Wabash more than 50 years. Still, it must have a bit of a downer when aerial photos taken in 1967 showed discolored soil in freshly plowed fields that suggested that the fort actually had actually stood about a mile to the west. After a little archaeological detective work confirmed it, the TCHA purchased that 20-acre property in 1972 and subsequent digs uncovered more details about the structure including some rough dimensions. But the excavations were hampered by the fact that the land around the historical association's plot was being farmed.

The TCHA dreamed of the day when a park might be located there, but then so does everybody who knows about the site of an old tribal village or trading post that is on someone else's property.

Fortunately, this story has happy ending. Rick Jones, the state archaeologist for the Indiana Department of Natural Resources, recommended land banking of the property in 2014, saying that it had been untouched by urban development and has "outstanding" historical and archaeological value. Colby Bartlett, then TCHA vice-president, confirmed that that's what the organization had been thinking for a long time, which might have been just another beautiful pipe dream. Then the land became available and, remarkably, so did the money to purchase it.

The Roy Whistler Foundation, established by the estate of a late Purdue University chemistry professor, kicked in $636,000, which was used to leverage $462,777 in matching grants from the Indiana Bicentennial Nature Trust and the Indiana Heritage Trust. The funds enabled the TCHA to purchase 200 acres surrounding the original fort site, which included former locations of nearby Kickapoo and Mascouten villages, and create the Ouiatenon Preserve. It is co-owned and operated by the TCHA and the Archaeological Conservancy.

"It was a four-year concerted effort, but I will tell you that the stars aligned and it was the right place and the right time," said Bartlett, now the preserve's director. "The project spoke to a lot of people and fortunately to the right people, not only because of its historic and archaeological importance, but also because of where it is located along the Wabash River, a critical environmental area. This was a project that killed a lot of birds with one

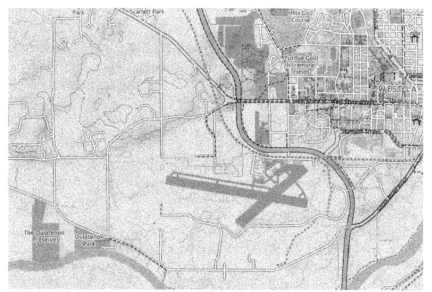

MAP SHOWS LOCATIONS OF THE PARK AND THE PRESERVE, AND THEIR PROXIMITY TO WEST LAFAYETTE AND THE PURDUE UNIVERSITY AIRPORT.

stone. We were able to protect and preserve the archaeological resources and have it as a place where we can interpret the history."

Unfortunately, all of that takes a while. Bartlett said that the initial focus has been on restoring 200 acres of farm fields to lowland prairie, and that it's going to take "four or five years" to get the prairie established.

"The seed mix was developed to be flood resistant but also not be deep rooted because we didn't want to disturb or destroy any subterranean archaeological features," he said.

That's important because this is one of those rare historic sites that has essentially been undisturbed by construction. An archaeological field school planned as a joint effort between the University of Southern Indiana and Purdue University for the summer of 2020 was cancelled because of the pandemic, but it was rescheduled for the summer of 2021. It is only the beginning.

"Even though Indiana University did two years of excavations and Michigan State University did seven or eight years of excavations through the mid to late 1970s, only about 15 percent of the area inside the stockade has been excavated archaeologically, and virtually nothing outside of the stockade had been done," Bartlett said. "There's an awful lot archaeology to be done there, and in keeping with what modern practices and strategies are, the goal is to preserve as much of it as we can for future generations of archaeologists."

The ground has quite a story to tell. It begins with French Ensign François Picote de Belestre. who came here in 1717 with four soldiers, three men, a blacksmith and supplies to trade with the Wea tribe, which is closely related to the Miami. The Weas had a village on the south bank of the Wabash across from the spot where the French built their fortification, the first fortified European settlement in what would eventually become the state of Indiana. Sometime in the 1720s François-Marie Bissot, the Sieur de Vincennes became commander of the fort, constructed to prevent British expansion in the region.

The fort flourished as a trading post under French control, with the Weas and other Native American tribes regarding it as a hub for the region. The settlement around it grew until it had as many as 3,000 residents at its high point in the middle of the eighteenth century.

It passed into British hands in September, 1760, when the French lost the French and Indian War and a contingent of soldiers under Lieutenant Edward Jenkins took control of it. But Jenkins and his troops were surprised on June 1, 1763, by a combined force of Wea, Kickapoo and Mascouten warriors who made this one of seven British posts captured during Pontiac's War. The British would get the post back, but they never made much use of it after that and never garrisoned it again.

In 1765, a band of Kickapoos and Mascoutens captured former British commander and now British Indian agent Colonel George Croghan on the Ohio River during his mission of peace to Fort de Chartres. They robbed him and took him as a prisoner first to Vincennes and then to Ouiatenon. The tribes released him two days later to resume his journey to Fort de Chartres, now accompanied by noted French trader Alexander Maisonville and a large number of Weas. They didn't get far before they happened across Ottawa chief Pontiac and a band of warriors on their way to Ouiatenon. Pontiac recognized Croghan and Maisonville, and after a brief conversation they all set out for Ouiatenon. They called together all of the tribal leaders in the region and commenced a grand council; Pontiac used it to announce that he had been deceived by the French king and that the French would fight no longer. He then hurled his tomahawk into the ground and said that he would never again go to war against the English. Croghan, Pontiac and the Pontiac's party left for Fort Detroit the following day. In a great council of Native American leaders there they confirmed the action taken at the Ouiatenon council. That ended the siege of Fort Detroit and the "Pontiac Conspiracy."

As his power ebbed in ensuing years, Pontiac returned to Ouiatenon to live in 1768 when he was forced to leave his Ottawa village on the Maumee River. In a letter to British officials, he explained that the people of his village no longer recognized him as a chief. A year later, a member of the Peoria tribe murdered him in Cahokia.

During the early years of the American Revolution, Native American war parties used Fort Ouiatenon as a staging ground while fighting for the British. American troops under Captain Leonard Helm and Lieutenant Bailey reached Fort Ouiatenon in 1778 to take the fort, and they captured a British Indian agent named Celeron and 40 men who controlled of the structure.

But the Americans didn't occupy it for long. During the 1780s, local Indian tribes again used it as a base of operations in resistance against the westward expansion of white American settlers. In 1791, President George Washington ordered a campaign to stop the attacks, and Northwest Territory Governor Arthur St. Clair subsequently sent General Charles Scott to attack villages along the Wabash River with those near Ouiatenon as the primary targets. Scott crossed the Ohio River with 750 Kentucky militia in May and marched to Ouiatenon. The troops burned down everything there including nearby crops and houses; the militia also destroyed other nearby tribal villages, including a major one called Keth-tio-e-ca-muck near the mouth of the Tippecanoe River in today's Prophetstown State Park.

"When Scott attacked and burned the Ouiatenon village, there was no reference to the fort being there," Bartlett said. "He referred to it as the old Kickapoo town. In the 1730s, the Kickapoo and Mascouten moved to Ouiatenon and set up villages around the fort, so we think sometime probably in the 1780s, the last remaining French families probably left Ouiatenon."

That closed the sometimes illustrious, sometimes minimal history of Fort Ouiatenon, and it didn't receive much thought again until a few graves, pieces of a military uniform, a silver crucifix and several utensils were uncovered in 1889. That subsequently led to the marker erected by the Lafayette branch of the D.A.R. in 1909, Dr. Wetherill's "replica" blockhouse in 1930 and a park that's not where it should be.

Today, a visitor to the reserve sees a large sign near River Road with an oval-shaped gravel driveway behind it next to a public overlook where the public can view the site from afar. The preserve itself is closed to the public, although it is opened to tours on occasion. For now, that nice walkway to the fort site pictured in a drawing at the top of the preserve's website is just that – a drawing.

"We're investigating the possibilities on building an interpretive trail that would go from the overlook down to the fort site and then loop back up," Bartlett said. "We're investigating how that can be done so that it is ADA (Americans with Disabilities Act) accessible, because in order to get any significant state or federal money for a trail system, it pretty much has to be ADA accessible.

"We have some engineering challenges that would need to be met with that. One would be how do you deal with the elevation drop from the bluff overlooking the river valley down to the river valley in a way that is ADA compliant. And at the base of the bluff we have about a 100-yard wide wetland, so we're investigating what type of material -- perhaps a pier-ed boardwalk -- could be used to transect that area."

There are a lot of things in the works. The preserve recently acquired a house adjacent to the public overlook, with the idea of possibly using it as a small interpretative center, museum and a place to do archaeological and environmental research. The Ouiatenon Preserve also received a unanimous recommendation from the National Park Service National Historic Landmark Commission to designate the site as a national historic landmark.

"It's actually a pretty big deal," Bartlett said. "Less than three per cent of historic sites that are the national register of historic places are eligible for national historic landmark status."

Given Ouiatenon's illustrious past, it seems ridiculous to say that the best is yet to come. But it is probably fair to say that the old trading post is finally going to get the memorial it deserved for over two centuries.

This time, it's even going to be in the right place.

52 LOCHRY'S DEFEAT

It's a good bet that most travelers who visit or pass through Aurora, Indiana, have never heard of Colonel Archibald Lochry. Aurora is a pretty little town that lies on a bend on the Ohio River that provides many of its houses and rental properties a picturesque view of "La Belle Riviere" as it wends its way east toward Cincinnati.

It is also a pit stop on Indiana Route 56 from the Hollywood Casino in Lawrenceburg to the Rising Star Casino Resort in Rising Sun, a distance of about 13 miles. This route was more important before the first casinos opened in Ohio in 2012, when many people looking for ways to lose their money routinely drove from Cincinnati, Dayton and Columbus for a chance to leave it in southern Indiana.

Maybe that's why the last time I drove this route it seemed considerably more crowded than it is today. Or maybe thousands of history lovers have already seen the roadside markers which commemorate the spot where the 107 men in Lochry's force were ambushed by Mohawk chief Joseph Brant and approximately 300 Indians in 1781 in a rout that came to be known either as Lochry's Defeat or the Lochry Massacre.

This skirmish occurred about two miles south of Aurora, near the mouth of Laughery Creek, the name meant to honor the commander of Westmoreland County, Pennsylvania, militia who lost his life there. Poor guy. He made the supreme sacrifice and lost his chance for geographic immortality because the government clerk who handled documents pertaining to the battle couldn't spell his name right.

It doesn't matter much. Most drivers on Route 56 – and again, this isn't Chicago's Dan Ryan Expressway – will cross Laughery Creek at 55 miles per hour and probably miss the competing signs that stand next to each other, a dark green historical marker with gold lettering for Lochry's Defeat and a green and white highway sign for Laughery Creek. You can't read the historical marker unless you stop the car, which might give you an immediate spot beside the good colonel in eternity. There is room for a car on the side of the road, but not enough to make stopping worth the risk. Besides, the road crosses the creek approximately 2000 feet from the Ohio River, so the real location of the massacre is probably, at the least, squinting distance away.

Or maybe not. Just before a Rising Sun-bound traveler reaches the bridge, Old Route 56 makes a right-turn and the narrow road takes a path parallel to the new route for about a mile. River View Cemetery lies a couple hundred yards up the road on the ground that fronts Laughery Creek, and it has a sign that claims this as the "Lochry Massacre Site." A sign to the left and a granite monument to right offer details of the battle and list the names of those who were killed here.

Is this the real massacre site? Maybe, although it's more likely that the markers were placed here as a matter of convenience before the new highway was built and the road (Old 56) passed by this way. The marker on the modern route dates from 1961, so that is probably when the new road by-passed the cemetery and the one-lane Triple Whipple Bridge, a structure that crosses the creek on the old route and dates from 1878. But even if it's not the battle site – and to be clear, no one is certain exactly where it is – it seems like a disservice to both the dead soldiers and to the modern curiosity-seeker to have these markers in this location, where many visitors would never find them. When I came here the first time I assumed the marker on modern Route 56 was the only one and only found out about the other ones later when a picture of them popped up during a Google search for information about the site.

It is important to note that while the exact location where Lochry's troops were killed is unclear, it seems likely that the spot was much nearer to the Ohio River than this. Early accounts of the battle place it at the mouth of Laughery Creek, and the cemetery is nearly a half-mile from the Ohio.

An adventurer determined to get a closer look at a more likely ambush site can turn into the entrance to the Lighthouse Point Yacht Club, which lies directly opposite the entrance of Old Route 56. The yacht club is located on the north side of the creek on a big chunk of riverfront property that fronts the creek at its mouth. A farm field occupies the opposite side of the creek nearly to the river's edge and the lack of signage doesn't necessarily mean that Lochry and his men didn't die over there. It may mean that the soil on that side of the creek is too rich to waste on monuments.

As is often the case, the event itself may have had a considerably larger impact on history than is indicated by either the location or the memorials. At the time, the frontier suffered from frequent Indian attacks supported by the British western headquarters at Detroit. Lochry created his force to be part of a George Rogers Clark force that planned to attack the British stronghold at Fort Detroit and end England's support of the Indians. Clark had initially been promised 2,000 troops by Virginia governor Thomas Jefferson, but because most Colonial troops were used to fight the British in the East, Clark had been able to raise a force of only about 400. They set out from Fort Pitt in early August, 1781.

Lochry raised his troops in Westmoreland County, Pennsylvania; the plan called for him to meet up with Clark's larger force at Fort Henry in Wheeling. But Lochry's force didn't arrive in time for some reason and while Clark awaited his arrival some of his soldiers deserted. Finally, after five days of waiting at Wheeling, Clark set out down the Ohio, leaving provisions and boats for Lochry's use along with directions to follow him.

Lochry's troops arrived in Wheeling a day after Clark's departure, but they were delayed again because of a shortage of boats and didn't leave until five days later. The delay caused them to miss Clark at the designated meeting spot by another day. This time, Clark intended to wait for Lochry's troops at the mouth of the Kanawha River, but because the desertions from his army continued, he kept moving. He left a letter, suspended from a pole, that directed the party to come down the river.

Lochry's group missed that note. With supplies dwindling and no sign of Clark, he sent Captain Samuel Shannon ahead with a party of seven men in a swift-moving boat to try to overtake him. In a note to Clark, Lochry asked him to leave more provisions because they were nearly out of flour and he wanted to avoid further delay by sending out hunters. Lochry did send two men on a hunt the next day but they never returned, a sign that Indians had probably either killed or captured them.

Meanwhile, Indians had also captured the Shannon party and with it they got the note describing Lochry's situation. The Indians knew of the intended expedition against Detroit, and they had been watching Clark's voyage down the river. Brant had been waiting for reinforcements being gathered in the Ohio interior by Simon Girty and British agent Alexander McKee. Because they had yet to arrive, he had been forced to watch Clark's larger army pass from the river's forested shores. Now that they understood the desperate situation involving Lochry's troops, they decided to attack the smaller party when the time was right.

They initially chose an island 11 miles below the mouth of the Great Miami River, where they planned to use some of Shannon's party to lure Lochry's troops ashore. But before they got there Lochry's troops stopped near the mouth of the creek; they had run out of feed for their horses and wanted to take them ashore to eat. The men were also hungry and had killed a buffalo they had spotted near the shore. Some of them were apparently in the process of cooking it when the Indians launched a surprise attack. The Indians killed 41 Americans and captured the rest. Lochry reportedly had his skull spit oven by a tomahawk blow from a Shawnee warrior as he disconsolately sat on a log after the surrender. An angry Brant reportedly stopped the Indians from slaughtering even more of the helpless militiamen.

Lieutenant Isaac Anderson, one of over 60 troops taken prisoner, kept a diary of the trip that is the source of most of the information on the battle. This was his entry from August 24, the day of the massacre:

"Colonel Lochry ordered the boats to land on the Indiana shore, about ten miles below the mouth of the Great Meyamee (Miami) river, to cook provisions and cut grass for the horses, when we were fired on by a party of Indians from the bank. We took to our boats, expecting to cross the river, and were fired on by another party in a number of canoes, and soon we became a prey to them. They killed the colonel and a number more after they were prisoners. The number of our killed was about forty. They marched us that night about eight miles up the river and encamped."

The Indians took the prisoners to a British and Indian camp on the eastern shore of the Great Miami River, about three miles from the current site of Cleves, Ohio. A historical marker about 150 yards from the intersection of Jordan Road and East River Road lists the names of the prisoners brought there. It says that they stayed for about a month before being taken to Fort Detroit.

Because of Lochry's losses, Clark abandoned his plans to attempt to take Fort Detroit in September. He led an expedition against the Shawnee towns on the Great Miami the following year, but never mounted an expedition against Fort Detroit. It remained in British hands even after the end of the American Revolution 1783 and continued to help Indian tribes in their attacks on American settlers until 1796, when it was finally surrendered under terms following the Treaty of Greenville.

VII.

FURS AND PORTAGES

53 LA POINTE

U.S. Route 2, the major east-west artery in the Upper Peninsula and northern Wisconsin, passes about 20 miles south of Bayfield, Wisconsin, the jumping off point for the ferry to La Pointe and Madeline Island. From Bayfield (population 487 in the 2010 census) it is 80 miles to Superior, Wisconsin, 279 miles to Green Bay and 206 miles to Marquette, Michigan. This is a roundabout way of saying that nobody ever winds up in La Pointe by accident, which doubtless was even more true in the seventeenth and eighteenth centuries than it is today.

Native Americans have lived here for thousands of years but the Ojibwa are the first people with a written history of it. They started their journey from near the mouth of the Saint Lawrence River in Quebec. Ojibwa legend says the tribe moved first to a place near Montreal, where it stayed for some time, and then to (Sault Ste. Marie) for another extended period before moving on to Moningwunakauning (Madeline Island). The island is partially shielded from Lake Superior by the Bayfield Peninsula and the rest of the Apostle Islands,

There, according to nineteenth century Ojibwa historian William Whipple Warren, "it has ever since reflected back the rays of the sun, and blessed our ancestors with life, light and wisdom." Warren, a native of La Pointe whose mother was French-Ojibwa (more on that later), used interviews with tribal elders to conclude in his *History of the Ojibway People*, written between 1849 and 1852, that La Pointe and Madeline Island is the spiritual home of the tribe.

"Moningwunakauning is the spot on which the Ojibway tribe first grew, and like a tree it has spread its branches in every direction in the bands that now occupy the vast extent of the Ojibway earth," Warren wrote. "It is the root from which all the far scattered villages of the tribe have sprung.'"

The Ojibwa still have a heavy presence in the area in the form of the Bad River Indian Reservation on the mainland, at 124,654 acres the largest reservation in the modern state of Michigan. But the tribe's share of the 15,360-acre island – which is 14 miles long and three miles wide -- has been reduced to a 200-acre sliver of land at the northeast corner set aside by the 1854 treaty as the tribe's traditional fishing grounds.

How the Ojibwa's "spiritual home" became a modern tourist destination with the tribe controlling only a small patch of land differs from many tales of tribal displacement, in part because of Ojibwa legends and in part of the vagaries of the fur trade that drew the white man here. At times, the Ojibwa vacated the island on their own accord for both economic and personal reasons, only to return later. So the tribe's final exodus to a nearby reservation on tribal lands on the shore of Chequamegon Bay where they had also lived is subject to interpretation.

Madeline Island, the largest of the 22 that came to be known as the Apostle Islands, was "discovered" by French traders Medard Chouart Sieur des Groseilliers and his brother-in-law Pierre Esprit Radisson. They arrived at Chequamegon Bay in the fall of 1659 accompanied by Ojibwa and Ottawa Indians. They went south for the winter, but when they returned to Montreal with a fortune in furs, it alerted the French to the riches that awaited them here.

Father Claude Allouez came here in 1665 and found a "great village" of seven Indian nations on the mainland, most of them likely having fled from the warring Iroquois. He became the first Jesuit priest to establish a mission at Chequamegon – La Pointe du St. Esprit -- which seems to have been on the mainland at the southwest corner of the bay, somewhere between the current towns of Ashland and Washburn. He apparently got the name for his mission from nearby Point Chequamegon. The region remained the focus of the growing French fur trade until 1668 when that shifted to Green Bay, partially because of a temporary peace between the French and the Iroquois. But a few traders remained in the region and Allouez stayed at his mission until the spring of 1669. Father Jacques Marquette took his place in the fall, and it was here that he learned of the route that would enable him and Joliet to reach the Mississippi River in 1673.

Apparently, the Ojibwa weren't living on the island at that point. The tribal elders Warren interviewed told him that the Ojibwa lived on Madeline Island for 120 years before the French arrived, so why weren't they there then?

This is where the story of this little piece of heaven gets a little dicey. Better to let Warren explain:

"At the end of this (120-year) period we come to a dark chapter in their

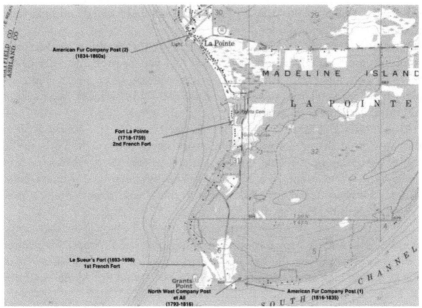

THIS FORTWIKI MAP BY JOHN STANTON SHOWS LOCATIONS OF FUR TRADE POSTS ON MADELINE ISLAND.

history, on which the old men (he interviewed for the book) dislike to linger. They are loath to tell the causes which led to the complete and sudden evacuation of the great village. . .

"The Evil Spirit had found a strong foothold among them. Evil practices became in vogue. Horrid feasts on human flesh became a custom. When the dead body of a victim had been interred, the murderer proceeded at night to the grave, disinterred it, and taking it to his lodge, he made a feast of it, to the relatives, which was eaten during the darkness of midnight, and if any of the invited guests became aware of the nature of the feast and refused to eat, he was sure to fall under the ill will of the feaster, and became the next victim. . . Such a taste did they at last acquire for human flesh, that parents did not dare refuse their children if demanded by the fearful medicine men for sacrifice."

Warren's sources illustrated their stories with several gruesome examples, and finally relate that "the Chi-be-ug, or souls of the victims, were at last heard nightly, traversing the village, weeping and wailing." He said because of this, "the inhabitants became panic-stricken and the consequence was that a complete and total desertion of their island of refuge took place."

Warren wrote that he didn't know how much of the nightly weeping of the dead was a product of their imagination, but "certain it is however that from that time the Ojibways considered the island as haunted, and never resided on it till after the first old French traders had located and built their trading establishment thereon."

It's difficult to say how many of the island's 300 year-round residents and 1,500 summertime inhabitants have heard that tale, or probably more to the point, actually believe it. Either way, it puts a macabre historical spin on a place that at first glance (and second, third and fourth glances) seems like a beautiful little chunk of paradise.

But it does emphasize a point that has been established over and over in this book, that that gorgeous seaside resort where you watched a beautiful sunset yesterday or the cute little restaurant where you ate breakfast this morning may be sitting on a site of unspeakable horrors you never knew about. That weird feeling you have in places that seem ordinary might not be as odd as it seems. History can be sneaky.

Fur traders will also be fur traders. If the "Chi-be-ug" exists, a little weeping and wailing probably wouldn't stop the traders' quest for profits. Only instability among the region's Indian tribes were likely to affect that, which is what happened when the Ojibwa living at Sault Ste. Marie expanded their territory westward and got into war with Sioux.

That warfare disrupted the fur trade in the region, but by 1680, the Ojibwa definitely had a village at Chequamegon, either on Madeline Island or on the mainland. The fur trade in the region bounced back in 1689 when the outbreak of King William's War between England and France caused the Iroquois to close the Green Bay trade route to the French and the French looked to build a trading post here. They first built one on the narrow point of land that juts from the mainland to the opening of Chequamegon Bay called a sandspit, by then known as La Pointe. The point reaches to within about a mile of the island. Pierre Le Sueur moved the trading post to a more defensible location on the southern end of Madeline Island in 1693. The post was built to maintain peace between the Ojibwa and the Sioux, and to protect the latter from attacks by their enemies, the Foxes and Mascoutens. To my knowledge, there is no mention in Le Sueur's "Mémoires" of being kept up at night by "wailing and weeping."

The fur trade flourished until 1696, when King Louis XIV of France revoked all trading licenses and closed this and the other trading posts in the region because of a glut of furs in the market. Archaeologist Robert Birmingham believes that this late seventeenth-century trading post and Ojibwa village stood at the lower end of the Winston-Cadotte excavation in the vicinity of Old Fort Road at the southern end of Madeline Island, although the evidence is not conclusive.

A historical marker is affixed to a rock in the grass on the west side of Old Fort Road that marks the spot of French-Canadian trader Michel Cadotte's trading post, which he started there in 1792. The plaque also erroneously notes that Fort La Pointe (the trading post) was built in 1718 about 500 feet west of the marker and lists the commanding officers there until 1759. But evidence of that eighteenth-century French trading post has been unearthed near the modern marina, about a mile north of here. The French trading post here, which preceded Cadotte's, likely was the one that operated near the end of the seventeenth century. The Cadotte- Fort La Pointe marker was erected in 1926.

Another war between France and England broke out in 1713, which was the catalyst for the French reestablishment of the La Pointe trading post at a new location on the west side of the island in 1718. The post remained as a trading center, military outpost and a home to traders and voyageurs until the last French commander left in 1762 following the French defeat in the Seven Years War (the French and Indian War) with England.

Again, the island's marina can be found at this location today. A large Ojibwa village has been excavated by archaeologists in the vicinity and because of the types of European trade goods found here, goods that include glass beads, gunflints, knives, cooking kettles and Jesuit rings, they have dated occupation of the site from 1718 to as late as 1775.

This Ojibwa village likely housed as many as 1,000 residents during the summer season. It served as the tribe's principal settlement and became the gathering place for the Ojibwas' annual religious ceremonies.

The British apparently destroyed the French trading post around 1765, which seems about right given the change in possession following the war. But Warren relates a dark tale that also results in the destruction of the post and may explain why the Ojibwa left the island again.

The clerk or trader in charge was a man named Joseph and he resided during his last winter there with his wife, two children and one Canadian coureur de bois. This man developed an "unlawful passion" for Joseph's wife, and one day when the clerk was gone to shoot ducks, he forced himself upon her. She grabbed a nearby Indian spear and defended herself with such force that her attacker killed her in defense.

Aware that his act wouldn't go unpunished, he seized a nearby gun and waited for her husband, hid behind the gateway of the post and shot him in the back and killed him upon his return. Then he sought the couple's six-year-old daughter and infant boy and murdered them both. With all of the Ojibwa away on their spring hunting trips, he tried to make his escape from the island, but spring was approaching and he broke through the thawing ice and was forced to remain. When the Indians returned and asked about the trader and his family, he told them that they had left on a dog train to visit the Indians' sugar camps while the ice was still intact, broke through and drowned. The Ojibwa bought this for a while and searched the shores for the bodies to no avail. But when the first trade shipments arrived from Montreal and the traders found blood on the walls of the room where the wife had been murdered, they conducted a search of the vicinity and discovered the bodies beneath a pile of rubbish. Confronted with the evidence, the murderer confessed and was taken to Montreal to be executed and the old fort was evacuated and the cannon and iron works thrown into an adjacent pond.

Whether this is true or not, another version of this tale appeared in the *Detroit Gazette* in August, 1822. This one dates the murder during the winter of 1760-61. Either way, the story must have reinforced the Ojibwa belief that evil spirits resided on the island and held sway over those who resided there.

When British trader Alexander Henry arrived in the region with plans to reopen the fur trade business here in August 1765, he found an Ojibwa village of 700 to 800 on the mainland near Chequamegon Bay, presumably many of those who had previously lived on the island.

Henry's partnership with French trader Jean Baptiste Cadotte (Michel's father) broke the ice with the Ojibwa, who had regularly dealt with Cadotte in Sault Ste. Marie. The French influence with the Indians remained strong and other British traders followed Henry's example. As the number of traders in the Lake Superior region increased, a group of traders and merchants based in Montreal formed the North West Company in 1783 to compete with the dominant British behemoth known as Hudson's Bay Company. Although the Treaty of Paris that ended the Revolutionary War that year established this as United States territory, the new partnership grew to dominate the fur trade here.

The North West Company established a trading post at La Pointe by 1791. Michel Cadotte took charge of the La Pointe post by 1793. He built his home and trading post near that historical marker on the southern end of Madeline Island and married Equaysayway, daughter of Ojibwa chief White Crane, who lived on Chequamegon Bay. Equaysayway had been baptized as Madeleine, and White Crane decreed that the Ojibwas' beloved home would be called Madeline Island. The Cadottes were Warren's grandparents.

Other Ojibwa returned to the island and came to live near Cadotte's trading post. The Michilimackinac Company took over most of the North West Company's posts, including La Pointe, after 1806, and in 1811 the two companies partnered with John Jacob Astor's American Fur Company to form the South West Company in an attempt to avoid American import taxes. After the War of 1812, Astor found that he could purchase the South West Company at low cost, and his new, larger American Fur Company dominated the American fur trade until 1834, when Astor sold it because of declining business.

By that time, the tiny town of La Pointe has grown up near Astor's trading post and two years later Father Frederick Baraga built the first Roman Catholic Church on the island near the old Ojibwa cemetery in the vicinity of the modern marina. Both Michel Cadotte and Kechewaishke, Ojibwa chief Great Buffalo (also known as Chief Buffalo), would be buried here. The chief's Protestant son, Little Buffalo, would be buried across the road to the south, his grave marked by four pine trees. Today, the cemetery is closed to the public, and visitors view it from the other side of a fence.

The Ojibwas themselves would soon be viewing their "spiritual home" about the same way. Ojibwa bands in Wisconsin, Michigan, and parts of eastern Minnesota were subject to terms of the Indian Removal Act of 1830, which pressured tribes to give up land claims and move west of the Mississippi. At the time, Americans weren't settling in the Lake Superior region in huge numbers, so there wasn't immediate political pressure for the Ojibwas' removal.

That began to change, however, and tribe signed the Pine Tree Treaty in 1837 and ceded approximately 11 million acres of land in north central Wisconsin and eastern Minnesota to the United States. The tribe's lands bordering Lake Superior weren't included in the sale, but that came next. Annuity payments due under this treaty were made at La Pointe beginning in 1838.

Times were changing rapidly. The Ojibwas ceded their lands along the southwestern shore of Lake Superior with their signing of the Copper Treaty in 1842. The American Fur Company ceased operations in 1847. The 1850 census listed the population of La Pointe as 463 with 40 of the residents named Cadotte. Four individuals were classified as "civilized Indians" and other Indians were not counted. A majority of the residents were of mixed French Canadian and Ojibwa ancestry.

But that was the year everything changed for the Ojibwa. With pressure increasing from American settlers to stop the Ojibwa from competing for resources and land – let that sink in for a moment – President Zachary Taylor and Secretary of Interior Thomas Ewing hatched a plan to expedite the Ojibwas' removal. They would change the location of the tribe's annual annuity payments from Madeline Island to a sub-agency at the more isolated trade-hub location of Sandy Lake, Minnesota, on the other side of the Mississippi River. By bringing the Ojibwa to Minnesota in late fall and then deliberately delaying the payments, the administration's Bureau of Indian Affairs knew the Ojibwa would be forced stay there for the winter. With Ojibwa detached from their "spiritual home," officials believed they would wear down the tribe's resistance to relocation.

The BIA told the Ojibwa to meet officials at Sandy Lake in late October and nearly 3,000 Ojibwa men made the trip. They waited several weeks before the first government agent arrived and when he did he told them that the annuities and supplies had been delayed. A small portion of the payment and food arrived in early December and much of the food was spoiled. By that point, 150 Ojibwa had already died of starvation, dysentery, measles or freezing. On a difficult winter return trip, an additional 200 to 250 Ojibway died.

This sad event became known as the Sandy Lake Tragedy and caused Ojibwa bands under Great Buffalo's leadership to pressure President Millard Fillmore to cancel the removal order. The chief asked Wisconsin residents to support the tribe's efforts and some did, but they didn't want Native Americans to live among them and encouraged the establishment of reservations.

The result was the Treaty of La Pointe in 1854 that established the Bad River, Red Cliff and at least five more reservations that enabled the Ojibwa to remain in the area, if not on Madeline Island. Prior to the treaty Ojibwa constituted a third of the population of La Pointe village, even though the Native Americans weren't counted in the census. After the reservations were created, only a few remained on the island.

Today, the Bad River reservation comprises 124,655 acres, most opposite the south shore of Madeline Island. The town of Odanah, located five miles east of Ashland on U.S. 2, became the cultural center for the tribe and home of the Bad River Lodge and Casino.

The island is a beautiful, peaceful place today, a paradise for fishermen and a lure to vacationers hoping to escape today's frantic pace. An astute visitor can almost breathe history in this place. But outside of the Madeline Island Museum, which occupies an 1835 American Fur Company building and chronicles the island's history, about the only visible reminders of the tribe and a once-flourishing fur trade are the French and Ojibwa names of some of the residents.

If the "Chi-be-ug" exist, a little weeping and wailing is probably in order.

54 GRAND PORTAGE

Grand Portage is as close as anyone on earth today can get to the Old Northwest.

This is a place surrounded by hundreds of miles of pine trees and lakes, perched on the Minnesota-Canada border on the northwestern shore of Lake Superior. It lies 145 miles north of Duluth, 300 miles northeast of Minneapolis and an eye blink from heaven. For that reason, its surroundings have probably changed less than any historically significant place within the modern six-state boundaries of this region.

The North West Company fur trading post has been rebuilt on the spot where its depot stood from about 1775 to 1805 and the eight-mile portage that brought Indian tribes and traders here for centuries is still intact in its original location. A modern road that crosses it even makes it accommodating for tenderfoot twenty-first century voyageurs who prefer to hike only three or five miles, without the inconvenience of a heavy canoe or 90-pound backpacks of furs or trade goods to lug.

The portage had been created by Native Americans before the first traders arrived. It offers a way around an unnavigable stretch of the Pigeon River, which almost from its mouth at Lake Superior plunges through basal chasms in an unpassable, foaming chain of cataracts. Bypassing this stretch brings the traveler to an almost uninterrupted chain of lakes and rivers that can take him all the way to Lake Winnipeg and the plains, hundreds of miles away.

When the early traders expanded their territory west and finally reached the western end of Lake Superior, they asked local tribes for the best inland routes and were shown the Grand Portage. As trade with the Indians grew over the years, Grand Portage stood out as the westernmost place where goods could be delivered by ship from the east and it grew in importance.

But that's getting ahead of the story. The white men who first brought attention to Grand Portage weren't interested in fur trading, but in finding the Northwest Passage, a shortcut to the Pacific Ocean. In 1729, a Cree named Auchagah gave the new French commandant at Fort Nipigon a map that offered a route from Lake Superior deep into the interior and beyond via the Grand Portage, and that officer, Pierre Gaultier de Varennes et de La Verendrye, tried to interest the French government in financing such an expedition. Louis XV wouldn't give La Verendrye any money, but instead offered him a monopoly on the fur trade west of Grand Portage. This would presumably enable him to give the king a valuable discovery and finance the expedition through the sale of furs.

La Verendrye accepted and put together a team that included his four sons and a nephew and Auchagah as a guide. All was well until they arrived at Grand Portage in August, 1731.

"All our people, in dismay at the length of the portage. . . mutinied and loudly demanded that I should turn back," he wrote.

Apparently they thought an eight-mile portage was more than they signed up for, Northwest Passage or not. After a delay of several months, La Verendrye finally won the argument – hey, four of them were his sons -- and by the following summer, he had crossed the portage and reached Rainy Lake, over 200 miles away. From there, the Cree guided him to the Lake of the Woods, where he built a trading post called Fort Charles. Here he got in the middle a conflict between the Dakota and the Ojibwa. His predicament annoyed the French government but didn't dissuade La Verendrye, who was still obsessed with finding a route to the Pacific. He never found one obviously, but by the time he died in Montreal in 1749, a heavy traffic of French fur traders who had purchased trade leases were using the Grand Portage. While traders, merchants and Indians held an annual rendezvous here every July for the exchange of furs and goods, there is no evidence that the French ever built a post here.

The Seven Years War between France and England intervened. French traders abandoned their western posts before the fall of Quebec in 1759 and France ceded Canada to the British in 1763. The forest near the shore of the bay hadn't been cleared by 1766; two or three years later the waterfront growth was gone. Whether the British erected the fort at that same time is not known.

When Guy Carleton became Canadian governor in 1769 and loosed the restrictions on trade, license applications from British traders exploded. The letters Laurent Ermatinger sent from his desk in Montreal to his partners at Michilimackinac and Grand Portage in 1775 show how the increased competition also took its toll on the Indians.

"The common heritage of these newcomers did not prevent their being ruthless adversaries," Erwin N. Thompson wrote. "None of them hesitated to employ liquor to bend whatever Indians to their ends. Ermatinger alone, in 1775, sent about 48 barrels of rum to his trader. The traders inflicted ruin upon one another as well as debauching the Indians with liquor whenever possible."

The brutal nature of the competition led to the formation of alliances. Details are sketchy, but it's clear that in 1775 a license was granted to a combine that included James McGill, Benjamin Frobisher, Maurice Blondeau, and Alexander Henry for 12 canoes with 78 men to go to Grand Portage and beyond. This convoy from Michilimackinac to Grand Portage received an escort from a military guard. The huge haul accumulated by this partnership led to other combines over the next several years.

While the American Revolution raged back east, trade shifted north and Grand Portage's share increased. A number of traders petitioned the Canadian government to send troops to protect their investments during the summer rendezvous. They didn't fear the rebel army – again, remember where this is – but the intense competition of their rivals, who sometimes convinced voyageurs and canoe men to ignore their contracts and take a job with the competition. The British government didn't care about that, but it was worried about the number of guns and ammo pouring through Grand Portage and acted. Lieutenant Thomas Bennett and another officer, five soldiers, seven gunners and two small cannon left Michilimackinac for Grand Portage in May, 1778. They enjoyed a relatively quiet summer and managed to erect a small fort before they departed in August. They never returned, called to duty in other places.

British officials issued new regulations on trade the following summer and trade consolidated into the hands of a few Montreal merchants. North West Company partner Simon McTavish was among Americans forced to move to Montreal to stay in business, and in 1779 he represented nine Montreal companies who met at Grand Portage and agreed to pool their resources for at least one year. Although this was called "little better than an armed truce," it marked the true beginnings of the North West Company.

During the next several years, new partners came in and the consortium grew in size and strength. While it was by no means the only company operating here, it gradually established its dominance. A petition of the merchants that year claimed that 800 men were involved in trade in the northwest, 300 of whom came to Grand Portage during the summer rendezvous. This would later grow to more than 1,000. More than anything that happened here in the past 400 years, these annual get-togethers were the high points of the region's history.

Representatives of the North West Company contacted government officials at Quebec in 1784- 1785 requesting a monopoly at Grand Portage. The request included a description of the company's fur trade business at Grand Portage:

"Two sets of men are employed. . . making upwards of 500; one half of which are occupied in the transport of Goods from Montreal to the Grand Portage, in Canoes of about Four Tons Burthen, Navigated by 8 to 10 men." The other half were "employed to take out such goods forward to every Post in the interior Country to the extent of 1,000 to 2,000 miles and upward . . . in Canoes of about one and a half Ton Burthen, made expressly for the inland service, and navigated by 4 to 5 men only."

In simple terms, traders who had spent the winter in remote locations among the Indian tribes brought their furs and skins to the rendezvous, where they received payment and exchanged them for more goods to trade for the next winter's haul. The Montreal merchants and their clerks came here with goods to exchange for the furs, which were weighed, sorted and trans ported back east for sale, usually to Europe. But the annual rendezvous became much more than that. The eastern consortiums, like the North West Company, usually held meetings of their directors here during this period. The Ojibwa controlled the region -- Grand Portage had an Ojibwa village by 1742 -- but it was by no means the only tribe represented at the rendezvous; Indian tribes from all over the region camped here. Some of the traders, after so many months of isolation, saw this as an opportunity for a month-long party before they returned to the remote locations where they spent most of their lives.

The trading post, the great hall and many of the small buildings that have been reconstructed for today's tourists were used by the North West Company, but other partnerships had smaller structures and camps at both ends of the portage. So many traders needed their goods transported over the portage during a relatively short period -- the goods were transported in 90-pound packs on their backs -- that a schedule had to be created in order to keep the trail from being clogged with workers and becoming impassable.

By 1795, the post within the palisades at Grand Portage had become a crowded, bustling village with 16 buildings inside. Some served as warehouses for the storage of goods and furs, some housed workers and others like the Great Hall hosted meetings and grand dinners and parties for the partners and the merchants. Although the palisades created a fort-like appearance it hadn't been built as protection from Indians; they were welcome and needed for their furs. The walls helped control traffic in and out of the area and provided a layer of protection for the company's merchandise.

At the western end of the portage near Pigeon River the company had another post for the traders called Fort Charlotte. Other smaller concerns also set up shop in this area to help expedite transport and trading.

The trading companies' impassive view of the Indians' role in this is probably best be summed up by trader Roderick Mackenzie, who succinctly noted on his arrival in 1785 that Ojibwa people were, "incamped within our limits. . . almost all their winter hunt in our possession."

When the American Revolution ended, the North West Company asked the British government (which effectively controlled the Great Lakes, despite what treaties said) for permission to establish a fleet of sailing ships to supply Grand Portage. That led to the launching of the 40-ton Athabasca in 1786 and 12- and 15-ton ships by 1790. Three years later, it launched the 75-ton sloop Otter, which made four trips between Sault Ste. Marie and Grand Portage each summer in from five to 18 days. The ship usually wintered at Grand Portage, where the crew maintained the buildings, took care of the animals, tended the gardens and traded with the Indians.

The end of the war brought another problem, albeit one whose effects wouldn't surface for several years. The treaty line placed Grand Portage on the American side of the border. This upset the traders and the merchants, whose businesses were based in Montreal, and the Indians, who had supported the British side in the war. The young republic had too many other pressing matters to worry about the west, but by the 1790s, concern had grown about British occupation of posts in American territory. John Jay's treaty in 1794 again declared the area south of the Great Lakes off limits to the British; this led to rumors about the Americans' imminent plans to take over the post. That happened in other places such as Fort Detroit and Fort Niagara but not here. Again, remember where this is.

As if all of this uncertainly weren't enough to roil the Grand Portage fur trade market, the traders themselves disrupted it further. A group of men disenchanted with Simon McTavish's leadership of the North West Company split off and formed a rival company in 1797. The new company came to be known as XY Company and it erected a building complex on the Pigeon River end of the Grand Portage across Snow Creek from Fort Charlotte.

This ignited a bitter trade war between the two companies, as can be seen from a diary entry from XY Company clerk George Nelson in 1802:

"One of our brigades, fitted out I belive (sic), for Fort des Prairies. Slept as usual at Portage la Perdrix, only a few hundred yards from our Stores at the north end of the Grand Portage, where they feasted & got drunk upon the regale that was always given them when they arrived from, or departed for, their winter quarters. When they arose the next morning they found thirty kegs of high Wines all run out! Upon examination it was found they had been bored with two gimlet holes each! The consternation & injury this occasioned may be imagined...It created an excessive bad feeling and led to retaliations some of which would have ended tragically but for providence, but nothing further ever followed."

The trade war at Grand Portage raged until 1804, when McTavish died suddenly at the age of 54. His successor, William McGillivray, immediately offered an olive branch to Alexander Mackenzie, leader of the rivals, and they negotiated a merger.

In the meantime, North West Company officials had also been working on their own solutions to the border problem. These was about as effective as crossing their fingers until the late 1790s when Roderick Mackenzie heard some Indians talking about another route from Lake Superior into the interior. They told him about the old Kaministiquia River route 45 miles to the north that the French sometimes used, site of the modern Canadian city of Thunder Bay.

The fact that the French only used it "sometimes" loudly hints that the route had its drawbacks. The river included brooks where the canoes had to be lightly-loaded because of shallow water and the route was also longer, so the voyageurs would have to be persuaded to use it. But it was on the Canadian side of the border, a condition that company officials felt they needed to survive. By 1800, the company had already started draining "the dead swampy flat" near the mouth of the river where it planned to build its new depot.

The 1802 rendezvous was the last one at Grand Portage for the North West Company. It moved its base of operations to the Kaministiquia River and eventually christened the new post as Fort William.

Although the North West Company "destroyed their forts and warehouses" at Grand Portage upon their departure, archaeologists have noted an absence of building fragments and believe that some of the structures may have been dismantled and reassembled them at its new site. The XY Company held its rendezvous at Grand Portage for two more years until the merger, when it abandoned its new depot there.

Grand Portage's days as a fur trade mecca had ended. The North West Company maintained a small Indian trading post there for a few years with a clerk and two or three men; they must have felt like the caretakers of a ghost town. When former company official David Thompson returned there in 1822 while surveying the U.S.-Canada boundary for the government, he found that "scarce a vestige remains of all the Factories; they are covered with rank Grass, and in places, a little fine red Clover."

The North West Company itself suffered the same fate. The decline of the fur trade business led to its merger (and loss of identity) with the Hudson's Bay Company in 1821, and HBC officials abandoned the Great Lakes shipping route in favor of the cheaper sea route via Hudson Bay. Fort William followed in the footsteps of Grand Portage and became an almost forgotten backwater post in a short time.

The American Fur Company had entered a pact with the Hudson's Bay Company that prevented it from competing with it in the area for furs. It had been trying to diversify for survival and set up Grand Portage as a fishing station. The fisheries boomed for five years until the market for fish plummeted during the Panic of 1837. The American Fur Company itself failed in 1842 and the area was again left to the Ojibwa.

The Grand Portage Reservation was created as part of the Treaty of La Pointe in 1854 with a land area of 74.396 square miles that includes the unincorporated community of Grand Portage. Today it also includes the Grand Portage National Monument, Grand Portage State Park and the tribal operated Grand Portage Lodge and Casino, which opened as a 90-room hotel in 1975 and added the casino in 1986.

The national monument that is the focus of it all might not have happened if a local resident hadn't sent a letter to Minnesota Historical Society director Solon J. Buck in 1922, expressing concern that many old rights-of-way on the reservation were being purchased, fenced and posted. A "closed" sign had even been posted on the old Grand Portage trail itself.

Buck sent a field representative and newspaper reporter to check out the historic trail, still visible despite its obstruction by fallen trees. The publicity brought an explosion of interest and another visit, this time for a systematic survey of all of the sites. A log cabin, two fish houses and two barns stood on the site of North West Company depot and a road ran across the southern part of it. Archaeological surveys of the sites finally started in 1936 and reconstruction of the depot began in 1938.

Progress from there to here hasn't always been a straight line; a lightning strike in 1969 burned down the reconstructed Great Hall. Ironically that allowed a more historically correct one (based on archaeology) to replace it. Consequently, today's visitor can see what it was like here over 200 years ago and walk in the footsteps of men whose raw courage are difficult to fathom today.

Fortunately, we have a colorful description of them by Canadian historian W. Stewart Wallace to remind us:

"The names of the North West Company partners sound like a roll call of the clans of Culloden. These men were hardy, courageous, shrewd and proud. They spent a good part of their lives travelling incredible distances in birch-bark canoes, shooting rapids, or navigating inland seas. They were wrecked and drowned. They suffered hunger and starvation, they were robbed and murdered by the Indians, and sometimes by one another. They fell the victims of smallpox, syphilis, and rum. Yet they conquered half a continent, and they built up a commercial empire, the like of which North America at least has never seen."

55 RED BANKS-MARINETTE

It's safe to say that most people don't visit Wisconsin's Door Peninsula, the 80-mile arm that separates Green Bay from Lake Michigan, in a search for Jean Nicolet's 1634 landing site. Most of the people who come here are vacationers looking to swim, fish, shop, eat and relax, not necessarily in that order. Nicolet is just a name on street sign to most of them, if that.

But the French explorer -- and not everyone agrees with that description of him – seems likely to have been the first white man to enter the bay and possibly the first to visit the modern state of Wisconsin. His journey from Quebec, probably in one canoe with seven Native Americans, came at a time when mapmakers were trying to figure out the size, shape and direction of Lake Superior and Lake Michigan, whether there was another great lake on the other side of Superior, and where the land ended and the Pacific Ocean began. For all they knew, the Pacific could have lapping at shores of today's Sioux Falls, South Dakota.

The details of Nicolet's visit seem a little sketchier today than they did to the historians of the nineteenth century. Those early chroniclers were convinced that Nicolet was sent here by French governor Samuel de Champlain to find the Northwest Passage to the Far East and that he even gave Nicolet a colorful Chinese robe to wear when he encountered the natives.

They also said that he landed on the southeastern shore of the bay at Red Banks, about eight miles north of the modern city of Green Bay. There are steep clay bluffs there that rise 80 feet or more from the beach. At the time the bluffs may have been topped by an imposing half-mile long palisaded fort, the remains of which made it on an 1844 map of the bay. Historians think the Puans built it as a defensive fortification.

There is actually a small park with a memorial that supposedly marks the spot where Nicolet came ashore in his Oriental robe and fired his two pistols into the air to impress the Indians who greeted him. This ostentatious display supposedly worked brilliantly. Nicolet's colleague Barthelemy Vimont wrote in 1642-43 that in a subsequent council, "four or five thousand warriors assembled, each of the chiefs gave a feast and at one of these not less than six score beaver were eaten. Peace was concluded."

Nicolet's landing inspired several paintings, including a famous one by E.W. Deming in 1907 with the colorfully-robed explorer holding his guns in air like some wild-eyed cowboy in Buffalo Bill's Wild West show. It appeared in some grade school textbooks and even on a 3-cent stamp issued by the U.S. Post Office in 1935.

The little park where this is supposed to have occurred is off Benderville Road, which runs off the aptly name Nicolet Drive (aka County Road A), and is easy miss if you're not looking for it. When you park in the small lot and walk up the short trail to the monument site, you can't help but think that this must be the spot where the natives welcomed Nicolet because no one in their right mind would choose to put a park and monument here if it wasn't.

But the deeper you get into this story, the more skeptical you are apt to become. About a mile to the east off nearby Wisconsin Route 57, the much larger Wequiock Falls County Park has another memorial and even a statue of Nicolet that was erected at Red Banks in 1951 and moved in 2009, after the reconstruction of Wisconsin 57. A plaque here makes it clear that the other park is the actual site of Nicolet's historic first landing on Green Bay, which would be convincing if modern historians hadn't cast so much doubt about it.

Using research in part done by the late anthropologist Nancy Oestreich Lurie with whom he had authored an earlier book, Patrick Jung wrote a 2018 book called *The Misunderstood Mission of Jean Nicolet* that explodes a lot of myths about Nicolet, including one that he was searching for the Northwest Passage to China. He also makes a case for the fact that Nicolet actually landed on the west side of the bay at the of the Menominee tribe, the site of the modern city of Marinette, Wisconsin.

While that theory is certainly plausible, he doesn't prove that Nicolet couldn't have landed at Red Banks, where the tablet says he did and a little park stands. Aaron C. Neville, who served as mayor of Green Bay in 1888 and 1889, "did a great deal of research into the early history of Green Bay," according to Jung, and he believed that Nicolet's landfall occurred at Red Banks. Hence, the marker was erected there in 1905.

For what it is worth, other historians have Nicolet landing in other places, including Horseshoe Island in Peninsula Park about 50 miles north on the Door Peninsula, and even on the shores of Lake Superior. There is also considerable dispute over what he did after he landed.

Jung believes he negotiated a treaty with the Puans, ancestors of the Winnebago tribe who are now known in Wisconsin as the Ho-Chunk, and immediately headed back to Quebec. Others believe he visited the site of modern Green Bay and journeyed a considerable distance up the Fox River. One nineteenth century historian believed he went all the way to the Mississippi River and others have him stopping short of the Fox-Wisconsin portage. Publius V. Lawson, a six-term mayor of Menasha, Wisconsin, who regularly researched the history of the Fox River, led an effort to put a monument to Nicolet on Doty Island near Neenah (where the Fox enters Lake Winnebago) in 1906 that supposedly marked the site of a Puan village that he visited on his trip. Whether any of this happened is subject to much conjecture.

"There are more questions and mysteries about Jean Nicolet than there are firm answers," Jung said, during a 2014 lecture on PBS Wisconsin.

One thing that isn't a mystery, at least in Jung's mind, is the notion that upon landing Nicolet wore a Chinese robe given him by Samuel de Champlain, presumably because he was looking for a route to China and the natives he encountered might be Chinese. He and Lurie wrote about that in their 2009 book, *The Nicolet Corrigenda*, and he talked about it that 2013 PBS video:

"In the description of his meeting with the Ho-Chunks, Father Barthelemy Vimont wrote that 'Nicolet wore a grand robe of China damask all strewn with flowers and birds of many colors.' This short passage has given birth to what Nancy and I call the 'Myth of the Chinese robe.' It is the textual foundation for the gravest of the factual errors.

"Vimont's description of Nicolet's meeting sat gathering dust for over 200 years. It was only in the 1850s that historians began to dust off the Jesuit Relations and examine them for what they had to say about North American history. The first historian to intimate that Nicolet wore a Chinese robe was the French-Canadian scholar Benjamin Sulte, who in 1876 wrote that Nicolet must have believed that he had arrived in China or someplace very close to it. Why? He wore a Chinese robe, of course. And Nicolet must have thought that the Ho-Chunk were Chinese, or at least Asian. Sulte asserted that Nicolet possessed "the belief that these people were not far from the Chinese, or they must have known them and Nicolet had put on a great robe of Chinese damask."

And with that, a small flood of distinguished historians began to echo Sulte or added their own versions of it. Jung believes that early historians improperly translated the French accounts written by Vimont, not realizing China damask was a merely a type of silk and that "cape" would have been a better translation than "robe." He believes these misinterpretations served as the basis for the erroneous conclusion that he was searching for a route to China.

E.W. DEMING PAINTED *THE LANDFALL OF JEAN NICOLET* IN 1907. IT HAS BEEN REPRODUCED MANY TIMES, INCLUDING ON A 1934 U.S. POSTAGE STAMP.

Jung also writes that Nicolet wasn't an explorer, but a diplomat, and that he had been sent there by Champlain because the Puans (and their minor partners, the Menominees) controlled Green Bay and were formidable enough and hostile enough to jeopardize French control of the region.

Other historians have seized upon Champlain's own obsession with finding the Northwest Passage as a younger man as the primary reason he sent Nicolet here and see the Chinese robe as proof of that. It's worth noting that other explorers during this period had China on the mind: Captain George Weymouth carried a tin box containing a finely illuminated letter from Queen Elizabeth to the Emperor of China when he sailed the Discovery into Hudson Straits in 1602 and his preacher, Reverend John Cartwright, wore a brand-new clerical gown to impress the natives upon their arrival in China. And Thomas James carried a similar letter from King James I addressed to the emperor of Japan when he entered Hudson Bay in 1631. So it doesn't require a giant leap of faith to believe that Nicolet might have dressed for such a landing in the Orient when he entered Green Bay.

But Jung, a professor at the Milwaukee School of Engineering, says Champlain's letters show that he had lost interest in that quest and was primarily interested securing peace for New France. Jung makes a compelling case for his theory, but in light of the scant data and correspondence that is available, it's difficult to see it as any more than that. It's just so hard to prove.

Nicolet's own log of his mission didn't survive. Consequently, a total of four printed pages in the 1640 and 1642-43 issues of the Jesuit Relations, an annual publication which chronicled the Jesuit missions in New France, described his journey into Wisconsin. Paul LeJeune told of Nicolet's trip in just less than two pages in the 1640 issue, and because place names had not been assigned by the French prior to this, the route is difficult to interpret. Vimont used about the same amount of space two years later in describing what occurred after Nicolet arrived, but again his descriptions are vague at best.

The various interpretations of these accounts explain how there can be so many different explanations of where Nicolet went and why. The interpretation of one French phrase used by LeJeune -- au dela – which Reuben Gold Thwaites translated between 1896 and 1901 as "beyond," seemed to indicate that Nicolet went "beyond" the St. Mary's River rapids and into Lake Superior. Another interpretation of the word is "past," as in travel past. That might mean that the party passed the entrance to the river and headed through the Straits of Mackinac and into Lake Michigan toward Green Bay.

Jung wrote an entire book about how historians have may have misinterpreted various aspects of Nicolet's journey; for my purposes here, it is probably sufficient to say that at this point there is no way to be sure exactly where he embarked and why.

Jung believes that he landed at Marinette because the Menominees – "the wild rice people" -- had their grand village there on the southern bank of the Menominee River near its confluence with the bay. Some Menominees also lived across the river in what is now Menominee, Michigan. While there is archaeological evidence of a Puan fortification at Red Banks and the presence of the Puans for miles along the shoreline of the Door Peninsula, artifacts indicating that as many 20,000 Puans (believed at the time to be the size of the tribe) lived at Red Bank haven't been found.

Unfortunately, the specific location of the Menominees' grand village hasn't been confirmed archaeologically either. Like the Puans at Red Bank, the tribe's presence there is confirmed by ethno-historical evidence and oral traditions, but not much archaeological evidence. That also doesn't prove that it didn't exist at some point. It's possible that evidence at Red Banks may have long been washed away by the water in the bay. The exact location of the Menominees' settlement at Marinette likely was lost during the rapid construction caused by the lumbering boom in the late nineteenth century when the little town exploded into one of more than 16,000 residents. Today, that has shrunk to about 10,600, although its "twin" city of Menominee, Michigan, has a population of 8,500.

So why is Jung convinced that Nicolet visited the grand village at the future Marinette?

In Vimont's 1642-43 account, he writes that when Nicolet arrived at the Indians' village they called him "Manitouiriniou," which means "the wonderful man" in the Algonquian dialect. He says the Menominees' language was Algonquian and that this word was specifically Menominee; the language of the Puans, on the other side of the bay, was Chiwere (a Siouan dialect).

This is a key piece of evidence, but it doesn't explain why if Nicolet was sent as a "diplomat" to make peace with the Puans he would venture to the Menominee village of their weaker allies. Jung's says he may have been looking for a neutral site and that the Puans simply had to cross the bay to get there, but it opens another avenue of speculation that he didn't address: Isn't it also possible that the Menominees crossed the bay to Grand Banks when they realized the Frenchman was headed there and that their greeting was what Vimont wrote about in the Jesuit Relations?

Again, as good as Jung's case is, the body of evidence seems too thin to come to a firm conclusion. Marinette would be as good a place as any to celebrate Nicolet's landing; it has a rich history of its own. A notable event in the state's fur trading industry occurred there in 1791 when two free African Americans set up a fur trading post among the Menominee. It did not end well for them. According to early Wisconsin fur trader Augustin Grignon, the pair used some sleight of hand performances to convince the local tribe that they were medicine men and could hold communication with the spirit world. This worked in their favor until some of the tribe's children became deathly ill, which the Indians attributed to the arrival of the newcomers. One Menominee and two Chippewas subsequently attacked the traders in their house, killing one and shooting the other while he was in the process of escaping through a window. The attacking trio was sent first to Fort Mackinac to answer for the murder and then to Montreal, where they were imprisoned for three years before being allowed to return to their people.

Stanislaus "Louis" Chappee (Chappieu), a French-Canadian fur trader, settled near the grand village site in 1794. He operated a log trading post there from 1794 and 1824 and is considered the first permanent white settler in the area. His log house has been described as "opposite" Queen Marinette's house, which is remembered by a historical marker on Riverside Avenue, approximately 200 feet east of the Hattie Street bridge. Queen Marinette (Marie Antoinette Chevalier), the namesake of the city, was the daughter of a Menominee Indian named Lucy and Barthelemy Chevalier, a French trapper; her grandfather was Menominee chief Wauba-Shish (Great Marten). She worked in the fur trade herself from the 1820s until 1854.

Of course, all of this activity took place long after Nicolet may or may not have visited the area.

Over in Menominee, on the Michigan side of the river, a marker titled "Menominee Area" on Bridge Street south of 10th Avenue sits in front of the Menominee Welcome Center/Claude Tobin Travel Information Center and offers its own take on the subject:

"This was the home of the Menominee Indians. Nicolet, the French explorer, visited them in 1634 on his futile search for Cathay. . ."

56 GREEN BAY

When I told a friend about my planned visit Green Bay, Wisconsin, to write about its history, he asked if I were doing a piece about Vince Lombardi, the legendary Green Bay Packers' football coach. His response didn't surprise me.

Ask 1,000 people the first thing they think of when asked about Green Bay and probably 999 of them would say the Packers. The only reason the famous National Football League team might not get a perfect score is the offhand chance of running across a guy who teaches a college course on American history, has French or Native American ancestry and has written a book on the fur trade industry. And truthfully, even then all bets are off if he's a football fan.

Just about anyone who has spent even a few hours in this Wisconsin city of 104,000 would understand. The Packers permeate the city. When you're not at Lambeau Field, the stadium the team calls home, a sign always seems to be directing you there. Even in the off-season, the team's gargantuan gift shop draws a steady stream of fans and tourists, many of whom are also attracted to the Packers Heritage Trail of 22 sites around Green Bay. Restaurants and bars constantly remind you, in every direction you look, where you are and which team rules the land (and water) here.

The history of the team is fascinating. The Packers were founded by former high-school football rivals Earl "Curly" Lambeau and George Whitney Calhoun on August 11, 1919, and joined the American Professional Football Association (renamed the National Football League in 1922) in its second season in 1921. Lambeau solicited funds for uniforms from his employer, the Indian Packing Company. It gave him $500 for uniforms and equipment on the condition that the team be named in the company's honor. It still is.

The Packers survive from an era when the NFL had teams in Canton, Ohio, Muncie, Indiana, and Rock Island, Illinois. All of the teams in those smaller cities eventually folded or moved to larger cities except for the Packers, who would seem out of place in a league with teams that represent places such as New York, Chicago, Boston and Los Angeles if they hadn't been so successful.

But there actually is a reason to dive deeply into Green Bay's history besides the Packers. This city at the foot of a bay of the same name has a history as rich as any place in the Old Northwest. It begins with Native American tribes who resided here for hundreds of years, continues with the arrival of French fur traders in the seventeenth century and was enriched by a permanent settlement that has lived under the flags of France, Britain and the United States.

Jean Nicolet is the first white man in recorded history to set foot on the shores of what the French called La Baye or La Baye des Puans in 1634 and some historians think he may have been the first to reach the site of the modern city of Green Bay and beyond on the Fox River. Whether Nicolet paddled up the Fox past the modern city or not, he would probably be amazed to know that he has his name on a Green Bay bank, elementary school, apartment complex and even a brand of bottled water, which as of this writing was the official bottled water of the Green Bay Packers.

Most historians credit French traders Nicolas Perrot and Toussaint Baudry with being the next white men to land near the mouth of the Fox, although their second-status probably merits an asterisk. While we know that Perrot and Baudry were there in 1668, we don't know how many coureurs de bois may have passed through or even lingered there in the time since Nicolet paddled into Green Bay. These were unlicensed French traders (as opposed to the licensed voyageurs) who wouldn't have wanted to do anything -- like write a log of their experiences -- that would alert the authorities that they were doing business there.

While working at Chequamegon Bay on Lake Superior, Perrot and Baudry accepted the invitation of some Potawatomis to visit Green Bay and they arrived in the spring of 1668. Perrot described it as a wonderful place with fertile soil that produced copious amounts of corn, squash and wild rice and had an abundance of ducks, pigeons and fish, a place where "the peoples of the bay can live in the utmost comfort."

Perrot and Baudry spent two years in the area and visited most of the surrounding tribes (the Fox, Miami, Illinois, Kickapoo, Mascouten, Puan and Menominee) and finally joined three other traders in forming a large flotilla of canoes that carried a huge load of furs back to Montreal. Unfortunately, their immense supply of furs flooded the market and prices dropped, leaving them with a much smaller return than they had hoped. That may explain why both men exited the trade business shortly thereafter, although Perrot returned to the area in 1685 as commandant-in-chief when war broke out between the Fox tribe and the Sioux and Ojibwa tribes.

By then, La Baye had become a destination for both fur traders and missionaries. Jesuit Father Claude Allouez had charge of the mission at La Pointe on Chequamegon Bay in 1669 when Father Claude Dablon was named superior of western missions headquartered at Sault Ste. Marie, where Father Jacques Marquette had created a mission the year before. Marquette moved on to La Pointe, while Allouez left to minister tribes on Green Bay and along the Fox River. Allouez first took up residence at a spot near a large multi-tribe Indian village on the shore of the Oconto River in modern day Oconto, Wisconsin, where he founded the St. Francois Xavier mission. A historical marker there next to the river on Brazeau Avenue, just south of Charles Street, says "six French fur traders happened to be here at that time," and notes that the "primitive chapel made of bark and cedar boughs remained until 1671 when the mission moved to Red Banks on the East shore of Green Bay."

This reflected Allouez' purpose. He spent two years traveling the area by canoe and on foot, creating the foundation for hoped-for missions on the Menominee and Oconto rivers, upper and lower Fox rivers, Lake Winnebago and at the modern site of Green Bay. He left the area for the Sault in the spring of 1670 to take part in the June ceremony where Sieur Saint Lusson claimed the western territory for Louis XIV of France and returned to the bay that fall.

This time, Father Louis Andre accompanied him and during the winter of 1671-72 they built the first permanent mission house on the lower Fox at the De Pere rapids in the modern Green Bay suburb of De Pere. This new St. Francois Xavier stood on a projection of land where the last series of rapids eddy before Fox makes its final sweep towards the bay six miles away.

Andre was a smart guy. He taught philosophy and Latin at the Jesuit College in Quebec for several years after his missionary tour ended, and his writings show that he knew how to effectively deal with face-painted Indians who showed up at his door.

"I found no better way of compelling them to clean their faces than to show them the painting of the devil to whom they made themselves similar," he wrote, "and to refuse them entrance into my cabin when they came to pray to God."

Marquette and Louis Joliet stopped here in June, 1673, on their way up the Fox to find and explore the upper Mississippi River. They returned to the mission in September to record their discoveries in their journals; Joliet left for Quebec the following spring, while an ailing Marquette stayed until the following October.

THE ROCK MARKS THE SITE OF THE LA BAYE BURIAL PLACE, 1720-1835.

A historical marker titled "Marquette-Joliet" on a pole once stood in Creviere Commons, a downtown De Pere park located on the northeast corner of George Street and Broadway. It had to be moved to the riverfront because of the 2016 construction of a five-story apartment/commercial building on the park site.

The marker offered information about their journey and their time at St. Francois Xavier and indicated that "the mission stood on the bank of the Fox River directly west of this spot." That places Allouez' mission near the river bank, just west of where George would intersect with Front. (George Street ends at Broadway and a parking lot now occupies the space.). The mission grounds are occupied by the concrete bike path, Front Street and/or part of the three-story, brick Fox River Terrace apartment building that stretches for a block from the parking lot to James Street.

The marker was moved a block north and a block west of its old location but left unchanged. From the spot it occupies today next to the riverfront bike path west of Front Street and just south of James, it stands less than 15 feet from the river. That makes it a bit of a head scratcher to anyone who happens upon it. Based on the directions on the plaque, the famous mission would have to have been located either in the water or on a narrow strip of land probably a hundred feet in the distance. While the marker itself isn't far from where the mission itself apparently stood, no marker is preferable to a confusing, erroneous one.

Work at St. Francois Xavier continued until at least 1687, when hostile tribes burned the mission. Some buildings must have survived or been rebuilt, however, because in 1690 Perrot apparently held council with the tribes there at the "house of Jesuits." The French priests continued to minister to the local tribes; Father Henri Nouvel was there in 1701 and Father Pierre Chardon worked in the vicinity from 1701 to 1728.

Life here during this period was anything but smooth. Resentful of French traders who did business with the Sioux on the upper Mississippi, the Fox made life miserable for the French. When the French finally dispatched a large force of soldiers, militia and Indians to Green Bay and defeated the Fox in 1716, they built Fort St. Francis on the west side of the river on the spot where Fort Howard stood 100 hundred years later. Modern historians believe the site is a little northeast of today's Titletown Brewery (in the old Chicago and Northwestern Railroad Terminal, on Dousman Street), about a mile south of the bay. At the same time the French erected a house for Father Chardon, the resident priest, who apparently had been living in the deserted St. Francois Xavier mission on the rapids at De Pere.

Another rebellion by the Fox and their allies in 1728 resulted in a second Fox war where the French and several Indian tribes dealt the Fox a crippling blow. The French dispatched a force of 450 soldiers and 1,000 Indians under Constant le Marchand de Lignery to La Baye to confront the Fox at their fortified village near the mouth of the Fox River, but the Fox fled. After failing to engage the enemy, Lignery's forces finally laid siege to a Fox fort 37 miles up the river. They executed four traitorous Indians and burned fields of corn, peas, beans and gourds. Lignery returned to La Baye and concluded his mission by burning the Winnebago village surrounding Fort St. Francis and later the fort itself. For this unauthorized act, the French government sharply censured him. The mutinous spirit shown there by the voyageurs, coupled with Father Chardon's recommendation that the post be abandoned because of its dissolute character, probably motivated Lignery to act.

Sieur de Villiers was sent to rebuild and re-establish the post in 1731, and he wrote that the Sauks had rebuilt t heir old village just across the river from the fort. The Sauks were the Fox long-time allies, and in 1733 they gave some Fox survivors refuge. French governor Marquis de Beauharnois' had given orders to Villiers, the arrogant commandant at La Baye, to kill all of the Fox. Villiers called the Sauk chiefs to the French fort, told them of his order and demanded that they deliver the refugee Fox to them. When they didn't appear within the specified time, Villiers, two of his sons, Jean-Baptiste René Legardeur de Repentigny and seven or eight French soldiers, crossed the river and approached the gate of the Sauk fortification. It stood on the sandy ridge where Main Street is today.

Three armed Sauks greeted him and told him to back off; when Villiers tried to enter anyway, he faced an uplifted tomahawk. The Sauks fired three shots, killing one of his sons. With that, both sides opened fire and Villiers was killed and three French soldiers were wounded. Repentigny, in his first year as commandant at Fort Michilimackinac, had been guarding the approaches on the side of the woods. He rushed up to offer assistance and was also killed by one of the Sauk volleys. When they heard the shots, two hundred Indians who had been living in or near the French fort came to the soldiers' assistance, and the Sauks withdrew inside their fort with three killed. Three days later, the Sauks and the Fox evacuated their fort and fled south up the river.

Today, the site of this skirmish lies just east of the Ray Nitschke Memorial Bridge, named for a legendary Packers' middle linebacker whose famous football battles never killed anyone. The bridge empties onto a wide section of Main flanked by a Hampton Inn, a five-story apartment building, a modern, five-story office building, a parking garage and the Green Bay Convention Center.

Fort St. Francis continued to be garrisoned for the next 37 years until the French turned it over to the English with other forts in 1761 at the conclusion of the French and Indian War. During the last four decades of French occupancy, it had a reputation for shameless mismanagement and corruption on the part of its commanders, many of whom demanded that the local tribes pay tribute to them with beaver skins.

By contrast, the level shores of the Fox River existed mostly as a delightful place for settlement and French-Canadian voyageurs constructed houses there, at least as early as 1744. Augustin de Langlade brought his family of eight (including his son Charles) here in 1745 and had a home and trading house on the east side of the river behind today's Johnson Bank Building on Washington Street, north of Crooks Street. (A plaque occupied a wall in front of the bank building.) While the Langlades conducted their trade business here as early as 1745, it seems unlikely that they were permanent, year-round residents prior to 1760.

Augustin obtained a fur trading license at Michilimackinac in 1728 and married Domitilde, a widow with six children who was the daughter of an Ottawa chief and the sister of another. Both Augustin and Charles seem to have resided at Mackinac in the 1850s; Augustin served as a church warden in the Mackinac parish in 1756 and is in the records as a prominent witness for several marriages conducted by parish priests. Like many Mackinac traders, Augustin likely alternated between Michilimackinac and La Baye for his trade business. At the age of 21, Charles received an appointment as a cadet in the French army in 1750 and a commission as an ensign in 1755. Two years later, he led a force of French soldiers and Indians in the capture of Pickawillany, a prominent Indian settlement on the Miami River where English traders conducted business.

The Fox River Trail of pink brick runs along the river here to De Pere and beyond and is a terrific place to take a walk through time. It passes modern sculptures that give a nod to the city's history and an occasional plaque that tells of the area's role in the fur trade. Nature still rules. On the day I visited one titled "Influence of the Fur Trade" sat on a pole in the water, a foot-and-a-half off-shore.

A half-block to the south, the Fox Harbor Bar and Grill occupies a two-story brick building on Washington Street. It was born as a hotel in 1898 and served as the Freimann Hotel for decades. A patio behind the building backs up to the Fox River Trail and the river, offering a nice view for a time traveler who wants make his journey with a burger and a brew. For those interested in a different kind of travel, a restored building just to the south once served as the Milwaukee Road railroad station.

Even though French traders set up business in log cabins on both sides of the river within hailing distance of the French fort, the area didn't become much of a permanent settlement until the English took control of the region in 1761. On October 12, 1761, Captain Henry Balfour arrived with a detachment of British troops and found the fort in wretched condition, with houses missing roofs and the stockade rotting and ready to fall. He stayed only two days before returning to Mackinac, leaving Ensign James Gorrell in charge with 17 soldiers and a French interpreter. The old outpost received a new name: Fort Edward Augustus. La Baye became Green Bay.

Gorrell found one family of Indians living there, the rest having gone hunting as they customarily did at that time of the year. Few, if any, would return before the spring. Two English traders also joined the French traders residing on both sides of the river.

Gorrell still commanded the post in May, 1763, when most of the area's Indian population assembled at Green Bay on their return from winter's hunt. Gorrell told them he had received word of an imminent attack on the little fort, and accepted the claims of the Ottawas and the Menominees that they knew nothing about it. But on June 15, he received a letter from Captain Etherington of Michilimackinac offering details of a surprise attack by the Ojibwas at that post that had killed Lieutenant Jamet and 20 others. Etherington instructed him to abandon Fort Edward Augustus immediately and proceed to L'Arbre Croche. Even though the Treaty of Paris confirmed British control in 1763, the British never regarrisoned the fort.

French traders stayed at the isolated outpost and profited by doing business with other Frenchmen in the French province of Louisiana by way of the Mississippi River. Jonathan Carver came here in 1766 and offered a description of what he found:

The "Fort. . . is only surrounded by a stockade and being much decayed is scarcely defensible against small arms. . . A few families live in the Fort, which lies on the west side of the Fox River, and opposite to it, on the east side of the entrance, are some French settlers who cultivate the land and appear to live very comfortably."

For a twenty-first century visitor, "comfortably" is a relative term. Augustin Grignon recalled a story his mother told him about Augustin de Langlade, his great-grandfather, at his Green Bay store:

"My mother, who was born in 1763, related to me, that when she was about seven years of age, she was once in the store, when an Indian came in, and expressed a desire to purchase a small Indian axe. When her grandfather, Augustin de Langlade, handed out one from under the counter, the Indian inquired if he had any more. M. De Langlade bent down to get some others, and as he arose, the Indian, in mere sport, made a motion as if to strike the old gentleman on the head with the first axe handed out. When my mother exclaimed, 'Grandpa, he is going to cut your neck!' He arose quickly, and, with one of the small axes, knocked the Indian over. Picking himself up, the Indian apologized to M. De Langlade, that he only intended it for a joke. He was told in reply, that such things were too serious for rude sport, and there the matter ended."

Grignon recalled that "about 1785" only seven families totaling 56 people lived at Green Bay so the absence of a military presence may have had an impact on settlement. That didn't change until the British occupied the area again during the War of 1812 and the Americans eventually built Fort Howard in 1816 on the site of the earlier French and British forts.

Grignon was born in Green Bay in 1780 and his writings give us a window into the eighteenth-century place he knew as a boy and a young man. There were three families living on the west side of the river above the fort and four on the east. East siders included his father (trader Pierre Grignon) and grandfather (Charles de Langlade.) The others were Amable Roy and "a young trader named Marchand, the agent of a Mackinaw trading company." The families of Baptist Brunet, Joseph Roy and a man named Lagral lived on the on the west side. Because Grignon and Marchand had the only trading stores, business was mostly conducted on the east side of the river.

Grignon said the group started to expand with the arrival of Jacques Porlier from Montreal in 1791 and Charles Reaume in 1792. Reaume would one day be appointed justice of the peace by Indiana Territory governor William Henry Harrison and serve as the only civic official at the Green Bay settlement for many years. He tried (and failed) to set up a successful trading business.

"At this time, there were no settlers at De Pere, nor anywhere on the Fox River, except those here mentioned at the Bay," Grignon wrote.

The Menominee village of Chakachokama (The Old King), grandfather of important Menominee chiefs Oshkosh and Tomah, stood just south of the residences on the west side of the river. A granite plaque embedded in the north face of an old, three-story brick office building at the southeast corner of Walnut Street and Pearl Street, next to the Canadian National railroad tracks, indicates that the village extended from there for three blocks to the south.

Chakachokama received a certificate in 1778 from Quebec governor Frederick Haldimand proclaiming him the Grand Chief of the Menominee. When he died in 1821 while visiting family members at Prairie du Chien in 1821, he was thought to be at least 100 years old.

A big chunk of the riverfront property that once held the Old King's Menominee village is now occupied by freight and shipbuilding companies. This is nearly opposite the site of Augustin and Charles de Langlade's property on the east side of the river, where it is much easier to get a sense of the history that permeates this place.

Two blocks south of the Fox Harbor Inn, Washington Street angles to the east and hits Adams Street, forming a somewhat distorted "Y" intersection. There, in the small, park-like grassy area in front of Green Bay City Fire Station No. 1, a rock marker on the ground announces this as the site of the "La Baye Burial Place, 1720-1835, land donated by Domatelle de Langlade Grignon-Langevin." The graves here were unmarked, and many of the bodies, including those of Augustin de Langlade and his son Charles, were moved to Allouez Catholic Cemetery in Green Bay, and buried in a trench with other unidentified remains. As is the case with other ancient, abandoned city cemeteries, construction workers sometimes uncover bones of those early traders and settlers that weren't moved in the nineteenth century. Adams Street occupies at least part of the ground where the cemetery sat.

The area sprouts historical markers like spring flowers. A metal plaque on a rock a few feet from the cemetery marker notes that the first Catholic church in Green Bay stood near this site in 1823, With so much history here, a bronze plaque on a non-descript two-story, brick building across the street from the Fox Harbor Inn seemed a likely place for another peek at ancient days of French traders and local Indian tribes.

The first few words told me that my distant time travel had ended and that I had arrived back in modern Green Bay:

"PACKERS OFFICE BUILDING. . . The Packers moved into the south side of this building, located at 349 South Washington St., in 1949, and occupied it until a new administration building was completed next to what is now Lambeau Field in 1963.

"Curly Lambeau was the first coach to have his office here in what was his final season with the Packers, and Vince Lombardi was the last. Lombardi worked here during his first four seasons as coach. . ."

I thought about my friend's earlier comment about Lombardi and laughed. Even while on the trail of the fur traders, French missionaries and Menominee chiefs who once inhabited this place, the Packers and their legends are never far away.

57 FOX-WISCONSIN PORTAGE

The drive from Green Bay to Portage, Wisconsin, takes about a little over two hours, no matter which route you take. Even with a gas stops, lazy lunches and potty breaks, it is faster and considerably more direct than the tortuous journey that Native Americans and early explorers and traders took on the Fox River.

Actually, the Fox doesn't take a traveler all the way to the heart of modern-day Portage, which is why the town is there in the first place and why it has its name. The Fox takes a jog to the south just east of town, a mile and a half from a similar jog by the Wisconsin River on the west side of Portage. So early Indian tribes portaged from one river to the other and hence found a way to link a canoe trip from anywhere on the Great Lakes to the Mississippi River.

When the French traders and missionaries arrived in the seventeenth century, this marshy patch of land between the two rivers may have been the most important place in the modern state of Wisconsin. Today, the old portage is a street called Wauona Trail on the southern edge of a city of 10,473 that is a pit stop on the way to tourist mecca Wisconsin Dells and a 30-minute commute to the state capital in Madison. The street name is derived from the Indians' reference to the portage as "Wau-wau-o-nah," which means "carry on the shoulder" in Winnebago."

The portage was widely known among Native Americans as an easy way to get from Green Bay to the Mississippi River. White men knew nothing about it until French traders became interested in the area that became the modern state of Wisconsin in the seventeenth century. Rumors about the existence of a "great river" circulated in New France after Jean Nicolet is presumed to have visited modern-day Green Bay in 1641 and canoed up the

Fox River; if he did, he apparently didn't reach the portage but he most certainly heard about it from the local tribes. When Illinois tribesmen at Chequamegon Bay on Lake Superior told Father Claude Allouez of the "Messipi" river and a Shawnee told Father Jacques Marquette about a "great river" discharging itself from the Illinois River into the South Sea, Jean Talon (who was in charge of internal affairs for New France) got interested. He commissioned Joliet to search for the "Sea of the South and the Great River which some Indians called 'Michiissipi.'" At the time, Joliet was a young trader who had been present at Simon-François Daumont de Saint Lusson's pageant Sault Ste. Marie that claimed thousands of miles of land and water for France in 1671. Father Claude Dablon, superior of the western missions with his headquarters as the Sault, found out about the assignment, and he told Marquette (who had started the mission at the Sault) to accompany Joliet on his journey.

Ironically Joliet's log of the trip was lost – the original in a canoe crash that nearly claimed Joliet's life and a copy in a fire at Sault Ste. Marie -- and a copy of Marquette's survived. So the Jesuit priest ended up getting most of the credit for their eventual "discovery" of the Mississippi.

They might not have reached the great river had they not stopped at the multi-tribal village of Maskouten near the present-day town of Berlin. There they were given the aid of two Miami guides, who agreed to escort them through the heavy wild rice growth of the upper reaches of the narrow winding stream to the site of the portage.

Marquette wrote: "We knew that, at three leagues from Maskoutens, was a river which discharged into the Missisipi. We knew also that the direction we were to follow in order to reach it was west-southwesterly. But the road is broken by so many swamps and small lakes that it is easy to lose one's way, especially as the river leading thither is so full of wild oats that it is difficult to find the channel. For this reason, we greatly needed our guides, who safely conducted us to a portage of 2,700 paces and helped us transport our canoes to enter that river, after which they returned home, leaving us alone in this unknown country, in the hands of Providence."

Marquette clearly understood the significance of their arrival at the Wisconsin River, adding: "Thus we left the waters flowing to Quebeq, four or five hundred leagues from here, to float on those that would thenceforth take us through strange lands."

With that, Marquette became the first white person to offer a written description of the Fox-Wisconsin portage. Today's traveler can walk in the footsteps of the seven Frenchmen and two Miami guides. A historical marker titled "Marquette" in a roadside park on the east side of the river and on the north side of Wisconsin Route 33 marks the "beginning" of the portage, which actually began on the west side of the Fox.

It reads: "On June 14, 1673 Jacques Marquette and Louis Joliet started

THIS PHOTO SHOWS THE RURAL NATURE OF THE WEST END OF THE PORTAGE IN 1905.

the portage (1.28 miles) from here to the Wisconsin River. The expedition, traveling in two birch bark canoes, discovered the Upper Mississippi River on June 17, 1673 at Prairie du Chien, continued south to the mouth of the Arkansas River. They correctly surmised that the great river led to the Gulf of Mexico and returned to St. Ignace, a trip of nearly 3000 miles. So began a new era of exploration, settlement and commerce for the Great Lakes region, the Mississippi Valley and the Far West. Stabilization of the fur trade followed and also the organization of numerous Indian tribes under French rule. Marquette, a talented Jesuit missionary, dedicated his life and energy ministering to the Indians. Born June 1, 1637 in Laon, France, he died near Ludington, Michigan May 18, 1675."

The marker is a good example of the treatment given Joliet by many historians. Even though Joliet was supposed to be leading the expedition, Marquette's journal was published in 1902 and has been reprinted many times. A savvy shopper could pick one up on eBay, AbeBooks or a hundred other Internet bookselling sites for $5 or $10. What we know of Joliet's part in the trip, we mostly know from Marquette.

Presumably, the marker was placed on the opposite side of the Fox because that was the best location for a wayside park and because it was also close to the site of Fort Winnebago. About 50 yards to the east of the Marquette marker another plaque marks the site of the fort. The fort was constructed there in 1828 primarily to control the portage and to protect American traders from interference by the Winnebago Indians following the conclusion of the Winnebago War the year before. The only part of the fort that remains is the restored Surgeon's Quarters on the hill across the highway. Troops from the fort participated in the Black Hawk War in 1832.

The portage actually began where Wisconsin 33 reaches the other side of the river; nothing about the spot even hints at the location's importance to the fur trade in in North America. The Fox River at this point when I visited in early July is little more than a glorified creek. Less than a quarter of a mile to the west, Wauona Trail turns to left off the highway, but it still doesn't seem like an ancient route that bridged two important watersheds. A used car lot on the right and a sign company on the left are the gateway to a rural setting with modest houses of various ages with no sidewalks and large yards. The road runs straight to the Wisconsin River past a trailer park, soccer fields, baseball diamonds and a restaurant. When it dead ends at Wisconsin 16, a high bank across the road guards the river.

Visions of Marquette, Joliet and the seven Frenchmen? Not here. A lumber company is on the left and a Dairy Queen parking lot is on the right. A four-foot high pink granite monument occupies a small spot on the corner of the lot, depriving DQ customers of another parking spot.

The river side of the stone explains its purpose: "This tablet marks the place near which Jacques Marquette and Louis Joliet entered the Wisconsin River, June 14, 1673. Erected by the Wau-Bun Chapter D.A.R. 1903."

Although the date tells us this wasn't initially erected in a Dairy Queen parking lot, an old black and white Wisconsin Historical Society photo of the monument taken in 1905 looking east offers visual proof. A dirt road stretches out behind the monument and there is no evidence of human activity – no Native Americans or Jesuit priests lugging canoes, kids riding bikes or farmers driving teams of horses -- on the road or on any of the ground beside it.

In fact, the portage ceased to be important in the 1870s when the long-held plans for a canal linking the Fox and Wisconsin rivers finally reached fruition. The first attempt to build a canal started with the authorization of the Portage Canal Company by the state legislature in 1834; digging began on a route that closely paralleled the Wauona Trail in 1838 and ended a short time later after $10,000 had been squandered.

A new route for the canal was chosen in 1849 and work began on the waterway that still exists today; it splits off the Fox River about a quarter of a mile north of the wayside park with the historical markers and continues straight until it reached the railroad tracks at the end of Agency House Road, where it veers to the right and runs just south of Mullet Street. It follows this path through the heart of town to the Wisconsin River.

Misunderstandings between the state and the contractor led to men being forced to work for months without being paid and the project was finally abandoned. Although the canal was left unfinished; Marquette, Joliet and the local tribes would have been satisfied with the result. Canoes used the waterway, even if larger boats couldn't.

A new company formed in 1853 to complete the canal went bankrupt. Finally, the U.S. Army Corps of Engineers started at the Fox River end of the old canal in 1874 and completed it in 1876; the finished product was 75 feet wide, 7 feet deep and 2 1/2 miles long.

Unfortunately, by then the railroads had largely taken the business that the canal could have had if it had been completed 40 years earlier, when the success of the Erie Canal had made the idea seem feasible. Still, the canal remained in use until 1951 when the Fort Winnebago Lock was bulldozed in and the Wisconsin River Locks were welded shut.

Today the portion of the canal that starts at Adams Street and splits downtown Portage has been beautifully restored and maintained; to the east of that point, it mostly resembles an overgrown creek that didn't dare dream about being the transportation answer to anything.

Nevertheless, the old Portage Canal is likely to be a modern visitor's lasting memory of a brief visit to Portage. Even a historically minded stranger who enters town from Interstate 39 west of town, would probably conclude that the old Fox-Wisconsin portage that gave the town its name had been located on or near where the old canal runs today, unaware of that the actual portage site is actually several blocks to the south.

If the Wauona Trail were human, it would know exactly what it is like to be Louis Joliet.

58 PRAIRIE DU CHIEN

On my way into Prairie du Chien, Wisconsin, I stopped at a Kwik Trip gas station/convenience store for a cup of coffee. As I prepared to pay for it, I noticed the name tag worn by the middle-aged woman working the cash register.

"Bridgette?" I pointed at her name tag. "Uh . . . you wouldn't be from a French family that has lived here for generations, would you?"

She smiled and gave me a sidelong glance.

"My family's Polish," she said.

I wasn't sure if she were kidding or truth-telling, but I should have known better than to ask. That would be a lot like asking a New York City hotel clerk named Peter if he were part of a Dutch family that came to Manhattan island when it was a dense forest.

I paid for the coffee with a dollar and a sheepish smile. "Sorry. I'm trying to write something about the city's history and I thought. . . "

"No problem," she said, "but I'm afraid I don't know anything about it."

This was my first clue that this riverfront town is living life as it is now and not as it was then, when it played a prominent role in the history of the Old Northwest. Today it is one of those pretty little places that really isn't on the way to anywhere and isn't a much of a destination on its own accord. That can be a source of confusion for a modern visitor trying to understand why this place on the Mississippi River could have ever been what it once was.

It practically dares you to understand it. It has French roots and a French name, but appears no more French than Madison or Milwaukee. The city owes its place in history to geography, but the confluence of the Wisconsin and Mississippi rivers is nearly three miles south of the center of town. The geography that meant as much to the town's importance as the two rivers is the broad, flat plain that stretches nine miles north of the confluence. Once the home of a large Fox settlement, it became the perfect location for fur traders and various Indian tribes to congregate in the spring and fall and conduct business.

Of course, to the modern eye this is no more noticeable than the absence of French architecture. When you first arrive in Prairie, especially if you're coming from the south or east, it looks like just another small Midwestern town (population 5,653 in 2017) with a Pizza Hut, McDonald's and Dairy Queen.

A drive to the heart of the heart of the business district abruptly changes that. Two east-west streets – Blackhawk Avenue and Washington Street -- cross short bridges west to St. Feriole Island, a huge greenspace that is surely one of the strangest parks on the planet. Once the home of the original town of Prairie du Chien, it features only a few scattered buildings and all of the streets as they existed in 1965 when the Mississippi reached an all-time crest of 25.38 feet and wiped out many of the old structures there in a devastating flood. In the wake of the disaster, the U.S. Army Corps of Engineers spent $500,000 relocating families, although the last residents didn't leave the island until the mid-1980s.

Once home to a fire department, a school, a swimming pool and scores of homes, all that remains are a few historic structures such as Villa Louise, an 1840s mansion; the Brisbois House (circa 1837), the Brisbois Store (once an 1850s fur trading post) and the Dousman House Hotel (circa 1864). They stand on the grid of mostly empty streets, which are marked by street signs and stop signs that give the park a ghost-town feel.

The "old Fourth Ward" is remembered in plaques shortly after you enter the park on West Blackburn Avenue, and while it's worth noting that this community was an important fur trading center until the middle of the nineteenth century, the history of this place goes back much further than that. When Father Jacques Marquette and Louis Joliet paddled their birch bark canoes down the Wisconsin and reached the Mississippi on June 17, 1673, the moment was remembered by many as the "discovery" of the Mississippi River. (As noted earlier, Spanish conquistador Hernando de Soto qualifies as the first European to reach the Mississippi when he crossed it south of Memphis, Tennessee, in May 1541.)

A statue of Marquette sits atop the tall stone monument in a little park adjacent to a visitor center, east of the bridge that takes U.S. 18 over the river to Iowa. It sits a long block south of the short bridge on Blackburn, and the plaque notes that "Rev. James Marquette S.J. discovered the Mississippi River at Prairie du Chien, Wisconsin." "The Business Men's Association" of Prairie du Chien which erected the statue in 1910 didn't see fit to even mention poor

Joliet, which again seems like a steep price to pay for losing your journal in a canoe crash.

Marquette and Joliet turned left at the Mississippi in search for a route to the Pacific so they may have not have made it to the prairie or even the site of a future Marquette monument. But they would soon be followed by other French explorers who recognized the enormous value in the location.

Nicolas Perrot, the French commander in the West, came here in May, 1683, and built Fort Nicolas (or Nicholas, depending on the source) as a trading post. He built it somewhere south of the modern town and relatively close to the confluence, or, according to an old Prairie du Chien resident "on the first high ground above Wyalusing (the area south of the Wisconsin River) suitable for such an establishment, and is the first dry prairie that could be reached by boat above that place."

Nineteenth century Wisconsin historians got into quite an academic scrap over whether that fort was located north or south of the confluence and whether a subsequent French fort supposedly built in Prairie du Chien in 1755, even existed. If they had been fur traders instead of historians, there would have been up-turned tables, knives, bruises and a full-scale brawl.

Most have since accepted the existence of Fort Nicolas on the north (or Prairie du Chien) side of the Wisconsin, although the length of its brief tenure is still in dispute. Some believe the fort may have been abandoned as soon as 1684, even though it appears on Jean-Baptiste-Louis Franquelin's 1688 map, north of the Wisconsin. Franquelin was the hydrographer of the King of France and he resided at Quebec, where he likely could best interview returning officers, explorers, missionaries and traders. According to Perrot, a trader named Bois-Guillot commanded the French there in May of 1789, so Fort Nicolas may have been there then and may not have been abandoned until Perrot stopped leading French fur trade operations in the area when a royal ordinance revoked all trading licenses in 1696.

Where was Fort Nicolas? Maps of that time place it a mile or more north and east of the confluence, which is difficult to precisely locate because of the existence of small islands and marshy ground in the area where the Wisconsin meets the Mississippi.

The location of the second French fort can be more easily located, if it existed. Several historical sources say that the French built it in 1755, and old Prairie residents claimed to have seen the charred remains of the old structure, supposedly burned during the American Revolution, and stockade ditches as late as the 1820s. Historian C.W. Butterfield disputed that in the 1880s, claiming that the remains were those of a large log house where furs were stored – and not a fort -- and the ditches and other fort-like land formations were built by the mound builders.

Noted longtime Wisconsin Historical Society secretary and co-founder Lyman C. Draper disagreed and interviewed several old-time residents of the area as to what they saw and where they saw it in repudiation of Butterfield's position in the same issue (Volume X) of the society's Report and Collections.

Most of them remembered the "old French fort" as being at the west end of Farm Lot 39 – I'll explain the system the French used to appropriate land in their early western settlements later – which would put it in the vicinity of today's Paquette Street, at the entrance to the Big River Campground. Mound-building Indians did construct earthworks in this area, but Draper cited the different characteristics between those and what the others believe were the remains of a French stockade. Old Fort Nicolas may have also been in the vicinity, which further complicates the debate.

Did the "old French fort" that many early prairie settlers heard about and think they even saw actually exist? The argument against it is that no one from the time it should have been standing mentioned it in their writings, an interesting but inconclusive position. Englishman Jonathan Carver visited the prairie in 1766 and found "about 300 Indian families (in) houses that are well-built, after the Indian manner, and pleasantly situated on very rich soil" that made the town the great mart for Indian trade – and made no mention of a fort. But he also didn't mention the ancient mounds in the vicinity, so it's possible that he simply didn't think it was pertinent to his discussion. He did, however, become the first person to record the name of the place as "Prairie du Chiens," or "Planes of the Dogs."

Carver also finds himself as a posthumous participant in another debate about when the town of Prairie du Chien was first settled. Although the prairie served as a spring and fall gathering place for fur traders and Indians soon after the first French explorers arrived, historians long believed the first permanent settlers arrived in Prairie du Chien in the 1750s. This was based in part on the recollections of an ancestor of one of those would-be settlers, which were later proven to be incorrect.

Carver's writings are again cited here as partial proof that there were no permanent French settlers here because he didn't write about them, instead focusing on the large Indian village located there. Rather than takes sides, it seems more productive to focus on the town that existed after the early 1770s, when everyone agrees that the area had permanent settlers. French from the Illinois country to the south began to move to the prairie and they brought the French method of land division that had been used in Kaskaskia, Cahokia and Prairie du Rocher with them. With this method, settlers owned both a village lot and a farm lot where they could raise crops.

Three villages developed: the main village on St. Feriole Island fronting on the Mississippi, a second village directly across the marsh or marais (the site of modern downtown Prairie du Chen) and a third, smaller village about three miles to the north. The farm lots were mostly located behind (east of) the village lots and extended to the bluffs that marked the end of the prairie to the east. Parts of each of the 43 farm lots were held in common by all the residents and cattle and horses grazed in common areas.

The prairie gained in importance throughout the eighteenth century as fur trading expanded. In the beginning, traders from Canada, Michilimackinac and Green Bay came to the prairie in their loaded canoes in the spring to trade. As the fur trade reached deeper into Minnesota and northern Wisconsin, the wintering traders began to use the prairie as a fall gathering place before they set out for remote winter posts on the Mississippi and its many tributaries. All gathered in the spring to exchange manufactured goods (traps, hatchets, muskets, beads, etc.) for furs, which were repacked for the long canoe trip back to Montreal.

Trader Peter Pond of Connecticut worked out of Prairie du Chien in 1774-75 and found it "Very Handsum." His written description is worth a look, including poor spelling that helps emphasize the idea that the isolated outpost wasn't an island of sophistication:

"All the traders that Youseis that Part of the Countrey & all the Indans of Several tribes Meat fall & Spring whare the Grateist Games are Plaid Both By french & Indans. The french Practis Billiards — ye latter Ball. Hear the Botes from New Orleans Cum. They are navagated By thirtey Six men who row as maney oarse. Thay Bring in a Boate Sixtey Hogseats of Wine on one. Besides Ham, Chese &c — all to trad with the french & Indans. Thay Cum up the River Eight Hundred Leages. These Amusements Last three or four weakes in the Spring of the Year."

If a historian could go back in time and attend some of those spring-fall gatherings on the prairie, he might return to the twenty-first century and plant historical markers all over the place. The cast of characters for these gatherings would be a roll-call of familiar names – French, English, American and Native American – from that time period.

While a twenty-first century reader might conjure the image of a crowd of suburbanites exchanging items at a weekend swap meet, this was, uh, a little less refined. When their business was concluded, the traders, Indians and in some cases their wives engaged in several days of partying, drinking, dancing and sometimes even brawling their way to happiness before departing.

At the conclusion of the French and Indian War in 1763, the area fell under British control. British and Scottish businessmen and merchants supplanted many of the French-Canadian businessmen in Montreal, and the area began to see more British traders. By the late 1790s, many traders from Mackinac and Montreal who regularly visited the prairie were acquiring property here and using it as their headquarters.

Although the area became part of the United States in 1783, the British valued the fur trade and went about their business here as they had at other western posts such as Mackinac and Green Bay. The prairie became part of the Northwest Territory in 1787 but again this didn't mean much until the Jay Treaty in 1794, when the British agreed to withdraw from five pre-Revolutionary War forts by 1796. But the treaty specifically guaranteed the rights of the British to engage in the fur trade in U.S. territory, so the influence of Canadian traders continued to be strong here.

St. Clair County (in the modern state of Illinois) was organized as the westernmost county of the Northwest Territory in 1790 and when it was re-organized in 1795 Prairie du Chien and its "65 souls" became part of the county. Cahokia, the county seat, was almost 400 miles away.

Through the descriptions of early visitors and residents, historian Mary Elise Antoine traced the slow growth of Prairie du Chien as a permanent settlement: Canadian trader Thomas Anderson wrote in 1801 that it consisted of between 10 and 15 houses, with three farms at a distance of three miles; American explorer Zebulon Pike came here in 1805 and made note of 18 houses on the two streets of the Main Village and eight houses across the pond (site of the second village and modern business district); U.S. Indian agent Nicolas Boilvin arrived in 1811 and recorded 30 to 40 houses and in 1816 American Fur Company employee James Lockwood found 25 to 30 houses in the traders' village, presumably meaning on the island.

None of these structures survive today, although a modern visitor can see what they must have been like at the Francois Vertefeuille log house on County Highway K, two and a half miles north of the city limits. The house is all that remains of the small upper village established by French-Canadian voyageurs in the early years of the nineteenth century. Indeed, a tourist who heads out Main Street (K) looking for it and begins passing farm fields north of town is apt to think he has gone too far.

The Upper Village consisted of seven village lots created from four farm lots in 1805, and the Vertefeuille house, constructed of hewn logs and an example of French-Canadian piece sur piece architecture, is the only structure from the village that has survived. Farm fields lie across the street from it, a trailer park sits just to the south and the Mississippi flows behind it to the west. Francois Vertefeuille, for whom the house is named, worked in the fur trade as early as 1797 as an employee of a British trading partnership named Parker, Gerrard & Ogilvy that was based in Montreal. He eventually retired from trading and lived at Upper Village Lot No. 4, where he and his wife worked the farm and raised three children.

He might be described as typical of the early residents, which explains why sentiment here (and in Green Bay) was mostly with the British when the War of 1812 broke out. Missouri governor William Clark (of "Lewis and Clark" fame) led a contingent of U.S. troops to Prairie du Chien in the spring of 1814 and immediately ordered the construction of Fort Shelby on a mound near the Main Village, in hopes of breaking the control of the British traders.

The British countered with a force of British troops from Mackinac under trader William McKay, a force that included some residents of Prairie du Chien and Green Bay. It lay siege to the fort and eventually threatened to burn it. Although the Americans surrendered, giving the British a victory in what came to be called the Battle of Prairie du Chien, the U.S. victory in the larger war eventually restored American sovereignty.

The British withdrew in May, 1815, and the renamed Fort McKay burned to the ground. The Americans established control over the fur trade with the construction of Fort Crawford on the same spot; flood damage eventually resulted in the construction of a replacement Fort Crawford on the south end of town. Today, there is a museum on South Beaumont Road where the second fort had stood.

Its three buildings of exhibits offer a nice salute to the history of Prairie du Chien. But it can't possibly satisfy the confused looks of modern visitors trying to wrap their head around the idea that this small town and the prairie it occupies was once as important as places such as St. Louis and New Orleans and a daily topic of conversation in Quebec and Montreal.

Few of today's geographically challenged people have probably even heard of Prairie du Chien. Everybody knew about it then.

59 CHICAGO PORTAGE

It's safe to say that 99 percent of the Chicago visitors who arrive at Midway airport are unaware that their drive or cab ride north on South Cicero Avenue toward the Stevenson Expressway takes them directly into an ancient swamp that earned the unflattering designation of Mud Lake.

To be fair, mud is about the last thing anyone thinks of in a rush of traffic on a six-lane sea of concrete. The same goes for history. With or without a mud quagmire to negotiate, this densely–populated area north of the airport just doesn't seem like a place where French missionaries, fur traders, British soldiers and Indian tribes spent a lot of time.

But the mud is only a small part of the story. The marshy area that stretched several miles through the place where the expressway – it is also known as Interstate 55 – takes travelers either to the Chicago lakefront or west to Joliet, Illinois, and beyond, was in fact an area that gave life to the Chicago portage. The route joined the Chicago River and the Des Plains River in creating a link between the Great Lakes and the Mississippi River. Depending upon the season, the portage usually covered three or four miles on the north edge of Mud Lake and is the primary reason that the city of Chicago is located where it is.

Today, the Chicago Sanitary and Ship Canal that was built in 1900 and runs just north of the expressway, serves as that connector. Its predecessor, the Illinois and Michigan Canal, opened to traffic in 1848 and is located beneath I-55.

Many of the most important local Indian trails were located near the Chicago portage. The South Portage Trail crossed the Des Plaines River at Summit Ford (the town of Summit is on the south shore of the river, just south of Portage Park). The North Portage Trail or Ottawa Trail crossed at

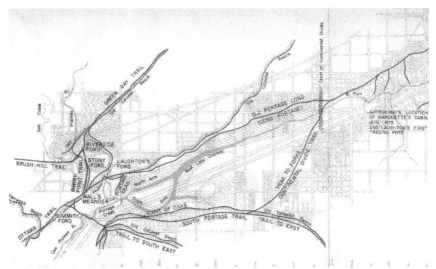

ROBERT KNIGHT AND LUCIUS H. ZEUCH CREATED THIS MAP OF THE CHICAGO PORTAGE OVER A MAP OF CITY STREETS IN 1923 FOR A PRESENTATION AND BOOK FOR THE CHICAGO HISTORICAL SOCIETY.

Stony Ford (near Joliet Road/Historic U.S. Route 66) and at Laughton's Ford f on the Illinois River. Portages were made on this trail during dry seasons; later it became a wagon road that became Route 66. The Ottawa Trail began at a point just east of the intersection of Joliet Road and Forty-Seventh Street. The east branch of the Green Bay Trail joined with Portage Road here to form this trail to the southeast; part of it is today's Ogden Road.

Father Jacques Marquette and Louis Joliet came through this area for the first time in September, 1673, on their way back to the Great Lakes from the Mississippi River. They had traveled to the Mississippi by way of Green Bay and the Fox and Wisconsin rivers, and Native Americans told them of a shorter return route while they canoed upstream on the Mississippi. The Indians eventually guided them up the Illinois and Des Plaines rivers to a landing spot where Portage Creek flowed into Mud Lake. Depending upon the time of the year, this could be either a shallow waterway or a muddy slough of eight miles.

Today, the explorers' landing spot is located in Portage Woods, a 91-acre park a mile and a half northwest of Midway. A monument to Marquette and Joliet and their Indian guides within sight of the landing spot marks this as the Chicago Portage National Historic Site. Beyond the monument, you can see a surviving fragment of Portage Creek where it joined the Des Plaines River. This small section was cut off from the main river by a levee during construction of the Sanitary and Ship Canal.

The explorers took the creek into and across Mud Lake to its eastern edge, a ridge that is site of a continental divide. The divide, which sends waters on the east side of it to Lake Michigan and waters west of it to the Mississippi, is located in the vicinity of South Kedzie Avenue about two miles east of Midway.

Marquette and Joliet began their actual portage on the east end of Mud Lake at South Albany Avenue and Thirty First Street, a nondescript corner with vacant weed-infested lots, chain link fences on two of the four corners and an overgrown inlet of the ship canal (behind another chain link fence) on a third. A concrete walkway serves as a long narrow entrance to La Villita Park on the fourth, next to another fenced-off parking lot. From a modern perspective, it seems like a heck of place to begin a portage over a mile and a half strip of prairie, which ended at the West Fork South Branch of the Chicago River at today's South Leavitt Street. From there it was an easy paddle to Lake Michigan.

Marquette had promised the Illinois tribe that he would return to their village near Starved Rock on the Illinois River and start a mission and he left Green Bay on October 25, 1674, to fulfill that pledge. But when the weather took a turn for the worse and Marquette came down with a bad case of dysentery, he and his two companions decided to spend the winter in a cabin they constructed just north of the Chicago River on what is today's South Damen Avenue.

The spot is marked by a 12-foot high concrete monument next to a sidewalk and in front of a lumber company's workshop, in an industrial area mostly devoid of trees. It's tempting to say that the monument couldn't look more out of place, stuck in a sea of concrete and asphalt. But then I tried to picture a fading missionary priest and his seventeenth century companions trying to wait out the winter in a log cabin on this spot and it struck me that they would be even more out of place here than the monument. They were the first white people of record to reside for any length of time in what is now the city of Chicago.

When the weather broke, Marquette and his party continued west in the spring. By this point, he needed help walking and suffered from bouts of temporary blindness. He arrived at the Illini village near Starved Rock on the Wednesday before Easter. He celebrated Easter mass on April 14 and told his Indian congregation that because of his worsening illness, he would be leaving for his mission at St. Ignace, Michigan, the next day. He never made it there, dying on May 18, 1675, near the modern town of Ludington, Michigan. He was 37.

The portage that Marquette and Joliet had been shown by the Indians may have changed the course of history. It made the area important to the

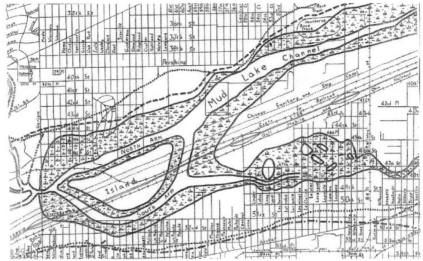

PHILLIP E. VIERLING CREATED THIS MAP OF MUD LAKE IN 1974. NOTE THE STEVENSON EXPRESSWAY (I-55) BETWEEN THE TWO RAILROADS.

early trappers and settlers, and European powers soon realized that a canal there would make it possible to control more territory. The French also saw control of the portage as an effective way to contain English expansion.

After Joliet returned to Quebec, he had reported that "it would only be necessary to cut a canal through half a league (about two miles) of prairie to go in a bark (canoe) by easy navigation from   to the Gulf of Mexico."

What Joliet didn't know couldn't hurt him; he had visited Mud Lake about September 1 between dry and wet seasons and he didn't know it could be vastly different at the extremes.

During the summer of 1818, fur trader Gurdon Hubbard retraced Joliet's route for the American Fur Company when the water was low. He followed the Chicago River until the water ended and had to portage seven miles through the mud and clay, battling schools of leeches and clouds of mosquitos almost the entire way. It took Hubbard and his bateau's twelve tons of trade goods three days to reach the welcome waters of the Des Plaines River.

During some wet seasons, travelers didn't have to portage. The waters of Mud Lake and the waters of the West Fork of the Chicago River connected and covered the divide near South Kedzie Avenue to a depth of four to five feet. Some estimates show this maximum water depth occurred for only four days per year, but for 48 days a year enough water covered the continental divide to permit boats drawing 15 inches or less to navigate the entire distance from Lake Michigan to the Illinois River. This offers quite a contrast to times when the portage became a slog through the mud and the leeches that covered the bottom, a rigorous and uncomfortable trek even for frontier travelers used to hardship.

Either way, the French considered this connecting link vital to control of the fur trade and they controlled both until the early 1700s when the hostile Fox tribe created problems. A four-year war with the Fox that began in 1712 and another war in 1728 that lasted five years caused the French to mostly abandon the portage in favor of safer routes to the Mississippi. After the French and Indian War, the British assumed control of the region's fur trade and by the time of the Revolutionary War both the British and the American colonists used the portage.

The Treaty of Paris gave the Americans official possession of it (and all lands east of the Mississippi) in 1783, but this was another place where the British refused to abide by the terms of the agreement. The Treaty of Greenville in 1795 finally put an end to British influence in the area and the nearby erection of Fort Dearborn in 1803-4 secured it, at least until the Indians burned the fort during the War of 1812. When the Treaty of Ghent ended that war, a second Fort Dearborn was built and the fur trade in the area exploded.

The draining of Mud Lake occurred in several stages, beginning with the construction of the Illinois and Michigan Canal which bisected it in 1848. Several other attempts were made to drain the area after that and it was finally accomplished with the building of the Chicago Sanitary and Ship Canal in 1900. A tiny remnant of Mud Lake exists today as a wetland area in Forest View, between the Stevenson Expressway, the railroad tracks, and West 51st Street, near the Forest View water tower.

Today, a journey through the area once occupied by Mud Lake can still be difficult, if drastically different. The ordeal now is mostly one for those who have to contend with heavy, slow-moving traffic on the Stevenson Expressway.

As frustrating as a traffic jam can be for a modern commuter, the sharp differences between then and now offers some welcome perspective. Personally, I'd take the annoyance of freeway logjam over a slog through mud, leeches and mosquitoes any day.

EPILOGUE

On a day for site visits of Colonel William Crawford's burning and the Indians' victory at Battle Island, I learned from a historical marker website on the Internet that a gravesite memorial to Wyandot chief Tarhe the Crane was only three miles away.

Because of a change in route numbers, a misleading address on the web site and my own impatience, getting there made it seem as if I had launched a search for the Northwest Passage. The GPS in my car showed a road that didn't exist and the one on my phone assigned a different route number to the current one.

I finally found myself heading northeast on Ohio Route 67, which a sign had earlier identified as the Tarhe Trail. I drove a couple of miles and didn't see anything resembling a memorial. I passed an aging, red brick church with boards on its windows and a small cemetery that protected it from encroaching cornfields. I continued on to the tiny crossroads settlement of Belle Vernon and knew I had gone too far. I backtracked nearly all the way to Battle Island, still looking at maps that showed both a wrong highway number and a road that didn't exist.

Heading back up Ohio 67, I took note of a brown, official-looking highway department sign that directed drivers left to the Parker Covered Bridge, saw the approaching one-lane turnoff veer left like the arm of a crooked "Y" and a tiny sign that announced this as "Township Highway 37." I wasn't sure this was the right way -- it was basically a one lane paved road between cornfields – but really, who doesn't enjoy a good covered bridge?

CORN ROWS VEER TO LEFT TO AVOID TARHE MONUMENT.

After about a half-mile, I came upon a granite grave marker sitting between the side of the road and a cornfield. Corn stalks stood within a few feet of the concrete base that surrounded it. You could read Tarhe's name from the car, but I turned off the ignition and paid my respects. If a five o'clock tour bus teeming with giddy passengers came this way on a covered bridge tour, it would have to wait.

One side of the monument indicated that it had been "Erected by Tarhe Tribe No. 145 IORM 1915." Another described him as the "Distinguished Wyandot chief AND loyal American." Beneath it was a granite plate that read only "Died here in Cranetown 1818."

That at least partially cleared up two questions: This used to be the site of Tarhe's Wyandot village and he may not have been buried precisely on the site of this marker; his Wyandot ancestors probably did the best they could to identify the site almost a century later.

But it was impossible not to feel uneasy about this. This had all been Native American land in the early days of Tarhe's life. A Wyandot village still occupied this ground when he died in 1818, twenty-five years before the Wyandots became the last tribe to be removed from what had become the state of Ohio. Now he has a memorial that makes him look like a trespasser who is rudely interrupting a farmer's corn crop.

The failure of the state and county to put a sign on Ohio 67 with an arrow to Tarhe's memorial, next to one for a covered bridge, is inexcusable. It says all we need to know about the general lack of respect for Native Americans and their history.

Tarhe is worth a sign. He was born about 1744 near Detroit and was a warrior from an early age. The French called him the Crane because he was tall and slender. He fought against new settlement in the Old Northwest during Lord Dunmore's war, assisting Cornstalk at the Battle of Point Pleasant. He served as one of the chiefs at St. Clair's defeat at modern Fort Recovery and in the Indians' losing effort at Fallen Timbers. He lost the use of an arm in that battle.

When war chief Half-King died in 1788, the Wyandot tribal council chose Tarhe as his successor, the first of his clan to be so honored. He represented the Wyandots at the signing of the Treaty of Greenville in 1795, and continually urged his people toward peace with the Americans after that. He rejected British offers and fought alongside William Henry Harrison during the war of 1812, actively participating in the Battle of the Thames at the age of 72.

When he died in 1818, chiefs from all Ohio tribes, the Delaware of Indiana and the Seneca of New York came to Cranetown and mourned his loss. Tribal historians described it as the largest gathering of leaders from Indian nations in the Great Lakes and Ohio Valley region and noted that Seneca chief Red Jacket made the trip from Buffalo to pay his respects.

In the decades that followed, Cranetown disappeared and memories of Tarhe faded, like those of many of his Native American counterparts. During my modern search of the Old Northwest, I didn't see a single statue of Tecumseh, Pontiac, Blue Jacket, Little Turtle or Cornstalk, possibly the five most prominent chiefs to have resided within its boundaries. There is a statue of an Indian in a residential neighborhood in the Cincinnati suburb of Saylor Park which is called Tecumseh; it was in fact one of a dozen manufactured by a New York company after a cigar store Indian and was erected by a local widow to honor her late husband. Tecumseh is honored with two statues in Ontario (where he was killed) and one at the U.S. Naval Academy in Annapolis, Maryland, which isn't actually Tecumseh but Tamanend. There is a statue of Little Turtle in Covington, Kentucky, across the Ohio from Cincinnati (that I have never seen), erected in 1988.

The sight of Tarhe's memorial, unannounced and unobtrusive, standing near the side of a one-lane road no more than three feet from the corn rows, stands in stark contrast to the impressive statues and memorials built to American soldiers and frontiersmen of his time period.

No one has to discover any of them on the way to see a covered bridge.

PHOTO AND MAP CREDITS

17 – Courtesy of the Ohio History Connection.
24 – author.
31 -- Etching published in Historical Collections of Ohio by Henry Howe, 1847.
37 – author.
42 – author.
63 – author.
69 – author.
79 – author.
90 – Courtesy of the Pickaway County Historical Society.
101- Courtesy of the Ohio History Connection.
105 – From History of the City of Columbus, Capital of Ohio, Vol. 1.
107 – Columbus Metropolitan Library.
112 – author.
118 – author.
136 – Wiki openstreetmap.
138 – author.
149 – Map by Rob Hunter, Wiki openstreetmap.
153 -- From Fort Washington at Cincinnati by Robert Ralston Jones, 1902.
158 – Postcard by Jacobi and Berry.
168 – author.
176 – Map by Rob Hunter, Wiki openstreetmap.
182 – Garst Museum, photo by author.
185 – Garst Museum, photo by author.

192 – Map by author, Wiki openstreetmap

193 – author.

199 – Courtesy of the Burton Historical Collection, Detroit Public Library.

202 – Map by Rob Hunter, Wiki openstreetmap.

217 – author.

225 – Wiki openstreetmap.

246 – author.

255 – Library of Congress, Detroit Publishing Co. Collection.

265 -- Plan de Missilimakinak avec la description de la route du Missisipi, Edward E. Ayer Digital Collection, Newberry Library.

271 – Photo by Joel Dinda.

274 – Map by Perkins Magra. Stephen S. Clark Library, University of Michigan Library.

284 – Library of Congress, Detroit Publishing Co. Collection.

293 -- E.A. Bishop, Bishop Pub. Co., Racine, Wisconsin.

305 -- The Abraham Lincoln Library and Museum / Southern Illinois University Press.

307 – Map by John H. Burnham, 1915. University of Illinois at Urbana-Champaign. Map Library.

317 – author.

324 – author.

329 – author.

340 – From Lost Maramech and earliest Chicago; a history of the Foxes and of their downfall near the great village of Maramech; original investigations and discoveries by John F. Steward, 1903.

345 – Wiki openstreetmap.

357 – FortWiki map, by John Stanton.

373 – Wisconsin Historical Society Museum Collection.

380 – author.

388 – Wisconsin Historical Society.

399 – May by Robert Knight and Lucius H. Zeuch for the Chicago Historical Society, 1923.

401 – Map by Philip E. Vierling for his book *A Self-Guided Loop Hiking Trail to the Chicago Portage National Historic Site*, 1974.

404 – author.

BIBLIOGRAPHY

Adams, Barry. "Famed French Explorer Jean Nicolet Gets a Historical Revision." Madison, Wis.: *Wisconsin State Journal*, June 24, 2019.

The Alliance Review. "History is unearthed in Ohio, Mysteries of largest stockade fortress in America investigated." Greenville, Ohio: August 20, 2008.

American Monthly Magazine. "Old Fort Massac." Washington, D.C.: Daughters of the American Revolution, Volume XXVI, No. 3, March, 1905.

Anderson, James H. "Colonel William Crawford." Columbus: *Ohio Archaeological and Historical Publications*, 1898.

Armour, David A. "100 Years at Mackinac: A Centennial History of the Mackinac Island State Park Commission." Mackinac Island: Mackinac State Historic Parks, 1995.

Associated Press. "Logan Elm in Ohio Killed by Heat." *New York Times*, August 9, 1964.
--------------------"Artifacts recovered from site of 1790s era Fort Greene Ville to go on display." Greenville, Ohio: April 15, 2008.

Averill, James. *History of Gallia County*. Chicago and Toledo: H. H. Hardesty & Co., 1882.

Babits, Lawrence E., and Gandulla, Stephanie. *The Archaeology of French and Indian War Frontier Forts*. Gainesville, Fla.: University Press of Florida, 2013.

Bailey, John R. *Mackinac, formerly Michilimackinac*. Lansing, Mich.: Darius D. Thorp, Publisher, 1895.

Banta, R.E. *The Ohio*. New York: Rinehart & Company, 1949.

Barrett, Carole, and Markowitz, Harvey. *American Indian Biographies*. Pasadena, Calif., and Hackensack, N.J.: Salem Press, 2005.

Baughn, James. "What does Cape Girardeau have in common with a small town in Ohio?" Cape Girardeau, Mo.: *Southeast Missourian*, October 15, 2009.

--------------------"Where the river drives a thousand mapmakers crazy." Cape Girardeau, Mo.: *Southeast Missourian*, July 30, 2010.

Bedford-Jones, H. *L'Arbre Croche Mission. A Memorable Relation Briefly Setting Form the Historical Facts and Eschewing All Fable & Legend, as Erected by Untutored Minds Touching Upon the Justly Famed Mission of the Crooked Tree.* Santa Barbara, Calif.: Printed by the author at the sign of the Crossed Quills, 1917.

Beeson, L.H. "Fort St. Joseph the Mission, Trading Post and Fort, Located About One Mile South of Niles, Michigan." Lansing, Mich.: *Michigan Historical Collections and Researches Made by the Michigan Pioneer and Historical Society*, Robert Smith and Company, 1900

Ben, David C. "Reconstruction of Fort Washington Way Redefined Cincinnati's Urban Core." Urban Cincy, July 7, 2010. urbancincy.com.

Bennett, Henry Holcomb. *History of the City of Chillicothe, Ohio.* Madison, Wis.: Selwyn A. Brant, 1902.

Bernstein, David. "Fort Steuben and U.S. Land Office." Tour 8 Section B - East Liverpool to Marietta. Davidbersteinphotographer.com.

Bienkowski, Brian. "Uncovering buried creek could spur Detroit development, ease sewer woes." Michigan River News/Great Lakes Echo, August 18, 2011.

Blount, Jim. "Indian Trails were basis for area roads, starting with St. Clair's army in 1791." Hamilton, Ohio: *The Journal-News*, June 12, 1996.
--------------- "First county jail in old powder magazine." Hamilton, Ohio: *The Journal-News*, October 1, 1997.

Bogan, Dallas. "Old Miami Trail Has Traversed the Ages." History of Campbell County, Tennessee. tngenweb.org.

Bond, Beverley W. *The Civilization of the Old Northwest.* New York: The Macmillan Company, 1934.
------------------------*The Correspondence of John Cleves Symmes.* New York: The Macmillan Company, 1926.

BonnieBlueFlag. "The Curse of Shawnee Chief Cornstalk.". Sunday, September 11, 2005. Bonnieblueflag.blogspot.com.

Booraem V, Hendrik. *A Child of the Revolution, William Henry Harrison and His World, 1773-1798.* Kent, Ohio: Kent State University Press, 2012.

Bowman, John. "A Ferryboat Ride to the Other Side." 2015. steamboat-birthplace-wheeling.com.
------------------- "Wheeling the Birthplace of the American Steamboat," 2008. steamboat-birthplace-wheeling.com.

Brant & Fuller (pub.), *History of the Upper Ohio Valley, 1890, Vol. II.* Madison, Wis.: Brant &Fuller.

Brice, Wallace A. *History of Fort Wayne.* Fort Wayne, Ind.: D.W. Jones and Son, 1868.

Briggs, John E. "Two Connecticut Yankees." *The Palimpsest, Volume 7, No.1.* State Historical Society of Iowa, 1926.

Brown, Parker B. "The Fate of Crawford Volunteers Captured by Indians Following the Battle of Sandusky in 1782." Western Pennsylvania History, 1982.
---------------------- "The Search for the Colonel William Crawford Burn Site: An Investigative Report." Western Pennsylvania History, 1982.

Brown, T.J. "Kenton's Gauntlet at Chillicothe." Columbus: Ohio *Archaeological and Historical Publications, Volume XIII*, 1904.

Buley, R. Carlyle. The Old Northwest, Pioneer Period, 1815-1840. Bloomington, Ind.: Indiana University Press, 1962.

Burnet, Jacob. *Notes on the Early Settlement of the North-western Territory.* Cincinnati: Derby, Bradley & Co., 1847.

Busch, Jane C. "Mackinac Island." National Historic Landmarks Nomination. January, 2000.
-------------------"People and Places: A Human History of the Apostle Islands Historic Resource Study of Apostle Islands National Lakeshore." National Park Service, 2008.

Butler, James, D. "French Fortifications Near the Mouth of the Wisconsin. Hold the Fort!" Madison, Wis.: *Reports and Collections of the State Historical Society of Wisconsin, Volume X*, 1888.

Butler, Scott E. *Mary Harris ~ The White Woman of the Coshocton Frontier.* Katonah, N.Y.: Katonah Publishing, 2016.

Burton, Clarence M. *The City of Detroit 1701-1922, Volume 3.* Detroit-Chicago: The S. J. Clarke Publishing Company, 1922.

Butterfield, Consul Willshire. "French Fort at Prairie du Chien a Myth." Madison, Wis.: *Reports and Collections of the State Historical Society of Wisconsin, Volume X*, 1888.
--------------------------------*An Historical Account of the Expedition against Sandusky under Col. William Crawford in 1782.* Cincinnati: Robert Clarke & Co., 1873.
--------------------------------*History of the Girtys.* Cincinnati: Robert Clarke & Co., 1890.

Calloway, Colin G. *The Victory with No Name, the Native American Defeat of the First American Army.* New York: Oxford University Press, 2015.

Carroll, George. "Lewis Wetzel: Warfare Tactics on the Frontier." Charleston, West Virginia: *West Virginia History, Volume 50*, 1991.

Castaldi, Tom. "The Beginnings of the Portage to the Wabash River." Fort Wayne, Ind.: Fort Wayne History Center, June 10, 2013.

Cauthorn, Henry Sullivan. *A History of the City of Vincennes, Indiana, from 1702 to 1901.* Vincennes, Ind.: M.C. Cauthorn, 1902.

Cayton, Andrew R.L. *Frontier Indiana.* Bloomington and Indianapolis: Indiana University Press, 1996.

Cayton, Andrew R.L. and Hobbs, Stuart D. *The Center of a Great Empire, the Ohio Country in the Early Republic.* Athens, Ohio: The Ohio University Press, 2005.

Charleston Gazette. "Fighting Chief Cornstalk's Remains Laid to Rest Again." September 21, 1954.

City of St. Ignace and Mackinac County, for the Year 1895, An Outline of the History, Advantages, Business Facilities, Attractions and Inducements Presented by this Charming Region. E. Jones. 1895

Clarke Historical Library. "Fort Greenville, Ohio, 1795. Fort Greenville in the Ohio Country, A Treaty of Peace." Central Michigan University. cmich.edu/library/clarke.

Coleman, Brent. "Cincinnati's Founding Fathers: Six men, from the prestigious to the penniless, helped mold region." Cincinnati: WCPO, January 5, 2017.

Crespel, Rev. Emanuel. "De Lingery's Expedition Against the Foxes, 1728." Madison, Wisconsin: *Reports and Collections of the State Historical Society of Wisconsin, Volume X*, 1888.

Cummings, William J. Menominee Range Memories 6: "Early Trading Posts and Half-way Houses from Menominee North." Iron Mountain, Mich.: Menominee Range Historical Foundation. dcl-lib.org.

Curry, William L. "The Wyandot Chief, Leather Lips, His Trial and Execution." Columbus: *Ohio Archaeological and Historical Publications. Volume XII,* 1903.

Darlington, William M. *Christopher Gist's Journals.* Pittsburgh: J.R. Weldin & Co., 1893.

Dawes. E.C. "Major John Burnham and Company" Columbus: Ohio *Archaeological and Historical Quarterly Volume III.* John L. Trauger, 1898.

De Hass, Wills. *History of the Early Settlement and Indian Wars of West Virginia.* Wheeling, W. Va.: H. Hoblitzell, 1851.

De Julio, Mary Antoine. National Register of Historic Places Registration Form, Francois Vertefeuille house. Prairie du Chien, Wis., 1993.

DeRegnaucourt, Tony. *Archaeology of the Fort at Greenville, Ohio.* Carthagena, Ohio: The Messenger Press, 2007.

Dickson, Kenneth R. "Indians crush soldiers sent to make Ohio safe for settlers." *Toledo Blade*, December 2, 2009.
-------------------------- "Wayne pulverized Indians, their bravado at Fallen Timbers." *Toledo Blade*, December 3, 2009.

Divine Jr., Lloyd E. *On the Back of a Turtle, A Narrative of the Huron-Wyandot People.* Columbus: Trillium, an imprint of The Ohio State University Press. 2019.

Drake, Benjamin. *The Life of Tecumseh and His Brother The Prophet.* Cincinnati: H. Rulison, Queen City Publishing House, 1855.

Draper, Lyman C. "Early French Forts in Western Wisconsin." Madison, Wis.: *Reports and Collections of the State Historical Society of Wisconsin, Volume X,* 1888.

"Early History of St. Ignatius Loyola Parish." St. Ignace, Mich. http://www.stigchurch.org/early-history.htm.

Eby, John. "Story of century-old Fort St. Joseph rock." *Niles Daily Star*, November 14, 2012.

Eckert, Allan W. *The Conquerors.* Boston: Little, Brown and Company, 1970.
---------------------*The Frontiersman.* Boston: Little, Brown and Company, 1967.
---------------------*That Dark and Bloody River, Chronicles of the Ohio River Valley.* New York: Bantam Books, 1995.

Edmunds, R. David. *American Indian Leaders, Studies in Diversity.* Lincoln, Neb.: University of Nebraska Press, 1980.

Edmunds, R. David, and Peyser, Joseph L. *The Fox Wars, the Mesquakie Challenge to New France.* Norman, Okla.: University of Oklahoma Press, 1993.

Ellison, Garret. "Rare 250-year-old rosary unearthed at Fort Michilimackinac dig site." Mackinaw City, Mich.: *Grand Rapids Press,* July 2, 2015.

Engeleken, Ruth. "The Old Stites House." *The Cincinnati Enquirer Magazine,* August 16, 1970.

Evans, Henry. "The French 500." Gallipolis, Ohio: Gallia County Genealogical Society OGS Chapter, Inc.

English, William Hayden. *Conquest of the Country Northwest of the River Ohio 1778-1783 and Life of Gen. George Rogers Clark, The Campaigns Against the British Posts, Showing Exact Land Allotted Each, Vol. 2.* Indianapolis: The Bowen-Merrill Company, 1896.

Ehler, Ralph B. "The Story of Fort St. Clair". Columbus: *Ohio Archaeological and Historical Publications, Vol. XXXII, No.3,* July 1923.

Erb, Robin. "War game; out-of-place battlefield may thwart developers." *Toledo Blade,* printed in the Chicago Tribune, July 9, 1995.

Faber, Charles. "Research gives better idea of where Crawford was burned." *Bucyrus Telegraph Forum,* June 8, 2007.

Farmer, Silas. *The History of Detroit and Michigan.* Detroit: Silas Farmer & Co., 1884.

Fausz, J. Frederick. *Founding St. Louis, First City of the New West.* Charleston, S.C.: History Press, 2011.

Feight, Andrew Lee, PhD. "Logan Elm & Commemorating Dunmore's War." sciotohistorical.org.

Feng, Patrick. "The Battle of the Wabash: The Forgotten Disaster of the Indian Wars." Army Historical Foundation, July 16, 2014.

Flechtner, Myron. Gallipolis. Being an account of the French Five Hundred
and of the town they established on La Belle Riviere. Columbus: The Ohio State Archaeological
and Historical Society. 1940.

Ford, Henry A. "Historical Detroit." Lansing, Mich.: *Michigan Pioneer and Historical Collections, Volume X,* 1908.

Ford, Henry A. and Kate B. *History of Cincinnati, Ohio.* Cincinnati: L. A. Williams and Company, 1881.

Gaff, Alan D. *Bayonets in the Wilderness. Anthony Wayne's Legion in the Old Northwest.* Norman, Okla.: University of Oklahoma Press, 2004.

Gale, Neil, PhD. "Indian Trails - Green Bay Trail, aka "Old Jambeau Trail," Chicago, Illinois to Green Bay, Wisconsin." Digital Research Library of the Illinois History Journal. November 11, 2019.
---------------------"The History of the Meskwaki (Fox) Indian Tribe and the Search for their Fort du Renards (Fort Fox) built in 1730." Digital Research Library of Illinois History Journal, October 27, 2018

Gilman, Carolyn. *The Grand Portage Story.* St. Paul, Minn.: Minnesota Historical Society, 1992.

Glaser, Susan. "In Marietta, Ohio, history and scenery merge." The *Plain Dealer,* September 23, 2012.
---------------- "Touring tiny North Bend, Ohio, home to presidents William Henry Harrison and grandson Benjamin." The *Plain Dealer,* July 13, 2016.

Greve, Charles Theodore. *Centennial History of Cincinnati.* Chicago: Biographical Publishing Co., 1904.

Gums, Bonnie L. *Archaeology at French Colonial Cahokia, Studies in Illinois Archaeology No. 3.* Springfield, Ill.: Illinois Preservation Agency, 1988.

Hall, Robert L. "The Archaeology of La Salle's Fort St. Louis on Starved Rock and the Problem of the Newell Fort." In *French Colonial Archaeology: The Illinois Country and the Western Great Lakes.* Urbana and Chicago: University of Illinois Press, 1991.

Hamilton Evening Journal. "Power Magazine Landed Safely South of Town." Hamilton: Ohio: April 18, 1913.
--------------------------------"Only Portico and Cupola of the Old Powder Magazine Damaged by its Wild Ride Down the Flooded Miami." Hamilton, Ohio: April 19, 1913.

Hatcher, Harlan. *The Buckeye Country, A Pageant of Ohio.* New York: G.P. Putnam's Sons, 1947.

Hare, A.J. *Atlas of Wyandot County, Ohio.* Philadelphia: Harrison & Hare, 1879.

Harrington, Hugh T. "Ambushed Victim's Bones at Fort Laurens". Journal of the American Revolution, February 7, 2014.

Havighurst, Walter. *The Heartland: Ohio, Indiana, Illinois.* New York: Harper & Row, 1974.
-----------------------*Wilderness for Sale, The Story of the First Western Land Rush.* New York: Hastings House, 1956.

Heiser, Alta Harvey. *West to Ohio.* Yellow Springs, Ohio: Antioch Press, 1954.

Hildreth, S.P. *Pioneer History, An Account of the First Examinations of the Ohio Valley and the Earliest Settlement of the Northwest Territory.* Cincinnati: Derby and Company, 1848.

Hildreth, Samuel P. *Contributions to the Early History of the North-west Including the Moravian Missions in Ohio.* Cincinnati: Hitchcock & Walden, 1864.

History of Tazewell County Illinois. Chicago: Charles C. Chapman & Co., 1879.

Howe, Henry. *Historical Collections of Ohio, Vols. 1,2,3.* Columbus: Henry Howe and Son, 1891.

Howells, W.D., *Three Villages.* Boston: James R. Osgood and Company, 1884.

Jacobs, James Ripley. *Tarnished Warrior, Major-General James Wilkinson.* New York: The Macmillan Company, 1938.

Jakucyk, Jeffrey B. "Streetcar Information." Cincinnati: http://jjakucyk.com/index.html.

Jones, Howard. "Logan and the Logan Elm." Columbus: *Ohio Archaeological and Historical Publications, Volume XXXII,* Number 2, April, 1923.

Jung, Patrick J. *The Misunderstood Mission of Jean Nicolet, Uncovering the Story of the 1634 Journey.* Madison, Wis.: Wisconsin Historical Society Press, 2018.

Jones, Meg. "History buffs launch search for Fort Howard's footprint." Green Bay, Wis.: *Milwaukee Journal-Sentinel,* September. 29, 2010.

Jones, Robert Ralston. *Fort Washington at Cincinnati, Ohio.* Society of Colonial Wars in the State of Ohio, 1902.

Keating, Barbara Cadot. "The Cadot Family of the French Five Hundred." Gallipolis, Ohio: Gallia County Genealogical Society OGS Chapter, Inc., October 5, 2009.

Keeler, Lucy Elliot. "The Sandusky River." Columbus: *Ohio Archaeological and Historical Publications, Volume XIII,* 1904.
------------------------"Old Fort Sandoski of 1745 and the Sandusky Country." Columbus: *Ohio Archaeological and Historical Quarterly, Volume XXI,* Sept. 15, 1912.

Kemp, Bill. "McLean Co. site of 1730 massacre of Fox Indians." *Bloomington Pantograph,* September 9, 2007.

Kendall County Now. "Maramech Hill one of Kendall County's local historical gems." Yorkville, Illinois: July 14, 2016

Kilbourn, John. *The Ohio Gazetteer, third edition.* Columbus: John Kilbourn. Printed at the office of the Intelligencer and Gazette by P.H. Olmstead, 1817.
--------------------*The Ohio Gazetteer, tenth edition,* Columbus: John Kilbourn. E. Glover, printer, 1831.

King, Arthur Gustave. "The Exact Site of Fort Washington and Daniel Drake's Error," Columbus: *Bulletin of the Historical and Philosophical Society of Ohio, Volume XI,* 1953

Kip, William Ingraham. The Early Jesuit Missions in North America. New York: Wiley and Putnam, 1846.

Kleist, Frederica Hart. Portage Canal History Since 1834. Portage, Wis.: Wisconsin Canal Society, 1983.

Knight, Robert, and Zeuch, *The Location of the Chicago Portage Route of the Seventeenth Century.* Chicago: Chicago Historical Society, 1928.

Knopf, Richard C. "The Rediscovery of Fort Washington," Columbus: *Bulletin of the Historical and Philosophical Society of Ohio,* Volume XI, 1953

LaKemper, Daniel A. (ed.) *The Centennial History of East Peoria.* East Peoria, Ill.: East Peoria Centennial Commission, 1984.

Lawe and Grignon papers, 1794-1821. Madison, Wis.: *Reports and Collections of the State Historical Society of Wisconsin, Volume X,* 1888.

Lewis, Virgil A. "Fort Randolph." First Biennial Report of the Department of Archives and History of the State of West Virginia. Charleston, W.Va.: The Tribune Printing Co., 1906.

Linehan, Thomas. "Early Catholic Missions in Emmet County." Lansing, Mich.: *Michigan History Magazine, Volume 2, No. 2,* April, 1918.

Local Columns. "Cornstalk's curse and other area legends." The *Marietta Times,* July 7, 2014.

Lockwood, James H. "Early Times and Events in Wisconsin." Madison, Wis.: *Wisconsin Historical Collections, Vol. II,* 1856.

Lockwood, Rod. "History on the rocks; Researcher says Turkey Foot Rock is upside down." *Toledo Blade,* February 27, 2008.

Lodge, David. "Pickawillany." Sidney, Ohio: Shelby County Historical Society, 1997. http://www.shelbycountyhistory.org/

Lore, David. "FORGOTTEN FORT, A pre-Revolutionary trading post may hold bloody details to Ohio's past." Piqua, Ohio: *Columbus Dispatch,* November 5, 2002.

Lossing, Benson John. *Pictorial Field Book of the War of 1812.* New York: Harper & Brothers, 1868.

Lott, Travis. "Kaskaskia: Where Illinois' rich history began 150 years before statehood." Springfield, Ill.: *The (Randolph) County Journal,* December 27, 2017.

Lowe, May. "Dedication of the Logan Elm." Columbus: *Ohio Archaeological and Historical Publications, Volume XXII,* 1912.

Lowry, R.E. *History of Preble County Ohio.* Indianapolis: B. F. Bowen & Company, Inc., 1915,

Lynn, Andrea. "Remains of St. Louis founder's home believed to have been located." Champaign, Ill.: Illinois News Bureau, October 2, 2006.

MacDonald, David and Waters, Raine. *Kaskaskia, The Lost Capital of Illinois.* Carbondale, Ill.: Shawnee Books, Southern Illinois University Press, 2019.

Marietta, Ohio's First Adventure. "Lewis Wetzel Frontier Hero…the Legend and the Dark Side." Marietta, Ohio: Marietta-Washington County Convention and Visitors Bureau. mariettaohio.org.

Martin, Deborah Beaumont. *History of Brown County, Wisconsin: Past and Present, two volumes.* Chicago: S.J. Clarke Publishing Company, 1913.

Martzolff, Clement L. "Zane's Trace." Columbus: *Ohio Archaeological and Historical Publications, Volume XIII,* 1904.

McCoy, Daniel. "Old Fort St. Joseph or Michigan Under Four Flags." Abstract delivered before the Michigan Pioneer and Historical Society at its 32nd Annual Meeting, June 7, 1906.

McCullough, David. *The Pioneers.* New York: Simon & Schuster. 2019.

McDermott, John Francis. *Old Cahokia, A Narrative and Documents Illustrating the First Century of its History.* St. Louis: The St. Louis Historical Documents Foundation, 1949.

McFarland, Prof. R.W. "Forts Loramie and Pickawillany." Columbus: *Ohio Archaeological and Historical Publications, Volume VIII,* 1900.
----------------------------"Simon Kenton." Columbus: *Ohio Archaeological and Historical Publications, Volume XIII,* 1904.

McIntosh, W.H. *The History of Darke County Ohio.* Chicago: W.H. Beers and Co., 1880.

McKendry, David Ian. "The Real Story of the Mothman (Parts 1 and 2): The Curse of Chief Cornstalk." December 1, 3, 2015. www.the13thfloor.tv

McNaull, Courtney, and Tuggle, Zach. "Colonel Crawford statue decapitated" Bucyrus, Ohio: *Mansfield News-Journal,* August 26, 2017.

Miami Baptist Association Minutes. "History of the Duck Creek Baptist Church." Cincinnati: 1890.

Miller, Michael. "Fort St. Joseph." Military History of the Upper Great Lakes, Michigan Tech University, October 16, 2016.

Miller, W.C. "History of Fort Hamilton." Columbus: *Ohio Archaeological and Historical Publications, Volume XIII,* 1904.

Morse, Harold. "Historian to survey area site for image of fort." Arrowsmith, Ill.: *The News-Gazette,* Champaign, Ill., January 12, 2003.

Nassaney, Michael S. "An Archaeological Reconnaissance Survey to Locate Remains of Fort St. Joseph (20BE23) in Niles, Michigan" Kalamazoo, Mich.: Western Michigan University, April, 1999.
------------------------*The Archaeology of the North American Fur Trade.* Gainesville, Fla.: University Press of Florida, 2015.
------------------------*Fort St. Joseph Revealed, The Historical Archaeology of a Fur Trading Post.* Gainesville, Fla.: University Press of Florida, 2019.

Nassaney, Michael S.; Cremin, William M.; Kurtzweil, Renee; Brandão, Jose Antonio; and Kurtweill, Renne. "The Search for Fort St. Joseph (1691-1781) in Niles, Michigan." *Midcontinental Journal of Archaeology, Vol. 28, No. 2, Fall, 2003.*

Neill, Rev. Edward D. "Notes on Early Wisconsin Exploration, Forts and Trading Posts." Madison, Wis.: *Reports and Collections of the State Historical Society of Wisconsin, Volume X,* 1888.

Newton, Stanley. *The Story of Sault Ste. Marie and Chippewa County.* Sault Ste. Marie, Mich.: Sault News Printing Co., 1923.

Northwest Ohio Quarterly. "Toledo and Fort Miami." Toledo, Ohio: Volume 16, No. 2, April, 1944.

Nunes, Bill. "Chief Pontiac and the legend of Starved Rock." *St. Louis Post-Dispatch,* June 14, 2007.

O'Brien, Ken. "Marquette's Mission Ends at Starved Rock." *Chicago Tribune*, April 7, 1996.

O'Connell, Patrick M. "Illinois' first capital is an island that's home to just 18 people. Recent flooding has made it even more isolated." Kaskaskia, Ill.: *Chicago Tribune*, July 3, 2019.

Oerichbauer, Edgar S. *Prairie Du Chien: A Historical Study.* Madison, Wis.: State Historical Society of Wisconsin, 1976.

Ogle, Gary. "Backyard history." *Bucyrus Telegraph Forum*, June 8, 2007.
----------------"Guns will blaze again in Battle of Olentangy." *Bucyrus Telegraph Forum.* April 14, 2007.

Olar, Jared. "Founding, and finding, Fort Crevecoeur." Pekin, Illinois: *Pekin Daily Times*, Dec. 15, 2017.

The Old Northwest Genealogical Quarterly. "Leatherlips. The Execution of the Wyandot Indian Chief, Sha-tey-ya-ron-yah, or Leatherlips, in 1810." January, 1904, Volume 7.

Osborn, Chase S. and Osborn, Stellanova. *Hiawatha with its Original Indian Legends.* Lancaster, Penn.: Jaques Cattell Press, 1944.

Parkersburg News and Sentinel. "Marietta's Putnam House provides glimpse at pioneer times." Parkersburg, W.Va.: February 1, 2016.
-------------------------------------- 'Survivor of Big Bottom Massacre remembered' Parkersburg, W.Va.: August 26, 2015

Peckham, Howard H. *Pontiac and the Indian Uprising.* Princeton, N.J.: Princeton University Press, 1947.

Perry, Robert E. *Treaty City, A Story of Old Fort Greenville.* Bradford, Ohio, 1945.

Pickard, Bill. "Some Thoughts on Pickawillany, 1748-1752, Part 1: The Setting." Columbus: Archaeology Blog, Ohio History Connection, 2007. ohiohistory.org/learn/collections/archaeology/archaeology-blog/2007/march-2007

Pieper, Thomas. "Christian Baatz, Fort Laurens' First Advocate." Bolivar, Ohio: Friends of Fort Laurens Foundation.

Pieper, Thomas I., and Gidney, James B. Fort Laurens 1778-1779, the Revolutionary War in Ohio. Kent, Ohio: Kent State University Press, 1976.

Poinsatte, Charles. *Outpost in the Wilderness: Fort Wayne, 1706-1828.* Fort Wayne, Ind.: Allen County, Fort Wayne Historical Society, 1976.

Quaife, M.M. "Marking the Site of Old Fort St. Joseph." Champaign, Ill.: *Journal of the Illinois Historical Society Volume 6, No. 4,* January, 1914.

Rezek, Rev. Antoine Ivan. *History of the Diocese of Sault Ste. Marie and Marquette.* Chicago: M.A. Donohue & Co., 1907.

Rice, Colonel James M. *Peoria City and County Illinois, A Record of Settlement, Organization, Progress and Achievement.* Chicago: S.J. Clarke Publishing Co., 1912.

Risinger, A.C. "Forty Foot Pitch." Columbus: *Ohio Archaeological and Historical Publications, Volume XXXII,* July 1923.

Romaker, Janet. "Roche de Boeuf to celebrate 'Buffalo Rock'; Up to 15,000 visitors, 100 volunteers expected." *Toledo Blade*, September 22, 2010.

Rosenberger, Tim. "Village Board hopes changes to Fort Crevecoeur Park will increase tourism." Creve Coeur, Ill.: *Peoria Journal-Star*, February 7, 2017.

Safford, William H. "An Outing on the Congo. A Visit to the Site of Dunmore's Treaty with the Shawnees 1774." Columbus: *Ohio Archaeological and Historical Publications, Volume VII*, April, 1899.

Sayre, Jim. "Loramie Had No Tender Feelings for Americans." Sidney, Ohio: Shelby County Historical Society, July 1998.

Scolaro, Joseph A. "Ancient road is about to receive a marker." Racine, Wis.: *The Journal-Times*, May 18, 1995

Sears, Alfred Byron. *Thomas Worthington, Father of Ohio Statehood*. Columbus: The Ohio State University Press, 1958.

Sheen, Dan R. *Location of Fort Crevecoeur*. Peoria, Ill.: The Author, 1919.

Simmons, David A. "An Orderly Book for Fort Washington and Fort Hamilton, 1792-1793." *Cincinnati Historical Society Bulletin, Volume 36, Number 2*, 1978

Smith, B. Wilson. "Old Ouiatenon." In *Past and Present of Tippecanoe County, Indiana, Vol. 1*. Indianapolis: B.F. Bowen and Company, 1909.

Smith, Isaac. "The story of Kaskaskia Island, Illinois' first state capital." The *Southern Illinoisan*, December 22, 2017.

Smith, William Henry. *The St. Clair Papers, the Life and Public Service of Arthur St. Clair*. Cincinnati: Robert Clarke & Co., 1882.
----------------------------"Vincennes, The Key to the Northwest," in *American Historic Towns Historic Towns of The Western States*. New York: G.P. Putnam Sons, The Knickerbocker Press, 1901.

Smythe, George F. "Mitchener's 'Legend of the White Woman and Newcomerstown." Columbus: *Ohio Archaeological and Historical Quarterly. Volume XXXIII*. 1924.

Snell, Samuel P., Jackson, Ryan L., and Krieger, Angie R. Lost and Forgotten Historic Roads: The Buffalo Trace, a case study. Indianapolis.
https://www.fs.usda.gov/Internet/FSE_DOCUMENTS/stelprdb5444947.pdf

Snyder, Fred L. "The Early Forts on Sandusky Bay (Parts 1, 2 and 3) Columbus: Ohio Sea Grant Extension, Ohio State University, 2004, 2005.

Soltow, Lee and Margaret. "A Settlement That Failed: The French in Early Gallipolis, an Enlightening Letter, and an Explanation." Columbus: *Ohio History Journal, Volume 94/Winter-Spring 1985*.

Southwest Corridor Northwest Passage. "Mud Lake." Southwestcorridornorthwestpassage.org.

Spencer, Oliver M. *Indian captivity: a true narrative of the capture of Rev. O. M. Spencer, by the Indians, in the neighborhood of Cincinnati*. New York: Carlton & Porter, 1834.

"Starved Rock: History, Legends, and Lore". Department of Anthropology - University of Illinois. 2002.

"State of Illinois Buys Starved Rock." *Journal of the Illinois State Historical Society, Volume 4*, 1912.

Stelle, Lenville J. "History and Archaeology: New Evidence of the 1730 Mesquakie (Renard, Fox) Fort." Champaign, Ill.: Parkland College Center for Social Research, 1992.

Stevenson, Mary Louise Cresap. "Colonel Thomas Cresap." Columbus: *Ohio Archaeological and Historical Publications, Volume X*, 1902.

Steward, John F. *Lost Maramech and earliest Chicago; a history of the Foxes and of their downfall near the great village of Maramech; original investigations and discoveries*. Chicago: F.H. Revell Co., 1903.

St. Louis Sage. "How and where did Chief Pontiac die?" St. Louis: *St. Louis Magazine*, August 1, 2019

Stockman, Dan. "Nonprofit makes history at old fort, builds on revival begun 9 years ago." *Fort Wayne Gazette*, March 3, 2013.

Straus, Frank. "Skull Cave Was Refuge for Englishman Alexander Henry." *Mackinac Island Town Crier*, July 3, 2010.
----------------"William Backhouse Astor House Is 200 Years Old This Year." *Mackinac Island Town Crier*, June 18, 2016.

Strickland, W.P. *Old Mackinaw, or The Fortress of the Lakes and its Surroundings*. Philadelphia: James Challen & Son, 1860.

Sugden, John. Tecumseh, A Life. New York: Henry Holt and Company, 1997.

Sulski, Jim. "Showing the Way." *Chicago Tribune*, December 18, 1997.

Sutherland, James. "Early Wisconsin Exploration and Settlement." Madison, Wis.: *Reports and Collections of the State Historical Society of Wisconsin, Volume X*, 1888.

Sword, Wiley. *President Washington's Indian War. The Struggle for the Old Northwest, 1790-1795*. Norma, Okla.: University of Oklahoma Press, 1985.

Tanks, Annie C. *Annie Tanks' Martins Ferry: A History of Martins Ferry, Ohio to the 1920s*. Martins Ferry, Ohio: Martins Ferry Area Historical Society, 2006.

Thompson, Erwin N. *Grand Portage: A History of the Sites, People and Fur Trade*. Washington, D.C. National Park Service, 1969.

Timman, Henry. "Fort Sandusky and its short-lived life." *Norwalk Reflector*, March 22, 2019.

Toledo Blade. "Progress on Fallen Timbers." Toledo, Ohio: August 20, 2004.

Vance, John L. "The French Settlement and Settlers of Gallipolis." Columbus: *Ohio Archaeological and Historical Quarterly Volume III*. John L. Trauger, 1898.

Vance, Will. "The Hidden History of the Battle of Point Pleasant, Parts 1-4" Charleston, W.Va.: May 23-26, 2018. WOWKTV.com.

Vezner, Tad. "Change bears down on historic battlefield, Main outcomes decided, but verbal clashes endure." *Toledo Blade*. August 8, 2004.

Vierling, Philip L. "The True Location of the Laughton Trading Post." *Chicago Portage Ledger*, May/August 2003

Wallace, Joseph A. "Fort de Chartres – Its Origin, Growth and Decline." *Transactions of the Illinois State Historical Society*, 1903.

Wallace, W. Stewart. *Documents Relating to the North West Company*. New York: Greenwood Press, 1968.

Warner, Beers & Co. *History of Defiance County Ohio*. Chicago: Warner, Beers & Co., 1883.

Warren, William Whipple. *History of the Ojibway People*. Minnesota Historical Society Press. 1885.

Westheider, James E. "The History of Fort Washington at Cincinnati, Ohio: A Case Study" Selected Papers from the 1989 and 1990 George Rogers Clark Trans-Appalachian Frontier History Conferences.

Wilcox, Frank N. *Ohio Indian Trails*. Kent, Ohio: Kent State University Press, 2015.

Wildow, Sam. "Area's Native American heritage one of many cultures." *Piqua Daily Call.* November 22, 2018.

William E. Rose and Associates. "The Chicago Portage - Historical Synopsis. The Chicago Portage and Laughton Trading Post Area. The Waterway West." Hinsdale, Ill.: Forest Preserve District of Cook County, River Forest, Ill., June, 1975.

Williams, Mark. "Eastern Ohio steel plant in line for investment, more workers from new owner." *Columbus Dispatch,* June 22, 2018.

Williamson, C.W. *History of Western Ohio and Auglaize County.* Columbus: Press of W. M. Linn and Sons, 1905.

Wilson, Frazer. "St. Clair's Defeat." Columbus: *Ohio Archaeological and Historical Publications, Volume X,* 1902.

Wilson, Frazer Ells. *Arthur St. Clair, Rugged Ruler of the Old Northwest.* Richmond, Va.: Garrett and Massie Publishers, 1944.

Wilson, George R. "Early Indiana trails and Surveys." Indianapolis: *Indiana Historical Society Publications, Vol. 6, No. 3.* C. E. Pauley and Co., 1919.

Winans, Vanessa. "Historian: Wayne was key to nation's growth; Subduing Indians led to expansion." *Toledo Blade,* February 9, 2005.

Withers, Alexander Scott. *Chronicles of Border Warfare.* Cincinnati: Stewart & Kidd Company, 1895.

Wood, Edwin O. *Historic Mackinac: The Historical, Picturesque, and Legendary Features of the Mackinac Country. 2 vols.* New York: The MacMillan Company, 1918.

Woolworth, Alan R. "Archeological Excavations at the Northwest Company's Fur Trade Post, Grand Portage, Minnesota, in 1936-37." Minnesota Historical Society, 1963.

Wyman, Mark. *The Wisconsin Frontier.* Bloomington, Ind.: Indiana University Press. 1998.

Yeager, Robert C. "A Historic River Town Where the West Began." *New York Times,* Nov. 5, 2009.

Young, David. "Time and the Tangles of History Obscure the Site of 1730 Massacre." *Chicago Tribune,* June 7, 1990.

INDEX